FIGHTER SQUADRON

FIGHTER SQUADRON

"POSSUNT QUIA POSSE VIDENTUR"

"They can because they think they can"

BADGE – Between wings elevated and conjoined in base, a dolphin, head downwards.

The Dolphin signifies the fact that it was the first Squadron to fly the Sopwith Dolphin, the wings showing that it was a flying unit.

DEREK PALMER

First published in 1990 by
The Self Publishing Association Ltd
Lloyds Bank Chambers
Upton-upon-Severn, Worcs
First re-printed 1991

A MEMBER OF

in conjunction with
Derek Palmer

British Library Cataloguing in Publication Data
Palmer, Derek *1936-*
       Fighter Squadron
       1. Great Britain. Royal Air Force. Fighter squadrons,
       history
       I. Title
       358.430941

ISBN: 1 85421 075 0

Designed & Produced by The Self Publishing Association Ltd
Printed & Bound in Great Britain by Devonshire Press Ltd., Torquay, Devon

"DOG FIGHT" by Joseph Simpson

This is a photograph of a page from the "Weekly Graphic", published in 1918, depicting the artist's impression of an engagement by Dolphin aircraft of No 19 Squadron. The details are as correct as they could be made at the time. The white dumbell on the side of the fuselage was the Squadron marking adopted in March, 1918. The aircraft numbers and letters are correct, and it is known that the occupants of three of the aircraft were, V – Captain J. Leacroft (now Group Captain J. Leacroft M.C.), N – Captain P. Huskinson (now Air Commodore P. Huskinson C.B.E., M.C.), I – Lieutenant Carter.

No 19 Squadron was the first to be equipped with the Sopwith Dolphin and when, in 1932 the Squadron Badge was chosen, a dolphin between elevated wings was adopted as its centre-piece.

To my wife Brenda
Thank you for your support,
patience and understanding

CONTENTS

FOREWORD

The writing of a detailed history of a Fighter Squadron, even one as illustrious as Number 19 Squadron, is not an easy undertaking. Derek Palmer has produced a truly comprehensive and readable account and past, present and future members of the Squadron are in his debt. He has had to do much painstaking research and despite the help given, and acknowledged by him, there must have been considerable frustration and disappointment at times for him in the course of gestation and publication. The subject is worthy of the effort but equally the author has produced a work which lives up to the subject.

The period of peace since 1945, albeit uneasy until very recently, far outweights in terms of time the years of active conflict but necessarily in the history of a fighting unit it is the periods of war which predominate. It is therefore natural that the activities of the Squadron during the 1914-1918 and 1939-1945 wars should be chronicled in detail and comprise a major part of this book. The history and traditions of No 19 Squadron, and indeed of the Royal Air Force, were forged largely by those two great conflicts which saw the emergence of nascent airpower and its rapid growth to maturity as a vital component of war winning forces. No 19 Squadron has played an important and illustrious part in that process as this book shows.

The sections of the book devoted to the peacetime Squadron illustrate clearly that the traditions of courage, endurance, professionalism and good humour which were forged in war, are in good hands and will remain so wherever No 19 Squadron happen to be in the future. However, should new or past members of the Squadron need reassurance of these traditions, this book will provide it.

Air Marshal Sir Laurence Jones, KCB, AFC, FBIM. (Ret'd)

AUTHOR'S NOTE

This is a story of 19 Fighter Squadron, of their courage and achievements. It is a true story, for I would not have written it any other way. How they came through two World Wars with honour, dignity and sacrifice. The men and machines are this story. From the first flimsy flying machines, with a machine gun that sometimes worked and bombs that had to be dropped over the side, to faster fighting machines with eight machine guns and cannons, and on to the supersonic sophisticated equipment which – without you ever having seen it – blasts you out of the air.

Some pilots are mentioned but that does not detract from those who are not, for they gave and did their share in the team effort. The groundcrews working in the background, although not fighting the enemy direct, were shelled and bombed, as they fought to keep the aircraft serviceable night and day.

The Squadron achieved many "firsts" with their machines and were responsible on many occasions for test flying them into service. The Squadrons' list of firsts include:–

*The first British Squadron to receive the French Spad.
*The first Squadron to be equipped with the Sopwith Dolphin. (From which is derived the squadron badge.)
*The first Squadron to perform synchronised flight-formation aerobatics with smoke.
*Service trials on the Gloster Gauntlet and pioneering of it into service.
*The first Squadron to receive the Spitfire.
*The intensive flying and reliability trials on the new Rotol constant speed airscrew on the Spitfire.
*The first cannon-armed Spitfires followed by service trials with this new weapon. (The constant stoppages cost the squadron dearly.)
*The first Squadron to be equipped with the Lightning F2.
*The first RAF supersonic-fighter Squadron in the 2nd T.A.F.
*First to receive the converted Lightning F2a.

The former Squadron Commander, Wing Commander R.L. Dixon who initiated my interest in the history of the Squadron, wrote to me after reading part of the manuscript on World War I – "One can easily imagine these young men in their frail machines seeing air combat as a personal challenge rather than an integral part of general war, as it would be now. Undoubtedly, they deserve that their accounts and exploits are recorded for the benefit and education of others."

My apologies for any omissions in this book. Either I didn't find it, or there was not space to include it. Had I entered all I wanted into this story, it could have become an encyclopedia of many volumes.

My sincere thanks to the Ministry of Defence (Air Historical Branch and Imperial War Museum) for the kind assistance they have given in documents and photographs. To all the members and ex-members, both aircrew and groundcrew, who are too numerous to list, but have all been very kind in their generous offer of assistance. To Jurgen Valley, Flight Magazine, The Yorkshire Evening Post, The Bon Accord and J.M. Bruce/G.S. Leslie Collection for their kind permission to use their photographs. To Flying Officer I. Halden for looking after me on my last visit and assisting me in the research. My special thanks to Wing Commander R.L. Dixon and 19 (F) Squadron for their support, encouragement and hospitality. To my brother, Group Captain J.K. Palmer, OBE, MBIM, for his help and knowledge.

May I urge the reader to bear in mind that, in the main, this book is taken directly from actual combat reports or the Squadron Record Book (F540). Such text is written verbatim with no attempt made to update or amplify what is sometimes unusual or even extravagant language. I point out, however, that owing to the Official Secrets Act and the attendant "Thirty Year Rule", the Squadron Diary beyond 1965 has not been available for personal research. The assistance of senior members of the Squadron has therefore been obtained to review this period.

In summary then I have – wherever possible – told the story as Squadron members over 75 years have told it. I hope you enjoy reading it that way.

THE FORMATION AND PREPARATION

1st September 1915

In May 1915 No 5 Reserve Squadron was formed at Castle Bromwich under the command of Captain R.M. Rodwell, and began at once to train pilots on Maurice Farmans. It was from this squadron that the nucleus of No 19 was obtained. On the 1st September the nucleus left the parent unit to start a separate existence as a service squadron. Captain Rodwell was transferred to command the new squadron, No 19, taking with him a few of his officers who could be spared from No 5.

At the time of the separation, in addition to the Maurice Farmans, several 80 Gnome Avros and Caudrons had been accumulated together with odd BEs, 70 Renault and Armstrong Whitworths and were all handed over to No 19. It is interesting to note that machines of these types had been out of Active Service for several months. Indeed, so acute was the shortage that it was not until a month later that the new squadron received its first service aeroplane, the 90 RAF BE2c, which was hailed with joy although already becoming obsolete in France.

Squadron Commanders of later days may be surprised to learn with what staff their predecessors were then accustomed to run their commands. There was no establishment for an Adjutant or Recording Officer. A half time instructor or pupil, more ready with his pen than his hands, being usually impressed for the duty. This arrangement was necessarily unsatisfactory. The temporary holder of office was liable to frequent moves; his chief interests lay outside and, receiving no extra pay for the increased work, he did not view it with pleasure. An Equipment Officer was a luxury which few enjoyed. An Establishment for one was soon authorised, but suitably trained officers were scarce. Shorthand Typists were almost unknown. A man who could look after the Pay and Mess Book was a treasure to be held at all costs. Stores, both Technical and 'Q', and Transport were dealt with by NCOs under the direct control of the Commanding Officer. Instructors or pupils were sometimes placed in charge of these departments with results which varied with their individual efficiency, so that it was generally better for a Squadron Commander with a large capacity for work to exercise direct control, until trained officers were available.

On the Aerodrome the Commanding Officer found himself the chief instructor, with perhaps two assistants to deal with 30 or 40 pupils. His time would be spent dashing between the Flight sheds and the telephone, and what with the strain of fighting against some muscular pupil who refused to flatten out on landing, and shouting through a dozen exchanges at a pilot lost on his first cross-country flight at the other end of England, it was no wonder his temper was sometimes short. As soon as the need was apparent and personnel available, proper establishments were authorised and filled but, until then, it is no way belittling to those of the present day to say that a squadron depended far more directly on its Commander than is now the case.

The higher training of pilots for their wings and for overseas was now taken up with energy and enthusiasm. It was hoped at first that all the best pilots so trained would be kept to go overseas with the squadron, but such was the demand from France and the other fronts that one by one they were all posted away long before the squadron was ready to go.

At that time training followed no hard and fast rules. It included night flying and was varied by alarms from Zeppelins when any pilot was liable to take the air in any sort of machine. Lieutenant Robinson, the future airship destroyer, joined the squadron in September and received his first training in night flying with the result that he was soon posted, very unwillingly, to a Home Defence Squadron near London. The need for night pilots was becoming urgent, but suitable machines were scarce and facilities for training poor. The arrangements were left largely to the discretion and initiative of Commanding Officers. In No 19 the first flights were made by the Squadron Commander in Maurice Farmans and Avros. The latter were very soon abandoned as being too dangerous except in the most experienced hands, though with the arrival of the BE2cs, flights were made on every suitable night.

December 1915

Night flying was never very popular with a Squadron which expected to go on active service in a few months. Only the best pilots (who, of course, were intended to remain with the squadron) proved a success, and they were promptly taken away. It was therefore with deep satisfaction that mobilization orders were received early in December.

January 1916

The Service machines were to be the RE7, with 120hp Beardmore, an improved edition of the RE5 which had been used in France since 1914. It seemed that the squadron's chief duty would be bombing. Some, impressed by the large wing area and the comparatively powerful engine, concluded that heavy bombs would be carried; and it appeared later that this view was also held in official quarters. Bombs of nearly 400lbs, and experts no less weighty in importance, were sent in quick succession to the squadron. After much hard work, inspired by the prospect of a speedy move to France, a number of the bombs were fitted and practice flights made. It was then realised that pilots and experts alike had been sadly optimistic. Only with a minimum of petrol and without an observer, could the bomb be persuaded to leave the ground. It needed no official orders cancelling the date of its departure to shatter the squadrons' dreams of bombing the Hun back to the Rhine. This was the day of Immelmann and the Fokker. A single pilot in the heavily loaded machine would have been 'easy meat', and yet so keen were all ranks that, had the choice been theirs, they would have gone at once. Eventually it was understood that mobilization was only postponed pending the delivery of a new and more powerful engine from which much was expected. In the meantime, the squadron had moved from Castle Bromwich to Netheravon on Salisbury Plain, at which station it was intended to undergo a few weeks strenuous training in the art of bombing before proceeding to France. When orders were cancelled, another squadron of RE7s had just gone overseas. Many of the pilots were sent to this squadron, and No 19 settled down to train others as reinforcements.

In the winter when the daylight hours are so few, a training squadron cannot afford to lose one of them assuming the weather is fit for flying. Even on the 'dud' days there is usually enough repair work to keep everyone at full pressure. This means that the men get little recreation or exercise outside that afforded by their work. When, therefore, a heavy fall of snow in February not only stopped flying but gave ample time for all the machines to be repaired, it afforded an opportunity for a holiday which could not be missed. On Salisbury Plain there are several hills with steep, smooth slopes well suited for toboggan runs, and others more gently graded to tempt the skiers. Every afternoon while the snow lasted, the squadron flocked to these hills. Carpenters and riggers were very busy with bobsleighs of ambitious design for Flight teams, while every enthusiast began to build his own single seater. Official encouragement was given by the Wing Commander, and everyone, from the Squadron Commander downwards, took part. While it lasted the fun was fast and furious: 'crashes' were frequent but harmless: budding pilots turned without bank and were not 'strafed': landings were sudden but no harm was done and altogether this interval in the ordinary routine was thoroughly enjoyed, and was always remembered with pleasure in aftertime.

4th April 1916

The squadron moved to Filton, near Bristol, and here No 19 gave birth to a new service squadron, No 42, which took over the Avros and the other old machines.

The new aerodrome was very different from Salisbury Plain. The ponderous REs could scarcely clear the trees which surrounded it, although no bomb of any description was now carried. Great efforts were made, with the assistance of a devoted band of elderly volunteers, to improve the surface and lay tracks through the mud, but little improvement was effected until the War Office took the matter properly in hand some months later. The buildings were still in course of completion, and the consequent difficulties at first bulked large in the minds of pilots somewhat enervated by the amenities of a permanent station on Salisbury Plain.

As an indication of the undeveloped state of the RFC in those days it should be mentioned that for two months, aeroplanes for co-operation training with the artillery on Salisbury Plain had to be flown by No 19 from Bristol. None more suitable were available on the Plain. Strange to say the RE7s, designed for bombing, proved quite successful and this work was very popular with pilots. The machines would be flown to the Plain in the early morning, carrying wireless and observers, and would return late in the afternoon. The training was very valuable to the observers, who had recently been attached. Several, after a few weeks being sent to join No 70 Squadron in France, where they did very gallant work in a squadron which soon became famous for its gallantry.

June 1916

Orders were received to mobilize at once, and to be ready to move about the middle of July. The service aeroplane was to be the BE12, a single seater with a 140hp engine designed by the Royal Aircraft Factory. Great things were rumoured of this machine, and when it first arrived they appeared fully justified to those who had hitherto only flown slow two seaters. The '12' was credited with a climb to 6,000 feet in eight minutes, and a ground speed of 104 miles per hour. A new machine with a good engine, handled by a skilful pilot, often reached these figures in practice. The factories turned them out with astonishing rapidity and they were collected as fast as pilots could be found to fly them.

Lieutenant Selous
(Crown Copyright – Sqdn Album)

The question of personnel now received great attention. Time was short, the 140hp RAF was a recent production; little was known of it, and little time remained to learn. Serious difficulties faced the Squadron Commander in completing his war establishments. The pilots then under his command were, for the most part, trained on the RE7 and quite unaccustomed to fast single seaters. There was no time to train any but the very best, and by force of circumstances, though with much regret, several pilots who had been with the squadron for a few months, and who looked forward to flying with it to France, had to be struck off the list of those who were to go. Application was made for others to be posted from outside, and it was answered in a very prompt manner. Amongst the newcomers was Captain Henderson, recently promoted to Flight Commander, who was to distinguish himself later as a very daring leader and skilful pilot.

Among the flying officers was Lieutenant Selous. Son of the famous big game hunter, he was destined to fight

15

and die in a manner worthy of his father. Several officers had already seen service with the RFC, and others with the Army. Amongst the former were Captain Tidswell, Captain Williams and Captain Henderson, and of the latter many of the flying officers whose quality as pilots was unusually high.

Although there was now little to complain of with regard to officers; and the NCOs and men were as fine a body as could be hoped for – many having nearly two years experience – very few of the fitters had seen the new engine. After nine months work on an engine with six cylinders and water-cooled, it was not to be expected that they would quickly learn the ways of one with 12 cylinders, cooled by air. It must be remembered that this was one of the first engines of its type to be produced and certainly the first to be fitted into a British aeroplane. Notwithstanding its merits and its eventual success, it was then in a comparatively experimental stage, containing not a few defects and requiring constant attention. This was proved by several alterations which were carried out at the last moment, but which even a very brief experience had shown to be essential. Short courses for the fitters were arranged at the factories; experts from Farnborough were in constant attendance, and every effort was made to master the intricacies of the engine before the date of departure. Nevertheless, the feeling of the squadron, confident in everything else, was dubious about the many-cylindered experiment.

About this time a curious incident occurred. In order to obtain practice in aerial firing and bomb dropping, the Squadron Commander had built a large raft and covered it with white canvas. This, supported by a number of empty barrels, was placed in the Severn estuary off a lonely part of the coast. The operation of mooring the target was personally superintended by the Recording Officer and the Squadron Commander, who also flew over to assure himself that it could be easily seen. Ample margin was allowed for the rise and fall of the tide. The next morning a young pilot was sent to test his machine gun, but returned in a short time to say he could not find the target. Not feeling entirely satisfied, the Squadron Commander flew over in the afternoon and found it a very conspicuous object floating in the correct position. The following day more pilots were sent, but all returned without finding it. In the afternoon an experienced Flight Commander was despatched, and reported that the raft was clearly visible at a distance and appeared in good condition. The erring pilots were hailed to the Orderly Room and told that they must find the target next day or there would be trouble. Nevertheless in the morning they came back with the same tale. Feeling very wrathful that his pet scheme should be in danger of falling through, the Squadron Commander at once jumped into a machine determined to solve the mystery. To his dismay his first search revealed nothing. After cruising for half an hour over the waters he saw a white object apparently lying on the river bed in the place where the target had been moored. He also noticed that the tide was running very strongly. Still unable to account for the raft being submerged he flew round for some time until he saw that it was becoming more visible as the current lessened. It then struck him that this part of the estuary was noted for the strength of its tides, and he concluded that their effect, when in full flow, must be to drag the raft below the water. As it was now visible he returned; explained the position and ordered several pilots out, adding that they were to do their best to fire all of their rounds. By this time, the chief topic of conversation in the Officers' Mess had become the question of whether or not the target still remained. The seniors for the most part, relying on the evidence of the Squadron and Flight Commanders were certain that it did: the juniors less audibly, but no less positively, asserted that it did not. The arrival of the Major settled the question. Both factions felt vindicated and a debate, which had threatened to become bitter, was now closed. In the meantime the Recording Officer, Lieutenant Morgan, had taken a side-car with the intention of discovering the cause of the trouble, by examining the target at close quarters. He was delayed by the strength of the current, and had great difficulty in finding his object. However, just as the Major flew away, he viewed it and after watching it rise as the force of the current subsided, he came to the same conclusion as his CO. He stayed some time examining the moorings, and had just began to row away, when he was suddenly startled by the sound of a machine gun. In a few seconds bullets were striking the water all round the target. The pilots, overjoyed at seeing it and mindful of the Squadron Commander's orders, had not noticed his small boat. For two minutes he pulled as he never had before and did not stop until he reached the safety of the beach.

About ten days before the squadron was due to move, it was noticed that the dope was peeling off the fabric of several machines. In a short time this spread to others, and the fabric itself became so rotten that it could be pierced with the finger. The trouble was confined to the machines delivered from one factory only, but as these formed the majority of the strength of the squadron, the position was serious. The matter was promptly taken up by the responsible department in London. It was discovered that some defect in one of its ingredients rendered the dope peculiarly sensitive to the actinic rays of the sun although in other respects it was quite innocuous. Orders were issued that the machines were not to be flown and were to be kept under cover.

Those whose fabric was already weakened were to be completely stripped and recovered; the remainder were to wait until a fresh dope could be supplied. In the meantime BE12s from other factories were collected by the Squadron as soon as possible, and the date of the departure was postponed. The hand of the enemy was strongly suspected although no proof was forthcoming; but, whether due to agents of Germany or negligence at home, it was equally criminal. During a long flight on a hot day before any warning sign could be detected, the fabric might have rotted and ripped away. Official visits of inspection were subsequently paid by Brigadier-General Salmond, GOC, Training Brigade, and Brigadier-General Brancher, from the Department of Military Aeronautics. Both were satisfied with the progress of mobilisation, but representation of the delay due to the faulty dope caused the latter to arrange a few further days postponement which were much needed.

No 19's history as a Training Squadron had now definitely ended. It had been varied and strenuous. Pilots had been taught to fly Avros, Caudrons, Bristol and Martinsyde Scouts, BE2cs, BE2bs, RE5s, RE7s, and BE12s. They had been sent overseas for work with the artillery – as fighting scouts – for long distance photographic reconnaissance, and as bombers. Every branch of technical training then employed in the Royal Flying Corps, such as wireless, artillery cooperation, the use of bomb sights, gunnery and photography, had all been taught in the squadron. It can be imagined that the varied nature of the training and the changing types of machines often threw a heavy strain on the resources of the unit, which could only be met by exceptional energy and adaptability on the part of all ranks. It is most satisfactory to add that during this period of 11 months not one fatal accident occurred to an officer or pupil on the strength of the squadron.

July 1916

On the 25th July the transport was safely embarked at Avonmouth under the care of the Equipment Officer. On the 26th, pilots and machines were drawn up ready to leave but after several attempts in a summer mist the departure was abandoned that day. Lieutenant-General Sir David Henderson, Director General of Military Aeronautics, came to see the squadron off, and stayed until the following day, when the weather improved. HQ, with the remainder of the squadron, entrained on the morning of the 26th and embarked the same afternoon at Southampton in one of the Great Eastern Railway's Packets, formerly on the service between Harwich and the Hook of Holland.

The Channel was crossed at full speed in a thick fog which prevented the ship from entering Le Havre until the 28th. During the wait outside, the possibilities of being torpedoed were much discussed. The ship's officers gave no comfort, rather emphasising the fact that this was the spot where two ships had been sunk quite recently; and, when the fog cleared away, the masts of no less than three vessels could be seen sticking out of the water in the near distance.

Men and transport were disembarked at Rouen where a stay of three days was made to complete equipment and overhaul the cars. On August 1st the squadron left by road for Abbeville, at which place final orders were received to proceed the next morning to Fienvillers near Doullens, no one until then being aware of the final destination. On arrival at the aerodrome it was found that the pilots had already flown over from St Omer on the previous day. Of the 18 machines which left Filton, in spite of minor mishaps at Farnborough and Folkestone, only one had failed to complete the journey. This was better than had been expected and compared favourably with other squadrons crossing at that time. The following are the names of the officers who were the pilots of the squadron on its first flight across the Channel:-

(It is assumed that Major Rodwell, the Squadron Commander, had gone to France earlier to prepare for the arrival of the aircraft)

Captain Williams

Lieutenant Bradley   Lieutenant Wadham

Lieutenant Williams

Lieutenant Briggs   Lieutenant Fellows

Captain Henderson

Lieutenant Reynell   Lieutenant Baker

Lieutenant Child

Lieutenant Selous   Lieutenant Callaghan

Captain Tidswell

Lieutenant Corbold   Lieutenant Talbot

Captain Allen

Lieutenant Green   Captain Hay

18

THE FIRST WORLD WAR

1st August 1916

At Fienvillers No 19 found itself in company with No 27 a squadron of single seater Martinsydes fitted with 120 and 160hp Beardmore engines, which had joined the EF in the spring. Also No 70, equipped with the first Sopwith 1½ Strutters, which had been needed so urgently that its Flights had been sent out independently, as soon as they were ready, the third flight having just crossed. No 27s chief role was long distance bombing; No 70s long distance and photographic reconnaissances. The part to be played by No 19 was not so defined. It depended on the behaviour of the 140 RAF engine – still a very unknown quantity. The machines were fitted to carry eight 20, or two 112lb bombs, and a camera. Their armament consisted of one Vickers gun firing through the propellor and a Lewis gun on a rear mounting, intended to meet attacks from behind. As was already the case with the other two squadrons, No 19 would be called upon to provide offensive and defensive patrols. The three units formed the 9th Wing, commanded by Lieutenant-Colonel H.C.T. Dowding. This Wing was attached for duty to RFC Headquarters then occupying an advanced position in a chateau in the village, which the GOC, Major-General Trenchard used throughout the Somme Battle.

On arrival in France, the officers of the squadron were distributed in Flights as follows:-

HEADQUARTERS FLIGHT

Major R.M. Rodwell .... Squadron Commander
Captain Hay .... Flying Officer
Captain Bowen .... Wireless Officer
Lieutenant Morgan .... Recording Officer
Lieutenant Western .... Equipment Officer
Lieutenant Johnson ....
Second Lieutenant Schell .... Flying Officer

'A' Flight	'B' Flight	'C' Flight
Captain G.G.A. Williams	Captain I.H.D. Henderson	Captain Tidswell
Lieutenant A.T. Williams	Lieutenant Child	Captain Allen
2nd Lieutenant Bradley	Lieutenant A.W. Reynell	Lieutenant Corbold
2nd Lieutenant Wadham	Lieutenant G.B.A. Baker	Lieutenant Talbot
2nd Lieutenant Briggs	Lieutenant F.O. Selous	2nd Lieutenant Green
2nd Lieutenant Fellows	Lieutenant Callaghan	2nd Lieutenant Downing

The Warrant Officers were Sergeant-Major F. Hudson and Sergeant-Major R.E. Norman.

THE BATTLE OF THE SOMME

Much had to be done before the squadron was allowed to take an active part in the Battle of the Somme, which was then at its height. Of first importance to the pilots was a knowledge of the country only to be obtained by constant flights between the aerodrome and the lines. Emphasis was laid on the necessity of being able to pick up their bearings without delay after fights in which they would not have time to see where they were going. Recent experience had lent much weight to the assumption that pilots had frequently been compelled to land on the other side because they had lost their bearings. It was almost of equal importance that they should quickly learn how to handle and fire their guns, and finally, practice in close formation flying was more than ever necessary. Luckily some of the older hands in the squadron had already considerable experience of formation work, and although far from perfection, the practice patrols were quite creditable; in fact the squadron flew from St Omer to Fienvillers on the day of its arrival in one big formation led by Colonel Dowding in a BE2c. In view of the slower speed of the leader's machine this was not easy.

In gunnery, there was very much more to be learnt. Although the practice of firing through a revolving propeller was not new, the principle adopted on the BE12 was; and the method by which it was carried out, virtually untried, with the exception of the Sopwith 1½ Strutter, which appeared in France about the same time, no gear had yet been fitted to synchronise the rate of fire with the revolutions of the propeller. Instead deflector plates had been made to protect the blades against the occasional round which hit them. Owing to the construction of the BE12, the gun was placed some six or seven feet behind the propeller. This necessitated a long intermediary push rod which became a frequent source of trouble. Again, the fact that nearly every British machine carried a Lewis Gun, did not give sufficient experience of a Vickers gun's performance at a height. In addition the method of fitting the ammunition on to the breech was entirely new. This was by means of an articulated belt formed of small links joined together by the rounds, the links being thrown out of the gun after the rounds had been fired. In view of its important bearing on the history on the squadron during the Somme Battle, the new and almost experimental state of the main armament must be remembered and appreciated.

Failing a more suitable place, practices in aerial firing were carried out over the sea, a distance of some 30 miles away. As the object was, primarily, to gain some knowledge of the gun under working conditions, and to accustom the pilots in remedying stoppages in the air, the sea was as good as elsewhere. When the gun could be trusted to fire properly, then a target would have to be made, but that would not be for some time.

Patrols were sent daily to the coast; and it was while on one of them that Lieutenant Baker had an exciting experience. He was firing into the sea some distance from the shore, when his engine completely failed. In spite of a long and flat glide he landed in the water not far from the beach. Luckily the machine sank slowly, so that by climbing up its tail he managed to keep above the water until a boat arrived just in time to pick him off the elevators, none the worse, except for his wetting. Although engine failures were not infrequent, this was the only occasion on which a BE12 of No 19 was dropped into the sea.

Much useful experience was gathered from these practice flights, particularly of the 140hp RAF. One defect soon appeared. This was over oiling on a glide, causing the plugs to 'soot up', often reducing the engine to firing on less than half its cylinders. The trouble arose from the fact that during a glide the oil collected at the forward end of the sump, thus uncovering the outlet pipe which drained it off. The front cylinders received far too much oil scattering it on to the points of the plugs and, the throttle being closed or the switch off, the spark was insufficient to burn off the accumulation. Pilots, who knew this defect or had been warned, never came down steeply or for long with the engine off, but always made a descent by easy stages. In spite of this it was quite common to see a machine returning from a patrol compelled to make a forced landing outside the aerodrome, because the pilot had 'undershot' and was unable to pick up his engine.

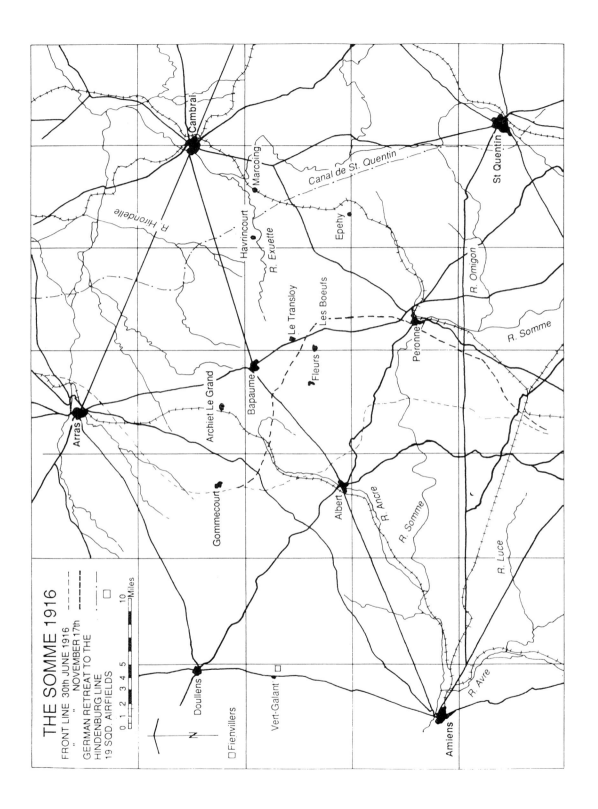

THE SOMME 1916

FRONT LINE 30th JUNE 1916
" " NOVEMBER 17th
GERMAN RETREAT TO THE
HINDENBURG LINE
19 SQD. AIRFIELDS

Miles
0 1 2 3 4 5   10

N

□ Fienvillers

Doullens

Vert-Galant □

Amiens

R. Avre

R. Luce

Albert

R. Ancre

R. Somme

Gommecourt

Arras

Archiet Le Grand

Bapaume

Fleurs

Le Transloy

Les Boeufs

Peronne

R. Somme

R. Omigon

R. Hirondelle

Havrincourt

R. Exuette

Marcoing

Cambrai

Canal de St. Quentin

Epehy

St Quentin

21

A partial remedy was found by arranging a restricted supply of oil when required. This was effected by connecting the throttle lever by means of a rod to the handle of a simple cock, which was fitted at a convenient place on the delivery pipe. The connection did not operate until the throttle lever was at the half way position, from which, as it was drawn further back, the oil cock was also shut down, so that when the throttle was completely closed only one third of the normal supply of oil was delivered. As the material for this device had to be bought locally, and worked and fitted in the squadron, it was some weeks before all the machines had been completed.

7th August 1916

The first contact with the enemy was made on an offensive patrol during the afternoon. Lieutenant Williams dived after a Fokker which had been attacking a Martinsyde and fired at it. The hostile aircraft went down apparently under control and was not seen to land. At 7.15pm, Lieutenant Downing reported his bombing mission unsuccessful due to the pilot injuring his nose, which bled profusely on looking over for bombing.

8th August 1916

Captain Henderson and Lieutenant Reynell took off at 10.10am to escort Martinsydes on a bombing raid. They reported the mission successful and bombs were seen to drop on the objective. One Fokker enemy aircraft was seen west of Bois de Havrincourt and engaged.

10th August 1916

Somewhat to their astonishment the pilots were now informed that they would also be required to do night flying. They felt that, in its present state, the engine did not inspire that confidence in its reliability which is so essential for this work. However, when it was pointed out that our policy was to allow the Huns no rest, even by night, and how much this was expected to weaken their morale, training was started without delay. Compensating advantages were discovered. The BE12 had a high degree of automatic stability, and the position of the pilot's seat left him with plenty of material in front to lessen his chances of injury in the event of a crash.

As the art of night flying was still in a rudimentary state, dependent on individual resources and ideas of each unit, it involved considerable organisation in a squadron. In No 19 the usual petrol flares were at first used for landing. Obstacles were also marked, but, as it was found that a number of lights only confused the pilots, they were kept as few as possible. Navigation lamps were fitted – one on each wing, and one in the rear on the fuselage behind the pilots' back. Parachute and wing tip flares were also carried. The former needed considerable judgment in choosing the moment of release to be of any use, and the latter, in spite of blackening the propeller blades and several parts, were found to confuse rather than help the pilot. Strange to say the engine then and afterwards always appeared to be more reliable at night. This may have been due to the comparatively low height at which operations were carried out, or to the fact that the best engines were detailed for the work; nevertheless, only the most experienced and skilful pilots were selected for this duty, which was then considered to be exceptionally dangerous.

At 10.10pm, Captain Williams whilst practicing night flying, came in to land testing the parachute light, but it was not sufficient over the aerodrome. He overshot the flares, ran into a hangar and wrecked the machine (6538).

Lieutenant Wadham, earlier in the day was testing a new machine, when he crashed on landing and totally wrecked the machine (6543).

12th August 1916

The first patrol was sent over the lines. Up to that date a few pilots had taken part in formations from the other squadrons, but this was the first time on which the squadron provided its own. It was an offensive patrol for two hours, chiefly on the line Bapaume-Peronne, and was uneventful, the only hostile aircraft in sight being too far behind their own lines to engage. After this formations were frequently sent until, in September the squadron was doing its full share in the Wing. The operations consisted of offensive and defensive patrols; to this was added escorts to bombers and reconnaissances, and at the end of August the squadron was carrying out its own bombing raids. Long distance reconnaissances were not demanded from the BE12s because this work could be done more efficiently by the two seaters of No 70, although it was sometimes their duty to escort the Sopwiths. Machines from No 27 frequently combined with those from No 19 to make up big formations for the purpose of bombing the enemy's billets and ammunition dumps. Including the escorts the number of machines would usually be eight to ten, although this was often exceeded.

To get such a formation into the air, successfully and without delay, was not an easy task. It was much helped by the comprehensive standing orders, existing in the 9th Wing and strictly enforced by the Wing Commander. Wing Orders would detail the nature and extent of the operation, the time of departure, the number of machines from each squadron, and which squadron commander was to be in charge on the ground. The position of the machines in formation and the height of their rendezvous would be arranged between the Squadron Commanders, who would each marshal his machines outside his own shed. When all was ready and the engines running, a signal would be sent to the officer in charge, who thereupon sent off his own machines, quickly followed by those of the other squadron. After taking up their position in the air at the required height, the pilots would look to the signals made by the ground officer. They were never allowed to proceed until the Squadron Commander in charge had signified, by means of signals, which were duly acknowledged by Very Lights from the leader, that he was satisfied with their formation.

Since the Battle of the Somme, the art of flying in formation has been greatly developed, and pupils receive many hours of instruction before they are passed as Service Pilots; but, in those days while the supreme importance of keeping formation was becoming obvious to everyone, its principles and practice were only learnt by bitter experience over the lines.

13th August 1916

The Squadron patrol of four BE12s attacked four hostile aircraft over Bapaume, dispersing them. The BE12s were in turn attacked from above by two other hostile aircraft, one of which was seen to side slip after a short encounter, and was lost sight of. Lieutenant Geen[*] is believed to have been forced to land from engine failure, but no one saw him go down.

Lieutenant Geen (6549) – is missing.

16th August 1916

The squadron took off at 7.44pm on an emergency patrol over Arras area, but no hostile aircraft were seen.

17th August 1916

The Squadron took off at 5.30am to escort Martinsydes on bombing mission on Grevillers, and then flew an offensive patrol at 6.15am over Lesboeufs and Rancourt. During this patrol

---

[*]   It seems likely that Geen is a misprint for Green in the official records but confirmation has not been possible.

Lieutenant Williams in BE12 No. 6562 could not keep up with the patrol due to a big hole in his fuselage from the A.A. The oil pipes were shot through and his engine seized up.

21st August, 1916

At 8.13am the Squadron took off to escort a bombing mission on Le Transloy. Lieutenant Corbold saw three hostile aircraft, one Roland and two twin engined machines. One of the twin engined machines passed very close and he fired both guns at it, but it went straight on. The Vickers gun jammed twice. Captain Allen fired at an Albatros but could not judge the effect. He was then fired on by a machine from behind, but did not see it. He had to return owing to a bullet through his petrol tank. Captain Tidswell saw five hostile aircraft trying to cross our lines but they were heavily fired on and turned back.

24th August 1916

At 4.15pm the Squadron took off for a bombing raid on Sailly Saillisel. Lieutenant Fellowes bombs were dropped from 9,000 feet, sights not used, and saw three bursts 100 yards east of the village. Lieutenant Chappell engaged hostile aircraft with Vickers gun, and it dived down towards its own lines, he accidently shot through his own tail with his Lewis gun. Second Lieutenant Selous saw his bombs burst in the village.

At 4.30pm on an Offensive Patrol, of Achiet Le Grand – Fleurs – Equancourt – Queany. Captain Henderson, Captain Allen, Second Lieutenant Callaghan and Captain Williams engaged several hostile aircraft. They were all driven away or forced to descend.

25th August 1916

At 9.15am on a bombing mission on Beaulencourt, Second Lieutenant Selous dropped his bombs from 8,000 feet. Lieutenant Williams saw them burst in the middle of the town. Lieutenant Corbold dropped his bombs and saw them burst in a camp on the outskirts of the village. Lieutenant Talbot's bombs burst on the road just outside the village. Second Lieutenant Johnson had to make six attempts to drop his bombs, and eventually did so on the village. He was attacked by three Rolands on his way back, and received a bullet through one of the struts and wires. He returned the fire.

26th August 1916

At 5.18pm on a bombing raid on Bois de Havrincourt, Captain Williams dropped his bombs on target and was attacked by hostile aircraft twice on his way back but was unable to return the fire. He landed at 34 aerodrome because of rainstorm. Second Lieutenant Johnson's bombs failed to release. His engine oiled up, and he force-landed in a field nearby. He was lost on other side of the lines for about one hour, fired at with fire balls, and his machine was shot through planes, main and tail, and longerons. His compass was out of adjustment which caused him to lose his way. Captain Henderson saw explosions in Holnon Wood, west of St Quentin.

Eleven BE12's took part in this bombing raid, five machines failed to return.

Lieutenant S.P. Briggs (6562) – is missing;
Second Lieutenant R. Talbot (6513) – is missing;
Lieutenant H.M. Corbold (6551) – is missing;
Second Lieutenant A.W. Reynell (6532) – is missing;
Lieutenant E. Callaghan (6545) – is missing.

Two of the pilots were killed, and a third died of wounds in hospital. Lieutenant S.P. Briggs and Second Lieutenant A.W. Reynell were taken as Prisoners of War.

B.E. 12 – 6562. Flown by Lt Briggs

The truth of this disastrous day did not come to light until some time later. One of the missing pilots on his return from imprisonment in Germany explained that as the leading machines of the formation entered the first thunder clouds, a large formation of enemy aircraft appeared out of the haze and severed the rear machines from the rest of the formation. Compelled to fight an unequal contest, all five machines were driven down in combat.

The following is a copy of a magazine feature of the time.

The Captive
by Peter G. Cooksley

In June 1916, No 19 Squadron of the Royal Flying Corps began to replace its RE7 bi-planes, used to train pilots for service in France, with BE12s flown as single-seaters. With these it went to France itself at the end of July. Here it participated in the Battle of the Somme in the following month where the aircraft proved almost useless as a fighter, the heavy losses forcing the Squadron to assume a new role as a bombing unit, also carrying out contact patrols.

Among the pilots of No 19 Squadron based at Fienvillers at this time, and attached to 'C' Flight was a youthful Second-Lieutenant Briggs, formerly of the Northamptonshire Regiment who, on 26 August found himself part of a formation detailed to bomb German troop billets near Mons.

Only two bombs could be carried by each aircraft, one of 20lb being slung under each wing. These bombs were aimed by means of the Central Flying School bombsight, training in the use of which had been given on the aerodrome with the aid of a camera obscura. Defensive armament of these BEs consisted of a forward-firing synchronised Vickers gun, while a Lewis was free-mounted on the fuselage aft of the pilots seat.

Poor weather meant that 'C' Flight was kept standing by for several hours. It did not finally take off until late in the afternoon, although the subsequent journey to the target was uneventful except for some poorly-aimed anti-aircraft fire. However, a formation of German interceptors was spotted which made no attempt to molest the British machines.

Having dropped their bombs from 700 feet, the flight re-formed and set course back to base only to run almost immediately into a heavy rainstorm with thunder and lightning. As the aircraft made their way through this, Lieutenant Briggs lost contact with his fellows and was destined not to see them again.

It was 2300 when his BE12 ran out of fuel and a forced landing had to be made almost at once. Fortunately this aircaft had a shallow gliding angle so getting down was not particularly hazardous, although the pilot had an uneasy moment when a tall chimney loomed out of the murk, causing him to take sharp evasive action.

The light-coloured patch on the ground at which Briggs had been aiming, turned out to be a field from which the corn had recently been harvested so the machine rolled to a halt across the stubble without mishap. Uppermost in the young Lieutenant's mind was the fact that, although he had no idea of his exact position, he had landed on the enemy side of the lines.

In such a situation it was the accepted thing to burn one's aircraft. Although a Very pistol was to hand that would do the trick efficiently, Briggs decided to delay, and instead try to discover his whereabouts. He seemed to be on the outskirts of a small town and a few minutes later he was cautiously walking down the main street, thankful that the darkness hid the tell-tale leather flying jacket of British cut that he wore.

Quite suddenly, four figures emerged from a house that later proved to be some sort of Batallion Headquarters. From their uniforms it was clear that they were German officers and they spotted the Englishman at the same moment as he saw them.

'Ach, Englander!' one of the four shouted, and all of them made a dive in his direction.

Deciding that the odds were too much in the Germans' favour, Briggs made no attempt to escape, merely making a token resistance by putting his head down and meeting their rush like a rugby player.

Having taken him into the house that they had been leaving, the Germans proceeded to attempt an interrogation, but this proved useless since none of them spoke any English, and Briggs no German. The only real communication was with a German medical officer who spoke a little French, and to whom Briggs gave his name before being allowed to sleep on a pile of straw in company with some other ranks.

The next morning, Lieutenant Briggs was conducted out of the house to a waiting car. His escort was a German officer of the type that was later to be portrayed in numerous films: stiff, with close-cropped hair and wearing a monocle. The two sat in silence as the car made its way to St Quentin. Here the prisoner was conducted into a house where he was faced by a group of German officers seated at desks before one of which he was given a chair. The German in front of him stood up and smiled.

'Good morning,' he said in perfect English, and went on to commiserate with Briggs at his misfortune at being captured.

'I'm sorry I can't offer you a cigarette,' said the German, 'but I don't smoke.'

'Nor do I,' replied Briggs, which seemed to surprise the other officer who observed that he had never met an Englishman that did not do so.

Further chat followed before the German asked to be excused as he had a lot of work to do, but added that another officer would arrive shortly to look after the prisoner.

The new German proved to be as friendly as the first, his opening remark being 'Bad luck, old boy' once again delivered in faultless English.

In the conversation that followed, Briggs complimented the German on his command of the language, and the other smiled as he explained that his grandmother was Irish and that he had lived for a number of years in that country.

Noting the row of medal ribbons that the German was wearing, the Lieutenant remarked that one of them was that of the Iron Cross, Third Class.

'When you're on the Staff, they throw them at you, old boy,' came the reply as he rose and invited his captive to another house nearby. Here the two had a cup of coffee before the German personally took the Englishman to the civil prison of St Quentin. There Briggs awaited transfer to the prisoner of war camp at Guteslloh where he joined about a thousand British, Russians, French and Belgians.

(Second-Lieutenant S.P. Briggs, later to rise to the rank of Major, was personally known to the author, and this feature was based on his notes and conversations with him.)

28th August 1916

At 7.35pm on a practice flight, Second Lieutenant Chappell in B.E.12 6552, made a forced landing outside the aerodrome. The machine was wrecked, and the pilot sustained serious injuries.

31st August 1916

The Squadron took off at 3.25pm on a bombing raid on the hutments and ammunition dumps at Bois de Havrincourt. Second Lieutenant Johnson dropped his bombs from 11,000 feet. Captain Tidswell and Captain Allen dropped from 10,500 feet. Second Lieutenant Carline was attacked by hostile aircraft after dropping his bombs and returned with a wound in the leg. He was admitted to hospital. Captain Henderson crossed the lines with the formation, dropped his bombs over the objective from 10,000 feet. Captain Henderson observed 6 hostile aircraft attacking two of ours, and at once returned to their help, and soon brought down one of the enemy aircraft apparently out of control, with the observer hanging out over the side. He escorted them back to the lines, endeavouring to ward off the attacks by the remaining five hostile aircraft.

The 9th (GHQ) Wing War Diary makes the following reference to this incident:-

"Captain Henderson apparently killed the observer in a Roland and the machine is believed to have been brought down. This Officer went back to assist two of his comrades whom he saw in difficulties, and in all probability, saved them from disaster".

2nd September 1916

The Squadron attacked the hutments and an ammunition dump in Bois de Havrincourt, dropping a total of 56 bombs. Second Lieutenant R.H. Johnson was slightly wounded and Lieutenant G.G. Downing was hit in the foot and compelled to land on a French aerodrome.

6th September 1916

Captain Williams was shot through the heel while leading a defensive and offensive patrol. The wound, though not serious, was sufficient to send him to hospital, from which he was later invalided to England. This officer had been with the squadron for several months, and while in France had taken part in several night operations. He was usually a patrol leader, in which position his previous experience was of great value. His wound deprived the squadron of a hard working Flight Commander and very popular officer.

Towards the middle of September there were rumours of a final and very determined effort on a large scale to break the Hun line before the winter. It was whispered that entirely new forms of frightfulness were to be employed, but so little was known, and the orders for secrecy so imperative, that they could only be described as 'hush hush' machines. Interest was further aroused when it was known that aeroplanes were to work in close co-operation with these mysterious engines of war. On the 13th September the Squadron Commander was informed that the date of the new attack was fixed for the 15th, and that a very special task was to be carried out by No 19 for which he was to select his most skilful pilots. This was no less than a continuous and very close patrol low over the trenches from the time the attack started, in order to report direct every movement of our advance, and, particularly, the position of the Tanks, as the 'hush hush' machines were now called. On the afternoon of the 14th all the officers of the three squadrons were collected together and were addressed by Major-General Trenchard himself. In grave tones he explained the great effort that was to be made the next morning and how it was dependent for its success on the help of the Corps. He called upon every pilot to do his utmost, and if need be to sacrifice himself loyally in the common cause. This address made a deep impression on the officers of the squadron.

15th September, 1916

During the night machines were sent with orders to drop bombs on the enemy billets, his railway junctions, aerodromes or any good target that could be found, and this was done from every aerodrome in the Somme area.

At 4.50am two machines left to attack Havrincourt Chateau. Four 112lb bombs were dropped from 1,400 feet. Captain G.W.D. Allen reports that one of his bombs exploded in the south-west corner of the Chateau, knocking out one of the walls. Second Lieutenant Edwards did not observe the bursts of his bombs.

THE OPENING DAY OF THE THIRD PHASE OF THE BATTLE OF THE SOMME

This day was marked by the first operational appearance of the tank. From the start of the attack, specially selected pilots of the squadron were allotted the task of flying a continuous and very low contact patrol over the trenches in order to report ever movement of our advance and, in particular, the position of the tanks. The system of contact patrols (close communication between aircraft and infantry, cavalry, tanks, etc) was now recognised as a tactical achievement and played its part accordingly in the Battle of the Somme. From this date the Squadron continued with its offensive fighter patrols and bombing raids as well as the special contact patrols. Officers and men were compelled to fly and to work day and night, repairing the damage caused by AA and machine gun fire in order to keep pace with the great offensive.

Captain Henderson was the first to go up on the special contact patrol. Before he returned Second Lieutenant Selous was sent to maintain the contact with the troops. He in his turn was succeeded by Lieutenant G.B.A. Baker; and so on. Captain Henderson, his machine riddled with bullets, reported seeing our troops leave the trenches and go ahead. Only a few, he said, were held up. On his second patrol, he reported seeing one of the tanks capture a village at the head of a column of men walking beside it, cheering and waving to him as he flew over.

As long as the push lasted and the weather held, those operations were continued night and day and everyone worked at their highest pressure. The strain on the NCOs and mechanics was very heavy. There was the handling of the machines, the starting up of their engines, (no easy task at any time with the 140hp RAF) and the fitting of bombs and guns. More than at any other time were machines damaged by anti-aircraft and the gun fire, and so badly were they needed that they had to be repaired at once without waiting until others could be delivered. This meant working night and day shifts, with several men on both. To this was added the night flying, which called for more time and energy from those on the ground than any other operations. Any man was lucky who obtained a full night's rest during the four days following the 15th.

22nd September 1916

On an offensive patrol at 7.00am, Second Lieutenant Stewart was attacked by a biplane. He replied and drove down the hostile aircraft east of Bapaume. This machine was seen by several pilots to burst into flames, and was doubtless destroyed. At 10.00am the same day another offensive patrol met four hostile aircraft. Second Lieutenant G. Edwards dived and attacked one using his Vickers gun and chased it east. Three pilots failed to return.

Second Lieutenant G. Hedderwick (6544) – is missing;
Second Lieutenant R.D. Herman (6561) – is missing;
Second Lieutenant R.H. Edwards (6591) – is missing.

The Squadron took off on another offensive patrol at 4.15pm
Second Lieutenant McClure (6580) – is missing.

24th September 1916

The squadron led by Captain Henderson at 3.15pm patrolled over Bapaume, Bourlon Wood and Epehy. They met two hostile aircraft. One of the British machines was seen to fall in flames, and another seen to fall and come to pieces in the air, during the fight over Havrincourt Wood.

Second Lieutenant T. West (6546) – is missing;
Second Lieutenant G. Edwards (6579) – is missing.

As a single seater fighter the BE12 was inferior to the enemy types which were now in use at the front, and in consequence the squadron were suffering heavy casualties. Towards the end of the month General Trenchard reported on the unsuitability of the BE12 as a single seater fighter and asked for a replacement. Pending the arrival of a new machine the Squadron devoted itself to bombing raids with an escort, supplemented by a few night bombing raids.

In October the shorter hours of daylight, and the general abatement of the fury of the Somme Battle, allowed work to resume a more normal course.

The Squadron confined itself during the month to bombing and night flying due to the heavy casualties suffered the preceding months.

Two months active service had taught pilots and mechanics alike some valuable lessons. Many of the earlier troubles with the engine had now been diagnosed and remedied. The Vickers Gun and synchronising gear was still far from satisfactory, but some improvement had been made, so that at last the pilots were beginning to bring down their opponents instead of having to return time after time, as before, with a hopeless stoppage or a jamb. The value of the Lewis gun on the rear mounting was much debated. There was a general feeling in the squadron that, for a single seater, it was not worth the extra weight. The Squadron Commander, going a step further, was for taking it off, fearing that its presence might destroy that offensive spirit to which Fighting Squadrons in the RFC owed so much of their success, by causing inexperienced pilots to rely on it and therefore fight defensive battles. When this view was placed before the GOC on one of his visits, he agreed heartily with the principles involved, but suggested that it would not be wise to do so until the front gun was thoroughly reliable. It remains to be noted that the BE12 was the last single seater to mount a rear gun.

10th October 1916

Three machines flown by Captain Allen, Lieutenant Buck and Lieutenant Cronyn carried out a night raid on Marcoing Station. Their bombs were seen to hit the station.

16th October 1916

The squadron lost its first Flight Commander, Captain Tidswell. He had led a number of offensive patrols, and had taken them through several scraps, in which he had one or two narrow escapes himself, bullets passing through his clothes in several places. He was shot down on one of these patrols when well over the other side, his machine bursting into flames.

In this connection it is worthy of record, to show how much the fighting in the air was done over the German lines, that not one of the casualties in action sustained by the squadron during its first six months occurred on our side.

Captain C.R. Tidswell (6620) – is missing.
Second Lieutenant F. Thompson (6580) – is missing.

20th October 1916

Second Lieutenant A.B. Drewery in BE12 (6179) was returning from patrol over the Bapaume-Peronne area with a Martinsyde and was killed, when he was involved in a collision in the air.

22nd October 1916

On an offensive patrol over the battle area
Second Lieutenant Watts (6180) – is missing.

In the November the squadron was the first British unit to be re–equipped with French Spad aircraft (S.VII), a fast single–seater with a fixed Vickers gun geared to fire through the airscrew. The Spad was then the fastest scout in the air. (NB. For technical data see page 357.)

During November and December, the pilots of the Squadron were busy getting used to the new Spads. The months were virtually taken up with test flights and practice, with an occasional line patrol and bombing escort.

Line up of SPADS

(J.M. Bruce/G.S. Leslie Collection)

10th November 1916

The Squadron's first success with the Spad came very quickly when Captain I.H.D. Henderson, on a practice flight in a Spad, attacked a hostile aircraft in the vicinity of Bapaume. The hostile aircraft had opened fire with Captain Henderson about 1,000 feet above him. He dived, came up below the tail of the hostile aircraft, the closing to about 150 yards, fired about 50 rounds in bursts. The hostile aircraft caught fire and fell in flames near Gueudecourt.

Second Lieutenant Reed dropped eight bombs on Arleux station and sidings; four of the bombs exploded on a train moving south, and the remaining four exploded in the station. He then, before returning, fired about 20 rounds from his machine gun into the train.

11th November 1916

Captain Allen, Lieutenant Orlebar and Lieutenant Buck, dropped 24 bombs on Havrincourt chateau. All bombs appeared to fall near the mark.

20th December 1916

On a Line Patrol, from Hebuterne to Sailly Saillisel. Second Lieutenant Reed saw a hostile aircraft over Hebuterne under our A.A. He went to engage but it returned to its own lines.

21st December 1916

12.12pm Captain Allen in Spad A263 took off to look for hostile aircraft reported between

Arras and Frevent. He flew over Vaulx, Framecourt, Mardevil, but no hostile aircraft seen.

22nd December 1916
During a test and practice flight, Second Lieutenant Capper in a Spad shot down a hostile aircraft out of control near Louveral. Lieutenant P.G. Robinson was wounded in the action.

25th December 1916
When Christmas arrived it found few of the original squadron left among the officers, and several new faces among the NCOs and men. Captain Henderson, who had received the M.C. for his work in the September 'push', and who was the first of the squadron to fly the Spad, had just left for a much deserved rest on the Home Establishment. The Flight Commanders were now – Captain Allen, Captain Davidson, and Captain Baker, who had all received their promotion in the squadron. Of the flying officers who had crossed over in July, Lieutenant Selous alone remained. He was one of the first Spad pilots and handled it remarkably well. Lieutenant Morgan and Lieutenant Western also remained as Recording Officer and Equipment Officer respectively.

Winter training was now in full swing. Every pilot was sent through a special course on Scouts at St Omer before flying the Spad, because as yet there were no Training Squadrons equipped with these machines in England. An Aerial Gunnery School had been opened at Camiers, and each flight was sent in turn to do a fortnight's course. This was badly needed, and the results were very encouraging. In addition arrangements were made to practise aerial firing at targets a short distance from the aerodrome, pilots then being able to test their guns in the air before leaving for the lines. The advantage of having a target near at hand was quickly appreciated and the fullest use was made of it.

27th December 1916
Second Lieutenant Binnie in BE12 6619 during a engine test flight. His engine began vibrating and the oil pressure was showing nothing, he misjudged the landing, broke the front lower longeron. The starboard undercarriage was wrecked, the propellor smashed, and the port lower fabric torn. Casualty report rendered.

5th January 1917
At 10.45am when patrolling the line between Hebuterne and Sailly Saillisel, Lieutenant Capper chased a fast hostile aircraft south east from Sailly Saillisel, lost him and recrossed lines north of Noyon. He landed at Cacy le Grand for petrol and then returned to base. Lieutenant Child had to make a forced landing at Vert Galand with engine trouble and returned the following day, Second Lieutenant Reed damaged his machine in a forced landing at Hesden.

7th January 1917
Captain Sison, Second Lieutenant Cheatle and Lieutenant Canning whilst on line patrol, saw two hostile aircraft at 1.30pm at 5,000 feet flying east. They followed them to the lines but they glided down and escaped.

8th-22nd January 1917
When the weather permitted, these two weeks were confined to returning the old BE12's to the Aircraft Depots and picking up the replacement Spads. The Squadron not yet being at full strength with Spads.

23rd January 1917

At 10.55am, Second Lieutenant J.W. Baker in BE12 6622, taxied out as far as No 27 shed when he saw a Martinsyde landing. He remained stationary, but the Martinsyde did not see him and crashed into him.

By February the Squadron was fully equipped with Spads.

The Squadron continued to do Offensive Patrols and escorting Bomb Raids. At that period four BE2c and one BE2e were on the strength of the Squadron for special duty and several important missions were carried out for the Intelligence by Lieutenant Reed. These were then handed over to a special duty flight then formed.

1st February 1917

At 1.07pm to 3.10pm Lieutenant Orlebar with Captain Sison patrolled the line between Gommecourt and Sailly Saillisel. Lieutenant Orlebar lost Captain Sison at about 2.35pm after diving to look at another machine. No hostile aircraft seen. A.A. fire over Bapaume and Warlencourt.

From 2.05pm to 3.33pm on the day before he officially took command, Major Harvey–Kelly patrolled the line Gommecourt – Le Transloy, at 10,000 to 12,000 feet.

2nd February 1917

Major R.M. Rodwell who had commanded the Squadron since its formation returned to England and *the command was taken over by Major H.D. Harvey–Kelly D.S.O.*

11.40am to 2.10pm Lieutenant Buck took Spad A6640 on test. Reported:–

Climbed to 16,000 feet in 35 minutes not full out. Very cold and very slow climbing at finish. Fired 30 rounds at this height, 2 No. 4 jambs, and 2 No. 3 jambs. After 2 hours 20 minutes pressure failed – service tank ran well for five minutes and then failed. Spad at 16,000 feet – 85 mph, revs 1,450. One pint of oil left in machine.

3.36pm Lieutenant Capper took Spad A6641 on test flight and climbed to 15,000 feet in 35 minutes. Gravity tank cut out after seven minutes. 4.15pm Lieutenant Browne first solo flight. Good landing.

6th February 1917

Test and practice flights.

2.45pm Lieutenant Child took Spad A6633 on test flight. Climbed to 10,000 feet in 11 minutes. Speed at 10,000 feet 103mph. Reached 15,000 feet. He throttled down over the village and owing to small residue of petrol in tank, pressure dropped at once and could not be pumped up or reserve tank used in time, so he was short and damaged machine on landing. Casualty.

8th February 1917

Lieutenant Cronyn in Spad A6642 took off at 10.00am for a two and half hour test flight. Only did two hours due to fact watch in machine gained half an hour in two. Frequent stoppages on gun. 10,000 feet in 13½ minutes, 15,000 feet in 30 minutes. At 10,000 feet – 103 mph, 1640 revs. Machine does not run on gravity tank.

11th February 1917

12.45pm Lieutenant Child with another Spad was heavily fired at by our AA over Doullens. No hostile aircraft seen.

12.45pm Lieutenant Bozman on a test flight had to make an forced landing near Bernay. The machine damaged. Pilot unhurt.

14th February 1917

At 9.35am Lieutenant Capper in Spad A6641. Wheel collapsed on taxi-ing in and wing tip touched ground and broke compression rib.

At 10.30am Lieutenant Browne in Spad A263 had to make a forced landing near Ligescourt, in which the undercarriage was damaged.

15th February 1917

10.30am Lieutenant Child in Spad A6627 whilst out practicing, had the side cowling blown off. He landed at St Andre for 20 minutes to see the damage and fill up with petrol. Told by CO that hostile aircraft had been reported over St Pol. Took off and patrolled for one hour. At 12.30pm over Doullens was fired at again by our AA and saw two distinct patches of AA one in front of him and one on his right. This was observed from the aerodrome by Lieutenant Buck.

At 11.58am Captain Sison in Spad A6681 whilst formation flying and gun testing, had a piece of cowling tore off in air and lodge in flying wires. He managed to land with it safely.

17th-28th February 1917

The weather closed in allowing only an occasional patrol, test or practice flight. It was so bad that on the 25th, Captain Allen took off at 11.50am on a test flight, and lost his way. He landed at Ervn between Hesden and St Pol. Landed at Lealvillers having lost his way again, owing to clouds being at 400 feet. He eventually managed to find his way back to base.

The month of March started quietly with line patrols between Gommecourt - Sailly Saillisel, and Gommecourt – Puisieuxam-Mont, Irles, Le Transloy.

6th March 1917

At 4.30pm, Major Harvey-Kelly on a line patrol, Heudiscourt, Roisel, saw villages reported burning by the morning patrol still burning. Also fires could be seen as far as fifteen to twenty miles south, averaging four to eight miles behind enemy lines. Captain Allen returned from this patrol early, due to his magneto cutting out, and was shelled by our own AA guns west of Peronne.

16th March 1917

At 2.30pm Major Harvey-Kelly on a practice mission reported:-
"Very little aerial activity over lines. No hostile aircraft seen. Fired gun about 150 - 200 rounds, satisfactory. The following villages were seen to be burning; Achiet-le Grand, Biefvilliersles, Bapaume, Behagnies, Sapignies, Favreuil, Fremicourt, Beugny, Hermies, Villers Plouich, Gouzeaucourt, Heudicourt, Epehy, Peronne, also a large number of villages stretching away to the South and South-East.

17th March 1917

Offensive patrol at 9.50am. Major Harvey-Kelly in formation with, Captain Baker, Lieutenant Child. At 10.30am saw a large two seater with an Albatros scout well above. He dived on the two seater and gave him a burst at long range, then climbed quickly and got on top of the scout, which he opened fire on from 200 yards. He then got a No 3 stoppage after the first round and so broke off the engagement. He rectified the fault and fired the gun satisfactorily. At 11.10 am he saw another Albatros scout above him at about 15,000 feet. He manoeuvred for position and easily outclimbed the Albatros. The hostile aircraft turned and made away, but Major Harvey-Kelly caught up with him, dived on him from 150 to 200 yards and got a No. 3 jam after the first round. He could not free this in the air so he returned. Captain Baker engaged several hostile aircraft Albatros and two seaters at 14,000 to 16,000 feet between Bertincourt and Hermies. He dived on one single seater and a two seater with several other Spads. The single seater tried to climb up behind him, he turned and out climbed it.

Albatros C 111
(Crown Copyright – MOD – AHB)

19th March, 1917

On an offensive patrol over Cambrai, Lieutenant Puıves (A6633) – is missing.

24th March 1917

At 9.36am Lieutenant J.W. Baker whilst on patrol with the squadron got as far as Arras when his pressure gave out. He turned round for home and used his hand pump to gain sufficient pressure, then tried the mechanical pump, which he found worked. At this result he turned to rejoin the patrol. He saw two aircraft which he thought was his patrol, he joined them and on reaching them, he found them to be hostile aircraft. On seeing him approach, one flew in an easterly direction, the other due south some distance south east of Amiens. After pursuing him for some time, but unable to make any progress, he flew due west, his intention being to fly until he reached the sea as he had lost his map and was not certain of his way. On reaching the coast, he flew north east but his petrol gave out and he was forced to land in a small field in Londiniere. He returned to the base on the 28th March.

Lieutenant R.P. Baker (A6706) – is missing.

SPAD – A6706

(Crown Copyright – MOD – AHB)

At 2.38pm Captain Allen on escort to Martinsyde made a forced landing at Guillaucourt. He reported that the machine gun refused to stop firing and eventually shot in half both planes of the propellor. This was caused by a lock spring breaking. It fired 300 rounds before it stopped.

2nd April 1917

The Squadron moved to Vert Galand.

8th April 1917

The Squadron carried out eight offensive patrols this day, over Arras, Vimy, Douai and Cambrai.

THE ARRAS OFFENSIVE

9th April 1917

This day saw the commencement of the Arras offensive (the Squadron took part both in the Battle of Arras and the Third Battle of Ypres). Aerial fighting at this time was very intense. Our air superiority, which was so marked on the Somme, was seriously challenged at this stage both by the introduction of new aircraft types and the launching of the new German 'circuses' under Baron von Richthofen. A circus was simply a formation consisting of about forty-eight machines led in the air by the Commander. This intense activity was, however, curbed by the arrival of new British squadrons equipped with the DH4's, the Bristol fighter and the SE5.

10th April 1917

At 5.55pm on an Offensive Patrol. Lieutenant Child saw an Albatros scout at 8,000 feet over Quiery, and chased it back to Douai. He lost the hostile aircraft in cloud. As heavy cloud threatened he came down to 2,500 feet but was not followed by patrol. He saw no unusual activity on the roads. Saw a white light fired at him from Heninel south east of Arras. He attacked an AA battery east of Recourt and fired about 100 rounds at it from about 1,800 feet. He was forced to land at Bellevue owing to bad snowstorm and left when conditions improved. Lieutenant Holmes in the same patrol, lost the patrol north east of Arras due to snowstorm, and was fired at by our AA at Arras although he flew round at 3,000 feet to show circles. He then saw another Spad which he followed and landed at No 23 squadron aerodrome in a snowstorm.

13th April 1917

Lieutenant Buck saw a hostile aircraft at 8.40am and dived on it. The hostile aircraft then went down in a spin, flattened out and was attacked by another machine and went down to earth.

14th April 1917

On an offensive patrol at 10.30am Lieutenant Hamilton followed Lieutenant Reed over the battle area at 15,000 feet, and passed over Dury four times, each time being fired at by enemy AA. The enemy AA was very accurate regarding height as a small piece of shell penetrated the fuselage just under Lieutenant Hamilton's seat. At 12 noon Lieutenant Reed engaged a hostile aircraft and Lieutenant Hamilton was climbing to assist when he noticed the hostile aircraft's observer was hit. Shortly after the machine banked excessively and flat spun, eventually disappearing into clouds at 4,000 feet in a spinning nose dive.

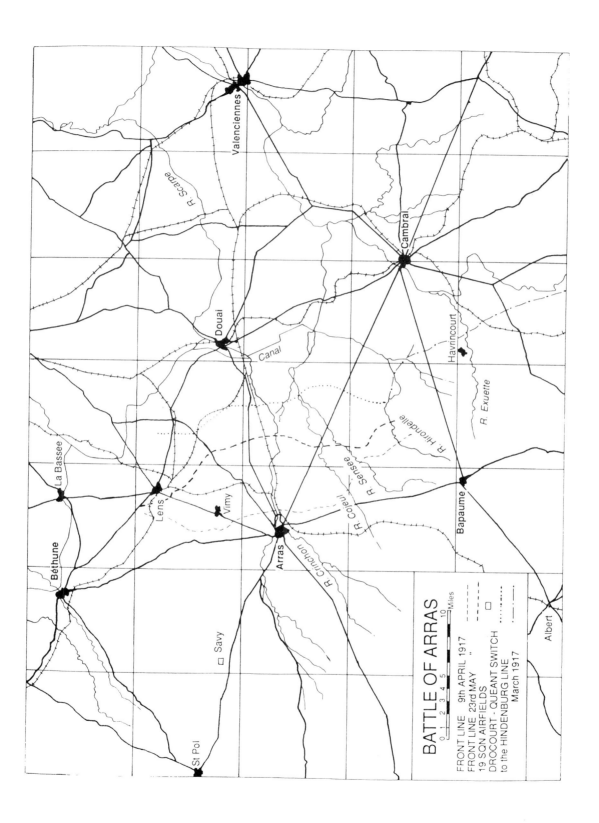

BATTLE OF ARRAS

FRONT LINE   9th APRIL 1917 ---------
FRONT LINE   23rd MAY   "   ---------
19 SQN AIRFIELDS   □
DROCOURT - QUEANT SWITCH   ···□···
to the HINDENBURG LINE
March 1917   ·—·—·—·

0 1 2 3 4 5   10
└─┴─┴─┴─┴─┴────────┘ Miles

Valenciennes

R. Scarpe

Cambrai

Douai

Canal

Havincourt

R. Exuette

La Bassee

R. Hirondelle

Béthune

Lens

Vimy

R. Sensee

R. Cojeul

Bapaume

Savy

Arras

R. Crinchon

St Pol

Albert

Lieutenant J.W. Baker (A6683) crash landed at Le Hameau, the machine was wrecked and the pilot taken to hospital unconscious.

Lieutenant Capper (A6746) – is missing.

22nd April 1917

In a combat area over Quiery, a two seater Albatros was destroyed by Lieutenant W.E. Reed.

Lieutenant W.E. Reed (Captain)
(Crown Copyright – Sqdn Album)

23rd April 1917

Lieutenant Reed on an offensive patrol was hit by AA fire after combat and landed at 8.30am with his machine damaged. He was wounded in the arm and admitted to hospital. Lieutenant Orlebar followed Lieutenant Reed over the area at 10,000 feet to 12,000 feet and saw him dive through AA fire. He lost him after that. Lieutenant Orlebar then saw a two seater Albatros over Vis-en-Artois, at 11,000 feet. He attacked but had to break off owing to his gun jamming after firing only 10 rounds. He saw another two seater later, firing two bursts at it from close range, but again had to break off owing to the gun jamming. On returning to base he found his propellor shot through by his own gun in twelve places.

At 4.50pm, Lieutenant Child attacked a hostile balloon adrift and brought it down near Vaucelles.

Major Harvey-Kelly at 5.32pm went out to meet Martinsydes but did not pick them up. He engaged a hostile aircraft at 10,000 feet over Graincourt, and got off a good burst of 60 to 80 rounds and it crashed about a mile out of Cambrai. The pilot attempted to flatten out before crashing.

29th April 1917

The squadron suffered a severe blow when they lost a patrol which included Major Harvey-Kelly D.S.O. – the Squadron Commander. On an offensive patrol at 10.00am, the three Spads engaged eleven red and grey Albatros's. Major Harvey-Kelly was shot down by Hans Wolff, Lieutenant Applin by Manfred Richthofen, and Lieutenant Hamilton by his brother Lothar Richthofen.

Major Harvey-Kelly (A6681) – is missing
Lieutenant Hamilton (A6753) – is missing
Lieutenant Applin (B1573) – is missing

Flying a BE2a machine, Major Harvey-Kelly was the first pilot to land in France on 13th August 1914 when the first three squadrons of the RFC flew over from England. He had, while in No 2 Squadron then a Lieutenant, taken part in the first aerial battle of the war on the 25th August 1914, forcing a German monoplane down by rifle fire, landed beside it and continued chasing the pilot on foot.

On a patrol at 11.30am Captain Davidson was seen to engage some hostile aircraft at 12.20pm. In the ensuing indecisive combat, his machine broke up in the air.

Captain Davidson (B1562) – is missing.

30th April 1917
Major W.G.S Sanday D.S.O., MC assumed command of the Squadron.

1st May 1917
The Squadron flew nine offensive patrols this day during which Lieutenant F.S. Wilkins, destroyed a two seater hostile aircraft.

2nd May 1917
The squadron flew ten offensive patrols. At 7.30pm, Captain Cairnes, with Lieutenants Hope and Anderson attacked a formation of seven hostile aircraft but without decisive results.

4th May 1917
Captain Hope brought a hostile aircraft down out of control.

11th May 1917
Major Sanday forced a two seater hostile aircraft to land.

12th May 1917
An offensive patrol at 6.33 pm over Croisilles, and Bailleul.
Captain Williams (B1560) – is missing.

18th May 1917
Second Lieutenant Holmes (B1588) – is missing.
Second Lieutenant Grandin – is missing.

SPAD – B1588. Captured by the Germans

(J.M. Bruce/G.S. Leslie Collection)

19th May 1917

Captain Cairnes on an offensive patrol, from 6.00am to 8.30am leading the formation saw a hostile aircraft ten miles east of the lines, east of Croiselles. He led the formation into the attack and the hostile aircraft went down completely out of control.

Lieutenant Allabarton (B1627) – is missing.

Major Mills in (A6749) had a fatal accident.

23rd May 1917

During offensive patrols one hostile aircraft destroyed by Lieutenant Orlebar and one driven down by Captain Cairnes.

25th May 1917

Captain Child on a patrol at 5.30am over Douai, attacked a hostile aircraft and drove it down out of control. During this combat Lieutenant Parry Okeden was seriously wounded in the head but flew back a distance of 34 miles, and landed without damaging his machine at No 32 Squadron Aerodrome. General Longcroft witnessed the landing and the severe conditions of his wounds. Lieutenant Parry Okeden was recommended for special recognition.

On a practice flight at 11.50am by Second Lieutenant Mearns, in B1620 he got his tail too high "getting off" and turned over. He was admitted to hospital with bad concussion and a dislocated shoulder.

27th May 1917

During offensive patrols this day Lieutenant McEntegart, Captain Hope, Captain Cairnes and Lieutenant Boeree all engage and attack hostile aircraft with indecisive results.

With the end of the Arras battle on the 15th May, 1917, the Squadrons of the 9th Wing moved north to take part in the forthcoming operations against the Messines-Wytschoete Ridge. 19 Squadron occupied the aerodrome at Liettres. For several days before the attack on the Messines-Wytschoete Ridge, which began on the 7th June, 1917, the squadron carried out offensive patrols over the area and engaged enemy aircraft in combat on many occasions. The squadron then took part in many successful ground strafing attacks during the attack on Messines.

June 1917

The squadron began to re-equip with the new 200hp engine SPAD.S.VII. This gave it a maximum speed of 138mph at 6,500 feet, a ceiling of 21,820 feet and an endurance of two hours. It was armed with two machine guns and had a crew of one.

4th June 1917

The 9th Wing was of the greatest value to the Second Army and on this date, General Trenchard sent the following telegram to Lieutenant Colonel C.L.N. Newall (OC 9th Wing):-
"Please congratulate yourself and all your pilots and observers on the excellent start made in this offensive".

Capt Chadwick was shot through the knee during combat and had to make a forced landing.

Lieutenant Sclater in B1537 returning with a bad engine, stalled and crashed very badly. He was sent to hospital.

5th June 1917

At 10.00am an offensive patrol was carried out over the battle area. Lieutenant Orlebar drove one hostile aircraft down out of control.

Lieutenant Grierson (A6747) – is missing.

6th June 1917

On an offensive patrol over Houthulst, Lieutenant Riggs drove a hostile aircraft down out of control.

MESSINES – WYTSCHOETE RIDGE

7th June 1917

The infantry offensive begins. Patrols were carried out over the area Houthulst Forest, Roulers, Menin, Quesnoy, and had many encounters with hostile aircraft. Much aerial fighting took place and the squadron drove down several hostile aircraft. Lieutenant G.S. Buck attacked the aerodrome at Marche from 800 feet, shot down an enemy machine that interfered with him, continued the attack on the sheds and shot up transport on the return journey. During this Messines attack low-flying began seriously and ground strafing played an important part in the work of the RFC. The Squadron accounted for three hostile aircraft one was destroyed by Captain Child, one was forced to land by Captain Buck, and one was driven down out of control by Lieutenants Orlebar, Rigg and Captain Cairnes.

14th June 1917

An offensive patrol of the squadron over Menin became engaged in a hot fight with hostile aircraft. Lieutenant Buck, flying a new 200hp Spad fitted with two synchronised guns, brought down a German machine above the fight.

15th June 1917

At 6.58am an offensive patrol led by Captain Young at 15,000 feet saw nine hostile aircraft at 9.00am north of Warneton. Captain Young had to break away due to pressure giving out, Lieutenant C.R.J. Thompson had his main petrol tank shot through and crashed on landing near Thiennes. One hostile aircraft was sent down out of control by Sergeant Clinch.

16th June 1917

Captain Hagon got the Bowden wires from the control stick caught behind the magneto when taking off, causing the gun to fire. The machine crashed, (B1586) (a complete write off), but the pilot was only shaken and cut about the nose.

17th June 1917

Captain Young in a patrol at 6.00pm with Lieutenants McEntegart, Foden, Thompson, Anderson and Captain Sowrey. They crossed the lines in good formation which was broken up during the combat with eight hostile aircraft near Wervicq. Captain Young destroyed one hostile aircraft and Captain Leacroft got another out of control.

18th June 1917

Lieutenant Orlebar brought down one hostile aircraft out of control.

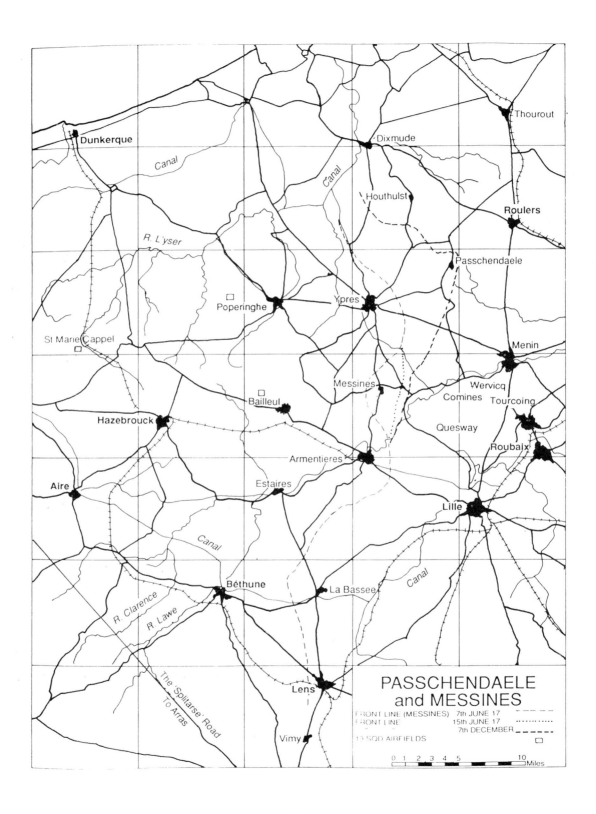

PASSCHENDAELE
and MESSINES

FRONT LINE (MESSINES)   7th JUNE 17 – – – –
FRONT LINE   15th JUNE 17 ·········
                                     7th DECEMBER – – – – –
13 SQD AIRFIELDS   □

0 1 2 3 4 5   10
                                        Miles

Reminiscences of a 19 Squadron Pilot
(original in Squadron Diary)

As a pilot in France I went over the lines,
And I met with an Albatros scout,
It seemed that he saw me or so I supposed,
His manouvre left small room for doubt,
He sat on my tail but with little detail, .
Of my subsequent actions I think I may say,
My turns approximated to the vertical,
As I deemed it expeditious to recede,
I frequently gyrated on my axis,
I attained prodigious atmospheric speed,
I descended with unparalled momentum,
My propellors point of rupture I surpassed,
I performed the most outstanding evolutions,
In other words splitassed.

21st June 1917

A patrol at 6.05am led by Captain Young in good formation, met a formation of eight hostile aircraft north of Wervicq at 7.00am. Lieutenant McEntegart followed by two other Spads attacked and dispersed the formation. Lieutenant Thompson returned after the combat with his machine considerably shot about.

27th June 1917

Captain Sowrey with four other Spads patrolled from 6.00pm to 8.00pm and attacked a formation of six hostile aircraft. Captain Sowrey shot down one hostile aircraft out of control.
Lieutenant Lowe (B1663) – is missing.

2nd July 1917

Between 10.30am and 12.20pm, Captains Young and Cairnes patrolled in the neighbourhood of four Sopwiths doing photography. They were seen safely over to our side of the lines when one hostile aircraft was seen crossing the lines. It was pursued east and attacked but with indecisive result. Six hostile aircraft were then seen by the Captains, east of the lines as the patrol reformed and again the combat was indecisive.

3rd July 1917

The squadron on patrol from 8.55am patrolled the battle area and saw a two seater hostile aircraft. Captain Young, Captain Cairnes, Lieutenants Thompson and Boeree all attacked this hostile aircraft which was driven down out of control.

6th July 1917

The patrol took off at 2.35pm and during the patrol, Captain Sowrey was dived on by an Albatros scout and attacked. He had to spin to get away and as a result his engine started to vibrate badly, causing him to return to base. Captain Leacroft attacked a hostile aircraft and drove it down out of control.

7th July 1917

The formation were patrolling at 16,000 to 10,000 feet near Lille at 8.55am, when a two seater hostile aircraft was seen and attacked by Captains Young and Leacroft. A second two seater was sighted near Armentieres and attacked but again with indecisive result. Lieutenant Riggs saw four hostile aircraft which he immediately attacked, driving three of them away. The fourth he drove down out of control east of Houthulst Forest. He was engaged several times by enemy formations. Later that day, Captain Sowrey saw two two seaters doing artillery observation about five miles east of the lines. He drove them off east but did not get close enough to engage.

12th July, 1917

Captain Hagon on patrol brought down a hostile aircraft out of control.
Lieutenant D.S. Weld (A6663) – is missing.

13th July, 1917

Aerial fighting continued and the number of hostile aircraft brought down by 19 Squadron was increased. One of the two hostile aircraft shot down on this day was accounted for by Major Sanday.
Major Sanday was on a practice flight at 11.15am and an enemy pilot was watching three

RE8's doing some photographic work over Lille. He then noticed the enemy pilot was about to attack from 21,000 feet and chased him for half an hour before finally shooting him down. He saw the hostile aircraft crash.

The early morning patrol, led by Captain Hagon had an indecisive combat with an Albatros scout, when his guns jammed. Lieutenant Best could not keep up with the patrol because his engine was running badly. While below the formation, he was attacked by four hostile aircraft and he dived away and recrossed the lines with his machine shot about, both front spars in bottom planes shot through, one rib in top plane shot through, one landing wire on port side also shot through.

Later that day, at 1.35pm Captain Sowrey in a 200hp Spad, attacked a two seater hostile aircraft and brought it down out of control.

The evening patrol at 6.45pm led by Captain Cairnes at 15,000 feet chased off a considerable number of hostile aircraft. A hostile aircraft being attacked by an SE5 spun downwards and as it came out of the spin, Captain Cairnes and Lieutenant Boeree attacked and chased it east. Lieutenant C.D. Thompson lost the formation during the combats and later when alone over Houthulst Forest attacked three hostile aircraft which climbed above. All four circle round each other for some time and the Spad was shot about. The hostile aircraft eventually went east, and they were faster and had a better climb than the Spad.

17th July 1917

At 8.25am, Captain Sowrey patrolled the area and saw one hostile aircraft. He attacked, firing about 20 rounds at it but it dived into a cloud and was lost.

19th July 1917

Lieutenant C.R.J. Thompson whilst on a patrol brought one hostile aircraft down out of control.

21st July 1917

The squadrons best day with four hostile aircraft accounted for. The patrols met considerable enemy aircraft activity, and Lieutenants C.D. Thompson and McEntegart both drove hostile aircraft down out of control. Captain Sowrey forced one two seater to land and drove one hostile aircraft scout down obviously out of control.

22nd July 1917

Lieutenant C.D. Thompson crashed on take off owing to the undercarriage giving way. Lieutenant Riggs on a test flight in Spad B1667 during the morning crashed in a field near the aerodrome. The machine was wrecked and the pilot killed.

Captain Young however, this day, brought down one hostile aircraft out of control.

26th July 1917

At 6.35pm. The squadron patrolled the area and joined a fight with two other Spads between Menin and the lines at 7.45pm. Lieutenant Wearne was last seen in close formation with Lieutenant McEntegart as they entered the fight.

Lieutenant Wearne (B3562) – is missing.

27th July 1917

Saw three hostile aircraft brought down out of control by the patrols. Lieutenants Kellogg, Harding and Boeree each accounting for one. Captain Leacroft patrolled the area in good formation at 7.45pm and led them into the attack on a large formation of enemy aircraft. The enemy aircraft were very active and one fight followed another.

28th July 1917
Patrol at 8.00am led by Lieutenant McEntegart over the area and they engaged several hostile aircraft. Lieutenant Waite joined in a fight between several FE's and about 12 enemy aircraft. The fighting was continuous thereafter. Lieutenant Best was much shot about during the combat and he landed at Bailleul. His machine, (B3565), was not repairable in the squadron. Lieutenant C.R.J. Thompson saw a Spad dive on a hostile aircraft and follow it down, which was last seen going east at 3,000 feet. He later attacked two formations of enemy aircraft and in the second attack either killed or wounded the observer in one machine.

29th July 1917
Lieutenants Best and Powers attacked and destroyed a single seater hostile aircraft.
Lieutenant F.B. Best (B3531) – is missing.

THE THIRD BATTLE OF YPRES

The 31st July 1917 – the first day of the Third Battle of Ypres, great assistance was given to the attacking infantry by low-flying machines, in spite of AA and machine-gun fire. The Wing received another telegram from General Trenchard couched in these words – "Today has shown very plainly how with good pilots the air can help the infantry on the ground even in the worst weather".
Lieutenant W.B. Kellogg (B3568) – is missing.

5th August 1917
A patrol at 6.37pm led by Captain Leacroft. Patrolled the area with three other Spads and dived on a formation of ten hostile aircraft which we chased down. Later saw six hostile aircraft and again dived on them, two of which went down in spins but it was impossible to see if out of control or not owing to bad visibility. Lieutenant Jerrard crashed his machine on landing. Machine wrecked (A8830) and the pilot admitted to hospital.

10th August 1917
A patrol at 6.00pm. Lieutenant Pentland in (B3566) crashed taking off and wrecked his machine. He went back for another, restarted and joined the formation, which had indecisive combat with some hostile aircraft. Major Sanday leading the patrol saw a large explosion near Zarren in which the smoke went up 500 feet and lasted for about 10 minutes. He attacked two hostile aircraft and sent one down possibly out of control.

12th August 1917
Escort patrol at 12.50pm led by Lieutenant C.D. Thompson, saw the Martinsydes over the lines and back. On the way four hostile aircraft were seen and the formation dived on two of these. Several other formations were seen and attacked. Lieutenant Pentland drove one hostile aircraft down out of control. Lieutenant Bryson in (B1593) collided with Lieutenant Barker, in (B3563) over the aerodrome.
Lieutenant Nichols (B3507) – is missing.

13th August 1917
Lieutenant Barker brought one hostile aircraft down out of control.

14th August 1917

The Squadron moved to Poperinghe to take part in the second attack East of Ypres. This was the 5th Army Area, so the squadron came under the orders of the OC 22nd (Army) Wing, 5th Brigade, RFC.

15th August 1917

At 2.27pm the squadron led by Captain Gordon-Kidd patrolled the area. Three enemy aircraft were seen and attacked. Lieutenant C.R.J. Thompson followed his leader and dived on two enemy aircraft and drove one down out of control. The formation later attacked another enemy aircraft formation.

16th August 1917

Enemy aircraft were so numerous on this date that combats went on almost continuously.

One early morning patrol led by Captain Gordon-Kidd with the rest of the formation attacked some enemy aircraft from close quarters and drove them down but it was impossible to observe the results owing to other enemy aircraft coming to attack. A further eight enemy aircraft were engaged in indecisive combat and a general combat ensued with many enemy aircraft with both British and French Spads.

Lieutenant H.C. Ainger attacked a two seater enemy aircraft east of Passchendaele at close range and forced him to land in a field east of Passchendaele and Ypres - Roulers road. He then attacked it on the ground. Later he attacked and dispersed some infantry on the Ypres - Roulers road, leaving four or five lying on the ground and also three lorries but did not see that result. Lieutenant Pentland followed Lieutenant Ainger also firing at the transport from a low altitude, sending it into a ditch. Lieutenant Pentland was then attacked by two enemy aircraft, which he drove off east and returned towards Menin to be attacked again by enemy aircraft. He fired on a party of troops scattering them and was again attacked by a formation of enemy aircraft. He returned with his machine (B3615) a write off as it was very much shot about. About the same time Lieutenant J. Manley together with a French Spad attacked 12 Albatros scouts south west of Roulers. Lieutenant Manley, diving and firing at one brought it down out of control. An enemy aircraft which was attacking an SE8 was also driven down out of control by Lieutenant Manley.

Lieutenant Bryson managed to get his machine back (B1622) but it was much shot about, a write off.

Lieutenant Waite was wounded in the patrol in the left side and arm. He managed to bring down an enemy aircraft out of control. He landed in a shell hole and his machine was damaged.

Lieutenant C.D. Thompson (B3471) – is missing.

Second Lieutenant A.T. Shipwright (A6634) – is missing.

17th August 1917

A patrol at 5.23am. Captain Sowrey the leader patrolled the area and fired at one two seater. He then joined in a fight between SE5's and several enemy aircraft and drove one down, which was seen to crash by Lieutenant Pentland. A little later, at 8.50am Lieutenant Manley followed his leader and joined in an attack on five enemy aircraft. He became alone and attacked a further five enemy aircraft, one of which he sent down probably out of control. Captain Gordon-Kidd encountered two enemy aircraft sending one down out of control. During the combat his rear spar in top plane of front centre section was shot through.

18th August 1917

7.34am patrol. Lieutenant Powers followed Lieutenant Harding and twice dived on enemy aircraft. The second time he fired right into one which disappeared and might have been shot down. The observer was killed or wounded.

20th August 1917

5.24am. Captain Sowrey led the formation up to a two seater enemy aircraft at 10,000 feet. He dived and drove it down to 8,000 feet, ten miles east of the lines but it escaped to the east. He then climbed and patrolled the Menin-Roulers road. Half an hour later with Lieutenants Pentland and Ainger, they dived on a two seater over the Houthulst Forest, following it down from 10,000 feet to 5,000 feet but had to break off owing to his gun jamming. Lieutenants Pentland and Ainger followed in down even further both firing at very close range, and last saw the enemy aircraft out of control disappearing into the ground mist.

21st August 1917

At 10.20am Captain Gordon-Kidd led the formation over the Menin-Roulers road. They encountered five enemy aircraft east of Polygon Wood who were diving to attack an RE8. They dived at the enemy formation and attacked. One machine burst into flames. Lieutenant C.R.J. Thompson followed his leader into this attack and saw the enemy aircraft go down in flames. Later they attacked two two-seaters, then three more enemy aircraft east of Houthulst Forest, followed by another formation of five enemy aircraft, driving one down to 3,000 feet, but with indecisive results. During this last attack, Captain Gordon-Kidd became separated from the formation, came back to Ypres to gain his height. Later he went north of Roulers to try for a balloon, coming down to 7,000 feet, but encountered two patrols of enemy aircraft which intercepted him. He returned through cloud.

22nd August 1917

9.40am. Lieutenant Pentland dived on one enemy aircraft but his gun jammed, and whilst clearing his gun was chased over the lines by the enemy aircraft. He attacked one two seater with Lieutenant Ainger and forced it to land in a damaged condition. Later he attacked an Albatros scout but without result. On the fourth patrol of the day at 4.16pm, Captain Gordon-Kidd led the formation and patrolled east of the artillery station at 8,000 feet. They encountered ten enemy aircraft south east of Houthulst Forest at 5,000 feet and attacked. Being outnumbered and below the majority of the enemy formation the combat was indecisive. The enemy aircraft climbed up east and approached the lines again over Houthulst Forest. Again an indecisive combat took place although the squadron were outnumbered. Lieutenant Van Der Byl fired a burst into one enemy aircraft, but was then attacked by ten other coming from above and had to break off, and so lost sight of the one he was attacking. Lieutenant Graham attacked a two seater at 3,000 feet, chased it down to 500 feet, firing bursts into it all the way. It went down apparently out of control but he was unable to watch it crash as his engine began to miss.

25th August 1917

Two enemy aircraft accounted for this day. Captain Leacroft attacked a two seater with Lieutenant Barker, and when his guns jammed, he left it to Lieutenant Barker who brought it down out of control. Lieutenant Bryson saw one enemy aircraft north west of Houthulst Forest and sent it down out of control.

26th August 1917

At dawn six machines of the squadron attacked the aerodromes at Bisseghem and Marche from a low altitude. On the return journey ground targets were attacked and several enemy aircraft were engaged - one of whom crashed. During this attack five enemy machines were brought down.

Take off was at 5.20am. Captain Leacroft on this special mission together with the other Spads accompanied the formation and attacked an enemy aircraft on the way out but result indecisive. After the attack, Captain Leacroft drove down one enemy aircraft out of control which was seen to crash by Lieutenant Ainger. Many enemy aircraft scouts came up from Bisseghem and Heule, several of which were engaged in turn. Captain Leacroft attacked two two seaters both of these were D111 and immediately after three others followed them back to the lines. Lieutenant Ainger met two enemy aircraft on the way out, which were attacked and one destroyed. On arrival at Courtrai, he fired at a train going into the town from the north. He then flew to Marke aerodrome with Lieutenant Pentland, dived and fired at eight Albatros scouts on the ground. He had fired only 10 rounds when his gun jammed. He freed this, turned, dived for a second time and again his gun jammed after ten rounds. He made for home and just east of Menin was fired at by a machine gun from inside a hospital flying a red cross flag.

Lieutenant McEntegart engaged three enemy aircraft in turn. The second he sent down out of control, the third hit his petrol tank so he returned home.

Lieutenant Graham attacked Bisseghem aerodrome, going down fired a long burst into the hangars. He followed Lieutenant Pentland when he dived on a troop train, but did not get off many rounds with a stoppage.

Lieutenant Pentland went down to within 20 feet of the ground as he attacked Marke aerodrome, firing at eight Albatros's on the ground. Leaving the aerodrome, he went down to 500 feet and attacked a troop train travelling alone the Courtrai-Menin railway until his gun jammed.

Lieutenant Barker returned from this mission with his machine wrecked (B3570) and himself shot in two places. He was admitted to hospital.

Second Lieutenant C.P. Williams (B3492) – is missing.

31st August 1917

Lieutenant Pentland brought one enemy aircraft down out of control, east of Moorslede.

Lieutenant Patterson on a practice flight crashed and wrecked his machine (A6641).

1st September 1917

A 6.30am patrol, led by Captain Leacroft. Patrolled the area and had five combats with enemy aircraft south of Houthulst Forest and east of Polygon. There being considerable fighting throughout the patrol with one enemy aircraft shot down, confirmed by the AA.

Lieutenant Sant (B3569) – is missing.

2nd September 1917

Lieutenant McEntegart brought down one enemy aircraft out of control. Captain Manley became separated from the formation owing to the clouds and encountered eight enemy aircraft.

Lieutenant Spencer (A312) – is missing.

3rd September 1917

At 7.31am Captain Leacroft with three other Spads met a formation of six enemy aircraft Albatros scouts. Lieutenant McEntegart followed Captain Leacroft and saw several formations of enemy aircraft and had three indecisive combats. On the third occasion he fired at an Albatros over Menin and it went down. He was unable to watch it as there were many machines about at the time and there was a big risk of colliding. This enemy aircraft was seen to go down out of control.

4th September 1917

At 3.13pm Captain Leacroft led the patrol and had three indecisive combats. He had one combat in which he fired at the enemy aircraft at very close range. The enemy aircraft turned completely on its back and went down vertically and at first out of control. The enemy aircraft pilot resumed control for a time but must finally have crashed or else been forced to land in a damaged condition.

At 8.07pm Lieutenant Pentland led the formation on the first section of the patrol over the lines and climbed to a higher altitude. A considerable amount of fighting ensued but with indecisive results.

5th September 1917

Moving to Bailleul the Squadron came under the orders of the OC 11th (Army) Wing, 2nd Brigade and took part in the Second Army operations, carrying out offensive patrols and low-flying.

6th September 1917

An unusual entry in the Squadron Record Book under Duty – "Aerial Sentry Patrol". For the next few days the squadron were settling in at their new home and familiarising themselves with the surrounding countryside.

11th September 1917

A message was received that enemy aircraft were working the area. Three Spads left the ground at 12.40pm to find the enemy aircraft. Lieutenant Pentland was delayed in starting and went north hoping to find another enemy aircraft which had been reported. He met two two seaters, one of which he destroyed south west of Menin. The other then boldly attacked him and after a long combat during which he was hindered by gun stoppages, the other Spads which had seen the combat going on, arrived and Captain Sowrey destroyed the two seater.

13th September 1917

Captain Manley took off at 6.25am with Lieutenant Van Der Byl on an offensive patrol. The weather was unfavourable, so they flew down to 500 feet over the trenches up the Lys and both fired at groups of men in shell holes and some trenches north of Warneton. They fired continually at a bridge crossing the Lys, just west of Comines, whenever enemy troops could be seen crossing it. Captain Manley was shot in the engine and force landed near Armentieres.

15th September 1917

At 10.44am the northern patrol saw a formation flying 2,000 feet above them at 7,500 feet and thought they were British. These turned out to be 2 seater enemy aircraft and Lieutenant Pentland climbed and attacked the formation, south west of Ypres. The enemy aircraft split up and headed east. He attacked one, severely damaging it and killing or wounding the observer. He drove it down to 3,000 feet but had to break off owing to his gun jamming. The enemy aircraft was still going down.

16th September 1917

Lieutenant Dawson flew east from Armentieres to Tourcoing, firing at some troops on the outskirts of the town. He then went on to Mouseron and there saw a large number of troops marching through the town on the Menin road. There was at least 2,000 of them, he came down to a very low altitude and fired at them heavily, scattering those who were on the main road clear of the town. He then proceeded north through Courtrai and west through Menin, but only a few troops were seen and fired at. He attacked an enemy scout but lost it in the clouds.

Lieutenant Pentland and Lieutenant Graham crossed the lines flying east to Bas Warneton and from there continued north firing at ground targets, descending to 200 feet on the east side of the enemy trenches while our barrage was on. They attacked the enemy troops continuing this for half an hour also attacking anything seen on the roads running east. Lieutenant Graham suddenly disappeared.

Captain Sowrey flew east of the trenches from east of Armentieres to Frelinghien, firing at some troops from 100 feet. He then climbed and flew east along the road to Lille, then turning west and coming down again to 100 feet, scattered some troops with his fire. He did not notice much troop movement on the roads but convoys of lorries, which he fired at. Later when over Questnoy he saw some teams dragging guns and broke up one team completely attacking from 100 feet.

The afternoon patrol were attacked by four enemy aircraft, one of which was shot down out of control by Lieutenant Pentland. He had to return immediately himself, his engine having been shot. Captain Leacroft also brought one down out of control.

Lieutenant Graham (B3618) – is missing.

17th September 1917

Northern area patrolled at first the weather was good, and enemy aircraft activity was normal, chiefly two seaters. Later thick clouds came up. Captain Leacroft attacked a two seater getting in so close he collided with it, breaking the top of the plane and one incidence wire. The enemy aircraft's observer got a burst into his fuselage breaking two struts. Lieutenants McEntegart and Kirby then attacked this enemy aircraft getting in some fairly good shooting, the later getting a stoppage when very close in. The enemy aircraft managed to get away but must have been damaged.

Southern patrol saw a good many two seaters doing artillery work. Captain Manley attacked one and drove it off. He then attacked a formation of three and fired at one from very close range, it went down completely out of control between Comines and Wervicq. Confirmed by Lieutenant Jones. The other two enemy aircraft attacked Captain Manley but he got away and then chased them east. Lieutenant Van Der Byl attacked a two seater north of Questnoy but after firing 50 rounds and while continuing to drive the enemy aircraft down got a stoppage and the enemy aircraft escaped.

18th September 1917

At 7.46am Captain Sowrey followed by Lieutenant Strang saw two two seaters at 5,000 feet, north of Wervicq. He attacked from the rear and fired a considerable burst into one. The enemy aircraft went down probably damaged, the observer who had been firing vigorously at first, having ceased to fire altogether. Captain Sowrey followed it down for some distance when four enemy aircraft scouts came down. There were four Sopwith Camels on the same level as the enemy aircraft but they did not appear to see them or attack them. Capt Sowrey afterwards dived on a single seater enemy aircraft into which he got a good burst but his gun jammed. Later still he attacked a balloon firing a long burst and following it down to 2,000 feet. The balloon was pulled down rapidly.

At 8.10am a message was received that enemy aircraft were working the area. Captain Leacroft on arrival at the lines saw four two seaters. He dived on one but they all made east towards Menin. He followed them diving and firing at them three times in succession. He got very near to one formation which was going down very erratically and rapidly, especially one enemy aircraft he had been firing at but he could not say if out of control. At 9.30am Captain Leacroft went up with his formation and on reaching the lines saw four blue Albatros scouts flying over the lines. He got into position but his gun fired one shot.

An enemy aircraft was seen to collide with a British aircraft and they crashed near Crucifix Corner, just east of Bailleul. The pilot Captain Manley being killed (B3503).

The afternoon patrols over the northern section met many enemy aircraft scouts having combats with formations of six, four and nine in turn. At 2.53pm a message was received that an enemy aircraft was working the area. Captain Sowrey had a burst top water tank and had to return. The rest of the formation without their leader, engaged five red nosed Albatros scouts having a violent combat, assisting one another in turn. Lieutenant Dawson followed one enemy aircraft down until it crashed. He then returned over the trenches at only 200 feet. Lieutenant Jones continued the combat with the other four enemy aircraft firing many rounds at them and being himself very much shot about. On reaching the lines, he turned once more at the enemy aircraft but they would not follow him over the west side of the lines. Lieutenant Paterson was shot through the shoulder early in the fight and landed at 23 Squadron, his machine being shot about to such an extent as being unrepairable in the squadron.

20th September 1917

Early in the morning, the weather was exceedingly bad with thick cloud and mist at 200 feet, and it was raining until 6.00am. Lieutenant Bryson was to take off on a special mission to attack Heule Aerodrome. As soon as there was any light, and the rain had stopped, Lieutenant Bryson set out. It was 6.12am and he climbed above the clouds to about 5,000 feet. He then flew east for about 20 minutes searching for a long time for Heule Aerodrome, but after repeatedly coming down through the clouds and looking for it, was quite unable to find it, or even determine his location at all accurately.

Lieutenant Bryson says:-

"At 6.35am I came down through a gap in the clouds and saw a village below me with a large farm near it, but as this offered no target that was worth engaging, I climbed up again and flew east for another five minutes. I then came down again and this time saw a first class road with an ammunition dump at one side of it, composed of boxes and things with one or two huts. There were also a good many people moving about the place. I dropped one 20lb Cooper's bomb on this dump from a height of 150 feet, but did not observe the result. I also fired about 70 rounds from my gun at some men who were moving about on the road not far off. After that I flew on and came to a larger camp which consisted of wooden huts and many tents, there was a considerable amount of people moving about the camp. I dropped a second 20lb Cooper's bomb from a height of 100 feet and saw it go off right in the middle of the camp. Thereafter, I fired many rounds into the camp and its surroundings, being still at a very low altitude."

The north patrol at 6.30am crossed the lines in very thick cloud with occasional gaps. The formation patrolled below the clouds but soon lost one another. Lieutenant Pentland saw a battery firing from a sunken road near the Comines canal. He tried to bomb this battery but for some reason his bomb would not drop. He then rendezvoused with Lieutenant Thompson and they patrolled together over Polygon Wood. They climbed through the clouds and went over Courtrai. They then came down through the cloud and followed the road from Moorslede to Becelaere, firing at one or two infantrymen from 400 feet. After this Lieutenant Pentland saw another battery firing and came down to 400 feet, dropped one Coopers bomb but did not observe the result. Lieutenant Thompson then fired a good burst into this battery.

The 9.12am patrol also became split up due to the cloud. Captain Sowrey came down through the clouds at 10.00am near Gheluewe and saw 150 infantrymen going north west along the road towards Terhand. These he fired at from a very low altitude and scattered them. These men seemed to be specially detailed for firing as a few of them stayed where they were and fired at him. Captain Sowrey went up into the clouds and continued north, came down again and found an AA battery near Oosthoek which seemed very active. He attacked the battery which consisted of three guns firing continuously from 200 to 100 feet until all his ammunition had been expended. There was an explosion on the ground as though some of the ammunition had exploded and all the crew disappeared. Lieutenant Strang became separated from the other Spads and while flying alone at 300 feet, trying to observe enemy movement behind their lines, he suddenly met a two seater enemy aircraft probably doing contact work as he was flying at only 150 feet. Lieutenant Strang dived right at the enemy aircraft and while firing right into it, it suddenly dived right into the ground as though the pilot had been killed. Lieutenant Strang was then at 100 feet and could see that the enemy aircraft was completely crashed. After this he turned to come home and was dived on by four other enemy aircraft which followed him back to the lines. He crossed the trenches at a very low altitude and returned with his machine very much shot about.

10.22am. Lieutenant Pentland with Lieutenant Van Der Byl met a two seater flying towards the lines at 1,500 feet and had an indecisive combat with it. He dropped one Cooper's bomb on some large sheds near a main road, then encountered three enemy aircraft at 3,000 feet and they dived on him. On turning round he saw another two red nose scouts below him. Some other Spads came up and a general combat followed in which all the enemy aircraft were driven east. Lieutenant Thompson became separated from the other Spads on this patrol owing to the clouds and he flew east. Coming through a gap in the clouds he saw 50 infantrymen marching towards the lines in fours with rifles and steel helmets. He fired a large number of rounds into them from 100 feet until his gun jammed.

The formation took off at 5.45pm and when flying at 8,000 feet suddenly noticed twelve enemy aircraft 2,000 feet above them. Two of the enemy aircraft dived down and Captain Sowrey got near to one and fired at it at close range. The enemy aircraft turned on its side and the other Spads saw it go down out of control, a little way north of Menin.

21st September 1917

The patrol took off at 9.15am and patrolled in two formations, a high and a low, with Lieutenant McLeod patrolling alone above the higher formation. The higher formation with two SE5's encountered many enemy aircraft scouts. A general fight ensued in which Captain Leacroft got one enemy aircraft, an Albatros D111 out of control over Dadizeele. The Spads and SE5's were outnumbered three to one. Captain Bryson fired at several of the enemy aircraft but with indecisive results.

Lieutenant McRea (B3642) – is missing.
Lieutenant Inglis (B3557) – is missing.
Lieutenant Kirby (B3533) – is missing.

A captured Albatros D111

22nd September 1917

An afternoon patrol in two layers took off at 4.46pm. Captain Sowrey was patrolling alone near the formations in a 180hp Spad. The formation joined some SE5's and dived with them on several two seater enemy aircraft and one enemy aircraft scout. Two two seaters were attacked by the Spads but they dived away east towards their lines and were lost. Lieutenant Dawson saw an enemy aircraft approaching a British balloon near Inverness copse. The enemy aircraft turned away as Lieutenant Dawson attacked and he fired at it from close range. The enemy aircraft spun down and Lieutenant Dawson followed it, firing again as it came out of the spin. It suddenly went down completely out of control over Cheluvelt (confirmed by AA Battery).

23rd September 1917

Lieutenant Strang brought an enemy aircraft down out of control near Lindselles.

24th September 1917

The Squadron took off at 1.38pm and patrolled again in two formations one above the other. As they approached the lines east of Ypres at 6,000 feet, about fifteen enemy aircraft dived on them. A general combat ensued during which Lieutenant Pentland was forced to land at Lalovie with his machine much shot about. The other Spads got together and again attacked eight of these enemy aircraft in indecisive combats, as they tried to do artillery work, near Menin. Lieutenant McEntegart thought he damaged one enemy aircraft, Lieutenant Thompson's combat being spoilt by a stoppage. Lieutenant Roberts on his way home from Ypres, ran into a thin balloon rope which swung him round, but he escaped before he became further entangled.

The 4.44pm patrol found the enemy aircraft less active. Two two seaters were seen and chased to Boelcappelle, where Lieutenant Dawson dived on one, a Rumpler, and got it down out of control. Captain Sowrey saw five SE5's fighting at 13,000 feet over Menin. He saw one enemy aircraft spinning down out of this fight and waited for it to flatten out. As it did so he dived on it and got in a good burst until he had a stoppage. This was corrected and some further rounds were fired, but again a stoppage. The enemy aircraft was still going down but Captain Sowrey does not think it was out of control.

25th September 1917

The north patrol at 10.40am found the visibility exceptionally bad. Lieutenant McLeod was dived on and fired at from a long range but was unable to see the machine that was firing at him.

The southern patrol at 10.45am. Lieutenant Pentland saw three enemy aircraft above to which he climbed and fired a burst at from below. The enemy aircraft dived east and escaped. Later he saw a two seater over Questnoy which was above him. He climbed to within 300 feet firing a few bursts up at it but was obliged to break off as his engine was overheating. He dived once or twice to try to cool his engine, but had to return as it began to overheat very badly. Lieutenant Powers went on and attacked a two seater enemy aircraft over St Marguerite just south of Comines at 11.45am. He was shot through the engine however and had to return.

At 3.15pm Lieutenant Holt was patrolling the 10th Corps Front and attacked a two seater enemy aircraft flying low and doing artillery work. He brought it down out of control just south east of Gheluvelt.

That afternoon at 4.08pm a message was received that the enemy troops were massing for an attack on the 10th Corps Front. Lieutenant Powers after studying the position on the map carefully for a minute or two, jumped into his machine which had been got ready for him and left the ground a few minutes after the message had been received. His orders were to fly low over the enemy ground in question and bring back information on their movements.

Lieutenant Powers (B3520) – is missing.

The southern patrol took off at 4.46pm, had indecisive combats with many enemy aircraft. Lieutenant Pentland had much fighting with the enemy aircraft and after driving three away got two on his tail. At this juncture, Captain Leacroft and Lieutenant Bryson on the northern patrol, caught sight of Lieutenant Pentland and went to his assistance. They fired several good bursts at close range and the enemy aircraft was seen to crash by a spotter of H Battery, 2nd Army AA south east of Houthem. Lieutenant McEntegart saw one machine break up and come down in flames between Zarren and Courtmarke.

26th September 1917

7.00am southern patrol with Lieutenant Dawson and Lieutenant Strang at 700 to 1,200 feet. Lieutenant Dawson soon after crossing the lines made towards a hostile balloon near Comines. He was subjected to very heavy machine gun fire which shot through the main petrol tank, top planes, main spar, while a flaming onion caught on his tail and nearly set his machine on fire. He was obliged to return home using his nourice[*]. He noticed very heavy transport on the road outside Comines. A new bridge was seen across the canal which this transport was proceeding to, heading north west.

Lieutenant Strang attacked the balloon with Lieutenant Dawson, which was brought down rapidly. He also was heavily engaged by the machine gun battery close by. He dived on it firing about 100 rounds from 500 feet. The men about the place immediately scattered, leaving

---

[*]   Intensive investigation has cast no light on what this might be – unless it means "nouse"

two stretched on the ground. Going on he had nine separate combats with enemy aircraft. Three indecisive with Albatros scouts, five indecisive with two seaters and one decisive with an Albatros two seater. In this last combat, he got right on the enemy aircraft, first killing the observer and then firing right into the pilot and engine. The enemy aircraft spun down with its engine full on and was seen to crash by the Officer i/c AA. After this fighting he returned to the aerodrome very much shot about, having actually a bullet hole right through the earpad of his flying cap.

The northern patrol, Lieutenant Pentland and Lieutenant Candy on a low patrol were looking carefully for any movement of enemy troops but none were seen. An enemy aircraft contact machine was seen flying near Becelaere by Lieutenant Candy and immediately afterwards, another one on the north east side of the Polygon Wood. Lieutenant Candy attacked the second enemy aircraft but was immediately dived upon by an Albatros D111. He swung round and fired about 20 rounds at the enemy aircraft but had a stoppage. At the same time six more enemy aircraft dived on him from the left driving him down to 50 feet. He put his nose down as though overheating very badly necessitating his return. Lieutenant Pentland as far as can be ascertained, dropped one 20lb Coopers bomb near a railway siding to the south of Ypres-Roulers Road, where there was an ammunition dump. The dump was seen to blow up. Immediately afterwards he was attacked and shot down by five enemy aircraft scout's, all his controls being shot through. He just managed to cross the lines and crashed (B3620). He had been shot in the face, one eye being affected and in the side. He was admitted to hospital.

Captain Leacroft and Lieutenant McEntegart took off at 9.27am to patrol the northern area. Captain Leacroft attacked a two seater at 800 feet but with indecisive results. He saw a third two seater and after firing at it from various positions for a time, got right on its tail and after firing from close quarters, brought it down out of control. Afterwards he engaged a circular concrete trench work, with a dozen men round it. He fired 200 rounds at it from 500 feet, scattering the men who fled in all directions. He then fired at 100 men, scattering them also. This target which was also engaged by Lieutenant McEntegart, being some sort of gun emplacement. The men had difficulty in getting out of it quickly.

Lieutenant Bryson and Lieutenant McLeod crossing the lines saw some men moving around a square patch of water. Lieutenant Bryson came down to 600 feet and dropped a 20lb Coopers bomb which burst a little distance from his target. Afterwards he saw a machine gun firing at him. He came down still lower and dropped a second Coopers bomb from 300 feet and saw it burst only a few yards away from the machine gun. It must have killed or wounded some men and may have damaged the gun. Later he saw four sections of infantrymen moving along the road in artillery formation. He fired at them from 500 feet and scattered them. After this he had an indecisive combat with a two seater enemy aircraft. Lieutenant McLeod followed Lieutenant Bryson and after crossing the lines saw a few men kindling a fire behind a trench just west of Houthem. He fired at them from under 800 feet and saw them all jump into the trench.

Captain Sowrey and Lieutenant Jones at 9.39am followed the road from Ypres to Menin at 2,000 feet and just in clouds until they reached Koelenberg. They then turned north and saw a large number of troops in fours behind the wood. Captain Sowrey came down very low and fired continuously at them from under 200 feet. The men scattered and he was then immediately attacked by eight enemy aircraft from above and driven down to within a few feet of the ground. He eventually managed to get back into the clouds again and fired several rounds at two of the enemy aircraft but without any effect. During this time there was very considerable machine gun fire and flaming onions from the ground. He returned to the aerodrome dropping a message on the way at the Army Report Centre, to give information of the men he had seen massed behind the wood. Lieutenant Jones who followed Captain Sowrey was wounded during this patrol in the left foot and returned to the aerodrome. Before going to hospital he stated that when flying near Polderhoek, he saw a two seater flying at 2,000 feet. He got close to it and after firing three good bursts into it, thought he had killed the pilot, as it suddenly went down completely out of control. He was then immediately attacked by three Albatros scouts from above and being shot through the foot. He managed to shake them off with difficulty.

Southern patrol at 10.07am. Lieutenant Dawson crossed the lines with Lieutenants Thompson and Holt, near Warneton keeping a sharp look out for the enemy movements on the ground. Nothing of any importance was seen and at 10.35am he attacked a two seater between Houthem and Comines. Following it down to 150 feet and forcing it to land, the observer having been killed. He was heavily fired at from the ground.

Northern patrol. Captain Leacroft suddenly saw a two seater enemy aircraft just above his head going through the cloud. He got in a good burst at it from underneath but it disappeared and as the clouds were very thick it was not seen again. Afterwards six Albatros scouts were encountered by four Spads. Lieutenant Holt was dived on by an Albatros D111 and he turned and fired at this from fairly long range. Three other enemy aircraft however, immediately got on his tail and he was very badly shot about. He returned to the aerodrome with his top plane, both bottom planes, centre section, petrol tank and mirror shot through. Also the petrol pipe from nourice. Lieutenant Bryson fired at one of these enemy aircraft finally losing them in the clouds. During this patrol weather conditions were very bad.

At 3.40pm, Lieutenant Dawson after returning from patrol immediately restarted of his own free will, and flew over the trenches on the southern area and saw a lot of men massed in trenches running along them towards the line. He flew up and down these trenches three times firing 250 rounds from 100 feet, until all the men he described had taken cover in the dugouts.

Second Lieutenant G.B. Roberts (A8863) – is missing.

27th September 1917

Taking off at 3.49pm on the southern patrol, eight Albatros scouts were seen between Roulers and Menin at 1,500 feet. The Spads climbed up and attacked but the enemy aircraft dived east into clouds. Afterwards, the enemy aircraft reappeared above and attacked the Spads. Lieutenant McLeod then attacked one enemy aircraft but broke off to attack a second which was lower down and offered a better opportunity. He brought the second enemy aircraft down out of control over Dadizeele.

Before returning Lieutenant Dawson saw 18 lorries moving from Menin to Gheleuwe. He also came down to 400 feet and fired at parties of men repairing the Gheluewe – Begelaere Road. The men scattered and ran away.

28th September 1917

A message was received at 10.05am that enemy aircraft were working the area. Captain Leacroft attacked one which went spinning slowly down but probably under control, just east of Zanvoorde. The other enemy aircraft went east.

Another message at 11.04am sent the Spads to 6,000 feet and eight enemy aircraft scouts were seen and later two 2 seaters near Gheluewe. These were attacked but they immediately dived east into cloud. Afterwards, three 2 seaters were seen north east of Lille at 4,000 feet. Captain Sowrey got on the tail of the rearmost enemy aircraft firing at close quarters until he got a stoppage. The observer of the enemy aircraft however being put of action. On returning to the aerodrome he saw that the arrow had been put on the ground and proceeded in its direction. He saw the enemy aircraft crossing the lines, high up near Armentieres but it went east.

At 12.17pm a message was received of enemy aircraft working the area. Lieutenant Dawson saw a two seater and attacked it near Zanvoorde but it cut off east. He later encountered five scouts near Begelaere which attacked the Spads. Lieutenant McLeod and Lieutenant Dawson had indecisive combat attacking three enemy aircraft in turn.

30th September 1917

At 8.26am the Spads saw a two seater near Gheluewe which was attacked and brought down out of control by the formation of Captain Sowrey, Lieutenants Strang, Delamere, Hewat and Candy.

1st October 1917

Northern patrol took off at 9.10am and crossed the lines at 8,000 feet. They immediately saw 12 enemy aircraft scouts in good formation 2,000 feet above them. The Spads climbed hard but the enemy aircraft outclimbed them. Later the Spads saw enemy aircraft at 5,000 feet south east of Gheluvet. The Spads attacked and had an indecisive combat. Captain Leacroft attacked one Albatros scout and got very close but he was attacked by an enemy scout of a new type (resembling the British Nieuport, with plane black crosses and small bottom planes). Captain Leacroft had a long indecisive combat with this machine which got on his tail and he found him very difficult to shake off. Many more enemy aircraft had by this time joined in from above, so that the Spads could not get a decisive fight. Two two seater enemy aircraft were also attacked but again indecisive.

4th October 1917

Weather conditions were very bad when the squadron took off at 8.20am on a ground patrol. The wind was an exceptionally strong west wind and thick clouds at a low altitude. Lieutenant Strang crossed the lines and managed to get as far as Moorslede. After a time he saw many troops massed just east of Moorslede village. This would be at 8.30am and he calculated that there must have been 2,500 men at this place. He patrolled the Roulers-Menin road but was unable to see any movement at all owing to the exceptionally bad weather. He had to give nearly all his attention to flying his machine and was twice thrown into a spin at only 1,000 feet. Lieutenant Candy also flew into the neighbourhood of Moorslede keeping at a low altitude and finding the weather condition extremely bad. He saw a large number of troops massed to the east and north east of Moorslede. There being as far as he could see about 2,000 men. At this time he was subjected to very heavy fire from the ground, both machine gun and phosphorus shells and a few minutes later ran into a violent rainstorm. He flew through the storm but it was so thick he could not see the ground again. He therefore returned to the aerodrome to give the information of the men he had seen near Moorslede. Lieutenant Dawson was circling round prior to leaving the aerodrome on this mission, when he was suddenly seen to spin and nose dive into a field not far from the aerodrome. The machine was completely crashed (B1533) and Lieutenant Dawson was killed.

Lieutenant Thompson flew along the Ypres-Menin road to Cheluewe and then turned north and patrolled Dadizeele and Polygon Wood. He recrossed the lines and returned to Cheluewe once more, this time he saw a two horse wagon with about a dozen troops going towards Menin. He opened fire on the troops from 200 feet firing about 200 rounds. They jumped into ditches at the side of the road. He turned round and attacked the wagon. He must have shot one of the horses, as it rolled over into the ditch, the other one reared up and fell into the ditch after it, pulling the wagon with it and turning the wagon onto its side with the wheels in the air. During the patrol, he was fired at by machine guns from the ground a great deal. He returned with his plane shot through.

Lieutenant Ainger (A6794) – is missing.

Captain Leacroft flew down the Menin road at 500 feet and there was heavy machine gun fire from both sides of the Menin road. He saw about 20 men with three machine guns which were firing at him. He scattered them after firing several rounds from 200 feet and must have wounded some of them although they put up a good fight. He saw a farmhouse of the usual French type with a large square yard in the centre. In this yard there were a great many men apparently forming up. He flew round for about five minutes firing about 200 rounds at them from about 100 feet. Many of them must have been killed or wounded as they were closely packed and made a good target. He next saw a good number of men in a large shell hole, north of the Menin road, he fired at these also. He then saw some transport coming from Moorslede to Vijfwegen which he attacked, but soon after his machine was hit and losing pressure completely, he had to return on his emergency tank alone. When returning at a very low altitude he saw German troops in large numbers moving up northwest through what appeared to be communication trenches or the reserve lines. He landed on a road by a level crossing and among shell holes, damaging one wheel and bottom plane. He had run out of petrol. Captain Sowrey also followed the Menin road in company with Captain Leacroft until he got to Gheluwe. He saw a two seater enemy aircraft and chased it, firing a few rounds at it but it climbed into cloud. He had now lost Captain Leacroft and was not certain of his bearings. He saw 50 men however on the Bousbecque Linselles and coming down to 200 feet he fired 150 rounds, scattering them. He then flew on thinking he was making for the lines and until he arrived over Lille, he corrected his course and returned.

A signal had been received and stuck on this day's page;

"To the OC 19 Squadron Flying Corps, – Tell your pilots what splendid work they did yesterday under impossible weather conditions" – Signed General Trenchard. 5th October 1917.

5th October 1917

Lieutenant Strang on line patrol kept low down keeping a sharp look out for low flying enemy aircraft and saw a two seater Albatros, flying very low on the east side of the lines. Lieutenant Strang attacked getting in some good bursts and probably hit the observer who ceased firing. The enemy aircraft escaped east towards Roulers. Later a second two seater was attacked near Becelaere but it made off towards Menin. Lieutenant Strang saw a gang of men on the Moorslede road, he went down to a low altitude firing one burst and scattering them.

At 9.50am a message was received that enemy aircraft were working the area. Captain Leacroft, Lieutenants Holt and Stevenson proceeded to the area but no enemy aircraft were seen. Lieutenant Stevenson was following Captain Leacroft but was seen to turn north towards Ypres and has not been heard of since.

Lieutenant Stevenson (B1536) – is missing.

6th October 1917

At 9.25am message received that two enemy aircraft were flying in the area. Spads took off and Captain Leacroft sighted a two seater flying near Wervicq. By this time the clouds were at 1,000 feet and it started to rain. Captain Leacroft gave chase, followed by Lieutenant Long and he caught the enemy aircraft over Lille and in spite of the erratic course taken, got in some good shooting. They dived over the town at 800 feet and went south east of Lille. The enemy aircraft went down but they got into a hailstorm. Captain Leacroft could see nothing until he picked up his bearings south of Douai and then again over Bois de Havrincourt.

Lieutenant Long (B3508) – is missing.

SPAD "B3508"

At 6.10pm, Lieutenant Hicks fetching a new Spad A6687 from No 1 Aircraft Depot, on landing, the propellor stopped in the middle of the aerodrome. Lieutenant Strang ran out to start the machine, the propellor hit his left arm and broke it. He has since lost the use of that arm.

7th October 1917

At 7.09am message that one enemy aircraft flying in the area at 4,000 feet. The Spads proceeded to the area and two two seaters were seen near Houthem. One immediately dived east. The Spads attacked the other which made no evasive action. Captain Leacroft got to close quarters and was firing into the machine when he had a stoppage. He corrected this but then the gun still refused to fire. Lieutenant Hicks followed the enemy aircraft still further and after getting in some good shooting at it, it went down very steeply out of control. Confirmed.

8th October 1917

The northern area was patrolled at 2.15pm keeping a sharp lookout for enemy troop movements. One hundred German infantry with transport was seen in the square at Moorslede by Captain Sowrey, and three trains were observed, two near Roulers and one near Menin. Only two enemy aircraft were seen but they made off before the Spads could get near.

9th October 1917

A patrol at 10.08am, enemy aircraft activity very slight. Two 2 seaters were seen over Roulers – Ypres railway. The Spads attacked and one enemy aircraft was brought down out of control by three Spads, (Captain Sowrey, Lieutenants Hewat and Candy) while the remaining Spad attacked the second. Lieutenant Delamere saw it disappear into a cloud going down vertically with the engine full on.

By 12.50pm the enemy aircraft were very active. One enemy aircraft seen above by two

Spads, and as the Spads maneouvred to close with the enemy aircraft, Lieutenant Olivier's gun jammed at the critical moment allowing the enemy aircraft to get in a burst at Lieutenant Van Der Byl. Lieutenant Van Der Byl was shot through the knee and forced to land near Ypres and admitted to Field Ambulance.

12th October 1917

9.00am patrol over northern area, Westroosebeke to Dadizeele by Lieutenants Candy and Delamere saw very little movement behind the enemy lines.

9.09am southern patrol, Lieutenants Thompson and Robertson. Lieutenant Thompson at first went towards Wervicq and going down to 100 feet attacked three lorries and some men travelling towards Menin. He fired at the targets and noticed the men disappear from the road. He later fired at 20 men on the ground near Tenbrielen, from 300 feet, they scattered. He was heavily fired at from the ground by machine guns and flaming onions. He returned with the incident wire and main plane shot through. Lieutenant Robertson flew round the same area, searching for movement on the ground. A few isolated men were seen on the tracks near Gheluewe, Comerenhoek and Coucou.

At 12.49pm on the northern patrol. Captain Leacroft saw many small groups of men lying in the open and in shell holes east of Passchendaele. He engaged them with machine gun fire from 300 feet and under. He must have killed or wounded some of them especially a group crowded together in a shell hole. He also saw a small shed and noticed as he swooped down on it, some men run out, he fired at them and they jumped into some trenches near the shed. He thinks it was a gun emplacement.

Major Carter when flying near Westroosebeke suddenly noticed 20 men marching in formation along a road. He went down to 100 feet and fired at them, scattering and wounding some of them. He was also almost immediately, attacked by an Albatros scout from above but on swinging round to engage the enemy aircraft, it made off east climbing hard.

Lieutenant Hicks (B3574) – is missing.

14th October 1917

3.40pm. On arriving at the lines, a good many enemy aircraft were seen above as though they had just stopped fighting. Captain Sowrey dived at an Albatros scout followed by Captain Leacroft. Captain Leacroft got in a short burst at this enemy aircraft but had sudden pressure trouble and was obliged to pull out and return. He must have hit this enemy aircraft however as Captain Sowrey saw it go down completely out of control and crash in the middle of Becalaere.

Twelve enemy aircraft were seen attacking an RE8 and the Spads dived on these enemy aircraft, driving them east but with indecisive results.

15th October 1917

The northern patrol at 3.45pm. The formation led by Captain Leacroft attacked a 2 seater enemy aircraft over Westroosebeke, who got very close to this enemy aircraft and fired five rounds when his gun jammed. Captain Sowrey saw a formation of five black and white Albatros scouts come up through a gap in the clouds about a mile to the east. He made for them and got behind them and dived on the rearmost enemy aircraft firing 120 rounds into it. It suddenly disappeared below. No 45 Squadron saw this attack and report the enemy aircraft was in flames after Captain Sowrey had left it.

16th October 1917

A message that three enemy aircraft were working the area was received at 8.56am. Three Spads proceeded to this locality and saw three two seaters. Captain Sowrey attacked the most favourable and got at fairly close range firing 100 rounds when he had a stoppage and had to break off. Two other two seater's were fired at from long range. As this formation was returning to the aerodrome, an enemy aircraft was sighted from the ground this side of the lines. An arrow was put out and the Spads turned in that direction but failed to catch the enemy aircraft.

20th October 1917

9.40am Northern patrol when near Dadizeele, Captain Huskinson saw 12 to 15 enemy aircraft scouts above them. These immediately dived down on the Spads, who at once protected the two RE8's doing photography. Captain Leacroft with the southern patrol saw the situation and dived on the enemy aircraft. The RE8's got back safely to the lines and a general combat ensued during which Captain Leacroft and Captain Huskinson both attacked enemy aircraft scouts from close range, seeing them go down and think they may have been out of control. The AA confirm one enemy aircraft brought down and it crashed between Oude and Menin, this was probably the enemy aircraft attacked by Captain Leacroft.

24th October 1917

At 8.00am 12 Spads went out in a strong formation with the intention of finding, if possible, the large enemy aircraft formation which usually patrolled east of the northern area. At 8.45am nine or ten Albatros scouts were sighted below north east of Menin and some white enemy aircraft with black crosses were seen at the same time a little above. The Spads at once attacked the former and an exceedingly hot combat ensued. The enemy aircraft being reinforced by the formation from above probably numbering 20 in all. The enemy aircraft however were obviously at a disadvantage as several of them were seen to fall out of control. A minimum of four have been claimed as undoubtedly out of control, but this is probably understating the case. Captain Leacroft first picked out one enemy aircraft and fired a good burst close on its tail, it went into a glide and at that moment he saw another enemy aircraft right in front of him. He then closed in and got in a good burst at very close range. It turned over and over with its propellor stopped. He watched it for some time and it seemed hopelessly out of control. The enemy aircraft he had attacked first was then seen gliding west and followed it, he caught it as it entered cloud, firing right into it but it made no attempt to manoeuvre and disappeared through the cloud out of control.

Major Carter followed closely on Captain Leacroft getting in many rounds at different aircraft, firing two bursts at one enemy aircraft which turned and went down east. Lieutenant Bryson saw a Spad pull off the tail of one enemy aircraft, he dived in and fired at it from very close quarters. It turned on its back and glided away very steeply appearing without doubt to be out of control. Captain Huskinson dived on an enemy aircraft and fired three bursts into it when it dived into cloud and was lost. He then immediately attacked a second and after firing two bursts at close range, brought it down out of control. All the Spads had much fighting and it is impossible to estimate the full result of the combat. Many of them returned much shot about. Lieutenant Candy after attacking an enemy aircraft was attacked by two enemy aircraft and his machine was much damaged, (B3615) written off. Lieutenant Hewat, who's engine was running badly was attacked and was much handicapped, the main spar was shot through. Lieutenant De'Pencier attacked an enemy aircraft at very close quarters and drove it spinning into a cloud. Lieutenant Holt attacked an enemy aircraft and when nicely placed got several jambs. Lieutenant Gartside-Tippinge attacked and drove an enemy aircraft down to 5,000 feet when several came down on him and drove him down to 2,000 feet over Tourcoing. He was unable to see what happened to the enemy aircraft he had attacked.

Lieutenant Golding (A6709) – is missing

Lieutenant Laing (A6627) – is missing.

Lieutenant Delamere was shot through the petrol tank early in the flight. He was trying to reach the lines without his engine, got half way when he was attacked by seven German Nieuports. These followed him all the way down, firing at him. He only just managed to cross the lines and land near our support trenches. The enemy aircraft continued firing at him after he had landed, this machine except for the undercarriage is undamaged, but is too near the front line and will be difficult to salvage (B3489).

26th October 1917

A patrol at 10.00am. Lieutenants Hewat and De Pencier. Weather conditions were very bad, with heavy rain and low clouds. Soon as it cleared a little and stopped raining the Spads set out for the central area. They made for Moorslede flying at low altitude. On the road south east of Moorslede, 40 troops were seen and these were fired at from 200 feet and scattered. They then proceeded to Moorslede. There were a number of German infantrymen on the main roads through the town. Both the Spads attacked these. Lieutenant De Pencier states that he saw Lieutenant Hewat flying low, below the level of the Moorslede church spire and on a level with the roofs of the houses. Flying as low as this, Lieutenant Hewat swept the street with machine gun fire from end to end. The men scattered and many doubtlessly hit. Afterwards near Gheluwe a two seater was encountered at 800 feet. Lieutenant Hewat dived and fired a burst from very close range and followed it down to 400 feet when it was falling out of control. Lieutenant De Pencier confirms this. During this time the fire from the ground was very heavy and Lieutenant Hewat was hit by a bullet which passed through his sights and windscreen, struck his goggles and wounded him in the face. He returned to the aerodrome safely and made a good landing but has been admitted to hospital.

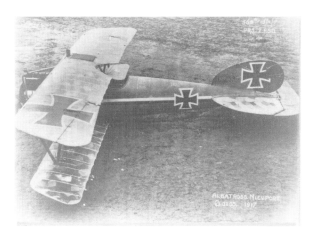

Albatros Nieuport
(Crown Copyright – MOD – AHB)

10.07am Southern patrol. Lieutenant Olivier and Jennings. Lieutenant Olivier flying at 600 feet saw some German infantrymen scattered in small groups south of Wervicq. He fired several bursts at them and they ran to take cover. Going on more infantrymen were found marching in artillery formation in sections of 20 each along the Menin – Gheluwe road. These he also fired at and saw them jump for the ditch at the roadside. Turning and going east he encountered a two seater enemy aircraft. He got on its tail and followed it down firing right into it until only 50 feet from the ground. The enemy aircraft went straight for the ground and Lieutenant Olivier, broke away being diverted by heavy enemy fire. Meanwhile Lieutenant Jennings also flying low engaged a machine gun battery near Werwicq from 600 feet and silenced it.

10.00am Northern patrol. Captain Huskinson and Lieutenant Candy. Captain Huskinson saw many infantrymen on the road near Moorslede. He went down to 500 feet and fired at them. As he turned round he saw many of them running into houses. Lieutenant Candy saw eight lorries near Westroosebeke and dived down and fired at them. His gun jammed after 3 rounds.

27th October 1917

Four Spads proceed to the lines at 6.16am, with a view to protecting the contact machine and attacking low flying enemy aircraft. On crossing the lines, Lieutenant Thompson saw a two seater Rumpler flying at 2,000 feet. He dived at it driving it down to 800 feet firing all the time and it went down out of control.

Lieutenant Whitehouse went to the lines on low flying practice.

Lieutenant Whitehouse (A6776) – is missing.

At 1.50pm on the southern patrol. Fourteen enemy aircraft and two Gothas appeared above the Spads. Some of these dived on the Spads but were lost in the clouds. A tracer exploded in front of Lieutenant Candy's gun and a spark flew back and hit him in the eye.

Lieutenant Rice has landed near Hondschoote, although no word has been received as yet it is believed the machine is damaged but he is unhurt.

30th October 1917

At 5.50am the low north patrol of four Spad took off and considerable difficulty was experienced getting into formation due to the strong winds and light. Major Carter attacked one low flying enemy aircraft and drove it east. After this he fired at a gun position at Westroosebeke, Moorslede and Dadizeele. Lieutenant Holt patrolled the area and saw 150 troops followed by three motor lorries advancing from Ghelewe towards Gheluvelt, three miles west of the former town. He fired at them from under 1,000 feet, scattering the troops. Lieutenant Bryson attacked a convoy just west of Moorslede from under 500 feet travelling towards Passchendaele. The transport turned off the road. He afterwards attacked a two seater north of Westroosebeke and followed it down to 500 feet firing. The enemy aircraft was damaged and possibly crashed but could not be claimed. Later Lieutenant Bryson attacked another two seater northwest of Dadizeele. Lieutenant De Pencier dived on a two seater enemy aircraft near Dadizeele with Lieutenant Thompson, followed it down to a very low altitude, the enemy aircraft was diving straight towards the ground but was unable to say what happened to it. AA confirm that this enemy aircraft went down out of control.

At 1.30pm the Spads on the northern patrol saw six enemy aircraft south of Houthulst and fired at them but they flew east. Just then a single seater was seen coming from the north. Major Carter and Lieutenant Bryson made for this scout. The enemy aircraft put its nose down as if to dive on them and dived through the formation. Major Carter had a single combat with it which resulted in him driving the machine down until it crashed near Gheluvelt. This enemy aircraft was a red nosed, salmon coloured fuselage, Albatros scout. The remainder of the formation climbed after six enemy aircraft scouts above Dadizeele, but they made off east. On turning back the Spads saw a formation of three Gothas and about fifteen enemy aircraft scouts returning from the west. Lieutenant Bryson dived on them but got a stoppage. Lieutenant Gartside-Tippinge dived on them and tried to break them up. He got a good number of rounds into a two seater in the middle of the formation but could not get them down.

31st October 1917

The northern patrol at 9.16am. Lieutenant Olivier engaged an Albatros scout and drove it down out of control. He was afterwards attacked by two Albatros scouts. His Aldis sight was shot away and main petrol tank shot through. He had to make a forced landing.

Major Carter, Lieutenants Bryson, Gartside-Tippinge and De Pencier had a combat with a two seater which went down damaged possibly out of control. At 10.20am Major Carter drove down an enemy aircraft two seater out of control (Confirmed). At the same time, Lieutenant Gartside-Tippinge had a long combat with an enemy aircraft single seater, followed it down to 300 feet, the enemy aircraft was then out of control. Lieutenant Bryson who climbed after a formation of enemy aircraft, he also brought one down out of control south of Westroosebeke. Lieutenant De Pencier whilst attacking a two seater had the leading edge of his right hand plane give way. He returned with difficulty to the aerodrome.

6th November 1917

At 6.21am Low North Offensive Patrol. Many two seater enemy aircraft were seen above and one formation of eleven Albatros scouts. Two two seaters were attacked by Lieutenants Robertson and Bryson but they dived away east and escaped. Later a DFW suddenly appeared directly above Lieutenant Bryson. He fired a burst into it from below but with no apparent damage. Major Carter while alone, had an indecisive combat with a two seater near Peldhock. He got in some good shooting at close range but no effect was observed and finally the enemy aircraft got away. An SE5 of 60 Squadron saw a Spad spin into the ground.

Lieutenant Gartside-Tippinge (B3641) – is missing.

At 10.07am two Spads flew in the neighbourhood of Westroosebeke at low altitude. Captain Robertson first fired on a small party of men on the edge of a wood from 800 feet. The men rushed back into the wood. Going on he next fired at a trench full of men and again at hostile batteries. He searched the road between Westroosebeke and Moorslede and the tracks in that neighbourhood but saw no activity. Lieutenant Holt followed Captain Robertson and fired at some men in a wood from 800 feet southwest of Westroosebeke. He was suddenly attacked by an Albatros scout which dived on him out of the mist. Swinging round and up however, he managed to get on the enemy aircraft's tail and put it down out of control.

The southern patrol of Lieutenants Jennings and Olivier. Lieutenant Jennings flying low down fired on a railway station. He searched the roads and villages in the neighbourhood of Moorslede but saw very little activity. Three motor lorries were seen on the road travelling west and a train was seen standing in a railway station, but otherwise activity of any sort was very slight, especially when compared with what was seen on the British side of the lines. Lieutenant Olivier soon after crossing the lines became lost in the clouds east of Moorslede. His compass evidently having guided him east instead of west. He flew for some time not knowing where he was and not knowing in which direction he was flying. He tried to climb in order to find the sun but being unable to do so, he decided to go down low again and found himself near a large town, probably Ghent. He landed in a large common and beckoned to a civilian who turned out to be a Belgian. He asked the man in French "Are there French people here?" but he received a negative reply. He asked him again "Are there English people here?". Again the reply was in the negative. He asked him a third time "Are the Allemandes (German) here?". "Yes, yes, yes" said the man, and with that Lieutenant Olivier opened out his engine and left the ground with all speed, being heavily fired at as he climbed. After this he flew for nearly two hours trying to find his way back to the British side of the lines. He very nearly lost heart and landed in despair, but by constantly urging himself on by repeatedly coming down very low to try to recognise the uniforms of men marching along the roads, he eventually got back via Tournin and recognised the khaki uniform of the men not far from Armentieres. He landed a little south of Bailluel without damaging his machine.

8th November 1917

On the northern patrol the Spads sighted three formations of enemy aircraft scouts at 8.45am, close together at 13,000 feet, south east of Westroosebeke. The Spads made for the nearest of these formations. An indecisive combat ensued during which Captain Robertson saw an enemy aircraft close on the tail of Lieutenant Cockburn's machine. He dived and succeeded in beating off the enemy aircraft but Lieutenant Cockburn went down vertically and steeply towards the west as though he had been hit. During the combat, Major Carter had much fighting with the enemy aircraft, many of which attacked him. He became separated from the formation after this fight and later had an indecisive combat with two two seater hostile aircraft.

Lieutenant Cockburn (A6777) – is missing.

9th November 1917

The northern area was patrolled at 9.39am, with clouds at 7 to 8,000 feet with occasional rain. Several enemy aircraft were seen, but soon lost in the clouds after a few rounds were fired at them. Major Carter however, attacked a two seater near Moorslede and after a hot combat in which the enemy aircraft was followed through clouds to within 300 feet of the ground, it was seen to go down completely out of control. Heavy fire from the troops on the ground prevented Major Carter at the last minute from seeing it crash. On one occasion five Albatros scouts suddenly dived onto the rear of the Spad formation from out of cloud. One of them attacked Lieutenant Jennings from behind. Lieutenant Thompson did a climbing turn and succeeded in getting on the tail of this enemy aircraft. Firing a burst from close range, the enemy aircraft went down out of control and was seen to crash. Later two RE8's were seen to be attacked by an Albatros scout. Lieutenant Thompson dived down and after firing two short bursts saw this enemy aircraft go down completely out of control.

11th November 1917

At 9.45am the area was patrolled but the visibility was very bad. Captain Robertson, Lieutenants De Pencier and Holt, and Major Carter attacked a two seater enemy aircraft at 10.30am over Spriet. Major Carter was unable to continue with the combat due to his engine not running well. Captain Robertson and Lieutenant De Pencier got in some good shooting at very close range. The observer was evidently shot and the machine may have been out of control. Six enemy aircraft scouts however, came down on them. Lieutenant De Pencier having to make a forced landing and his machine turned over.

The 3.12pm patrol saw four or five groups of six enemy aircraft scouts and three or four two seaters. Lieutenant Bryson had an indecisive combat with five enemy aircraft scouts. He then dived on six enemy aircraft near Menin with Lieutenant Candy. Afterwards chasing a two seater east from Comines but it was too dark to see the result. Lieutenant Candy and Lieutenant Rice attacked five enemy aircraft east of Moorslede, but Lieutenant Candy's gun would not fire. They then saw six enemy aircraft over Gheluewe, but Lieutenant Candy got two jams and the enemy aircraft dived into cloud. They then chased three enemy aircraft which were lost but finally drove down one of two Albatros scouts out of control near Menin.

12th November 1917

On the northern patrol at 10.30am Lieutenant Bryson saw three RE8's going towards Cheluvelt. He immediately went down and was just in time to engage four Albatros scouts which were attacking them. He drove one of these enemy aircraft down out of control and then chased the other three east.

Lieutenant Blythe was only a few hundred feet up when his engine cut out. He crashed into a telegraph post, the machine (B3573) was wrecked but the pilot was only shaken.

13th November 1917

9.50am Major Carter led the formation on patrol 3 to 4,000 feet east of Passchendaele and Westroosebeke. There were practically none of our artillery machines working. He saw twelve low flying enemy aircraft, flying in pairs, which tried to approach our lines. All of these were driven east. He noticed a large formation of Gothas and enemy aircraft two seaters crossing our lines as far as Ypres at 7,000 feet and another formation of six two seaters and several scouts cross over our salient from north to south. He only saw Spads attacking these. Captain Huskinson shortly after crossing the lines saw a formation of twelve enemy aircraft machines and attacked one which was separated from these and destroyed it, between Moorslede and Beythem. After this he climbed hard and pursued the enemy aircraft formation going west and fired 70 rounds at point blank range into a Gotha over Ypres. His gun then stopped firing and he had to break off, leaving the Spads well on top of the Gothas. Lieutenant Thompson just as he was attacking this formation had to break off with a big end gone in his engine. Lieutenants Holt, Candy and Bryson followed Captain Huskinson and each attacked a large two seater driving them east. Lieutenant Holt's enemy aircraft went down very steeply and Lieutenant Candy observed one of these two seaters over Moorslede going down in a vertical dive, probably the one engaged by Lieutenant Holt and disappear into the clouds. Lieutenant De Pencier attacked a Gotha just west of Ypres, followed it to Moorslede and finally getting to close quarters when six Albatros scouts dived on him and he had difficulty in getting away.

During the afternoon, at 1.45pm, Lieutenants Thompson, Holt and Bryson with Captain Huskinson attacked three two seaters over Comines. The two later Spads were unable to get close, but Lieutenants Thompson and Holt drove them down to 2,000 feet east of Menin. Lieutenant Bryson had pressure failure, lost his propellor and had trouble in getting back.

At 2.45pm Major Carter, Lieutenant Candy, Captain Huskinson and Lieutenant Bryson saw four Albatros scouts between Ypres and Comines. The two former drove one of these down out of control and just before it disappeared at 1,000 feet large volumes of smoke came out of it.

15th November 1917

A low line patrol at 6.15am. The patrol left the ground as soon as it was sufficiently light but the visibility was very bad. Very few enemy aircraft were seen and they were chased east. Captain Huskinson had been firing on the roads and as he climbed up again received a direct hit from one of our shells which carried away his petrol tank, part of the radiator and half his propellor and threw him into the most violent spin. He recovered, glided west and turned over in a shell hole four feet deep in water. He was pinned fast and almost drowned. On being rescued, he worked until 3.0pm, although wet through and salvaged the engine of his machine (A6773).

Lieutenant Stone whilst returning with the other machines stalled and crashed. The pilot was killed.

At 10.00am a message was received that enemy aircraft were working our area. Major Carter and Lieutenant Olivier saw a two seater near Zanvoorde and immediately attacked. Major Carter attacked from above and then below. The enemy aircraft started downwards but he had to give up the attack owing to engine trouble. Lieutenant Olivier however continued firing at very close range, following the enemy aircraft down to 500 feet, leaving it out of control. 2nd Army reported that the enemy aircraft crashed.

Seventeen minutes later another message was received. The Spads attacked a two seater over Gheluvelt but were immediately attacked by several Albatros scouts from above. Spads attacked another enemy aircraft over the Comines canal, it went into a spin but flattened out after going down 1,000 feet.

Lieutenant Hearn was shot down, pilot wounded in the arm and admitted to hospital, the machine (B3646) crashed.

23rd November 1917

At 8.40am Major Carter followed by the other Spad had two short combats with six Albatros scouts and again at 9.25am when he drove one Albatros scout down possibly out of control.

29th November 1917

11.30am Ypres patrol. Six Albatros scouts seen. One attacked from the rear by Lieutenant Fairclough, he fired several rounds into it. Captain Bryson attacked another enemy aircraft at the same time, this enemy aircraft was also attacked by Captain Taylor and Lieutenant Hustings and was seen to go down out of control near Becelaere. Lieutenant Galer had to make a forced landing, his engine seized.

Lieutenant Rice (A6758) – is missing.

2nd December 1917

An offensive patrol at 10.44am saw only one enemy aircraft. Lieutenant Spiro was last seen as the patrol returned over Ypres and was at the rear of the formation.

Lieutenant Spiro (A6662) – is missing.

3rd December 1917

Shortly after crossing the lines on an offensive patrol at 11.44am, a fight was seen to be taking place in the distance between DH4's and enemy aircraft. On approaching two DH4's were seen coming west. The enemy aircraft were then attacked and one being driven down completely out of control by Captain Huskinson near Menin. The other enemy aircraft were chased east and Captain Huskinson dived on another enemy aircraft scout which escaped owing to Captain Huskinson's engine being too cold from the dive. All pilots suffered very much from the cold.

6th December 1917

The Spads attacked a two seater near Gheluewe at 12.45pm. After firing at close range the enemy aircraft went down vertically. Ten Albatros scouts immediately dived on the formation. In the combat which ensued, Lieutenant Puckridge drove one down out of control, Lieutenant Candy sent one down in a spin. Lieutenant Yeo's machine was hit in several places.

7th December 1917

At 9.45am southern offensive patrol. The patrol was much hindered by low cloud and poor visibility. One two seater and six enemy aircraft were seen but the conditions so favoured the enemy aircraft that the two seater could not be properly attacked. AA and machine gun fire from the ground was so accurate that all machines were hit.

At 9.50am northern offensive patrol. At 10.30am Lieutenant Jennings and the other Spads attacked a two seater enemy aircraft probably the same one as the northern patrol drove east, but six enemy aircraft came down on them. Later at 10.50am an attempt was made to engage the six enemy aircraft with indecisive results owing to weather conditions.

Lieutenant Yeo (B3559) – is missing.

12th December 1917

Several Gotha's were seen approaching the aerodrome at 2.10pm. Four Spads and one DOLPHIN (the Squadrons' first "development" machine) left the ground. Captain Huskinson was catching up with the Gothas as they approached the lines but did not follow up the chase as he was not allowed to cross the lines in this machine. Lieutenant Irving (A6784) ran into Lieutenant Blythe (B3563) on leaving the ground, both machines having all planes smashed and the fuselages twisted.

15th December 1917

At 9.35am a message was received that enemy aircraft were working in the neighbourhood of Gheluvelt and south to Houthem. Three Spads proceeded to the area and at 9.50am attacked one of the 2 seaters. Major Carter attacked one two seater following it to Comines where he brought it down out of control. A group of three were attacked, one of these became separated from the rest and had a long combat with Major Carter and was finally sent down out of control. Later at 3.30pm in company with an SE5, the two Spads attacked seven Albatros scouts. During this combat, one enemy aircraft was driven down completely out of control by Major Carter.

18th December 1917

At 9.30am a message received that two enemy aircraft were working between Cheluvelt and Houthem. Three Spads proceeded to the area and attacked the two seater enemy aircraft northeast of Houthem. The result of this combat was not fully observed. Later a two seater was attacked near Combines, Captain Bryson fired into it at close range, it turned to the left and was also fired into by Lieutenant Fairclough and it was then seen by all three Spads to go down out of control.

19th December 1917

A low line patrol at 7.25am. No enemy aircraft were seen near the lines but three two seaters were seen just west of Roulers. These were attacked, two got away and one was brought down by Lieutenant Fairclough. Five minutes later, the other two seaters were seen again and engaged. One being brought down out of control and the other being badly damaged but the pilot could not be certain of this one being out of control.

At 10.15am a message was received that three enemy aircraft were working between Becelaere and Houthem and one south of Comines. Major Carter saw two two seaters 10,000 feet between Messines and Ploegsthert and climbed up and beneath them. When getting within range the enemy aircraft saw the Spad, opened fire and turned east. Major Carter climbed and fired several bursts from close range at one of these. The enemy aircraft dived and each time it flattened out, Major Carter fired again, finally the enemy aircraft went into a vertical dive through haze near Comines.

Lieutenant Olivier crashed on landing.

22nd December 1917

The 1.48pm patrol. At 2.20pm five Spads encountered eight Albatros scouts, south of Questnoy. A hot combat ensued during which one enemy aircraft was brought down by the formation in flames.

25th December 1917

On Christmas Day, the squadron left Bailleul and moved to St Marie Cappel.

28th December 1917

An offensive patrol at 8.36am. At 10.00am the Spads engaged four Albatros scouts. Major Carter got on the tail of one of these and followed it down until he saw it crash in the snow.

29th December 1917

At 10.00am Major Carter sighted at least six Albatros scouts north of Houthulst Forest and about 1,000 feet above his formation. He immediately led his formation under the enemy scouts and began climbing to attack. The enemy aircraft came down and attacked the Spads, being joined by at least eight more enemy aircraft scouts. A general fight ensued, lasting for nearly 20 minutes. Captain Huskinson who left the ground later also joined in the fight and after much hot combating, Lieutenant Fairclough, Lieutenant Candy, Lieutenant De Pencier, Major Carter and Captain Huskinson each got one enemy aircraft out of control. In addition, Lieutenant Fairclough brought one enemy aircraft down in flames, this enemy aircraft was also seen to be on fire by Lieutenant De Pencier. Captain Huskinson got a second enemy aircraft out of control.

Lieutenant Galer was last seen during the combat with two enemy aircraft on his tail.

Lieutenant Galer (A6786) – is missing.

Only six Spads were on this offensive patrol when they attacked a formation of twelve enemy aircraft and accounted for seven (confirmed). Captain J. Leacroft, Captain H.P. Huskinson, and Major A.D. Carter being the Flight Commanders.

Two signals were attached to this day's record sheets:-

"To the Officer OC 19 Squadron. The Officers of 57 Squadron send their heartiest congratulations to 19 Squadron on their fine show today. Signed by the OC 57 Squadron".

The following is a translation of a message to the officer commanding 19 Squadron;

"New Year, 1918. We should be greatly pleased to meet the Squadron of twelve Spads again over Houthulst Forest in the near future. Sporting greetings, the four Albatros".

January 1918

The squadron again re-equipped, this time with the Sopwith Dolphin. (NB. For technical data see page 358)

The month was taken up in collecting and practicing with the new aircraft and returning the Spads to the Aircraft Depot. Many days flying was lost due to the bad weather conditions.

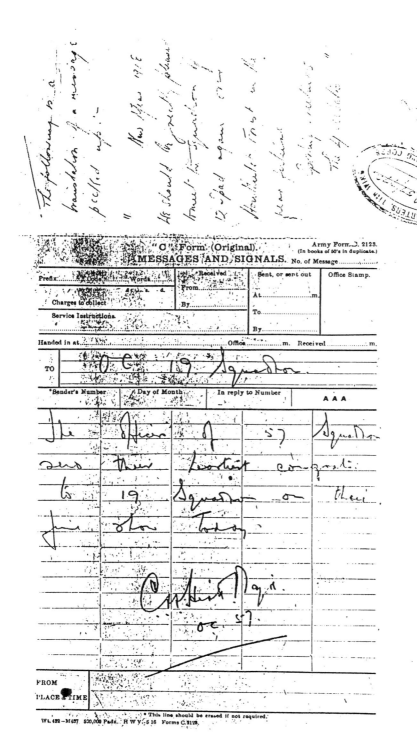

The following is a translation of a message picked up.

"Nov 17th 1916

He should be very pleased [...] trust [...] formation [...] 12 spad again [...] formula in first [...] his [...] spray victories [...] The A Coffee"

[Round stamp:] HEADQUARTERS 11th WING · ROYAL FLYING CORPS

"C" Form (Original).   Army Form C. 2123.
(In books of 50's in duplicate.)

MESSAGES AND SIGNALS.   No. of Message...........

Prefix...... Code...... Words......	Received... From......	Sent, or sent out	Office Stamp.
Charges to collect	By......	At...............m.	
Service Instructions.		To......	
		By......	

Handed in at............ Office............m. Received............m.

TO   O C 19 Squadron

*Sender's Number	Day of Month	In reply to Number	A A A

The Officer of 57 Squadron
send their heartiest congratulations
to 19 Squadron on their
fine show today.

Arthur Major
OC 57

FROM
PLACE TIME

* This line should be erased if not required.
Wt. 432—M 437 500,000 Pads. H W V. 5 16 Forms C. 2123.

It takes three to start this Dolphin

6th January 1918

At 1.45pm on practice flight for the new pilots, Captain Huskinson saw a fight going on over Houthulst Forest. He fired a light for the new pilots who were with him to return, and entered the fight himself. Saw a Camel bring a enemy aircraft down out of control near our lines. The enemy aircraft in question were unusually offensive, coming well west of our lines. Captain Huskinson attacked one of them near St Julien, driving it down to 3,000 feet but losing it at the last moment due to a No 3 stoppage. Later he saw two enemy aircraft firing into our trenches, while a third enemy aircraft flew above them. He attacked this enemy aircraft bringing it down completely out of control over Waterdamhoek at about 2.07pm.

22nd January 1918

10.35am Lieutenant Veale in (C3826) on practice flight crashed. Pilot killed. Weather permitted no flying during the last week of the month.

13th February 1918

The squadron returned to Bailleul.

16th February 1918

Major Carter whilst on a practice flight at 10.43am saw six enemy aircraft two seater this side of the lines at different times. He attacked three from long range and three at close range, but with indecisive results, being much hampered with a broken sight.

17th February 1918

10.30am Patrol Bailleul – Poperinghe. During patrol Major Carter saw three enemy aircraft and fired at one from below at long range, when he saw another 4,000 feet below him.

He dived onto this one, came up underneath it and was within 20 feet of the enemy aircraft, when the engine completely failed, pressure trouble. Lieutenant Blythe and Lieutenant Reed-Walker did not follow Major Carter and they saw the enemy aircraft above. Lieutenant Blythe's left hand inner flying wire broke and he was obliged to return. Lieutenant Reed-Walker climbed after the enemy aircraft which recrossed the lines however before he could catch them. Captain Bryson with remaining two Dolphins saw a enemy aircraft two seater at 11,000 feet, between Ploegsteert and Armentieres, being attacked by an SE5. The enemy aircraft spiralled down and Captain Bryson attacked it driving it down to 4,000 feet, until he was obliged to break off being blinded by oil. The enemy aircraft however was seen by the AA to descend onto the enemy side of the lines, but were unable to say whether or not it crashed.

19th February 1918
10.49am patrol. At 11.55am Major Carter attacked four Albatros scouts north of Messines, ended by his engine cutting out whenever he attempted to climb.

1.30pm Patrol Bailleul – Poperinghe. Area patrolled and two red nosed Albatros scouts were seen, just west of the lines, and fired at from long range. But having the advantage of height they dived away east and escaped.

26th February 1918
8.50am. The area patrolled in two layers of three machines each. The higher formation being joined by six Bristol fighters from the 9th Wing. The lower formation engaged two 2 seater enemy aircraft from long range when patrolling near the lines, but were attacked by a triplane and three other enemy aircraft scouts at about 10.05am. A fight ensued during which the triplane was seen to be diving on Lieutenant McLintock's tail by Lieutenant De Pencier. He immediately attacked and is believed to have brought it down out of control. Lieutenant McLintock was last seen gliding southwest of Comines.

Lieutenant McLintock (A6871) – is missing.

28th February 1918
A patrol at 3.14pm. Captain Taylor engaged five enemy aircraft but as his Vickers gun would not fire he had to return. Captain Bryson and Lieutenant Fairclough had an indecisive combat with eight enemy aircraft over Passchendaele. Later Captain Taylor was engaged with eight enemy aircraft but owing to petrol trouble had to return.

Captain Huskinson went up on patrol at 3.30pm on his own and had an indecisive combat with a 2 seater enemy aircraft over Comines. He drove it down through the clouds but then lost it.

1st March 1918
Two or three enemy aircraft bombing machines were observed from the ground to be crossing our lines. Weather conditions were unfavourable for patrol, but at 6.30am Captain Bryson and Lieutenant De Pencier took off to look for these enemy aircraft. Weather became even worse, no enemy aircraft were seen and the patrol returned at 7.30am.

5th March 1918
2.55pm Patrol – One two seater enemy aircraft was seen working between Gheluwe and Menin. All three Dolphins dived on this machine, Lieutenants Fairclough and Olivier firing at fairly close range. The enemy aircraft went down almost vertically, emitting white smoke or steam and may have been hit.

6th March 1918

9.38am Two single seater enemy aircraft were attacked, the first at 10.25am near Westroosebeke, the second at 10.45am near Moorslede with indecisive results. At 11.30am Lieutenant Fairclough dived on a 2 seater enemy aircraft north east of Wervicq. The enemy aircraft at once fired several signal lights. Lieutenant Fairclough got several good bursts at close range. The enemy aircraft went down very steeply without firing back. It was last seen very low down but could not be watched further owing to five enemy aircraft above.

1.52pm At about 2.45pm whilst patrolling at 14,000 feet near Houthulst Forest, seven Albatros scouts were sighted. Captain Huskinson immediately dived and drove one enemy aircraft down in indecisive combat. He then had gun trouble. Five enemy aircraft then attacked the other two Dolphins (two new pilots), Lieutenant Gardner and Lieutenant McConnell, but Captain Huskinson drove them away with his top gun.

8th March 1918

The squadron's first Dolphin victory, as the German 1918 offensive began. In this battle the squadron was involved almost exclusively in low-attack work endeavouring to repulse the advancing German armies.

9.44am Offensive patrol. Captain Bryson's formation attacked six enemy aircraft north east of Roulers, which got away east in an indecisive combat. One enemy aircraft spun down. At 11.10am four red tailed enemy aircraft were encountered, during the fight which followed, Captain Bryson destroyed one Albatros scout, the wings of the aircraft being seen to come off in the air, confirmed by other pilots and the AA 'T' Battery. Captain Huskinson drove one of these enemy aircraft down out of control. Lieutenant Jenkinson's formation chased six Albatros scouts, which disappeared east. The Dolphins then climbed after a enemy aircraft triplane, but at 17,000 feet the triplane was still above them and climbing much faster than the Dolphins.

9th March 1918

11.55am Offensive patrol. At 1.15pm Captain Huskinson saw 11 enemy aircraft near Wervicq attacking a RE8. Lieutenant Olivier attacked one of these, as they were flying west, and it went down spinning. He was then attacked from above. Captain Huskinson, Lieutenant Puckridge, and Lieutenant Blythe got onto two Pfalz and an Albatros, all of which flew straight, giving them splendid shooting. Two enemy aircraft were destroyed and one sent down out of control. Camels came up as this fight was ending. Lieutenant Irving diving on the enemy aircraft with the others, his pressure went low, and he turned west pumping this up. One Camel got on his tail and started firing. Lieutenant Irving banked up to show his markings but had to continue going west pumping up his pressure. This Camel continued to fire and was joined by another. They then shot him through his radiator and the engine began to run very badly. These two Camels followed him firing continuously. Lieutenant Irving being powerless to do anything but show them his markings and wave to them. Finally they followed him down to within a 100 feet of the ground still firing, they then left him and went off. Lieutenant Irving landed near Hazebrouck as his engine seized and the machine wrecked being shot through the radiator and main spars of the planes, one round being evidently a Buckingham or tracer as it had burnt the spar. Six bombs were dropped near Menin.

10th March 1918

A message was received at 3.15pm that enemy aircraft were working in the Westroosebeke and Houthem area. Three Dolphins patrolled the area and saw two Camels driving a enemy aircraft scout east. The Dolphins then attacked a train with bombs which was going east from Wervicq, but the results were unobserved.

11th March 1918

7.15am Lieutenant Reed-Walker on Line patrol. In bad weather, and due to engine trouble, had to make a forced landing near Locre. The machine turned over and pinned him underneath. He escaped with injuries to his arm.

12th March 1918

10.40am Squadron scrambled as a report had come in at 10.35 that two enemy aircraft were working the Westroosebeke – Passchendaele – Houthulst Forest – Westroosebeke areas. Lieutenant Jennings, Blythe and Irving patrolled the area but no enemy aircraft seen. All machines dropped their bombs on Westroosebeke, whilst doing this six enemy aircraft scouts dived from the sun. Lieutenant Irving was shot through all three ailerons. The enemy aircraft turned east and disappeared.

11.50am Message received enemy aircraft in the Becelaere – Zanvoorde – Houthem – Warneton area at 4,000 feet. Led by Captain Leacroft, three Dolphins took off, and proceeded by ground signal station, which worked very well. Two 2 seater enemy aircraft were seen and immediately chased. They fired numerous lights and immediately fled. They were pursued and fired at from long range, got away without being caught. Eight enemy aircraft above, failed to attack the Dolphins.

4.53pm Captain Huskinson on patrol saw six enemy aircraft flying 15,000 feet about a mile over the lines near Houthulst Forest. On approaching he noticed that they were of a new type, and had white top planes and one had a black tail. They had a light purple cross on a black background. The enemy aircraft seemed faster than the Dolphin but not such a good climber. (A drawing of the design on the Record Book overleaf).

13th March 1918

10.04am Bombs dropped on Wervicq. Captain Taylor landed very fast, sheered a nut off his undercarriage. The aircraft turned over, injuring him. He was admitted to hospital.

15th March 1918

10.42am Offensive patrol. Three formations led by Major Carter, Captain Huskinson, and Captain Leacroft. Captain Huskinson's and Captain Leacroft's formations flew together, with Major Carter's above. Soon after 11.00am a large formation of enemy aircraft were encountered south east of Halluin, and completely broken up. Later another formation of 13 enemy aircraft were encountered and dealt with in a similar way. The enemy aircraft were poor performers and many casualties were undoubtedly inflicted. The following decisive combats are claimed although several other are thought to have been much damaged. One destroyed and one out of control – Major Carter, two out of control – Captain Leacroft, two out of control – Captain Huskinson and Lieutenant Hustings. Six bombs dropped on Comines and six on Wervicq.

16th March 1918

11.18am Major Sanday took off for a practice flight and attacked a two seater enemy aircraft south of Perenchies with two Camels. The enemy aircraft was hit and may have crashed but no confirmation could be obtained.

(6304) Wt. W2637/M2210 200,000 6/17 McA & W Ltd. (E.1386), orms/W3343/2

Army Form. W.3343.

Pilots available _____

Aeroplanes { S _____ { U _____

No. 1c _____ Squadron.

SQUADRON RECORD BOOK.

Date 16th May 1918.

Type and Number	Pilot and Observer	Duty	Hour of Start	Hour of Return	Time in Air	Remarks
3620	Lt. Herrman	Practice	4.07 p.	5.67 p.	1.0	Practice for new pilot.
S. 43	Lt. Helmsby	Practice	4.33 p.	4.48 p.	15	Practice for new pilot.
3792	Capt. Hutchinson.	Line Patrol	4.53 p.	6.6 p.	1.13	Capt. Hutchinson saw 6 E/A flying at 15,000 feet about a mile over the lines near HOUTHULST FOREST. On approaching he noticed they were of a new type and had white top planes, and one had a black tail; they had a light purple cross on a black background. E/A seemed faster than a Dolphin but not such a good climb; they looked like this:-

Double struts.

17th March 1918

Twelve Dolphins left the ground at 11.37am in three flights led by Major Carter, Captain Huskinson and Captain Leacroft. Captain Leacroft first saw a formation of enemy aircraft north east of Menin and pursued these well east of Menin. He was supported by Major Carter's formation 2,000 or 3,000 feet above and Captain Huskinson's formation on the west of him. The enemy aircraft continued east till they were nearly at Courtrai; one of them then turned west to attack, the others leaving him to his fate. Lieutenant Fairclough drove this enemy aircraft down in a spin and then reformed on Captain Leacroft, who turned north west as four more enemy aircraft were seen coming from that direction. One of these turned back and dived under Captain Leacroft, who overshot it, but Lieutenants Fairclough and Olivier, shot it down in a mass of flames in full view of our own, and the enemy formations. At this moment a large enemy aircraft formation was suddenly seen chasing six Camels in the Ypres district. The enemy aircraft 15 to 20 strong, turned east and coming from a north westerly direction quickly met Captain Leacroft's formation, Captain Huskinson's being on the left and Major Carter's above. A rather spread out contest ensued which gradually developed into a "Dog Fight".

Captain Leacroft got one enemy aircraft completely in flames. Both Lieutenants Olivier and Fairclough saw this, and Major Carter who had come down from above also saw this. Captain Leacroft afterwards had many combats, but was unable, owing to the heat of the contest to make any other definite claims.

Captain Huskinson attacked one white coloured enemy aircraft Pfalz and followed it down to 3,500 feet and saw it crash west of Roulers. He started to climb up and had climbed up 500 feet when another Pfalz with a white top plane passed him under partial control, and crashed about half a mile from where the first one was seen to crash. Captain Huskinson is absolutely certain of the colours and types of these machines but cannot say the times for certain, about 12.15pm.

Lieutenant Olivier after having shared in shooting the enemy aircraft scout down in flames (as above) attacked one which was diving on another Dolphin and drove it down out of control; and again about five to ten minutes later saw an enemy aircraft come floating past him out of control and on fire.

Lieutenant Hustings attacked a Pfalz scout which he drove down out of control. He did not see it crash but suddenly saw an enemy aircraft crashed on the ground in the neighbourhood of where he was looking (but it is uncertain if it was his).

Major Carter after having seen two enemy aircraft completely in flames, was attacked by a white Pfalz scout. After a good fight this went down out of control. He did not see this crash.

Lieutenant Blythe states with absolute confidence, that he saw the following enemy aircraft crash:-

1. At 12.17pm. A Dolphin engaged a battleship coloured Pfalz with a red nose; he watched it go down until it crashed. After this he was considerably shot about himself. He joined Lieutenant Jennings.

2. Saw Lieutenant Jennings attack an Albatros which went down out of control, and he saw it crash. Neither of these two enemy aircraft were on fire.

DEDUCTIONS:-

Seven enemy aircraft were undoubtedly crashed.

Three in flames	{1.	Lieutenant Fairclough & Lieutenant Olivier
	{2.	Captain Leacroft
	{3.	It is uncertain to prove to whom to credit this, possibly Captain Leacroft or Major Carter.

	{1.	Lieutenant Jennings (Albatros)
	{2.	Captain Huskinson
Four destroyed	{3.	White Pfalz. It is uncertain to whom to credit this, possibly Lieutenant Olivier's out of control, Major Carter's out of control or Lieutenant Husting's out of control.
	{4.	Grey Pfalz with red nose. It is uncertain to whom to credit this; possibly one engaged by Captain Leacroft.

Seven enemy aircraft destroyed without loss to the Squadron.

19th March, 1918
Major Sanday D.S.O., M.C., left the squadron and Major E.R. Pretyman took command.

THE GERMAN SPRING OFFENSIVE

The 21st March, 1918, the German Spring Offensive began along the Western Front. In this offensive the advancing Germans were continuously harassed by the aircraft of the squadron, who strafed and bombed their troops causing severe casualties and great confusion.

23rd March 1918
Owing to the continued shelling of Bailleul aerodrome, the squadron had to retire to St Marie Cappel.

2.51pm Offensive patrol led by Major Carter, Captains Leacroft and Jennings. Captain Leacroft and Lieutenant Fairclough attacked a two seater enemy aircraft near Lille and shot it down in flames. It was seen to break into pieces and crash. Five enemy aircraft were later seen at 17,000 feet, these made off to the east. Nine 20lb Cooper's bombs were dropped on a gun position near Wervicq, results not observed.

24th March 1918
9.45am Offensive patrol led by Major Carter, Captain Jennings and Captain Leacroft. Thirteen aircraft – the Dolphins flying in three layers proceeded to Staden and dropped 11 x 20lb Cooper's bombs on the town. Afterwards, turning south, Major Carter's formation dived on a 2 seater enemy aircraft which was driven down out of control by Major Carter and Lieutenant Irving. Continuing the patrol, Captain Leacroft saw eight enemy aircraft and a few minutes later, 10 other enemy aircraft coming north from Menin. He climbed hard and collecting his formation in good order, attacked from the sun. A general dogfight ensued in which one enemy aircraft was destroyed by Captain Leacroft and seen to crash. Other enemy aircraft were driven down out of control by Captain Leacroft and Lieutenant Blythe. Lieutenant Puckridge drove one enemy aircraft down and forced it to land and saw it turn over in a field near Coucou. Other enemy aircraft were attacked by the remaining pilots of all three formations but owing to the heat of contest no other decisive results can be claimed. Lieutenant Irving crashed on landing and was slightly cut about the face.

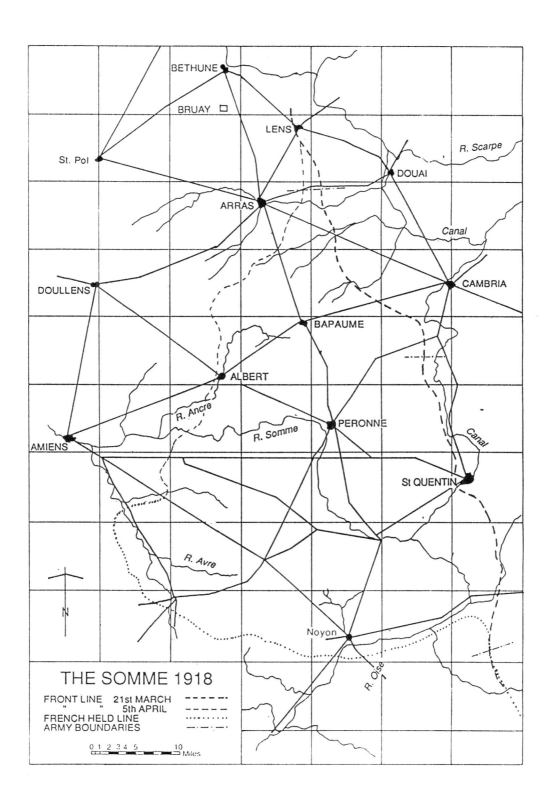

THE SOMME 1918

FRONT LINE   21st MARCH   – – – –
   "   "   5th APRIL   – – –
FRENCH HELD LINE   · · · · ·
ARMY BOUNDARIES   – · – · –

0 1 2 3 4 5   10
⌐⌐⌐⌐⌐⌐   ⌐⌐ Miles

1.32pm Offensive patrol led by Major Carter, Captains Jennings and Leacroft – 11 aircraft and dropped 10 x 20lb bombs Cooper's on Staden. One enemy aircraft two seater was seen and attacked by Captain Leacroft, with Lieutenant Olivier and others in close support. The enemy aircraft went down and glided west as though hit, but when very near the ground he turned slowly east and Dolphins did not see him crash.

26th March 1918

From this date to the end of March, the Squadron's work was mainly low-flying along the Bapaume front. Machines flew to Bruay each morning and returned at night.

Summary of work carried out by low flying patrols of Nos 1, 19 and 40 Squadrons over Bapaume Front; the weather was fine in the morning with detached clouds in the afternoon and visibility good. In all 150 bombs were dropped on groups of enemy troops massing for a counter attack, and columns on the roads, also on transport of various kinds. In most cases general panic ensued and men and horses scattered and ran about in disorder. 30,000 rounds of ammunition were fired also into enemy troops, in trenches and behind shelters, also marching along roads. Pilots report that as a result of the concentrated bombing up on the main Bapaume – Albert road, the enemy has been obliged to take to smaller side roads to bring up his troops. The Dolphins patrolled the Albert-Bapaume area from 10.00am to 12 noon.

Major Carter attacked troops at Bapaume with bombs, causing much disorder and panic. He also fired all ammunition into transport, men with horses and cattle which were moving west. British troops were thought to be retiring.

Lieutenant Blythe attacked troops at Le Sars with bombs, also observing bombs fall amongst some transport – some troops fell down, others scattered. All ammunition was fired at troops which scattered in complete disorder.

Captain Jennings dropped one bomb on a body of troops at Le Sars dispersing same and continuing attack with machine gun fire in trenches and on roads – results were good and in all cases the enemy scattered or fell down. He also dropped one bomb on Bapaume road where men were seen moving west, continuing attack with gun fire creating a panic.

Lieutenant Puckridge dived and attacked massed troops near Vaulx-Vraucourt firing all round troops, of which some fell down or ran in all directions – and on second dive a general panic ensued. Four bombs were dropped on Favreuil, where road movement was observed. Captain Leacroft dropped bombs on German Infantry causing a panic and general disorder, he also fired all ammunition on enemy.

Lieutenant Hainsby dropped bombs on Infantry marching west, and scattered them completely.

Lieutenant Olivier fired all his ammunition and dropped bombs on Infantry from 100 feet at Fremicourt – Hemies road – Enemy immediately scattered in all directions and stampeded.

Lieutenant Ross dropped bombs and attacked troops at Le Sars with gun fire, causing general panic.

Lieutenant De Pencier attacked troops on Bapaume roads with bombs and gun fire – dispersing same and causing great panic.

One Pilot (Lieutenant Fairclough) forced landed.

The area was again patrolled from 1.50pm to 3.05pm, firing into transport and troops on the roads – scattering men and horses and dropped 26 bombs amongst troops and transport.

Major Carter at an altitude of 150 feet over Bapaume attacked troops and vehicles – the latter were damaged and the troops dispersed.

Lieutenants Hardman & Captain Jennings dropped six bombs and fired into transport at Le Sars – transport stopped movements and troops ran. Lieutenant Gardner attacked massed troops on Bapaume roads fired 15 long bursts and dropped four bombs amongst troops – Enemy ran in complete disorder.

Captain Leacroft fired into troops on Bapaume – Albert road, also dropped bombs on them – enemy fell down and he inflicted severe casualties with machine gun fire.

Lieutenant Hainsby fired on troops also dropped four bombs amongst them causing panic and great disorder.

Lieutenant Olivier attacked massed troops on Bapaume – Albert road with machine gun fire, and when directly above them at about 50 feet caused severe casualties by dropping four bombs and causing panic and general disorder.

Seven machines patrolled from 4.40pm to 6.20pm with the following results:-

Lieutenant de Pencier dropped one bomb on troops in a camp east of Bihecourt – troops scattered. With two other pilots he attacked five Albatros scouts, one of which crashed at Achiet le Grand. He also fired 100 rounds at troops at Beifvillers.

Major Carter dropped bombs on Bapaume and shot at troops on roads SE of Bapaume, firing all together 500 rounds and causing a panic and stampede.

Lieutenant Hardman dropped his bombs near Bapaume and fired at enemy troops along the road, causing them to scatter in all directions. Captain Jennings had forced landing – but he is reported to have shot down an enemy aircraft in flames.

Two pilots are missing.

7.10am 12 machines left for temporary duty at Bruay.

4.40pm Captain Jennings had to make a forced landing at Mazingarbe, and reported that he had shot down an Albatros scout in flames. This was confirmed by Lieutenant Warden of 40 Squadron.

6.45pm Returning from Bruay, Lieutenant Blythe is believed to have been shot down in flames. Lieutenant Fairclough landed well behind our lines, heard from him, but he has not yet returned.

Lieutenant Blythe (C3793) – is missing.

Lieutenant Hainsby (C3790) – is missing.

Lieutenant Fairclough (C3940) – is missing.

27th March 1918

Summary of work carried out by Low-Flying Patrols over Bapaume Front:

Weather conditions in the morning were unfavourable with much low cloud and some considerable wind. As soon as weather conditions would permit, nine Dolphins proceeded to Bruay Aerodrome, and on arrival they were immediately filled up and made ready for a patrol, which left the ground at 10.00am.

The patrol proceeded to the neighbourhood of Albert and dropped a total of 34 bombs on enemy troops in massed formation along the roads leading to Albert, and in the neighbourhood of Marmetz.

The German Infantry were seen to scatter and run about looking for shelter, while in one case a large fire was seen to break out east of Albert as the result of a bomb dropped by Captain Leacroft. A total of 2,450 rounds were also fired into enemy troops marching along the roads in the same neighbourhood, and casualties were seen to be caused in a severe degree.

Captain Leacroft leading the patrol, dropped four bombs on Albert – Pozieres road where very large numbers of German Infantry were seen to be massed:- and as a result of one of these bombs a large fire was seen to be caused by Lieutenant Olivier and other pilots. With the Bristol fighters above and in and out of a circus of other machines, he dived repeatedly at the German troops firing 700 rounds into them from under 1,000 feet and noticing many casualties being caused to the enemy.

Lieutenant Olivier with Captain Leacroft, also dropped four bombs south east of Albert and following hard after Captain Leacroft dived in and out repeatedly firing short bursts into the German Infantry which were in large numbers in this neighbourhood and expending a total of 320 rounds at such targets.

Lieutenant Hardman dropped four bombs near Albert and keeping with Lieutenant Olivier and Captain Leacroft fired 40 rounds into German Infantry on the ground from under 1,000 feet. Being strange to the country he afterwards became lost and landed at Vert Galand, leaving there again 45 minutes later. During his second attempt to regain Bruay aerodrome he became lost once more and spent a considerable time working his way home. Having unknowingly crossed the German lines he was heavily fired at by Anti Aircraft and machine guns, and when flying at 3,000 feet his pressure gave out and he only succeeded in recrossing the lines and returning home by using his auxiliary tank.

Major Carter dropped four bombs on German Infantry which were seen marching along the Bapaume-Albert road and afterwards he traversed another portion of the same road several times firing into troops (which were in close formation) from 900 feet, and completely scattering the German formations. A total of 300 rounds was fired by this pilot.

Lieutenant Ross also dropped four bombs on the road leading into Albert and fired 180 rounds inflicting casualties on German Infantry and transport.

Captain Jennings and Lieutenant de Pencier each dropped four bombs on the Mematz-Albert road. Captain Jennings fired 160 rounds and Lieutenant Pencier fired 140 rounds at German Infantry and Transport on the road round Mametz, where the German Infantry were very crowded and would have little chance of escape from attack from above.

Lieutenant Puckridge along with Lieutenant Gardner attacked similar groups of German Infantry with equal success and together dropped six bombs upon the German Infantry in the neighbourhood. 500 rounds were fired by Lieutenant Puckridge and Lieutenant Gardner fired 110 rounds.

The patrol returned to Bruay at 12 noon.

The 2nd patrol left the ground at 1.45pm. A total of 27 x 20lb Cooper bombs were dropped on Mametz and Maricourt and neighbourhood wherever enemy troops were observed. In addition a total of 1,850 rounds were fired by six pilots at enemy forces and transport on the ground. In one case a bomb dropped by Lieutenant de Pencier was seen to get a direct hit on a column of German Infantry marching along a road near Montauban, and much damage must have been done in this case. General impression of the pilots was that activity on the ground was less than in the morning and things in this sector appeared to be more orderly.

All machines returned OK.

Captain Leacroft attacked one enemy aircraft at long range but although this enemy aircraft appeared to have been hit and dived away very suddenly it cannot definitely be claimed as out of control. He dropped 4 x 20lb bombs on some troops observed on the road Avelay-La Boisselle and fired 500 rounds from his machine guns at German Infantry and transport which were seen to scatter.

Captain Jennings was obliged to return early owing to engine trouble.

Lieutenant Puckridge dropped four bombs on a camp near Mametz where enemy movement was noticed and seeing some troops coming along the Maricourt – Albert road he repeatedly swooped down at them, firing a total of 270 rounds in short bursts.

Lieutenant Gardner followed Lieutenant Puckridge and dropped three bombs on some corrugated iron sheds and a fourth bomb was aimed at an AA Battery but result not observed. 190 rounds were also fired from a very low altitude at enemy troops.

Captain Carter dropped four bombs at Montauban where he observed a number of enemy troops apparently resting by the road-side. Afterwards he dived several times at some troops moving in the outskirts of this village and fired 230 rounds from under 1,000 feet.

Lieutenant de Pencier dropped four bombs on enemy troops one of which was seen to get a direct hit on a column moving along a road near Montauban. He also fired 350 rounds at ground targets repeatedly going down and firing wherever enemy movement was seen.

Lieutenant Ross also dropped four bombs to the east of Albert and going down to a low altitude fired 310 rounds at ground targets.

Only one enemy aircraft was seen. Patrol returned at 3.00pm.

A third patrol left Bruay aerodrome at 5.00pm. Eleven 20lb Cooper's bombs were dropped where enemy movement was noticed and in addition 1,400 rounds were fired at ground targets.

During this patrol more shelling from British guns was noticed and no enemy aircraft were seen.

Captain Leacroft dropped four 20lb bombs near a group of men and some transport south east of Albert, and fired 550 rounds at other movement seen on the roads in the same neighbourhood.

Lieutenant Olivier following Captain Leacroft also dropped three bombs and fired 420 rounds at various ground targets.

Captain Jennings and Lieutenant de Pencier were obliged to return early owing to engine trouble. (LH distributor loose on one machine and engine missing; engine not giving revs on the other machine).

Lieutenant Gardner has landed at Authies with his machine unserviceable owing to his engine having given out.

The patrol returned to Bruay aerodrome at 6.10pm.

28th March 1918

Report by Lieutenant A.B. Fairclough M.C.

I followed Captain Leacroft on patrol to the area just south east of Bapaume flying at low altitude. I dropped four bombs there on some troops which I saw on a road from about 3,000 feet, and afterwards, diving down I engaged them with my Vickers guns.

While still flying low down I was attacked at 1,500 feet by one of several Albatros scouts from above. I turned to engage it with my top gun and may have hit him as he dived steeply and did not appear again.

A second then attacked me, and I fired several bursts at him from close range; my engine was then overheating badly and turning to come home, I became lost. I landed at once to try and ascertain my locality but could not understand the French peasants who were the only people about. I finally landed at Grandcourt near Abbeville at 12.15pm.

Being unable to communicate with my Squadron I was obliged to remain there till the following day when I succeeded in obtaining some petrol and oil.

I returned to St Marie Cappelle aerodrome, landing there at 6.50pm 27.3.18.

Signed A.B. Fairclough. Lieutenant.

30th March 1918

Special Summary of work carried out by pilots of 19 Squadron.

Nine Dolphins left St Marie Cappelle at 8.45am and carried out a low flying patrol over Bapaume area, afterwards returning to Bruay aerodrome.

During the patrol enemy transport was observed east and south east of Albert and this transport and infantry were engaged with machine gun fire and bombs from low altitudes.

Nissen huts occupied by the enemy were also fired into, and two hostile balloons were attacked with machine gun fire. In the case of the balloons however, no decisive results were observed.

A total of 3,030 rounds were fired from machine guns at German infantry and transport, and 28 25lb bombs were dropped on ground targets.

One enemy aircraft was seen (Triplane) disappearing into a cloud in far east.

Captain Leacroft who led the patrol, went down low over the Albert – Pozieres road and dropped four bombs where movement was seen. He also saw considerable numbers of German Infantry in a village (thought to be Hardecourt) and diving at them several times, fired 360 rounds into their ranks, and at transport in the same place.

Lieutenant Olivier following Captain Leacroft first dropped four bombs into the village of Ovillers (north east of Albert) where enemy movement was observed, and then afterwards he searched the Albert – Bray road from 1,500 feet firing into some Nissen huts and at German Infantry seen in small parties on this road, expending a total of 300 rounds.

Lieutenant de Pencier was unable to release his bombs but fired 150 rounds at some troops located south east of Albert. He also attacked an enemy balloon but with indecisive result.

Captain Jennings dropped two bombs on the Albert-Bapaume road and going down to a still lower altitude fired into some transport seen at a cross roads using 180 rounds, some Nissen huts south east of Albert were also fired at, although this pilot was hampered by gun trouble (No 3 stoppage and broken belt on the other gun).

Lieutenant Gardner, Lieutenant Hardman and Lieutenant Aldridge all dropped bombs at similar targets and fired at transport east of Albert. Lieutenant Gardner fired 360 rounds, Lieutenant Hardman fired 280 and Lieutenant Aldridge fired 300. Major Carter searching the roads dropped four bombs where movement was seen and diving again and again wherever transport of infantry movement was observed, fired a total of 600 rounds at such targets. He also attacked an enemy balloon but with indecisive result.

Lieutenant Fairclough dropped four bombs and fired 550 rounds at ground targets with good effect.

During the patrol the movement of enemy infantry observed was comparatively slight; but some considerable activity in transport was noticed. The Patrol returned at 10.30am.

31st March 1918

The squadron moved to Savy, where it came under the orders of the OC 10th (Army) Wing, 6th Brigade. From the aerodrome at Savy escorts to bombing missions were provided by the squadron as well as the usual patrols.

1st April 1918

A momentus month in terms of political decisions. On this date, the RAF was officially formed to replace the RFC. Lord Trenchard resigned as a Chief of Air Staff on the 14th April to be succeeded by General F.H. Sykes. (On the 5th June the Independant Air Force was promulgated under Trenchard).

3rd April 1918

3.05pm Escort for DH4's on bombing raid on Cambrai. One two seater enemy aircraft was attacked over Douai at close range, but escaped east apparently unhurt.

BAILLEUL – March 1918 – Squadron Officers celebrating the shooting down of 100 enemy aircraft within 6 months. BACK ROW, LEFT TO RIGHT: Capt. J.D. Hardman, Lieuts. Hainsby, Hastings, Aldridge, Blythe, Jennings, Gardner and Jones. MIDDLE ROW, LEFT TO RIGHT: Lieut. Reed (Equipment Officer) AT BACK OF: Lieuts. Olivier, Ross, Fairclough, Capt. J. Leacroft, Lieuts. Irving and Lord (Armament Officer). FRONT ROW, LEFT TO RIGHT: Major A.D. Carter D.S.O., Major W.D. Sanday D.S.O., M.C., Capt P. Huskinson M.C., and Lieut. Puckridge (Only one standing) Capt O. Bryson M.C., D.F.C., was on leave at this time.

(Crown Copyright – Sqdn Album)

85

7th April 1918

9.00am Major Carter led a patrol of 14 Dolphins between Scarpe River and Le Bassee canal. About 12 enemy aircraft triplanes were encountered and some fighting ensued. The triplanes however, avoided combat for most part and spun away into the clouds, so that the results were indecisive.

The 6.40pm patrol saw 12 enemy aircraft triplanes, 5 to 6,000 feet above the Dolphins, but these kept too high to be engaged.

10th April 1918

6.44am The Dolphins set out on patrol east of the battle lines from Le Bassee northwards, but the weather conditions were found to be too unfavourable for patrol and were obliged to come back. When returning, Major Carter, Lieutenant Irving, Lieutenant Hardman and Lieutenant Aldridge took advantage of a clearance in the local haze and each dropped four bombs on the Arras – Cambrai road.

9.00am Area the north of La Bassee was patrolled and visibility was exceedingly bad throughout the patrol owing to a thick haze. When flying at a low altitude, a very small two seater enemy aircraft was suddenly seen, Lieutenant Hardman swung round and got a good burst into it seeing it going down vertically. It was almost immediately lost in the haze however, and can not be claimed as out of control for this reason. Lieutenant Hardman and Lieutenant Aldridge were much shot about by machine gun fire from the ground and were obliged to fly very low the whole time owing to the mist. They each dropped four bombs on enemy ground targets. Major Carter became separated from the other Dolphins in the haze, he dropped his four bombs north east of La Bassee and attacked a two seater enemy aircraft near Neuve Chapelle. The enemy aircraft was seen to crash with its tail sticking up in the air. During the patrol the infantrymen were observed on the ground and many corpses were seen lying in the open and in shells on the ground held by the enemy.

11th April 1918

2.28pm the area north of La Bassee was patrolled and seven enemy aircraft Pfalz were seen. These kept too high to be engaged and would not come down for combat. Major Carter fired at one of two 2 seaters from long range, but they both went east. Lieutenant Rogers's engine cut out when almost home, and making a forced landing in a field, he turned over and was badly bruised and shaken. (C3837) He was admitted to No 57 CCS.

5.35pm Escort to RE8's on bombing mission to Douai. No enemy aircraft seen.

12th April 1918

6.30am patrol saw one 2 seater enemy aircraft and this was attacked by Captain Jenning, who had gun trouble and the enemy aircraft escaped east.

9.30am The area north of La Bassee was patrolled and several enemy aircraft were seen about 4 to 5,000 feet above the Dolphins, but they remained there and no combat ensued. Many fires were seen burning in the neighbourhood of St Venant, and bombs were observed exploding on the road between St Venant and Foret de Nieppe. More fires spread over the country from Vieux Berquin to Bailluel and west of Lille.

1.30pm Offensive patrol. The area north of La Bassee was patrolled. Captain Leacroft's formation engaged 10 to 12 enemy aircraft (Albatros and Pfalz). Three of these were attacked at close range, and Captain Leacroft followed one Pfalz down to 4,000 feet. This aircraft was last seen spinning very close to the ground and may have been out of control. Captain Leacroft however did not see it crash. Captain Leacroft was then badly hit by "Archie", and returned with the main spar shot through.

5.00pm Offensive patrol. Four Dolphins patrolled the area east of Foret de Nieppe, and many Camels were seen in this neighbourhood and later eight enemy aircraft were seen west of Armentieres. The Dolphins attacked these enemy aircraft assisted by four SE5's. Driving the enemy east, Captain Leacroft in particular, fired at several in turn, one of these at very close range, this aircraft went down out of control at first but is thought to have flattened out again when near the ground.

17th April 1918

Whilst on patrol, Lieutenant Blake was shot through the propeller by AA fire and had to return early.

19th April 1918

At 7.21am ten Dolphins took off on an offensive patrol.
Lieutenant Lye (C4048) – is missing.

The following letter arrived later:
To OC 19 Squadron
Lieutenant Lye is just off to the base and has given me the following statement:-
"Early on the morning of the 19th April I was doing early morning OP with Major Carter as leader, when I noticed an allied Camel in the sun. I took no particular notice of this machine and kept up with my formation. Less than a minute after this, there was a large explosion in my cockpit. This was the first indication I had of having been fired at. I felt paralysed all over my body and could not turn round to look for the Camel or even make sure whether or not it was the Camel which had fired at me. Explosions continued in my cockpit and so I shut off my engine and landed near some reserve trenches being dug by the French. I was picked out of my machine by French soldiers, taken to a road nearby and put into a motor ambulance which took me to hospital".

Lieutenant Lye has a bullet wound in the neck. He has made good progress and is going down to the base today. Signed W.R.P. Goodwin, Lieutenant Colonel. OC No 22 Casualty Clearing Station.

21st April 1918

At 6.30pm Lieutenant Irving on patrol saw a machine falling in flames, south west of Ypres, later the Dolphins engaged a formation of five enemy aircraft (Pfalz Scouts), which were subsequently joined by 15 or 16 other enemy aircraft scouts from above.

During the fight which ensued, Lieutenant Irving brought down one enemy aircraft which was seen by Major Carter to fall in flames. Major Carter, Lieutenant Aldridge, Lieutenant Hustings and Lieutenant de Pencier each brought one enemy aircraft down out of control. Many other enemy aircraft were engaged but the results in these other cases were not observed.

10.30am Three Armstrong Whitworths were escorted on a photography patrol, and afterwards the Army area was patrolled. Captain Leacroft saw four or five enemy aircraft Pfalz scouts and got right onto the tail of one of these but had gun failure and had to break off. Two 2 seaters were also attacked, and a third was attacked by Lieutenants Gardner and Hustings but with indecisive results.

Lieutenant Blake (C3843) – is missing.

22nd April 1918

The area was patrolled and six or seven enemy aircraft (Albatros and Pfalz scouts) were engaged over Bois de Biez. During the fight which ensued, many enemy aircraft were fired at at close range by the Dolphins. These chiefly spun down, and were lost out of sight into the clouds. Lieutenant Fairclough however, saw one go down completely out of control, a piece of fabric coming off the fuselage as it did so.

23rd April 1918

5.46pm During this patrol the Dolphins saw 15 Pfalz scouts and later six enemy aircraft triplanes. Unfortunately, Captain Leacroft had both his Vickers guns hopelessly jammed, but in spite of this he continued to lead the patrol and after they had fought the Pfalz scouts, led the Dolphins against the triplanes. During both these fights there was a great deal of round and round fighting. All pilots firing at least two enemy aircraft from close range. In all cases the results were not observed due to the heat of the contest. Major Carter and Lieutenant Irving, together brought down one enemy aircraft in flames and afterwards Major Carter followed another enemy aircraft down a 1,000 feet and saw it crash completely in a green field. In addition Lieutenant Hall and Lieutenant Fairclough each shot down one enemy aircraft each completely out of control. Several of the Dolphins returned much shot about. Lieutenant Hall (C3940) turned over on landing.

2nd May 1918

4.53pm Offensive patrol. At about 5.45pm two large enemy aircraft formations were engaged consisting of eight to ten Albatros scouts and six or seven triplanes respectively. A general dog fight ensued during which there was much round and round fighting. All the Dolphin pilots engaging several enemy aircraft in turn. Visibility was poor and results in many cases were not observed. Lieutenant Fairclough and Lieutenant Blake however, simultaneously attacked one enemy aircraft which was seen by all pilots to burst into flames, and a few seconds later to break into innumerable pieces. Captain Leacroft, Major Carter, and Lieutenant Hustings also attacked an enemy aircraft which went down obviously out of control, while four other enemy aircraft are definitely known to have been fired into from very close range. The results in each of these cases being unobserved owing to the heat of combat.

3rd May 1918

9.30am Captain Leacroft was the officer leading an offensive patrol which later saw a formation of Pfalz scouts but they avoided combat. Major Carter's formation attacked three enemy aircraft two seaters, firing a great many rounds but with indecisive results. Captain Leacroft also attacked a two seater enemy aircraft but the result was indecisive.

An offensive patrol at 4.56pm engaged six or seven enemy aircraft Pfalz scouts with indecisive results. Captain Chadwick was seen by Lieutenant Irving to have fabric torn from the righthand top plane and go down under partial control, subsequently seen to be attacked by further enemy aircraft and go down spinning near Neuve Chappelle, east of the lines.

Captain Chadwick (C3828) – is missing.

Dolphin – C3828

(J.M. Bruce/G.S. Leslie Collection)

7th May 1918

At 5.21pm Lieutenant Brown on a practice flight in (C3841). When flying at a low altitude, machine dived into the ground some distance from the Aerodrome. Lieutenant Brown was killed and the machine wrecked.

8th May 1918

Offensive patrol. The Dolphins engaged 15 or more enemy aircraft from below and much round and round fighting ensued, during which it was almost impossible to observe results chiefly due to the poor visibility. Major Carter however, supported by Lieutenant Irving, successfully attacked and destroyed one of the many enemy aircraft. Pieces were seen to come from the fuselage of this enemy aircraft as it went down vertically.

9th May 1918

9.25am The Dolphins patrolled the whole of the Army area and saw no enemy aircraft. The total absence of enemy activity in the area this morning was most remarkable. Lieutenant Hardman however, who was delayed in starting, came upon an enemy aircraft two seater whilst trying to regain the Dolphin formation. He attacked the enemy aircraft and saw it go down completely out of control. While still watching it, his attention was distracted and so did not actually see it crash but he thinks it probably did so in the neighbourhood of Plouvain.

14th May 1918

5.15pm Offensive patrol. The area was patrolled and the Dolphins encountered six enemy aircraft which immediately dived into a thick bank of cloud below. Lieutenant McQuistan however, managed to get a good burst into one of the enemy aircraft from very close range. This enemy aircraft also spun into the cloud and was lost from view. Major Carter was delayed in starting and patrolled with some Bristol fighters and while flying with them engaged in an indecisive combat near Menin.

15th May 1918

9.20am Offensive patrol. The Dolphins patrolled from Lens to Bailleul in three layers from 7,000 to 11,000 feet. Six 2 seater enemy aircraft were seen, three of which were dived on by the two lower Dolphin formations but with indecisive results. Major Carter says enemy activity of six 2 seaters. "I attacked three enemy 2 seaters and fired several bursts from different angles but could not observe any effect. All these enemy aircraft were flying very low at 3,000 feet, and well behind their own lines."

5.24pm Offensive patrol. The Dolphins patrolled in two formations at 15,000 feet east of the lines from Arras to Bailleul. About 15 enemy aircraft were encountered between Wervicq and Quesnoy, at 6.25pm. During the fight which ensued Major Carter destroyed one triplane, the righthand planes of which were seen to leave the fuselage and drove a Fokker biplane down completely out of control. He also attacked a third enemy aircraft getting in a good burst at very close range but did not observe the result in this case. Later an enemy aircraft two seater was attacked by Lieutenant Aldridge and Major Carter but it is thought to have escaped east under control.

16th May 1918

9.30am Offensive patrol. Only one enemy aircraft 2 seater was seen and this was attacked by Major Carter and Lieutenant Hardman over Bucqucy. It was fired into from close range and it disappeared into a cloud with streams of smoke coming from its fuselage, which was evidently on fire.

5.30pm Patrol saw nine enemy aircraft Pfalz, east of Comines. The combat was indecisive due to poor visibility.

17th May 1918

9.34am The Dolphins patrolled in two formations. The lower formation encountered four Pfalz and one Albatros scout. The Albatros scout was brought down out of control by Lieutenant McQuistan. Later 20 enemy aircraft (Pfalz, Albatros and Fokker) were seen at about 2,000 feet above four of the Dolphins, but these enemy aircraft did not attack. Lieutenant Hustings reported that when he was on patrol that morning, he joined in the attack against five enemy aircraft scouts and had a very hot combat with two of them. One of these he shot down out of control, but he had sudden engine failure and after which he was much set about by three or four enemy scouts as he regained the lines and landed north of Cassel. He saw Lieutenant Hunter recross the lines with him, enter a cloud over Foret de Nieppe. He landed at Roly with his engine seized up.

18th May 1918

8.58am The Dolphins patrolled from Arras to Bailleul in two formations. Enemy aircraft were active. The lower formation first encountered three Hannover two seater enemy aircraft, south west of Estaires, at 10.15am. These were attacked at close range by Major Carter, Lieutenant Aldridge and Lieutenant de Pencier, who followed them east but with indecisive results. One appeared to be going down as though badly hit. Major Carter also fired at one 2 seater, south of Arras. At 10.30am 10 Pfalz scouts came over the Dolphin formation about 2,000 feet above. The Dolphins tried to climb up to them and fired a considerable number of rounds from their top guns. Some Camels joined in the engagement but all the enemy aircraft went east under control.

19th May 1918

9.04am Offensive Patrol. The Dolphins this morning encountered nine enemy aircraft scouts and two 2 seaters. At the time they were flying in three formations, 'A' flight – two machines on top, 'B' flight – five machines in the centre, and 'C' flight – six machines below. The enemy aircraft were at 10,000 feet when the Dolphins attacked. 'B' and 'C' flights dived onto the enemy aircraft whilst 'A' flight remained above to deal with any enemy aircraft that became detached. Captain Leacroft who was leading the formation dived onto one enemy aircraft but got stoppages on both guns. He corrected this and started firing again but had further gun trouble. Later he saw a Dolphin very low down at about 2,000 feet, it appeared to be diving as though with engine failure. At the same time, Captain Leacroft saw a piece of fabric or something in the air. An enemy aircraft dived down after the Dolphin but the Dolphin spiralled away. The enemy aircraft went east, and the Dolphin continued down appearing under control. Meanwhile Lieutenant Blake

Major A.D. Carter. D.S.O
(Crown Copyright – Sqdn Album)

followed Captain Leacroft, firing bursts at about five different enemy aircraft but did not observe any result, then he got at close range to what was clearly a Pfalz scout, he fired right into it as it passed in front of him, he saw a piece of fabric or something fly from this machine and it rolled over several times and went down completely out of control. After this, as he turned round, he saw a Dolphin going down into a big spiral, fairly steep. Two enemy aircraft dived down after this Dolphin and Lieutenant Blake dived after them. One of these enemy aircraft turned off and made away, the other dived past the Dolphin and shot away east. The Dolphin was seen to be going down still in the same way, but after this Lieutenant Blake lost sight of it. As the fight ended, Lieutenant Blake saw a machine on the ground as though it had landed there. His impression of it was only a passing one, and he did not notice the markings or type. Lieutenant Pierce got well onto an Albatros scout and fired a long burst into its tail. The shots seem to enter the cockpit and it went down completely out of control. This enemy aircraft was confirmed by the AA. Lieutenant Barlow entered the fight with Major Carter. They first went for two 2 seater enemy aircraft firing together at one first. Lieutenant Barlow who was on the right of and slightly above Major Carter, turned off to the left after the second 2 seater as it came nearer, while Major Carter continued on, under him, to the right after the first 2 seater. Lieutenant Barlow did not see the first 2 seater fire at all and lost sight of it and Major Carter after this. Now however, he got very close to the second which fired wildly, well over their heads. The observer in it presently ceased firing and may have been killed. This was the juncture however, when Lieutenant Barlow was suddenly attacked from behind by another enemy aircraft an Albatros, which shot him about considerably. Captain de L'Haye as the fight finished saw a brown machine sitting on the ground below which had landed OK. He only caught a passing glimpse of it however, but his general impression at the time was that it was a British machine.

Major Carter did not return from this patrol. The evidence seems almost in favour that he had engine failure and being very low was obliged to land. AA battery reported seeing the fight but owing to poor visibility are unable to give information other than one Albatros scout was driven down out of control and another machine, nationality not known, went down in a very steep dive. Lieutenant Hardman, who also saw the incident, is not as hopeful as the other pilots states that he saw Major Carter make no effort to avoid an enemy aircraft which was firing at him but continued down in a slow spiral.

Major Carter (C4017) – is missing.

20th May 1918

5.06pm Offensive patrol. The Dolphins patrolled in two formations, the lower formation remained over the battle area protecting Camels flying low. The other formation flying at 10,000 feet had two combats with five or six enemy aircraft Pfalz scouts. During the first of these, Lieutenant de Pencier destroyed one enemy aircraft, seen to crash by a pilot of 46 Squadron. During the second combat, Lieutenant Hustings brought down an enemy aircraft out of control.

7.43pm Offensive patrol. The Dolphins patrolled in two formations. The lower formation encountered five or six enemy aircraft, of which three made east at once as the Dolphins attacked. An indecisive combat took place with the other three. Lieutenant de Pencier forcing one down which seemed to go east at about only 100 feet. All three enemy aircraft were fired into at close range by the Dolphins but escaped.

21st May 1918

5.33pm Offensive patrol. At 6.20pm the Dolphins saw eight enemy aircraft scouts at about 3,000 feet below them going due east. They met them again north of La Bassee ten minutes later, and also ten enemy aircraft scouts above the Dolphins. The enemy aircraft above made off to the east, the Dolphins then attacked the enemy aircraft below, though no decisive results were observed. One enemy aircraft was seen to go east smoking but this cannot be claimed as an out of control or on fire. Lieutenant de Pencier's engine cut out north of Bethune, and being forced to land at Hesdigneu, he crashed in doing so but was OK.

22nd May 1918

The Dolphins took off at 9.10am on an offensive patrol. They saw four enemy aircraft below them, but were obliged at the time to give their attention to six enemy aircraft above them. Afterwards they followed the lower enemy aircraft but they made due east and escaped. Later the Dolphins attacked two two seater enemy aircraft north of Arras, but no decisive result was observed.

The 6.27pm patrol had an indecisive combat with six enemy aircraft scouts, which had the advantage in height. When landing an enemy aircraft Triplane was seen from the ground in the neighbourhood, but the Dolphins were too late to be able to attack this enemy aircraft.

27th May 1918

9.48am Offensive patrol. The Dolphins encountered six or seven enemy aircraft scouts at 12,000 feet, nine miles east of Arras. An exceptionally hot combat ensued during which the Dolphins attacked all the enemy aircraft at close quarters. Climbing again and again to attack others. Owing to the nature of this combat, only one enemy aircraft is claimed as out of control since though several of the Dolphin pilots fired right into the enemy aircraft at close range, they were in every case, obliged to turn at once to engage others and were thus unable to observe enemy aircraft long enough to claim definite results. It is nevertheless significant that after the fight was over, Captain de L'Haye could only count three enemy aircraft going east. Lieutenant Aldridge brought down one enemy aircraft completely out of control and this was confirmed by 64 Squadron. Lieutenant Barlow was shot through his left leg during the combat and managed to get back to base. He was admitted to hospital. Lieutenant Devitalis and Lieutenant Laird went supernumerary into the lines.

29th May 1918
Lieutenant White a new pilot, crashed his machine (C3820) on landing whilst practicing.

30th May 1918
Three Dolphins on Line Patrol at 10.20am. Lieutenant Hardman had to return, his engine overheated badly and caught fire for a moment. The two Dolphins continued the patrol and saw six enemy aircraft in the neighbourhood of Lens. They chased one enemy aircraft over Arras but it escaped. The 10.39am patrol south east of Arras saw two two seater enemy aircraft at 8,000 feet. They attacked these enemy aircraft which made off east and low. In spite of heavy fire from the Dolphins they escaped. Lieutenant Gardner returned to the aerodrome, filled up with petrol and ammunition and went up again looking for enemy aircraft. He patrolled as far north as Ypres and chased two enemy aircraft east of Bethune, but they escaped.

31st May 1918
6.38am Offensive patrol. The Dolphins had two encounters with formations of enemy aircraft. They first attacked 8 enemy aircraft scouts east of La Bassee. During this encounter, Captain Irving, brought one enemy aircraft down completely out of control. After a short fight however, the other enemy aircraft made off east. Later the Dolphins attacked four Pfalz and three Albatros scouts near Armentieres. Captain Irving brought an enemy aircraft down completely out of control, seeing pieces coming from its fuselage as it went down. Lieutenant Blake also supported by Lieutenant Ray had a very sharp contest with a Pfalz scout and after firing right into it saw it go down out of control and break up into many pieces as it did so. Lieutenant Pierce, Lieutenant Hustings and Lieutenant Fitchat all fired into enemy aircraft at very close range, but these cases definite results were not observed. One enemy aircraft attacked by Lieutenant Aldridge, went down in a steep dive and was seen to land in a field by Lieutenant Fitchat. Lieutenant De Pencier becoming separated from the Dolphins during the fight, brought two enemy aircraft down to 1,500 feet and recrossed the lines at a low altitude.

1st June 1918
The squadron escorted DH's on a bombing mission to Mouchin.

5th June 1918
At 11.00am on an offensive patrol the Dolphins encountered seven enemy aircraft triplane's. During the fight which ensued, Captain Irving fired several bursts at one enemy aircraft from close range, but his pipe line then broke and he was obliged to return home. Another enemy aircraft was engaged at close range by Captain De Pencier.

6th June 1918
On an offensive patrol at 5.30pm the Dolphins saw a two seater enemy aircraft north east of La Bassee. They followed this enemy aircraft as it came west and attacked it together. It dived east and Lieutenant Gardner who remained close on the enemy aircraft tail for a long time, fired many bursts into it and finally saw it go down completely out of control, with much smoke coming from it. Captain Irving and Lieutenant McQuistan also fired at the enemy

aircraft from close range, while Captain De Pencier leading the patrol followed the enemy aircraft down to 3,500 ft firing at it and last saw the enemy aircraft completely out of control 300 ft near Bleue. Lieutenant Hewson was forced to land north of Pernes and turned over and crashed. (C3940)

7th June 1918

9.56am Offensive patrol. The Dolphins encountered six to seven Albatros scouts which were attacked at close quarters. Captain Irving and Lieutenant Aldridge in particular, got in some good shooting but did not observe results definitely. Lieutenant Hustings put two short bursts into one enemy aircraft which he saw go down into a steep glide and crash in the middle of a wood. From the appearance of the machine which he was once very close to, he thinks the pilot must have been killed.

17th June 1918

8.00am Offensive patrol. The Dolphins flying in three formations saw six or seven Pfalz scouts 1,000 ft above them and about seven miles east of the lines between Douai and Le Bassee. They tried to climb up to these enemy aircraft and the enemy aircraft started to come down on the two Dolphin formations. Some fighting ensued during which Captain Irving, after chasing one enemy aircraft near to Lille, shot another one down out of control, at the same time the remaining Dolphin formation, led by Captain De L'Haye had seen in the west a formation of twelve enemy aircraft, triplanes and Albatros scouts, which had come between them and the lines and were 3,000 ft above them. The Dolphin formation turned west towards the lines and in order to prevent the other two formations from being cut off, attacked these enemy aircraft and fought them from 14,000 ft down to 3,000 ft although greatly outnumbered. During this fight, Captain De L'Haye brought one down out of control, later the other Dolphins turned back from the east and there was some further fighting but decisive results were not observed.

Lieutenant Blake and Lieutenant Ray fired at enemy aircraft from very close range. One enemy aircraft which attacked Lieutenant Laird was driven off by Lieutenant Ross who got in some good shooting at it.

Lieutenant Laird (C4062).crashed near Ricquinghem.

Lieutenant Hewson (C3843) landed near Lillers and turned over on landing.

Lieutenant Leach was wounded during the fight and landed near Loos where he has been admitted to hospital.

26th June 1918

An evening patrol at 5.55pm found the weather conditions very unfavourable owing to too much cloud, but the lower flight saw four enemy aircraft near Comines and nine other enemy aircraft in the distance near Messines. They attacked the four enemy aircraft and during the short time the fight lasted, got in some good shooting. Lieutenant Hardman brought one down out of control.

27th June 1918

4.55pm. The Dolphins encountered five Pfalz scouts between Bailluel and Estaires. These enemy aircraft did not observe the Dolphins but flew right underneath them and a short fight ensued. The Dolphins dived from above and Captain Irving and Lieutenant McQuistan each brought one down completely out of control.

28th June 1918

Special Offensive patrol at 5.00am. The Dolphins patrolled towards the neighbourhood of a British attack near Merville but before they had been out many minutes a thick mist came up and they were obliged to make their way home again. Lieutenant Lansbury became detached from the other Dolphins and was completely lost in the mist, which at times extended down to the ground. He made two attempts to land, each time however, he was just in time to see that landing was impossible and climbed again, narrowly missing trees and houses that were obscured in the mist. For the third time he was gliding down and he noticed his aneroid was only showing 100 ft, even then he was unable to see any ground. He continued to glide carefully looking for the ground, when he suddenly crashed into a wheat field 10 yards from a row of tall trees near Houdain. The pilot was only shaken but the machine was completely wrecked (C3840).

Lieutenant Gardner had his engine cut out at 2,000 ft and he crashed near Ablain St Nazaire. (C4057)

30th June 1918

At 6.58pm offensive patrol. The Dolphins saw ten Pfalz scouts at 18,000 ft, four of these came down on the Dolphin formation and in a short fight which took place at 14,000 ft over Armentieres, at 8.00pm one enemy aircraft was brought down completely out of control by Captain De L'Haye.

1st July 1918

On an offensive patrol at 2.20pm the Dolphins saw a two seater enemy aircraft crossing the lines, they followed it and it flew round the neighbourhood of Cassel at 16,000 ft. The Dolphins watched and attacked it over Killeo, they followed it down to 5,000 ft over Steenwercke where it went down completely out of control and was seen by Lieutenant Aldridge to burn on the ground.

At 5.00pm when crossing the lines on another offensive patrol at 12,000 ft near Bailluel, the Dolphins saw twelve enemy aircraft a long way above them. These enemy aircraft stayed above the Dolphins until they were over Fluerbaix, when some of the enemy aircraft dived down. The Dolphins attacked and during the fight which ensued, Lieutenant Gregory fired at one enemy aircraft which was afterwards shot down out of control by Lieutenant Gardner. Lieutenant Gregory then attacked a second enemy aircraft at close range. The enemy aircraft spun down and a moment later Lieutenant Gregory saw it spin into the ground.

2nd July 1918

Two 2 seater enemy aircraft were seen at 5.10 am north of the Forest De Nieppe flying at 17 to 18,000 ft. Later the Dolphins· engaged six enemy aircraft triplanes at 13,000 ft over Estaires. A sharp contest took place and Captain Irving and Lieutenant Aldridge both shot enemy aircraft down out of control. Towards the end of the patrol an enemy aircraft, probably a Rumpler, was seen working between St Omer and Aire at 18 to 19,000 ft. This enemy aircraft made off east while the Dolphins were still climbing.

4th July 1918

Offensive Patrol at 4.00pm. The lower Dolphin formation encountered five Pfalz scouts which they attacked from above. During the fight one enemy aircraft was brought down in flames by Captain De L'Haye and one enemy aircraft was brought down out of control by Lieutenant Gardner.

Pfalz D111

13th July 1918

At 6.55pm. The Dolphin formations patrolled the area in three layers. At 8.05pm at 11,000 ft over Bois de Biez, Captain De Pencier leading the bottom layer and squadron formation attacked six enemy aircraft scout's which were slightly below him. The middle layer led by Lieutenant Gardner came down while the top formation stayed above. A very hot combat ensued during which Lieutenant Gardner, Gregory and Pierce each destroyed one enemy aircraft each and Captain De Pencier and Lieutenant Crane each brought one enemy aircraft down out of control.

16th July 1918

Captain De L'Haye patrolled alone at 10.56am at 17,000 feet. He saw five Pfalz scouts at 12.30pm at 15,000 ft and dived down on the last machine of the enemy aircraft formation and brought it down completely out of control. He then attacked at very close range another enemy aircraft scout firing 200 rounds into it and saw the enemy aircraft left bottom plane fall off. The enemy aircraft fell in a spinning nosedive completely out of control and must have been destroyed.

17th July 1918

5.00pm Offensive patrol. The Dolphins patrolled in two layers, the higher formation at 15,000 ft over Estaires met six Fokker biplanes at 17,000 ft which they attacked. They drove five of the enemy aircraft down to the lower formation who immediately engaged them, while the higher formation stayed above as protection there being twelve enemy aircraft scouts a little further east and higher up, which however did not come down. The lower Dolphins got in some good shooting. Lieutenant Hardman firing into one enemy aircraft and followed it down to 4,500 feet was obliged to pull out and lost sight of the enemy aircraft.

Lieutenant White (C3792) – is missing.

31st July 1918

Lieutenant Northridge on a line patrol at 2.31pm, whilst flying alone, north of Bethune he saw six Fokker biplanes flying in two formations of three. He attacked the last enemy aircraft of the higher formation and fired bursts into it from less than 25 yards range. The enemy aircraft spun and crashed into the earth northeast of Bethune. An offensive patrol at

6.25pm, the Dolphins engaged five enemy aircraft south of Douai at 16,000 feet, at 7.50pm. Lieutenant Blake shot one enemy aircraft down in smoke which burst into flames on striking the ground. Lieutenant Gardner and Lieutenant Ray each destroyed one enemy aircraft and in both cases were seen to crash.

7th August 1918

10.00am offensive patrol. The Dolphins met seven Fokker biplanes and Pfalz scout's east of Arras at 15,000 feet. Captain Irving, Lieutenant Hardman, Lieutenant Northridge forced several of the enemy aircraft to spin down with their top guns. These enemy aircraft were subsequently attacked by a flight in the middle layer. Lieutenant Gardner, Lieutenant Gregory and Lieutenant Ross had indecisive combats. One of the enemy aircraft Pfalz scouts forced down by the top layer was engaged by Lieutenant McQuistan who brought it down completely out of control and observed pieces coming from its tail. Later another Pfalz was engaged by Captain De Pencier, Lieutenant Blake and Lieutenant Pierce and two SE5's. This enemy aircraft floated about the sky loosing height and making no effort to dodge the Dolphins or SE5's. In the opinion of all the Dolphin pilots engaged, the pilot of the enemy aircraft must have been dead or his controls jammed.

9th August 1918

The Dolphins took off at 8.05am on a patrol and no enemy aircraft were seen. Forty eight 20lb bombs were dropped just west of Douai. Lieutenant Northridge's engine failed when attempting to turn into the aerodrome, his machine (D3748) was wrecked and the pilot was admitted to hospital with injuries to the face and head.

Lieutenant Lance in (D3796) had a forced landing near the aerodrome and turned over.

11th August 1918

4.12pm offensive patrol. The Dolphins started out in three layers east of Albert. The top layer was attacked by five Pfalz scouts at 11,000 feet. Lieutenant Gardner and Lieutenant Graham fired several bursts at the enemy aircraft and Lieutenant Gardner finally drove one down in flames. The pilot of which descended by parachute. Captain Irving drove one down out of control. The formation reformed and carried on with its patrol. At 5.55pm they encountered six enemy aircraft Pfalz and Fokkers over Flaucourt at 7,000 ft. All Dolphins dived on the enemy aircraft and a dogfight ensued in which Captain McQuistan destroyed one enemy aircraft, Lieutenant Pierce drove one down completely out of control but was unable to see it crash. During this fight twelve more enemy aircraft, Pfalz and Fokkers dived on the Dolphins from a considerable height. Lieutenant Gardner destroyed one of these, a Fokker. During this fight, a Dolphin was seen to go down in flames and the letters of which could not be distinguished but it was thought by several pilots to be Captain Irving.

Lieutenant Gregory (B7876) – is missing
Lieutenant Douglas (C4043) – is missing
Captain Irving (E4432) – is missing

13th August 1918

SECOND BATTLE OF AMIENS

Machines were flown to Allonville to take part in the Second Battle of Amiens.

On arrival at Allonville a thick mist covered the aerodrome. Lieutenant Pierce (D3762) and Lieutenant Lance (C3902) collided in the air, both pilots being killed.

18th August 1918

A further move was now made to Cappelle near Dunkerque. Here the Squadron came under the orders of the OC 65th Wing, 10th Brigade: and provided escorts for the DH9's bombing Bruges and Thourout.

Right through to the end of August the Dolphins escorted the DH9's on their missions and on most occasions without sighting any enemy aircraft. The weather closed in and little flying was done until the 14th September.

15th September 1918

The Dolphins led by Captain Gardner patrolled the area in three layers at 15.45. The DH9's were seen crossing the lines at Dixmude and escorted to Bruge and back. At 16.10 four Dolphins engaged five enemy aircraft Pfalz and Fokkers biplanes with indecisive results.

Lieutenant Anderson (D5314) – is missing.

16th September 1918

7.57am Dolphins led by Captain McQuistan patrolled the area in three layers. At 9.45am a formation of eight to ten Pfalz and Fokker enemy aircraft were engaged at 15,000 feet north of Lille. During the fight which ensued, one enemy aircraft was destroyed by Captain De L'Haye, this enemy aircraft was seen to crash by Captain McQuinstan near Fort Carnot. Lieutenant Hardman assisted by Captain Gardner shot down one enemy aircraft out of control, a piece of the machine was seen to come off in the air. Lieutenant Laird sent one enemy aircraft down out of control with smoke coming from it. Lieutenant Ray also brought down one enemy aircraft out control. The remaining Dolphins joined in the fight and got in some good shooting with indecisive results.

Lieutenant Farrand made a forced landing in a ploughed field and the machine was wrecked (D5306).

21st September 1918

At 10.45am the Dolphins led by Captain Gardner patrolled the area in three layers. When the patrol was returning at 11.55am, twelve Fokker biplanes attacked the DH9's east of Thourout. The top layer of Dolphins dived on the enemy aircraft and Captain McQuistan brought one down out of control emitting black smoke. Lieutenant Duff and Lieutenant Ray got in some good shooting but with indecisive results.

23rd September 1918

The Squadron moved from Cappelle to Savy. Enroute Lieutenant Farrand is believed to have crashed in a field due west of Ryveld. (C3818)

27th September 1918

6.20am Dolphins patrolled the battle area in conjunction with Bristol Fighters and at 7.35am, twelve Pfalz and Fokker enemy aircraft were seen near Haynecourt, north of Cambrai. These enemy aircraft were engaged and a dogfight ensued. Captain De L'Haye and Lieutenant Moore destroyed one enemy aircraft. Lieutenant Aldridge and Captain Gardner each shot one enemy aircraft down out of control. At 7.15am Lieutenant Ray saw three Fokker triplanes, northeast of Cambrai, he attacked these enemy aircraft destroying one and shooting the remaining two down out of control. Immediately after this in the same locality he saw a balloon ascending through the clouds. He attacked it and shot it down in flames.

The 11.20am patrol. Dolphins patrolled the area with DH4's. At 12.50am ten enemy aircraft were seen diving on the DH4's. Captain De L'Haye dived with his formation on the enemy aircraft and shot down one out of control over Aubigny.

Captain Gardner (E4501) – is missing.

Offensive patrol that took off at 4.10pm.

Lieutenant Boyd (C8087) – is missing.

Dolphin – C8087. Flown by Capt Gardner
Left to right: J.A. Aldridge, Capt R.A. De L'Haye, Lt. Montgomery-Moore, Capt J.W. Crane, Lt. W.F. Gordon.
(J.M. Bruce/G.S. Leslie Collection)

1st October 1918

8.00am 15 Dolphins were led by Captain De L'Haye and patrolled in three layers. At about 8.55am 10,500 feet east of Cambrai, the bottom and middle layers engaged ten to twelve enemy aircraft formation of Fokkers, Pfalz and triplanes. During the fight which ensued, Captain De L'Haye brought a Pfalz scout down completely out of control, at the same time 12 enemy aircraft were seen in the sun at 18,000 feet. The top formation of Dolphins climbed to 17,000 feet but the enemy aircraft made off to the east and escaped. Lieutenant Baird was wounded, but landed safely.

3rd October 1918

8.00am The Dolphins led by Lieutenant Ray, patrolled the area. Between 8.45am and 9.00am whilst over the neighbourhood of Cambrai, two separate formations of about 20 Albatros, Fokker and Pfalz were engaged. During the two engagements which ensued, Lieutenant Moore destroyed two enemy aircraft, seeing the first crash into the ground north east of Cambrai, and the second burst into flames on striking the ground. Lieutenant Crane also destroyed one enemy aircraft, confirmed by 203 Squadron as coming down in flames, and brought a second enemy aircraft down completely out of control. Lieutenants Mercer and Duff each brought one enemy aircraft down completely out of control. Lieutenant Farrand was last seen being forced down by Fokkers over Aubigny-au-Bac.

Lieutenant Farrand (D3769) – is missing.

4th October 1918

10.00am The Dolphins led by Captain McQuistan patrolled the area following Camels. At 11.15 the lower Dolphin formation dived on eight to 10 enemy aircraft at 12,000 feet on the Cambrai-Le Cateau road. Captain McQuistan destroyed one enemy aircraft a Pfalz scout, half the enemies aircraft, the top right hand plane folded back and broke up in the air. The remaining enemy aircraft made off east. At 11.20 eight enemy aircraft Pfalz and Albatros's appeared above the Dolphins and were drawn west of Cambrai, where the fighting ensued. Captain McQuistan drove an enemy aircraft Albatros scout down completely out of control, confirmed by six other pilots. Lieutenant Ray attacked a enemy aircraft which had been forced down by the top Dolphin formation, the aircraft went into a spin, then pulled out and dived east. Lieutenant Ray followed the aircraft, firing all the time, and the enemy aircraft landed in a field east of Cambrai.

5th October 1918

6.30am The Dolphins formation led by Captain McQuistan, and following Camels patrolled the area. At 7.40am eight or ten enemy aircraft were seen north of Cambrai at 14,000 feet and climbing. The Dolphins climbed after them to 18,500 feet and engaged the enemy aircraft about eight miles due east of Cambrai. Captain McQuistan destroyed one enemy aircraft Fokker biplane in flames. Lieutenants Crane and Mercer each shot one enemy aircraft down out of control. Lieutenant Boyd (E4715) crashed near Hendicourt, pilot believed to be alright.

9th October 1918

7.00am The Dolphins led by Captain McQuistan. At 7.45am eight enemy aircraft Fokkers were seen north east of Cambrai at 8,000 feet. These enemy aircraft avoided combat and dived away east on the approach of the Dolphins.

At 3.15pm eleven Dolphins led by Captains Crane and Hardman in three layers escorted 18 Squadron on a bombing mission. At 4.25pm several enemy scouts were seen well east of Cambrai but were not engaged.

14th October 1918

6.30am Captain McQuistan led 14 Dolphins in three layers and patrolled the battle area. At 7.45 Lieutenant Duff dived on an enemy balloon just west of Valenciennes and fired several bursts into it from close range. It was pulled down very quickly. When the Dolphins were returning, five enemy aircraft followed the middle layer, Captain Hardman and Lieutenant Brown to the lines keeping well east.

24th October 1918

The squadron moved to Abscon, which had just been evacuated by the Germans four days previously. Large enemy aircraft formations were frequently met with.

27th October 1918

10.45am Offensive patrol of nine Dolphins led by Captain Hardman patrolled the battle area. An enemy formation of eight Fokkers were engaged at about 12 noon 13,500 feet north east of Valenciennes near Quaroubles. Captain Hardman destroyed one enemy aircraft in flames, confirmed by Lieutenant McDonald. Lieutenant Hewson fired one burst at a Fokker "head on" and when the enemy machine turned he fired two long bursts into it from the side. The machine hung in the air and then went down in a slow spin completely out of control.

Lieutenant Duff also shot one enemy aircraft down completely out of control.

Lieutenant Nesbitt was last seen during the combat, diving very steeply, his aircraft pouring smoke.

Lieutenant Nesbitt (D5236) – is missing.

At 3.00pm. Offensive patrol. The Dolphins patrolled the battle area in three layers. At 3.35pm twelve enemy aircraft attacked the top Dolphin formation which was then at 10,000 feet north of LeQuesnoy. Lieutenant Miller shot down one enemy aircraft a Fokker biplane completely out of control. This was confirmed by Captain Hardman. Other pilots got in some good shooting at close range, with indecisive results. The enemy finally made off east. The weather was very thick.

30th October 1918

10.15am Nine Dolphins led by Captain Crane on an offensive patrol and escort to DH9s on a bombing mission to Mons and return. While over Mons at 11.20am, 14 Fokker biplanes attacked the DH9s, and as the Dolphins were attacking these enemy aircraft, another large formation of enemy aircraft joined in the scrap. A dogfight ensued in which the Dolphins got in some very good shooting. Five enemy aircraft being destroyed, and one enemy aircraft shot down completely out of control. Captain Hardman shot down two enemy aircraft in flames, Lieutenant Moore destroyed one enemy aircraft in flames, and Lieutenant Davies destroyed one enemy aircraft which was seen to crash, and shot down one enemy aircraft out of control.

Captain Crane (B7855) – is missing
Lieutenant Lynn (E4511) – is missing
Lieutenant Murray (E4637) – is missing
Lieutenant Duff (D3768) – is missing
Lieutenant Boyd (E4552) – is missing.

The remaining pilots on their return were warmly congratulated by the DH9 pilots who declared that the Dolphins saved their life they only loosing two machines.

On the night of the 10th November 1918, news was received that Lieutenant Duff, one of the missing pilots had escaped and on return to the Squadron much valuable information was obtained from him and also news of the remaining four pilots, two being prisoners of war (unwounded), one wounded slightly in the left arm and the remaining one is feared a casualty.

4th November 1918

8.55am Offensive patrol led by Captain McQuistan, the Dolphins working with 22 Squadron patrolled the battle area. At 9.45am eight enemy aircraft Fokker were seen north east of Valenciennes at 13,000 feet. The enemy aircraft were above the Dolphins, climbed into the sun and were not seen again.

1.30pm Offensive patrol led by Captain McQuistan. Eight Dolphins patrolled with 22 Squadron and at 2.20pm dived on nine enemy aircraft Fokkers who were seen south east of Valenciennes at 11,000 feet. At 2.35pm attacked seven Fokkers, probably the same enemy aircraft who were a little further south, at 10,500 feet. Captain McQuistan got in some good shooting, one enemy aircraft he sent spinning down into a cloud, but no decisive result can be claimed.

10th November 1918

About this date, Major E.R. Pretyman left the squadron (sick)

ARMISTICE DAY

11.15am Lieutenant Mercer in (C8188) on practice flight, had to make a forced landing at Chasse-Farm. Machine and pilot alright. Machine being dismantled and brought back by road.

12th November 1918
Major H.W.G. Jones, M.C., assumed command of the Squadron.

10th January 1919
At 9.40am Lieutenant Hendershot and Lieutenant Wilson took off on a reconnaissance fight to observe the condition of bridges along the canal from Cambrai to Lille, via Douai and Pont-A-Venden. The original bridges had been destroyed but it was observed that temporary bridges had been erected on all important thoroughfares, main roads and railway bridges leading to Cambrai from Douai and Arras were temporary but in good condition. Temporary bridges across the canal at Aubigny, Courcheletts, Douai, Dourges, Courrieres, Wingles, Maubourin, and Lille, were in good condition. The bridges at Point-A-Venden and Don, had been destroyed and no temporary bridges erected. The Dolphins returned via Douai and Aberchicourt.

13th January 1919
Lieutenant Morris took off at 11.05am in Dolphin (F7056) for a practice flight. He was doing some low flying when he hit the hangar, stalled the machine, crashed and was killed.

15th January 1919
An Inspection took place by the Officer Commanding 91st Wing, RAF of the Squadron's personnel and machines.

20th January 1919
Saw the start of the return to England when Captain Hamersley led nine machines to Marquise for eventual delivery to England. Eight days later on the 28th, Captain Busk led the remaining six machines, for delivery to England via Marquise.

9th February 1919
The squadron arrived at Genech.

17th February 1919
The Squadron moved to Ternhill where it was reduced to cadre.

31st December 1919
The Squadron was disbanded.

The following Decorations and Awards were made to Officers for duties carried out while serving with the Squadron.

Captain I.H.D. Henderson	Military Cross.
Captain G.B.A. Baker	Military Cross and Bar.
Captain J. Leacroft	Military Cross and Bar.
Major A. D. Carter	Distinguished Service Order and Bar, and Belgium Croix de Guerre.
Captain M.R.N. Jennings	Military Cross.
Captain F. Sowrey	Military Cross.
Captain O.C. Bryson	Military Cross.
Lieutenant A.B. Fairclough	Military Cross.
Captain P. Huskinson	Bar to the Military Cross.
Captain A.A.N. Pentland	Military Cross.
Captain G.S. Buck	Military Cross.
Captain F.H.B. Selous	Italian Order for Valour.
Captain R.A. De L'Haye	Distinguished Flying Cross and Bar.
Captain F. McQuistan	Distinguished Flying Cross.
Captain J.D.I. Hardman	Distinguished Flying Cross.
Captain G.B. Irving	Distinguished Flying Cross.
Captain C.V. Gardner	Distinguished Flying Cross.
Lieutenant J.A. Aldridge	Belgium Croix de Guerre.
Lieutenant R.M. Strang	Belgium Croix de Guerre.

Photocopies of the original recommendations for most of the above awards (and some not approved) are shown in the following pages.

To
Headquarters
11th Wing,
Royal Flying Corps.

file

        2/Lieut. R.M.STRANG: I wish to strongly recommend
this young Officer for award as he did very excellent and gallant work
(as below) until he broke his arm in an accident,and has now lost the use
of it.

20/9/17.   Two-seater E/A.   Destroyed at 28 E.28.   Confirmed.

26/9/17.   Two-seater E/A.   Destroyed at 28 V.12.   Confirmed.

23/9/17.   Scout E/A.   Out of Control near LINDSELLES.

      On 26/9/17 he attacked a balloon firing about 100 rounds; it was
pulled down rapidly to a low altitude. Whilst still attacking the balloon
Lt. Strang was heavily engaged by a machine gun battery close by. He dived
down on it, firing over 100 rounds from a height of 500 feet. The men about
the place immediately scattered leaving two stretched on the ground.
      Going on, he had 9 separate combats with E/A - 3 indecisive with
Albatross Scouts, 5 indecisive with E/A two-seaters, and one decisive with
an Albatross two-seater. In this last combat, he got right on to the E/A,
first killing the observer, and then firing right into the pilot and engine.
The E/A spun down with it's engine full on, and was seen to crash by the
Officer i/c 88th Section "J" Battery, 2nd Army A.A.
      After continuous fighting he returned to the Aerodrome very much
shot about, having actually a bullet hole right through the ear pad of his
flying cap. He had himself fired 450 rounds.

      On the 4/10/17.   Under the most unfavourable weather conditions,
(Low clouds with a 60 m.p.h. gale blowing), he flew at a very low altitude
to East of MOORSLEDE, where he discovered 2,500 Enemy troops massing for
a counter-attack; he returned with this valuable information to the Report
Centre.   The Army Commander afterwards stated that this information
was of the greatest value.

      On 5/10/17.   He attacked about 100 Enemy troops on the
MOORSLEDE road firing at them from 200 feet, killing some and scattering the
remainder.

In the Field.
5th January 1917.

                       Major,
           Commanding No.19 Squadron,R.F.C.

               (Crown Copyright – PRO – Air 1)

To
  Headquarters,
    9th Wing,
      Royal Flying Corps.
      _____

    I herewith attach combat report from Lieutenant
H.D.Parry Okeden. It has been impossible to obtain
this before,owing to the serious nature of his wound.
                                                    25.5.17
This Officer showed very gallant conduct on this occasion,
as after having probably driven an E.A. down out of control,
was very severely wounded; but flew back a distance of
34 miles, landing without damaging his machine at No.32
Squadron Aerodrome; and I wish to bring his name before
you,for special recognition.   I understand General
Longcroft witnessed this Officer landing and the severe
condition of his wounds.

                              (signature)

                                      Major,
In the Field.   Commanding No.19 Squadron,
28th June 1917.   Royal Flying Corps.

                          (Crown Copyright – PRO – Air 1)

105

To
Officer Commanding,
11th. Wing,
Royal Flying Corps.

Captain John Leacroft, M.C.

This Officer has proved himself of such inestimable value to
the Corps, in that he has set the most splendid example of keeness,
courage and skill in leading his patrols to combat, and by his own deeds,
that I feel it my duty to bring his name before you for consideration
for further award.
Below I enumerate some special deeds since 10-10-17.

14-10-17, 1 Single Seater   DESTROYED.   Seen to crash
                                                in BECALAERE.

2? ?-17, 1 Single Seater   DESTROYED.   Seen to crash by
                                                II Army A/A.

24-10-17. He led his Patrol to attack two E/A Formations of
approximately 20 machines. During this Combat he was seen by
others to engage three E/A at close range, bringing two down
out of control, which without a doubt must have crashed . (This
was confirmed by Major Carter,)   In this combat 4 E/A were
driven down out of control and many more badly damaged.

12-10-17. He searched East of PASSCHENDALE and found many German
Infantrymen in small groups lying in the open and in shell-holes.
Although himself heavily fired at, he repeatedly engaged these men
from under 100 ft,, and must have killed and wounded numbers of
them, especially one group which were crowded together in a shell-
hole. He also engaged what was probably a gun emplacement, with good
effect, and returning home was able to give valuable information as
to the enemy's dispositions.

As an example of determination, on 6-10-17, while on wireless
interupting he saw the two-seater going East just as a storm
burst. He followed it through the storm, catching it up, and drove
it down through the clouds and rain to under 800 ft East of LILLE.
The E/A was then going down as if out of control, when they both
got into a blinding storm.   Captain,returned near BOIS D'HAVRINCOURT.

(Signed) W D S Sanday.
                                        Major,
                        Commanding No 19 Squadron,
                        Royal Flying Corps.

In the Field
25-10-17.

Officer Commanding,
11th Wing,
Royal Flying Corps.

Temp Capt   I beg to submit to your favourable notice the name of
Lieutenant OLIVER CAMPBELL BRYSON (Albert Medal) DORSET YEOMANRY and
R.F.C. Acting Flight Commander, No.19 Squadron, who was posted to this
Squadron on 1st August 1917.

He has proved himself a determined and undaunted leader.
He has carried out several missions in the most unfavourable weather in
which only sheer determination has carried him through and he has at all
times set a fine example of pluck.

On 25/9/17 he destroyed an Albatross Scout S.E. of HOUTHEM
which was seen to crash by an A.A. Battery.
On 26/8/17, 24/10/17, 31/10/17, 12/11/17, 29/11/17 and
8/12/17, he shot down E/A out of control.

On 27/8/17, 20/9/17 and 6/11/17, and again on 21/9/17 he
carried out patrols at a very low altitude, firing upwards of 1,200 rounds
at enemy troops, and on his return bringing back valuable information
regarding the enemy's dispositions.

On 26/9/17 flying in extremely bad weather, he dropped a
20lb Coopers Bomb from 150 feet on an active enemy dump, in the midst
✱ of much activity, and one 20lb Coopers Bomb from 100 feet in the middle
of an enemy camp near COURTRAI, doing very considerable damage.

On 20/9/17 he dropped one 20lb Coopers Bomb from 600 feet
on a group of enemy troops and one 20lb Coopers Bomb from 300 feet on a
group of men round a machine gun.

And, one 21/9/17 he dropped one 20lb Coopers Bomb from
2,000 feet on an active cross roads, and one 20lb Coopers Bomb from
2,000 feet on a shell hole full of enemy troops.

✱   On this occasion he flew for 1½ hours behind the enemy lines with
clouds at 200 feet, trying to find HEULE aerodrome.

This Officer is good in all branches of his work and I beg
to recommend him for immediate award.

In the Field.

9th December 1917.

                                        Major,
                        Commanding No.19 Squadron,
                            Royal Flying Corps.

                    (Crown Copyright – PRO – Air 1)

CONFIDENTIAL.

To
Headquarters,
11th Wing,
Royal Flying Corps

I wish to bring Major Albert Desbrisay Carter's, (New Brunswick Regt. & R.F.C.,) name before you.

This Officer joined this Squadron 1-10-17; having previously served with his Regiment in France, until severely wounded.

He was promoted to the rank of Major in February 1916.
This Officer has considerable character and since joining the Squadron has shown the utmost keenness and dash, setting a very high example.

On
31-10-17 He destroyed an Albatross Scout at 1.40 p.m. near GHELUWE.

8-11-17   "   " a two-seater E/A at 9.15 a.m. South of
GHELUWE.

15-12-17 "   " " two-seater E/A at 9.50 a.m. at COMINES.

He has driven down 7 E/A Scouts "out of control" on the following dates:-   31-10-17, 9-11-17, 13-11-17, 16-11-17, 18-11-17, 23-11-17, 2 on 18-12-17.

On 12-10-17 and 6-11-17 he flew at a very low altitude behind the enemy's lines, firing at troops, and bringing back highly important information.

This Officer's work in all it's branches, is of an exceptionally high standard, and I wish to very strongly recommend him for immediate award.

W.D.S. Sanday
Major,
Commanding No.19 Squadron,
Royal Flying Corps.

In the Field.
18th December 1917.

(Crown Copyright – PRO – Air 1)

108

Copy

<u>CONFIDENTIAL REPORT ON MAJOR A.D.CARTER,</u>

<u>NEW BRUNSWICK REGT. & R.F.C.   RECOMMENDED</u>

<u>FOR PROMOTION TO SQUADRON COMMANDER.</u>

This Officer obtained his Commission in March 1911, and his majority in February 1916.

He was severely wounded in October 1915, obtained his Wings in September 1917, and was posted to this Squadron on October 1st; and was posted to this Squadron on October 1st; and was promoted Flight Commander 14/11/17.

He is now recommended for further promotion, as he is an officer of exceptional character.   He is a first-rate Pilot,an exceedingly keen and skillful fighter, and is very conscientious.

His qualities as an officer are exceptional, and I strongly recommend him for promotion to Squadron Commander.

In the Field.
23rd December 1917.

Major,
Commanding No.19 Squadron,
Royal Flying Corps.

(Crown Copyright – PRO – Air 1)

Ruetchley Kings.

Headquarters,
    11th Wing,
    Royal Flying Corps.
    _____

        I beg to bring the name of Captain Patrick
Huskinson, M.C, Notts & Derby Regiment & R.F.C., before
you for recognition for continuous good work.
        Since joining the Squadron on 11th October 1917
he has proved himself a very gallant and keen Patrol leader.
        He has had the following decisive combats ;-

24-10-17	One single seater	Out of control	N.N.E.of Menin.
27-10-17	One twoseater	Out of control	OOSTHOEK.
13-11-17	One two seater	Destroyed	Near MOORSLEDE 10-35a
3-12-17	One single seater	Out of control	MENIN.
29-12-17	One single seater	Out of control	HOUTHULST FOREST
again	One single seater	Out of control	" "
6-1-18	One single seater	Out of control	WATERDAMHOEK.

        On 26-10-17 during an attack by the 2nd Army Capt.
Huskinson carried out a ground patrol flying at a very low
altitude and searching for enemy movement. He engaged a German
Infantry Company on a Road near MOORSLEDE with machine gun
fire from under 500 feet, and as he swooped down he saw numbers
of them running into the houses and scrambling to take cover.
Without doubt many of them were hit. Returning, he dropped a
message reporting the presence of these men and giving a "G.F
call" on the houses in question.

        On 15-11-17 at 6-15 am. when firing at roads etc. from a
low altitude, he got a direct hit from a shell which carried
the propeller undercarriage and lower parts of the radiator away.
He however regained control and landed upside down in a shell hole
full of water, being suspended in the water till he was almost drowned
Having been rescued he remained all day, working in the shell hole and
under fire, till he had salved the engine, only returning to the
Squadron at 6-30 pm.

        This officer's general work has been excellent, and I
strongly recommend him for immediate award.

In the Field.   Major,
                                        Commanding No.19 Squadron,
4th March 1918.   Royal Flying Corps.

                                        (Crown Copyright – PRO – Air 1)

110

Friend of Robert
December

To
Headquarters,
11th Wing, R.F.C.

With reference to your A8/1361.

I beg to bring the name of 2/Lieut. ERIC OLIVIER, GENERAL LIST & R.F.C. to your notice, as I consider that his work has been deserving of recognition. I would like to draw particular attention to the following episode, as I think this is one of the only known cases of a machine landing behind the enemy's lines and then escaping.

On the 6th November 1917, in spite of very bad weather and low clouds Lt. Olivier set out to do a Ground Patrol. While engaging a ground target East of MOORSLEDE he became lost; his compass would not direct him properly. He flew for an hour hopelessly lost, and finally, thinking he was behind our lines he landed on the Common at GHENT. But finding from a Belgian that he was in enemy territory, he started up and got away in spite of very heavy ground fire.

After flying for another three-quarters of an hour, practically despairing of getting back, he managed to cross our lines at ARMENTIERES and landed as his petrol gave out.

He carried out Ground Patrols on 12-10-17 and 26-10-17, firing at small groups of infantry and doing considerable damage.

He has had the following decisive combats:-

10-11-17	One two-seater E/A.	Destroyed at ZANVOORDE.	Confirmed by 2nd Army A.A.
26-10-17	One two-seater E/A.	Out of control.	
6-12-17,	One two-seater E/A.	Out of control.	

I also wish to bring the name of Capt. JOHN LEACROFT, GENERAL LIST & R.F.C. before you.

This Officer as you will see from the following list, has a fine record of good work. He was only awarded the Military Cross for this, and I consider he is deserving of a Foreign Decoration.

On the 17-6-17	1 Two-seater E/A.	Out of control.
6-7-17	1 Single-seater	Out of control.
26-8-17	1 Single seater	Destroyed.
1-9-17	1 Single-seater	Destroyed.
3-9-17	1 Single-seater	Out of control.
14-9-17	1 single-seater	Driven down.
16-9-17	1 Single-seater	Out of control.
19-9-17	1 Single-seater	Out of control.
19-9-17 again	1 single-seater	Out of control.
21-9-17	1 Single-seater	Out of control.
26-9-17	1 Two-seater	Out of control.
14-10-17	1 Single-seater	Destroyed.
21-10-17	1 Single-seater	Destroyed.
24-10-17	1 Single-seater	Out of control.
again 24-10-17	1 Single-seater	Out of control.

On the 1st, 16th and 19th of September 1917, 26-9-17, 4-10-17 and 12-10-17 he carried out Ground Patrols for a long distance behind the enemy lines; he engaged many enemy troops from a low altitude and brought back exceedingly valuable information, on several occasions being much shot about; and on one occasion when East of MOORSLEDE was shot through the petrol tank. He, however managed to recross the lines and land on the MENIN ROAD without damaging his machine, and on another occasion during a combat he got so close to the machine he was attacking that he collided with it, damaging his plane but managed to return safely to the Aerodrome.

In the Field,
8th March 1918.

Major,
Commanding No.19 Squadron, R.F.C.

(Crown Copyright – PRO – Air 1)

Officer Commanding,
11th Wing, R.F.C.
_____

   I beg to bring the name of Captain JOHN LEACROFT M.C.
General List & R.F.C. before you for IMMEDIATE AWARD, in view of
his continuous good work, leadership, and gallantry, culminating
in a brilliant fight again this morning, in which he destroyed
one E/A and drove a second down out of control.

   He is exceptional in his abilities as a leader in
formation, and his example, determination, skill and gallantry have
always been altogether magnificent.

   While with this Squadron he has brought down the following
E/A. :-

17-6-17	One two-seater	Out of control.	PROVEN - CARVIN.
		(Confirmed by Lt. Buck).	
6-7-17	One single-seater	Out of Control.	HOUTHULST FOREST.
		(Confirmed by No.23 Squadron).	
28-8-17	One single-seater	Destroyed.	BISSEGHEM.
		(Seen to crash by Lt. Ainger).	
1-9-17	One single-seater	Destroyed.	SOUTH OF HOUTHULST FOREST.
		(Confirmed by A.A.).	
3-9-17	One single-seater	Out of Control.	SOUTH EAST OF COMINES.
4-9-17	One two-seater	Damaged & forced to land.	
14-9-17	One single-seater	Driven down damaged.	QUESNOY.
16-9-17	One single-seater	Out of Control.	GHELUVELT.
19-9-17	TWO single-seaters	Out of Control.	BECELAERE.
		(One of these seen to crash by another pilot).	
21-9-17	One single-seater	Out of Control.	DADIZEELE.
26-9-17	One two-seater	Out of Control.	WERVICQ.
14-10-17	One single-seater	Destroyed.	Seen to crash in BECELAERE.
21-10-17	One single-seater	Destroyed.	S.E. of DADIZEELE.
		(Confirmed by A.A.).	
24-10-17	TWO single-seaters	Out of Control	N.E. of MENIN.
15-3-18	TWO single-seaters	Out of Control.	TOURCOING.
17-3-18	One single-seater	Destroyed in Flames.	DE RUITER.
		(Confirmed by Major Carter).	
23-3-18	One two-seater	Destroyed in Flames.	LILLE.
24-3-18	One single-seater	Destroyed.	MENIN.
24-3-18	One single-seater	Out of Control.	MENIN.

On the 1st, 16th and 19th of September 1917, 26-9-17, 4-10-17
and 12-10-17 he carried out low flying Ground Patrols for a long
distance behind the enemy lines; he engaged many enemy troops from
a low altitude and brought back exceedingly valuable information,
on several occasions being much shot about; and on one occasion when
East of MOORSLEDE being shot through the petrol tank.
On this last occasion however he managed to recross the lines and
land on the MENIN Road without damaging his machine, and on another
occasion during a combat he got so close to the machine he was
attacking, that he collided with it, damaging his plane but managing
to return safely to the Aerodrome.

His leadership in the two big fights of 17-3-18 and again today
was largely responsible for the excellent results achieved.

This Officer is conspicuous in all branches of his work -
both in the air and on the ground, and I beg to recommend him most
strongly for immediate award.

In the Field.
24th March 1918.

Major,
Commanding No.19 Squadron,
Royal Flying Corps.

Headquarters,
11th Wing, R.F.C.

_____

I wish to bring the name of Lieut. ARTHUR BRAD.
FAIRCLOUGH, Canadian Machine Gun Corps & R.F.C. before you for
IMMEDIATE AWARD.
This Officer has always shown the utmost dash and courage;
he has done continuous good work for several months, being determined
to attack and destroy the enemy at every possible opportunity, and
yesterday afternoon he was instrumental in completely destroying an
enemy machine for the fifth time.
While with this Squadron he has brought down machines as
under :-

18-12-17	One single-seater	Destroyed (Confirmed by A.A.)	Near GHELUWE.
19-12-17	One two-seater	Out of Control	East of HOOGLEDE.
19-12-17	One two-seater	Destroyed	Near PASSCHENDAELE.
29-12-17	One single-seater	Destroyed	HOUTHULST.
29-12-17	One single-seater	Out of Control	HOUTHULST.
17-3-18	One single-seater	Destroyed in Flames	N.E. of MENIN.
23-3-18	One two-seater	Destroyed in Flames	LILLE.

He is hard working in all branches of his work.
His qualities as an Officer are very good, and I recommend
him most strongly for immediate award.

In the Field.
24th March 1918.

Major,
Commanding No.19 Squadron,
Royal Flying Corps.

114

To
Headquarters,
10th Wing,
Royal Air Force.

I wish to bring the name of Capt.MONTAGUE RIGHTON NEVILL
JENNINGS (Flight Commander) Royal Air Force S.R., before you for
IMMEDIATE AWARD; in view of his continuous good service, leadership
and gallantry.

Last Autumn, all through the Winter and during the Spring
Offensive, his work in this Squadron has been altogether invaluable;
while by his examp'- determination and skilful leadership he has won
very considerabl.. ..cess with his formation until today, when,after
seven and a h'. r-aths of War flying, he is being transferred to the
Home Establis ort for a period of rest.

During the offensive actions in the PASSCHENDAELE Sector
last autumn he on four occasions carried out low flying ground patrols
over the enemy lines, searching for enemy movement in the ROULERS-MENIN
neighbourhood and firing into trenches, at groups of men on the roads,
and at enemy trnasport, from under 800 feet.

On one of these occasions although heavily fired at from the
ground he engaged and silenced a machine gun battery near WERVICQ from
600 feet; afterwards going on and searching the town of MENIN for enemy
concentration.

Besides carrying out a very considerable amount of low flying
work over the enemy lines, this Officer has completely destroyed three
E/A.

On 15-18-17 when flying North West of JESNOY he approached
a two-seater E/A to within 250 yards firing a good burst into it.
Overshooting the E/A he swung round a second time and as the E/A was
coming straight towards him, he fired two more bursts into it and it
was seen to go down vertically and crash completely. (Confirmed by
pilot of another Squadron).

On 17-3-18 he joined in a very hot combat and brought down
one of the seven E/A which were destroyed by the Dolphins on this pccasion.
The E/A was seen to crash completely.

On 26-3-18 during the enemy offensive in the BAPAUME Sector
he went out three times and flying at under 800 feet dropped bombs and
fired into the enemy infantry which were in large numbers on all the roads.
The same evening he attacked an enemy Scout which was seen to crash
completely by a Pilot of No.40 Squadron.

On 27-3-18 he again carried out low flying patrols, and on one
of many occasions went down very low and fired into the mass of German
infantry which in this case were particularly crowded and would have but
little chance of escape.

Throughout his work in France this Officer has shown the
utmost courage, being determined always to force a fight.
His undiminished daring in connection with low flying has itself proved
him worthy of recognition. He is excellent in all branches of his work,
both in the air and on the ground and I beg to recommend him most strongly
for immediate award.

Major,
Commanding No.19 Squadron,
Royal Air Force.

In the Field.
5th May 1918.

115

To
Officer Commanding,
No.23 Squadron,
Royal Air Force.

_____

TRANSFER REPORT ON LT. TEMP. CAPT. A. B. FAIRCLOUGH M.C.

While with this Squadron the above named officer has destroy the following E/A.:-

18-12-17	One single-seater	Confirmed crashed by A.A.
19-12-17	One two-seater	Confirmed by 2nd Army A.A
29-12-17	One single-seater	In flames.
17-3-18	One single-seater	In flames. Seen by all Pilots.
23-3-18	One two-seater	In flames.(With Capt. Leacroft).
2-5-18	One single-seater	In flames.

He has also got the following E/A "Out of Control":-

19-12-18	One two-seater
29-12-17	One single-seater
21-4-18	One single-seater
23-4-18	One single-seater

On 19-12-17 he also forced one E/A two-seater down damaged.

This Officer has served with this Squadron since 17th November 1917

He last returned from leave 12th February 1918.

He was awarded the Military Cross 20th March 1918.

Major,
Commanding No.19 Squadron,
Royal Air Force.

In the Field.
9th May 1918.

(Crown Copyright – PRO – Air 1)

116

CONFIDENTIAL.

NO. 19 SQUADRON
R.F.C.

To
Headquarters,
10th Wing,
Royal Air Force.

   I wish to bring the name of Major ALBERT DESBRISAY CARTER
D.S.O,,Croix de Guerre NEW BRUNSWICK REGT. & R.A.F. before you
for further IMMEDIATE AWARD.

   This Officer obtained his Commission in March 1911, and
his Majority in February 1916.

   He was severely wounded in October 1915, obtained his
Wings in September 1917, and was posted to this Squadron on September
29th 1917. He was promoted Flight Commander on 4-11-17 and was
awarded the D.S.O. on 2nd January 1918. He was subsequently awarded
the Croix de Guerre on 4th February 1918.

   Throughout his service with this Squadron Major Carter has
always shown the most striking keenness and dash, setting a very high
example to his brother pilots. His character is altogether exceptional
and his daring is unequalled.

   Since the 1st of October 1917 he has completely destroyed
eleven enemy machines, and has driven no less than fifteen enemy
machines down completely out of control - making a total of
twenty six E/A accounted for.

   Since Major Carter was awarded D.S.O. and the Croix de Guerre
he has accounted for the following E/A:-

15-3-18	One single-seater	Destroyed (Wing came off).
15-3-18	One single-seater	Out of Control.
17-3-18	One single-seater	Destroyed (Seen to crash).
24-3-18	One two-seater	Out of Control.
10-4-18	One two-seater	Destroyed (Seen to crash).
21-4-18	One single-seater	Out of Control.
23-4-18	One single-seater	Destroyed in Flames.
23-4-18	One single-seater	Destroyed (Seen to crash).
2-5-18	One Triplane	Out of Control.
8-5-18	One single-seater	Destroyed.
15-5-18	One Triplane	Destroyed.(Wings came off).
15-5-18	One single-seater	Out of Control.

   As will be seen from the above list Major Carter's record
is a very fine one. His work has been splendid. On every occasion
he goes out with the one intention of hunting down and destroying
the enemy. He is full of enthusiasm and has shown the most
remarkable gallantry over and over again. I feel that I cannot
recommend him too strongly for further IMMEDIATE AWARD.

In the Field.
16th May 1918.

             Major,
     Commanding No.19 Squadron,R.A.F.

(Crown Copyright – PRO – Air 1)

To

Headquarters,

10th Wing,

Royal Air Force.

I wish to bring the name of TEMP.CAPTAIN GORDON IRVING

ROYAL AIR FORCE (FLIGHT COMMANDER) before you for IMMEDIATE AWARD,

in view of his continuous good service, leadership and gallantry.

This officer has always shown the utmost dash and courage.

He has done continuous good work since he joined the Squadron in

November 1917, being determined to attack and destroy the enemy

whenever possible, and this evening he was successful in bringing

down an enemy machine for the eighth time.

The E/A which he has accounted for while with this Squadron

are as follows:-

24-3-18	One two-seater	Out of Control.	Near ROULERS.
21-4-18	One Pfalz Scout	Destroyed. (Seen by Major Carter to fall in flames).	STEENWERCKE.
23-4-18	One single-seater	Destroyed. (Seen to go down in flames by Major Carter & Lieut.Fairclough).	N.of LA BASSEE.
8-5-18	One single-seater	Destroyed. (With Major Carter).	S.E.of BAILLEUL.
31-5-18	One single-seater	Out of Control.	S.E.of ESTAIRES.
again on 31-5-18	One single-seater	Out of Control.	S.W.of ARMENTIERES.
17-6-18	One Pfalz Scout	Out of Control.	LILLE.
27-6-18	One Pfalz Scout	Out of Control.	Between BAILLEUL and ESTAIRES.

This officer is hard-working in all branches of his work -

both in the air and on the ground.

His qualities as an officer are very good and I wish to

recommend him most strongly for Immediate Award.

Major,

Commanding No.19 Squadron,

Royal Air Force.

In the Field.
27th June 1918.

(Crown Copyright – PRO – Air 1)

118

To

Headquarters,

10th Wing, R.A.F.
_____

       I wish to bring the name of LIEUT. CECIL VERVON GARDNER
R.A.F. (Pilot) before you for IMMEDIATE AWARD for gallantry in
the Field when attacking enemy aircraft and for continuous good
service.

       This Officer was posted to this Squadron on 22nd January
1917 and carried out much steady and very valuable work during the
months following.

       During the last few weeks however he has shown unusual
determination to attack and destroy E/A, and his enthusiasm has met
with considerable success. He has accounted for the undermentioned
E/A :-

6-6-18	One Two-seater	Out of Control.	VIEUX BERQUIN.
9-6-18	One D.F.W.	Destroyed. (Seen to crash into ground).	NEUF BERQUIN.
1-7-18	One Pfalz Scout.	Destroyed.	FLEURBAIX.
4-7-18	One Pfalz Scout.	Out of Control.	ESTERELLES.
13-7-18	One Fokker Biplane Destroyed. (in flames -)		BOIS DE BIEZ.

       This Officer is keen, "dashing" and absolutely without
fear. He sets the right example and his zeal is altogether most
praiseworthy. He is good in all branches of his work and I feel
that I can recommend him most strongly for IMMEDIATE AWARD.

In the Field.

                  Major,
Commanding No.19 Squadron,
Royal Air Force.

(Crown Copyright – PRO – Air 1)

119

To
Headquarters,
1 h Wing, R.A.F.
_____

I wish to bring the name of CAPTAIN ROGER DE L'HAYE R.A.F. S.R.
(Flight Commander) before you for IMMEDIATE AWARD in view of his prolonged
good service,leadership, skill and gallantry.

This Officer joined this Squadron from ENGLAND on 4-5-18. He has
done continuous good work since then, leading his Flight very skilfully
and attacking and destroying the enemy whenever possible. During a
comparatively short period he has accounted for the undermentioned E/A:-

19-6-18	One Triplane	Destroyed. (Confirmed as crashed by A.A.)	DOUAI.
30-6-18	One Pfalz Scout	Out of Control.	ARMENTIERES.
4-7-18	One Pfalz Scout	Destroyed in Flames.	ESTRELLES.
16-7-18	One Pfalz Scout	Destroyed.	ARMENTIERES.
16-7-18	One Pfalz Scout	Out of Control.	ARMENTIERES.

On 17-6-18 the Dolphins, when pursuing some Pfalz Scouts were cut
off from the lines by 12 E/A Triplanes which had the advantage in height.
Capt. De L'Haye with much skill turned against these Triplanes and fought
them with his Flight from 14,000 down to 3,000 feet, although greatly outnumbered, thus allowing the other two Dolphin flights which were much
further East to carry out their work and return safely.

On 16-7-18 whilst patrolling by himself Capt. De L'Haye saw 5 E/A
Scouts which he immediately attacked. He shot down one out of control and
then attacked the remainder and by great skill and pluck shot down one
of them whose left bottom plane was seen to fall off. Capt. De L'Haye was
then forced to break off the combat as he had used all his ammunition.

Not only has Capt. De L'Haye excelled with this Squadron, but his
previous record is worthy of some recognition. He served as an Artillery
Pilot in No.13 Squadron for nine months, from July 1916 until March 1917,
being promoted towards the end of that time to the rank of Flight Commander.
During this period he carried out much valuable work during the battle of
the SOMME in July 1916, and during the fighting at ARRAS in the Spring of
1917, being engaged in Artillery Observation, Contact Patrol and Day and
Night Bombing. He was also responsible for bringing down a two-seater
E/A which crashed in "No Man's Land". His total flying time in FRANCE
is 670 hours.

This Officer is good in all branches of his work, both
in the air and in his duties as a Flight Commander on the ground.
I wish to recommend him most strongly for IMMEDIATE AWARD.

In the Field.

5th July 1918.

Major,
Commanding No.19 Squadron,
Royal Air Force.

Dear Colonel,

In answer to your letter I wish to put forward the following names of officers to be recommended for Decoration, with a short resume of their work.

Capt.R.A.DE L'HAYE has personally destroyed 3 E/A and driven down 2 others out of control while serving in this Squadron, and he has also destroyed 1 E/A while serving with No.13 Squadron. He has seen 15 months active service in FRANCE with the R.F.C. Whilst with this Squadron he has shown great skill and dash in leading both the flight and Squadron formation. I strongly recommend this officer for a Decoration.

Capt. F.MC.QUISTAN served for fourteen months in the R.F.C. in FRANCE, having served in both No.12 & 55 Squadrons before joining this Squadron. Whilst with this Squadron Capt. Mc.Quistan has set the highest example to the other pilots, especially during the present SOMME Offensive in August. He has led over 28 successful flights in the Squadron formation and has personally destroyed 1 E/A and has driven down 3 others out of control, besided which he has destroyed one E/A while serving with No.55 Squadron.

I strongly recommend this officer for a Decoration.

I also wish to put forward the following officer for Mention in Despatches Lieut.J.A.ALDRIDGE and Lieut.J.D.HARDMAN.

Lieut.J.A.ALDRIDGE has carried out very good work with this Squadron for seven months and has often led his flight with marked success during the absence of his Flight Commander. He has personall driven down 4 E/A out of control.

Lieut.J.D.HARDMAN has shown great gallantry and keenness whilst serving with this Squadron for the last six months and has personally destroyed one E/A and driven down two others out of control

Yours sincerely,

R.R.Leighman.

12.9.18.

(Crown Copyright – PRO – Air 1)

122

Headquarters.
  10th Wing,
  ROYAL AIR FORCE.

        I wish to bring the name of Lieutenant Temp. Captain
ROGER AMEDEE DEL'HAYE Royal Air Force before you for immediate
award in view of his prolonged good service and leadership, skill
and gallantry.
        This Officer joined the Squadron from England on
4-5-1918. He has done conspicuously gallant and plucky work
since then, leading both his flight and Squadron Formations very
skillfully; attacking and destroying E/A whenever possible.
        During the time he has been with the Squadron he
has destroyed the undermentioned E/A :-

        17-6-1918 1 Triplane Destroyed (Confirmed by A.A.)
               DOUAI.
        30-6-1918 1 Pfalz Scout out of control. ARMENTIERES.
         4-7-1918 1 Pfalz Scout destroyed in flames.ESTRELLES.
        16-7-1918 1 Pfalz Scout destroyed ARMENTIERES.
        16-7-1918 1 Pfalz Scout out of control ARMENTIERES.
        16-9-1918 1 Pfalz Scout destroyed LILLE.
        27-9-1918 1 Pfalz Scout destroyed with Lt.Moore CAMBRAI
        27-9-1918 1 Pfalz Scout out of control AUBIGNY N.W.
               CAMBRAI.

        In addition to the above Captain Del'Haye shot down one
E/A in No-Mans-Land while serving with No.13 Squadron.
Not only has Captain Del'Haye excelled in this Squadron but his
previous record of service is worthly of recognition.
He served as an Artillery Pilot in No.13 Squadron for 9 months from
July 1916 to March 1917; being promoted to the end of that time
to the rank of Flight Commander.
        During this period he carried out much valuable work
during the battle of the SOMME 1916 and the battle of ARRAS in 1917,
being engaged in Artillery Observation, Contact Patrol,day and
night bombing.
        I wish to recommend this Officer most strongly for im -
mediate award.

                              Major.
In the Field.   Commanding No.19 Squadron,
27th September 1918.   Royal Air Force.

(Crown Copyright – PRO – Air 1)

To
Headquarters,
10thnWing,
Royal Air Force.

     I wish to bring the name of Temp.2/Lieutenant LEWIS HECTOR RAY R.A.F. before you for IMMEDIATE AWARD.
     This Officer joined this Squadron from England on 2-4-18 and has always shown the utmost dash and courage during combats and the greatest keen-ness to destroy E/A.
     On 27-9-18 this officer with great gallantry, by himself attacked three Fokker Biplanes at a comparatively low altitude. The first he destroyed; the remaining two he sent down completely out of control and it was only due to ground mist and shell smoke that he did not see them crash. As he was climbing again he observed a hostile balloon coming up which he immediately destroyed in flames.
     Altogether this Officer has accounted for the following E/A :-

31-5-18	1 E/A Scout.		Out of Control.
31-7-18	1 E/A Scout.		Destroyed.
16-9-18	1 E/A Scout.		Out of Control.
27-9-18	1 E/A Scout.		Destroyed.
27-9-18	1 E/A Scout.		Out of Control.
27-9-18	1 E/A Scout.		Out of Control.
27-9-18	1 Hostile Balloon.		Destroyed in Flames.
4-10-18	1 E/A Scout.		Driven down - seen to land.

     I strongly recommend this officer for Immediate Award.

Major,
Commanding No.19 Squadron,
Royal Air Force.

In the Field.

4th October 1918.

(Crown Copyright – PRO – Air 1)

124

CONFIDENTIAL.

To
Headquarters,
10th Wing,
Royal Air Force.

_____

      I wish to bring the name of Lieutenant Temp.Captain
F.MC.QUISTAN R.F.A. & R.A.F. before you for IMMEDIATE AWARD for
gallantry when attacking enemy aircraft and for continual good
leadership.
      This Officer was posted this Squadron from Home Establishment
on April 20th 1918. Since joining this Squadron this Officer has
been invaluable. By his example, determination and devotion to duty,
he has inspired the greatest confidence in the other pilots of the
Squadron, especially during the British SOMME Offensive in August
and the present CAMBRAI Battle. He has already led over thirty
successful Squadron Patrols, and the E/A destroyed by this Squadron
during the past three months are largely due to his skilful leadership.
      While serving with this Squadron he has accounted for the
following E/A :-

17-5-18	1 E/A Scout.	Out of Control.
27-6-18	1 E/A Scout.	Out of Control.
7-8-18	1 E/A Scout.	Out of Control.
11-8-18	1 E/A Scout.	Destroyed in Flames.
21-9-18	1 E/A Scout.	Out of Control.
27-9-18	1 E/A Scout.	Out of Control.
4-10-18	1 E/A Scout.	Destroyed - broke up in air.
4-10-18	1 E/A Scout.	Out of control.

      This Officer has served twice before overseas with the R.F.C.
the first time with No.12 Squadron from June to September 1916 when
he was very severely wounded, and again with No.55 Squadron from
March to July 1917. When serving with No.55 Squadron he was again
wounded whilst engaged in a fight with an E/A which he, although
wounded in the head, shot down and it was seen to crash.

      I wish to recommend this Officer most strongly for Immediate
Award.

                              Major,
               Commanding No.19 Squadron,
                   Royal Air Force.

In the Field.

4th October 1918.

CONFIDENTIAL,

To
~~Headquarters,~~
10th Wing,R.A.F.
_____

     I beg to submit the name of LIEUT.TEMP.CAPT. JOHN

DONALD HARDMAN R.A.F. for IMMEDIATE AWARD.

     This Officer has in the seven months that he has been
with the Squadron done conspicuously gallant and hard work. He has
on all occasions set a very high example of determination and
tenacity inspiring his pilots with the greatest confidence.
     During the retreat in March 1918 this Officer did
exceedingly useful and courageous work in attacking both with bombs
and machine gun fire, enemy troops from very low altitudes.
     Captain Hardman also has done very hard and useful
work during the present battle from August till the present time.
     While serving with this Squadron he has personally
shot down the following E/A :-

16-5-18	One two-seater	In flames (Destroyed).
31-5-18	One single-seater	Out of Control.
20-6-18	One single-seater	Out of Control.
16-9-18	One single-seater	Out of Control.
27-10-18	One single-seater	Destroyed (in flames).
30-10-18	One single-seater	Destroyed (in flames).
30-10-18	One single-seater	Destroyed (in flames).

     On 30-10-18 whilst escorting D.H.9's on a bombing raid
to MONS, Capt. Hardman with his flight met about 40 E/A,
Capt. Hardman personally shot down 3 E/A in flames; and it was
entirely due to his foresight and judgement and great skill in
leading the formation that the patrol destroyed 5 E/A and one E/A was
shot down out of control.

     I wish to recommend this Officer most strongly for
IMMEDIATE AWARD.

                             Major,
                Commanding No.19 Squadron,
                    Royal Air Force.

In the Field,

30-10-18.

ENEMY AIRCRAFT

brought down and by whom – in date order

	Date	Type	Result	By Whom
1	13.4.17	1 single seater	Out of control	Captain G.S. Buck
2	14.4.17	1 two seater	Out of control	Lieutenant W.E. Reed
3	22.4.17	1 two seater	Destroyed	Lieutenant W.E. Reed
4	24.4.17	1 single seater	Destroyed	Major Harvey-Kelly
5	1.5.17	1 two seater	Destroyed	Lieutenant F.S. Wilkins
6	4.5.17	1 single seater	Out of control	Captain A.T. Hope
7	11.5.17	1 two seater	Forced to land	Major W.W.S. Sanday
8	19.5.17	1 single seater	Destroyed	Captain W.J. Cairnes
9	23.5.17	1 single seater	Driven down	Captain W.J. Cairnes
10	23.5.17	1 single seater	Destroyed	Lieutenant A.H. Orlebar
11	25.5.17	1 single seater	Out of control	Captain J.M. Child
12	5.6.17	1 single seater	Out of control	Lieutenant A.H. Orlebar
13	6.6.17	1 single seater	Out of control	Lieutenant R.R. Riggs
14	7.6.17	1 two seater	Forced to land	Captain G.S. Buck
15	7.6.17	1 two seater	Out of control	Captain W.J. Cairnes
16	7.6.17	1 two seater	Destroyed	Captain J.M. Child
17	14.6.17	1 single seater	Destroyed	Captain G.S. Buck
18	15.6.17	1 two seater	Out of control	Sergeant S.J. Clinch
19	17.6.17	1 single seater	Destroyed	Captain W.E. Young
20	17.6.17	1 two seater	Out of control	Captain J. Leacroft
21	18.6.17	1 single seater	Out of control	Lieutenant A.H. Orlebar
22	27.6.17	1 single seater	Out of control	Captain F. Sowrey
23	3.7.17	1 two seater	Out of control	19 Squadron patrol
24	6.7.17	1 single seater	Out of control	Captain J. Leacroft
25	7.7.17	1 single seater	Out of control	Lieutenant R.R. Riggs
26	12.7.17	1 single seater	Out of control	Captain A.C. Hagon
27	13.7.17	1 two seater	Out of control	Captain F. Sowrey
28	13.7.17	1 two seater	Destroyed	Major W.W.S. Sanday
29	19.7.17	1 single seater	Out of control	Lieutenant C.R.J. Thompson
30	21.7.17	1 single seater	Out of control	Lieutenant C.D. Thompson
31	21.7.17	1 two seater	Driven down	Captain F. Sowrey
32	21.7.17	1 single seater	Out of control	Captain F. Sowrey
33	21.7.17	1 single seater	Out of control	Lieutenant B. McEntegart
34	22.7.17	Unknown	Out of control	Captain W.E. Young
35	27.7.17	1 two seater	Out of control	Lieutenant W.B. Kellogg
36	27.7.17	1 single seater	Out of control	Lieutenant T.L. Harding
37	27.7.17	1 single seater	Out of control	Lieutenant A.R. Boeree
38	28.7.17	1 single seater	Forced to land	Captain F. Sowrey
39	29.7.17	1 single seater	Destroyed	Lieutenants Best & Powers

40	12.8.17	1 single seater	Out of control	Lieutenant A. Pentland
41	13.8.17	1 single seater	Out of control	Lieutenant T.E. Barker
42	15.8.17	1 single seater	Out of control	Lieutenant C.R.J. Thompson
43	16.8.17	1 two seater	Forced to land	Lieutenant H.C. Ainger
44	16.8.17	1 single seater	Out of control	Lieutenant J. Manley
45	16.8.17	1 single seater	Destroyed	Lieutenant J. Manley
46	16.8.17	1 single seater	Out of control	Lieutenant C.R.J. Thompson
47	16.8.17	1 single seater	Out of control	Lieutenant H.L. Waite
48	17.8.17	1 two seater	Destroyed	Captain F. Sowrey
49	17.8.17	1 single seater	Out of control	Captain Gordon-Kidd
50	18.8.17	1 two seater	Out of control	Lieutenant B.A. Powers
51	20.8.17	1 two seater	Out of control	Captain Sowrey/L. Pentland
52	22.8.17	1 two seater	Forced to Land	Lieutenant A. Pentland
53	22.8.17	1 single seater	Out of control	Lieutenant J. Manley
54	22.8.17	1 two seater	Out of control	Lieutenant Graham
55	22.8.17	1 Balloon	Forced down	Lieutenant A. Pentland
56	25.8.17	1 two seater	Out of control	Lieutenant A.C. Bryson
57	25.8.17	1 single seater	Destroyed	Lieutenant Barker
58	26.8.17	1 two seater	Destroyed	Lieutenant H.C. Ainger
59	26.8.17	1 single seater	Destroyed	Captain J. Leacroft
60	26.8.17	1 single seater	Out of control	Lieutenant B. McEntegart
61	26.8.17	1 two seater	Destroyed	19 Squadron patrol
62	31.8.17	1 single seater	Out of control	Lieutenant A. Pentland
63	1.9.17	1 single seater	Destroyed	Captain J. Leacroft
64	2.9.17	1 single seater	Out of control	Lieutenant B. McEntegart
65	3.9.17	1 single seater	Out of control	Captain J. Leacroft
66	4.9.17	1 single seater	Out of control	Lieutenant B. McEntegart
67	11.9.17	1 two seater	Destroyed	Lieutenant A. Pentland
68	11.9.17	1 two seater	Destroyed	Captain F. Sowrey
69	14.9.17	1 single seater	Forced to land	Captain J. Leacroft
70	15.9.17	1 two seater	Out of control	Lieutenant A. Pentland
71	16.9.17	1 single seater	Out of control	Lieutenant A. Pentland
72	16.9.17	1 single seater	Out of control	Captain J. Leacroft
73	17.9.17	1 two seater	Out of control	Captain J. Manley
74	19.9.17	1 single seater	Out of control	Captain J. Leacroft
75	19.9.17	1 single seater	Out of control	Captain J. Leacroft
76	19.9.17	1 single seater	Destroyed	Lieutenant H.W. Dawson
77	20.9.17	1 two seater	Destroyed	Lieutenant R.M. Strang
78	20.9.17	1 single seater	Out of control	Captain F. Sowrey
79	21.9.17	1 single seater	Out of control	Captain J. Leacroft
80	22.9.17	1 single seater	Out of control	Lieutenant H.W. Dawson
81	23.9.17	1 single seater	Out of control	Lieutenant R.M. Strang
82	23.9.17	1 two seater	Out of control	Lieutenant A. Pentland
83	24.9.17	1 two seater	Out of control	Lieutenant H.W. Dawson
84	25.9.17	1 two seater	Destroyed	Lieutenant R.G. Holt
85	25.9.17	1 two seater	Destroyed	Lieutenant O.C. Bryson
86	26.9.17	1 two seater	Destroyed	Lieutenant R.M. Strang
87	26.9.17	1 two seater	Out of control	Lieutenant Jones

88	26.9.17	1 two seater	Out of control	Captain J. Leacroft
89	27.9.17	1 single seater	Out of control	Lieutenant N. McLeod
90	30.9.17	1 two seater	Out of control	Captain F. Sowrey
91	7.10.17	1 two seater	Out of control	Lieutenant H.R. Hicks
92	7.10.17	1 single seater	Destroyed	Captain Sowrey
93	9.10.17	1 two seater	Out of control	Captain Sowrey
94	14.10.17	1 single seater	Destroyed	Captain J. Leacroft
95	14.10.17	1 single seater	Destroyed	Lieutenant Thompson
96	15.10.17	1 single seater	Destroyed	Captain Sowrey
97	16.10.17	1 two seater	Forced to land	Captain Sowrey
98	21.10.17	1 single seater	Destroyed	Captain J. Leacroft
99	24.10.17	1 single seater	Out of control	Captain J. Leacroft
100	24.10.17	1 single seater	Out of control	Captain J. Leacroft
101	24.10.17	1 two eng Gotha	Forced to land	Lieutenant Hewat
102	24.10.17	1 single seater	Out of control	Captain P. Huskinson
103	26.10.17	1 two seater	Out of control	Lieutenant E. Olivier
104	27.10.17	1 two seater	Out of control	Captain P. Huskinson
105	30.10.17	1 two seater	Out of control	Lieutenant De Pencier
106	31.10.17	1 single seater	Destroyed	Major A.D. Carter
107	31.10.17	1 two seater	Out of control	Major A.D. Carter
108	31.10.17	1 single seater	Out of control	Lieutenant Gartside-Tipping
109	31.10.17	1 single seater	Out of control	Lieutenant E. Olivier
110	31.10.17	1 single seater	Out of control	Lieutenant O.C. Bryson
111	6.11.17	1 single seater	Out of control	Lieutenant R.G. Holt
112	8.11.17	1 two seater	Destroyed	Major A.D. Carter
113	9.11.17	1 single seater	Destroyed	Lieutenant C.R.J. Thompson
114	9.11.17	1 single seater	Out of control	Lieutenant C.R.J. Thompson
115	9.11.17	1 two seater	Out of control	Major A.D. Carter
116	11.11.17	1 single seater	Out of control	Lieutenant Candy
117	12.11.17	1 single seater	Out of control	Lieutenant Bryson
118	13.11.17	1 two seater	Destroyed	Captain Huskinson
119	13.11.17	1 single seater	Out of control	Major A.D. Carter
120	15.11.17	1 two seater	Destroyed	Lieutenant Olivier
121	18.11.17	1 two seater	Out of control	Major A.D. Carter
122	18.11.17	1 two seater	Driven down	Major A.D. Carter
123	23.11.17	1 single seater	Out of control	Major A.D. Carter
124	29.11.17	1 single seater	Out of control	Captain Bryson
125	3.12.17	1 single seater	Out of control	Captain Huskinson
126	6.12.17	1 single seater	Out of control	Lieutenant Puckridge
127	6.12.17	1 two seater	Out of control	Lieutenant Olivier
128	8.12.17	1 two seater	Out of control	Captain Bryson
129	15.12.17	1 two seater	Destroyed	Major A.D. Carter
130	15.12.17	1 two seater	Destroyed	Lieutenant Jennings
131	17.12.17	1 single seater	Driven down	Captain Huskinson
132	18.12.17	1 two seater	Out of control	Captain Bryson
133	18.12.17	1 single seater	Destroyed	Lieutenant Fairclough
134	18.12.17	1 single seater	Destroyed	Captain G.W. Taylor
135	18.12. 17	1 single seater	Out of control	Major A.D. Carter

136	18.12.17	1 single seater	Out of control	Major A.D. Carter
137	19.12.17	1 two seater	Out of control	2nd Lieutenant H.E. Galer
138	19.12.17	1 two seater	Out of control	Lieutenant A.B. Fairclough
139	19.12.17	1 two seater	Driven down	Lieutenant A.B. Fairclough
140	19.12.17	1 two seater	Out of control	Major A.D. Carter
141	19.12.17	1 two seater	Destroyed	L F'clough/Captain Bryson
142	19.12.17	1 single seater	Out of control	Major A.D. Carter
143	22.12.17	1 two seater	Destroyed	19 Squadron patrol
144	28.12.17	1 single seater	Out of control	Major A.D. Carter
145	29.12.17	1 single seater	Destroyed	Lieutenant Fairclough
146	29.12.17	1 single seater	Out of control	Lieutenant Fairclough
147	29.12.17	1 single seater	Out of control	Major A.D. Carter
148	29.12.17	1 single seater	Out of control	Lieutenant J.G.S. Candy
149	29.12.17	1 single seater	Out of control	Lieutenant De Pencier
150	29.12.17	1 single seater	Out of control	Captain Huskinson
151	29.12.17	1 single seater	Out of control	Captain Huskinson
152	6.1.18	1 single seater	Out of control	Captain Huskinson
153	25.2.18	Fokker Tri	Out of control	Lieutenant De Pencier
154	8.3.18	1 single seater	Destroyed	Captain Bryson
155	8.3.18	1 single seater	Out of control	Captain Huskinson
156	9.3.18	Pfalz scout	Destroyed	Captain Huskinson
157	9.3.18	1 single seater	Destroyed	Lieutenant Puckridge
158	9.3.18	1 single seater	Out of control	Lieutenant Blythe
159	15.3.18	1 single seater	Destroyed	Major A.D. Carter
160	15.3.18	1 single seater	Out of control	Major A.D. Carter
161	15.3.18	1 single seater	Out of control	Captain J. Leacroft
162	15.3.18	1 single seater	Out of control	Captain J. Leacroft
163	17.3.18	1 single seater	Destroyed	Major A.D. Carter
164	17.3.18	1 single seater	Destroyed	Lieutenants F'clough/ Olivier
165	17.3.18	1 single seater	Destroyed	Captain J. Leacroft
166	17.3.18	1 single seater	Destroyed	Captain Huskinson
167	17.3.18	1 single seater	Destroyed	Lieutenant Jennings
168	17.3.18	1 single seater	Destroyed	Lieutenant Hustings
169	17.3.18	1 single seater	Out of control	Lieutenant Olivier
170	23.3.18	1 two seater	Destroyed	Captain Leacroft Lieutenant F'clough
171	24.3.18	1 single seater	Destroyed	Captain J. Leacroft
172	24.3.18	1 single seater	Out of control	Captain J. Leacroft
173	24.3.18	1 single seater	Driven down	Lieutenant Puckridge
174	24.3.18	1 two seater	Out of control	Major Carter Lieutenant Irving
175	24.3.18	1 single seater	Out of control	Lieutenant Blythe
176	27.3.18	1 single seater	Destroyed	Captain Jennings
177	10.4.18	1 two seater	Destroyed	Major A.D. Carter
178	12.4.18	1 single seater	Out of control	Captain J. Leacroft
179	21.4.18	1 single seater	Destroyed	Lieutenant G.B. Irving
180	21.4.18	1 single seater	Out of control	Lieutenant Aldridge

181	21.4.18	1 single seater	Out of control	Major A.D. Carter
182	21.4.18	1 single seater	Out of control	Lieutenant De Pencier
183	21.4.18	1 single seater	Out of control	Lieutenant Hustings
184	22.4.18	1 single seater	Out of control	Lieutenant Fairclough
185	23.4.18	1 single seater	Destroyed	Major Carter Lieutenant Irving
186	23.4.18	1 single seater	Destroyed	Major A.D. Carter
187	23.4.18	1 single seater	Out of control	Lieutenant· Fairclough
188	23.4.18	1 single seater	Out of control	Lieutenant C.S. Hall
189	2.5.18	1 Triplane	Out of control	Major A.D. Carter
190	2.5.18	1 Triplane	Out of control	Lieutenant Hustings
191	2.5.18	1 single seater	Out of control	Captain J. Leacroft
192	2.5.18	1 single seater	Destroyed	Lieutenants Fairclough/ Blake
193	8.5.18	1 single seater	Destroyed	Major Carter Lieutenant Irving
194	9.5.18	1 two seater	Out of control	Lieutenant Hardman
195	15.5.18	1 Triplane	Destroyed	Major A.D. Carter
196	15.5.18	1 single seater	Out of control	Major A.D. Carter
197	16.5.18	1 two seater	Destroyed	Major Carter Lieutenant Hardman
198	17.5.18	1 single seater	Out of control	Lieutenant Hustings
199	17.5.18	1 single seater	Out of control	Lieutenant McQuistan
200	19.5.18	1 single seater	Out of control	Lieutenant De Pencier
201	19.5.18	1 single seater	Out of control	Lieutenant A.W. Blake
202	20.5.18	1 single seater	Out of control	Lieutenant Hustings
203	20.5.18	1 single seater	Destroyed	Lieutenant De Pencier
204	27.5.18	1 single seater	Out of control	Lieutenant J. Aldridge
205	31.5.18	1 single seater	Out of control	Lieutenants Hardman/Ray
206	31.5.18	1 single seater	Driven down	Lieutenant Aldridge
207	31.5.18	1 single seater	Out of control	Lieutenant Blake
208	31.5.18	1 single seater	Out of control	Captain G.B. Irving
209	31.5.18	1 single seater	Out of control	Captain G.B. Irving
210	5.6.18	1 Triplane	Out of control	Captain De Pencier Lieutenant Blake
211	6.6.18	1 two seater	Out of control	Lieutenant Gardner
212	7.6.18	1 single seater	Destroyed	Lieutenant Hustings
213	9.6.18	1 two seater	Destroyed	Lieutenant Gardner
214	17.6.18	1 single seater	Out of control	Captain Irving
215	17.6.18	1 Triplane	Destroyed	Captain de L'Haye
216	17.6.18	1 single seater	Out of control	Lieutenant Leach
217	20.6.18	1 single seater	Out of control	Lieutenant Hardman
218	27.6.18	1 single seater	Out of control	Lieutenant McQuistan
219	27.6.18	1 single seater	Out of control	Captain Irving
220	30.6.18	1 single seater	Out of control	Captain de L'Haye
221	1.7.18	1 two seater	Destroyed	Captain Irving
222	1.7.18	1 single seater	Out of control	Lieutenant Gardner
223	1.7.18	1 single seater	Destroyed	Lieutenant Gregory

224	2.7.18	1 single seater	Out of control	Lieutenant Aldridge
225	2.7.18	1 single seater	Out of control	Captain G.B. Irving
226	4.7.18	1 single seater	Out of control	Lieutenant Gardner
227	4.7.18	1 single seater	Destroyed	Captain de L'Haye
228	13.7.18	Fokker Biplane	Out of control	Lieutenant J.W. Crane
229	13.7.18	Fokker Biplane	Out of control	Captain De Pencier
230	13.7.18	Fokker Biplane	Destroyed	Lieutenant Gardner
231	13.7.18	Fokker Biplane	Destroyed	Lieutenant Pearce
232	13.7.18	Fokker Biplane	Destroyed	Lieutenant Gregory
233	16.7.18	Pfalz scout	Destroyed	Captain de L'Haye
234	16.7.18	Pfalz scout	Out of control	Captain de L'Haye
235	31.7.18	Pfalz scout	Destroyed	Lieutenant C.V. Gardner
236	31.7.18	Pfalz scout	Destroyed	Lieutenant L.H. Ray
237	31.7.18	Pfalz scout	Destroyed	Lieutenant A.W. Blake
238	31.7.18	Fokker Biplane	Destroyed	Lieutenant G.W. Northridge
239	7.9.18	Pfalz scout	Out of control	Lieutenant McQuistan
240	11.8.18	1 scout	Out of control	Lieutenant P.J.E. Pierce
241	11.8.18	Pfalz scout	Destroyed	Captain McQuistan
242	11.8.18	Pfalz scout	Destroyed	Lieutenant C.V. Gardner
243	11.8.18	Fokker Biplane	Destroyed	Lieutenant C.V. Gardner
244	11.8.18	Pfalz scout	Out of control	Captain G.B. Irving
245	16.9.18	Pfalz scout	Out of control	Lieutenant D.P. Laird
246	16.9.18	Fokker Biplane	Out of control	Lieutenant J.D. Hardman
247	16.9.18	Pfalz scout	Destroyed	Captain de L'Haye
248	16.9.18	Pfalz scout	Out of control	Lieutenant L.H. Ray
249	21.9.18	Fokker Biplane	Out of control	Captain McQuistan
250	27.9.18	Fokker Biplane	Destroyed	Lieutenant L.H. Ray
251	27.9.18	Fokker Biplane	Out of control	Lieutenant L.H. Ray
252	27.9.18	Fokker Biplane	Out of control	Lieutenant L.H. Ray
253	27.9.18	1 Balloon	Destroyed	Lieutenant L.H. Ray
254	27.9.18	Fokker Biplane	Out of control	Captain C.V. Gardner
255	27.9.18	Fokker Biplane	Out of control	Lieutenant J.A. Aldridge
256	27.9.18	Pfalz scout	Destroyed	Captain de L'Haye Lieutenant Moore
257	27.9.18	Pfalz scout	Out of control	Captain de L'Haye
258	27.9.18	Pfalz scout	Out of control	Captain McQuistan
259	1.10.18	Pfalz scout	Out of control	Captain de L'Haye
260	3.10.18	Pfalz scout	Destroyed	Lieutenant J.W. Crane
261	3.10.18	Fokker Biplane	Out of control	Lieutenant J.W. Crane
262	3.10.18	Pfalz scout	Destroyed	Lieutenant C.M. Moore
263	3.10.18	Albatros	Destroyed	Lieutenant C.M. Moore
264	3.10.18	Pfalz scout	Out of control	Lieutenant R.W. Duff
265	3.10.18	Pfalz scout	Out of control	Lieutenant T.H. Mercer
266	4.10.18	Fokker Biplane	Forced to land	Lieutenant L.H. Ray
267	4.10.18	Albatros	Out of control	Captain McQuistan
268	4.10.18	Pfalz scout	Destroyed	Captain McQuistan
269	5.10.18	Pfalz scout	Out of control	Lieutenant T.H. Mercer
270	5.10.18	Fokker Biplane	Out of control	Lieutenant J.W. Crane

271	5.10.18	Fokker Biplane Destroyed	Captain McQuistan
272	26.10.18	Fokker Biplane Out of control	Lieutenant M.E. Miller
273	27.10.18	Fokker Biplane Out of control	Lieutenant R.W. Duff
274	27.10.18	Fokker Biplane Out of control	Lieutenant J.S. Hewson
275	27.10.18	Fokker Biplane Destroyed	Captain J.D. Hardman
276	30.10.18	Fokker Biplane Destroyed	Lieutenant C.M. Moore
277	30.10.18	Fokker Biplane Destroyed	Captain J.D. Hardman
278	30.10.18	Fokker Biplane Destroyed	Captain J.D. Hardman
279	30.10.18	Fokker Biplane Destroyed	Lieutenant R.C. Davies
280	30.10.18	Fokker Biplane Destroyed	Lieutenant W.F. Hendershot
281	30.10.18	Fokker Biplane Out of control	Lieutenant W.F. Hendershot

The Official Records show 281 enemy aircraft accounted for.

The following four are shown in the Squadron's Record Book but missed of the Official List.

282	22.9.16	Destroyed	Second Lieutenant Stewart
283	10.11.16	Destroyed	Captain Henderson
284	22.12.16	Out of control	Second Lieutenant Capper
285	21.8.17	Destroyed	Captain Gordon-Kidd

Flying Casualties sustained by No 19 Squadron, RFC and RAF during their period of service on the Western Front, July 1916 to Armistice.

KILLED IN ACTION

RICE, A. H. Second Lieutenant   29th November 1917

WOUNDED IN ACTION

CARLINE, S.W. Second Lieutenant   31st August 1916
DOWNING, G.G.B. Lieutenant   2nd September 1916
JOHNSON, R.H. Second Lieutenant   2nd September 1916
WILLIAMS, G.G.A. Captain   6th September 1916
REED, W.E. Lieutenant   23rd April 1917
OKEDEN, H.G.P. Lieutenant   25th May 1917
CHADWICK, G. Captain   4th June 1917
YOUNG, W.E. Captain   22nd July 1917
GORDON-KIDD, A.L. Captain   23rd August 1917 died 27th August
                                                 1917

BARKER, F.E. Second Lieutenant   26th August 1917
PATERSON, R.J. Second Lieutenant   19th September 1917
PENTLAND, A.A.N. Lieutenant   26th September 1917
JONES, W. Lieutenant   26th September 1917
VAN DER BYL, R.I. Lieutenant   9th October 1917
HEWAT, R.A. Second Lieutenant   26th October 1917
ELDER-HEARN, T. Second Lieutenant   15th November 1917
DE PENCIER, J.D. Second Lieutenant   23rd November 1917
LYE, R.G. Second Lieutenant   19th April 1918
BARLOW, W.H. Second Lieutenant   27th May 1918
HUNTER, W.A. Second Lieutenant   9th June 1918
LEACH, F.W. Second Lieutenant   17th June 1918
LAIRD, D.P. Second Lieutenant   1st October 1918
WALMSLEY, H. Second Lieutenant   30th October 1918

MISSING – SUBSEQUENTLY REPORTED DEAD OR PRESUMED DEAD

CORBOLD, H.M. Lieutenant   26th August 1916
TALBOT, R.F.R. Second Lieutenant   26th August 1916
CALLAGHAN, E.C. Second Lieutenant   26th August 1916
HEDDERWICK, G. Second Lieutenant   22nd September 1916
HERMAN, R.D. Second Lieutenant   22nd September 1916
WEST, T. Second Lieutenant   24th September 1916
EDWARDS, G. Second Lieutenant   24th September 1916
TIDSWELL, C.R. Captain   16th October 1916
THOMPSON, J. Second Lieutenant   16th October 1916
CAPPER, E.W. Lieutenant   14th April 1917
APPLIN, R. Second Lieutenant   29th April 1917
HARVEY-KELLY, H.D. Major, D.S.O.   29th April 1917
DAVIDSON, D.A.L. Captain   30th April 1917

WILLIAMS, W.G.B. Captain	12th May 1917
LAWE, M. Lieutenant	27th June 1917
BEST, F.B. Lieutenant	29th July 1917
NICHOLS, S.L. Second Lieutenant	12th August 1917
WILLIAMS, C.P. Second Lieutenant	26th August 1917
SANT, E.M. Second Lieutenant	1st September 1917
GRAHAM, R.L. Lieutenant	16th September 1917
KIRBY, F.W. Second Lieutenant	21st September 1917
INGLIS, R.A. Second Lieutenant	21st September 1917
POWERS, B.A. Lieutenant	25th September 1917
ROBERTS, G.B. Second Lieutenant	26th September 1917
AINGER, H.C. Lieutenant	4th October 1917
HICKS, H.R. Second Lieutenant	12th October 1917
GOLDING, K.L. Second Lieutenant	24th October 1917
LAING, J.D. Second Lieutenant	24th October 1917
GARTSIDE-TIPPINGE, F. Second Lieutenant	6th November 1917
COCKBURN, G.A. Lieutenant	8th November 1917
McLINTOCK, J.L. Lieutenant	26th February 1918
BLYTH, E.J. Second Lieutenant	26th March 1918
HAINSBY, F.W. Second Lieutenant	26th March 1918
IRVING, G.B. Captain	11th August 1918
GREGORY, M.S. Second Lieutenant	11th August 1918
NESBITT, W.J. Second Lieutenant	27th October 1918

PRISONERS OF WAR

GEEN, C. Second Lieutenant	13th August 1916
REYNELL, A.W. Second Lieutenant	26th August 1916
BRIGGS, S.P. Second Lieutenant	26th August 1916
EDWARDS, R.H. Second Lieutenant	22nd September 1916
WATTS, R. Second Lieutenant	22nd October 1916
PURVES, S.S.B. Second Lieutenant	19th March 1917
BAKER, R.P. Lieutenant	24th March 1917
HAMILTON, W.N. Lieutenant	29th April 1917
HOLMES, J.D.V. Second Lieutenant	18th May 1917
GRANDIN, R.J. Second Lieutenant	18th May 1917
ALLABARTON, S.F. Second Lieutenant	19th May 1917
GRIERSON, C.D. Second Lieutenant	5th June 1917
WELD, D.S. Lieutenant	12th July 1917
WEARNE, A. Second Lieutenant	26th July 1917
KELLOGG, W.B. Second Lieutenant	31st July 1917
THOMPSON, C.D. Lieutenant	16th August 1917
SHIPWRIGHT, A.T. Second Lieutenant	16th August 1917
SPENCER, W.A.L. Second Lieutenant	2nd September 1917
McCRAE, W.G. Second Lieutenant	21st September 1917 died 26th October 1917
STEVENSON, J.G. Second Lieutenant	5th October 1917
LONG, C.R. Lieutenant	6th October 1917

WHITEHOUSE, S.L. Second Lieutenant	27th October 1917
SPIRO, S.G. Second Lieutenant	2nd December 1917
YEO, H.A. Second Lieutenant	7th December 1917
GALER, H.E. Second Lieutenant	29th December 1917
CHADWICK, G. Captain	3rd May 1918
CARTER, A.D. Major, D. S. O.	19th May 1918
WHITE, R.E. Second Lieutenant	17th July 1918
DOUGLAS, R.K. Second Lieutenant	11th August 1918
ANDERSON, G.F. Lieutenant	15th September 1918
FARRAND, E.S. Second Lieutenant	3rd October 1918
LYNN, F. Lieutenant	30th October 1918
BOYD, C.N. Second Lieutenant	30th October 1918

ACCIDENTALLY KILLED

DREWERY, A.B. Second Lieutenant	20th October 1916 collision in the air
HALL, W.T. Captain	19th May 1917
RIGGS, R.R. Lieutenant	22nd July 1917
MANLEY, J. Captain	18th September 1917
DAWSON, H.W. Second Lieutenant	4th October 1917
STONE, H.J. Second Lieutenant	15th November 1917
VEALE, A.A. Second Lieutenant	22nd January 1918
PIERCE, P.J.E. Second Lieutenant	13th August 1918 collision in the air
LANCE, W.G. Second Lieutenant	13th August 1918 collision in the air

ACCIDENTALLY INJURED

CHAPPELL, S. Second Lieutenant	27th August 1916
BAKER, J.W. Lieutenant	14th April 1917
MEARNS, E.A. Second Lieutenant	25th May 1917
SCLATER, T.W. Second Lieutenant	4th June 1917
BROWN, A.D.C. Second Lieutenant	6th June 1917
JERRARD, A. Second Lieutenant	5th August 1917
GALER, H.E. Second Lieutenant	3rd December 1917
McCONNELL, F.J. Second Lieutenant	8th March 1918
TAYLOR, G.W. Captain	13th March 1918
ROGERS, G.H. Second Lieutenant	11th April 1918
NORTHRIDGE, G.W. Second Lieutenant	9th August 1918

THE "IN-BETWEEN" YEARS
1923-1939

1923

On the 1st April, the Squadron was reformed at Duxford, which was to remain its permanent home – with the exception of short redeployments – until February 1941. The Squadron was attached to No. 2 Flying Training School for the purpose of training pilots to fly single seater fighter machines.

1924

On the 1st June, the Squadron was brought up to full strength. *Flight Lieutenant T.V. West assumed command until the arrival of Squadron Leader P. Babington, M.C., A.F.C., on the 28th July.* The equipment consisted of Sopwith Snipes and Avro 504 machines. The Squadron remained at Duxford when No. 2 Flying School moved on the 30th June 1924.

In December the Squadron began to re-equip with the new Gloster Grebe. Training was still continued on the unit which had one flight of Avros in addition to a two seater Grebe dual-trainer.

Grebe

(Crown Copyright – Sqdn Album)

1925

In January, a Meteorological flight, consisting of two machines arrived from A. & G. School, Eastchurch and were attached to the Squadron.

Squadron Leader P. Babington was promoted to Wing Commander on the 1st July, and assumed command of the RAF Station, Duxford. *Command of the Squadron passed to Squadron Leader H.W.J. Jones M.C.*, who as a Major, had previously been commanding officer from November 1918 to February 1919.

1926

The Squadron were second in the Efficiency Cup of No. 6 Group; while in the same year they won the Converging Bombing Cup open to all Fighter Squadrons, both in Inland and Coastal Areas; in spite of the fact that the leader of the team had injured himself in a crash just before the event and another leader had to be found.

There were two fatal accidents during the year; On the 18th August, Pilot Officer R.N.T. Gape was killed on a practice flight and on the 30th November, Flying Officer C.T. Crowden was killed whilst on an Instructors Course at Central Flying School.

The RAF Display at Hendon that year saw the Squadron participate in two events; Low Bombing and Group Evolutions.

1927

They appeared again in 1927 — as they did in all subsequent years up to 1938 — this time involved shooting down a Kite Balloon and a simulated Air Attack on London. July saw them busy at Sutton Bridge carrying out the Annual Firing practice and at the end of the month, they took part in the ADGB Tactical Exercises.

On the 24th September, a collision took place between one of the Squadron's Avro machines, piloted by Sergeant O.C. Tostevin, with L.A.C. Cleland as passenger under instruction, and a Siskin machine belonging to No. 111 Squadron. The Avro was flying normally over the aerodrome when it was struck by the Siskin, piloted by Sergeant Kelly of No. 111 Squadron. The Avro came down under partial control, neither of the occupants being injured. Sergeant Kelly in the Siskin was killed.

In November the Squadron competed in the final of the Pin Pointing Competition for a Cup presented by Sir Philip Sassoon. The Squadron with No. 41 Squadron shared the first place having obtained 100%.

1928

Two pilots of the Squadron, Flying Officer J.E. Clayton and Sergeant Pilot Parsons took part in an Air Combat at an Air Display on the 17th March, given to King Ammanullah, HM the King of Afghanistan. Flying Officers P.P. Grey and P.R. Barwell gave a demonstration of aerobatics, being warmly congratulated by the King of Afghanistan for their fine display.

Later that month the Squadron began to re-equip with the Armstrong Whitworth Siskin. These machines were fitted with the non-supercharged Mark IV Jaguar engines. By early April the Squadron had been fully equipped with the Siskin and co-operated with No. 39 (B) Squadron at Bircham Newton.

On the 1st May Squadron Leader H.W.G. Jones took over temporary command of the

Station when the Station Commander, Wing Commander Barton, was posted to the Air Ministry. Flight Lieutenant Coote assumed temporary command of the Squadron.

The Squadron again participated at the RAF Air Display at Hendon on the 30th June. The Squadron with Nos. 56 & 111 (F) Squadrons took part in the event in the "Evolution by a Wing of Fighter Squadrons".

August and September were taken up with first the ADGB Tactical Exercise at Hornchurch, then to Tangmere to take part in the Aldershot Command Manoeuvres. In between which *Squadron Leader E.C. Emmett M.C., D.F.C., assumed command of the Squadron*, while Squadron Leader Jones was posted to No. 216 (B) Squadron, Middle East.

On the 10th December 1928 two Siskins collided in the air over Whittlesford, Cambs., involving Flying Officer E.G. Cayley of the Squadron and Flight Sergeant Pilot Tostevin of the Station Meteorological Flight. Flight Sergeant Tostevin was killed and Flying Officer E.G. Cayley made a safe parachute descent. *

1929

Ironically the squadron's first member of the 'Caterpillar Club', died six weeks later, on the 20th January. Flying Officer E.G. Cayley was killed as a result of a flying accident and Mr P.A. Wells seriously injured when a Moth, owned by Mr Wells, crashed on the aerodrome.

In February, the Squadron took part in the Map Reading Test for the Cup presented by Sir Philip Sassoon, and obtained a percentage of 74.5%. Flying Officer J.W. Bayes and Sergeant Pilot Parsons both scoring 100 points.

On the 28th of that month, while performing aerobatics over the aerodrome in a Siskin IIIa aircraft, Flight Lieutenant G.A.F. Bucknall crashed on diving after a spin and was killed. The machine burst into flames.

In April the Air Officer Commanding Fighting Area (Air Vice Marshal F.R. Scarlett, C.B., D.S.O.), carried out the annual inspection of the Squadron, after which the Squadron flew past in formation.

On the 16th May, two pilots, Flying Officer J.W. Bayes and Sergeant Pilot E.G. Parsons, competed in a competition held at Northolt by Fighting Area to select a team of two pilots to give a display of aerobatics at the annual RAF Display. Flying Officer J.W. Bayes was killed as a result of his machine failing to right itself after completing inverted flying.

---

* Flying Officer Cayley appears to be the first 19 Squadron member to "hit the silk". Todays aviator on reading of the exploits of his 1914/18 counterpart will doubtless marvel at his courage in going into combat without an escape route. It's one thing to think of the old aircraft as being so slow and uncomplicated, that an engine failure merely meant location of a reasonably flat small field. But as the aircraft performance and weapon technology advanced – and combat became a daily occurrence – the absence of a parachute takes on special significance. In April 1917, the life expectancy of British airmen on the Western Front was 13 days and almost unbelievably, so it seems today, combat in 1917/18 was taking place regularly at 20,000 feet. At best, the problem would be attempting to control and land a crippled machine, probably in hostile territory; at worst it could be the consciously taken decision at altitude either to jump over the side to certain death or stay and be burned alive; although it was known that some pilots carried a revolver for such an eventuality. Literally thousands of pilots perished in the war and over 400 more RAF pilots alone were to die before the RAF received its first "operational" 'chute in May 1926. The saddest footnote is that the technology and experience had been available some 10 years earlier for successful production and use of a parachute for the crew of combat aircraft. (The Germans incidentally were using parachutes in their fighters before the end of the war.)

The Air Officer Commanding-in-Chief ADGB (Air Vice Marshal Sir E.L. Ellington, K.C.B., C.M.G., C.B.E.), inspected the Squadron on taking over command of the Air Defence of Great Britain on the 27th May. The following day Sergeant Pilot E.G. Parsons competed in the race for Single Seater Fighters held at Northolt for the cup presented by Sir Philip Sassoon. He was placed 9th at an average speed of 127.6mph.

During June and July the Squadron proceeded to Sutton Bridge to carry out the Annual Firing Exercises obtaining 38.96%. The highest scores were obtained by Flight Lieutenant Openshaw 67.66% and Flying Officer Lindley 65.66%. Flying Officer Lindley and Sergeant Lott took part in the RAF Station, Andover "At Home" in conjunction with a Sidestrand of No 101 (B) Squadron, carrying out an "Air Combat" and again a week later at the Annual RAF Display, Hendon.

"A" Flight, Commanded by Flight Lieutenant A.J. Rankin A.F.C., proceeded to Aldergrove, Ireland via Catterick, North Berwick and Turnhouse to carry out affiliation exercises with No. 502 (Ulster) (Bombing) Squadron during their summer camp from the 15th to the 27th July. On the 30th of the month *Squadron Leader L.H. Slatter, O.B.E., D.S.C., D.F.C., assumed command of the Squadron.*

During September, the Squadron operating from Worthy Down in conjunction with No. 16 (AC) Squadron participated in the Southern Command Exercises carrying out low flying attacks on ground targets. Later operating from Tangmere, they participated in the 1st Air Defence Brigade Exercises carrying out low flying attacks on AA guns. Flight Lieutenant E.R. Openshaw and Flying Officer W.J.H. Lindley competed in the competition for best firers for the Brooke-Popham Cup, being placed 16th and 21st respectively.

On the 9th December Squadron Leader C. R. Keary assumed command of the Squadron.

A.C.2 Aircrafthand L.O. Boughey recalls:-

"I was posted to 19 Squadron on the 20th December 1929. That Christmas Eve I was on 24 hour Guard Duty. At one stage during the night, I was the only person within sight of the Guard Room. A raw 'Rookie' marching up and down as I had been taught, too scared to question the absence of the Corporal Guard Commander or the rest of the 'Old Sweat' guard. I had been informed that my punishment for leaving my post would be reporting to the Guard Room at 9.00pm every night for a month to whitewash the 'Last Post'. I must have been solid ivory from the neck upwards.

During 1930, there was one fatal accident, when three Siskins were taking off in formation. One peeled off as they climbed, turned to land again, lost flying speed and crashed onto the end of the 'drome. The pilot was Flying Officer Roger Teale, who was buried at Whittlesford Churchyard, the first Military Funeral I had attended."

1930

On the 8th April, as a result of stalling his machine on landing from a gliding turn, Flying Officer R.P. Teale spun into the ground and was killed.

The Annual Inspection of the Squadron took place on the 23rd April by the AOC Fighting Area, Air Vice-Marshal H.C.T. Dowding C.B., C.M.G., p.s.c. After the inspection the Squadron flew past in formation.

During May No. 35 (B) Squadron visited Duxford and carried out affiliation exercises with the Squadron. The 29th May to 9th June "A" Flight, commanded by Flight Lieutenant E.R. Openshaw with Pilot Officers Brackenbury, McIntyre and Sergeant Buchan proceeded to

Turnhouse and carried out affiliated exercises with No. 603 (City of Edinburgh) (Bomber) Squadron.

On the occasion of the opening of the Bristol Municipal Aerodrome on the 31st May, four Siskins, piloted by Flight Lieutenant J.S.L. Adams, Flying Officer Adnams and Sergeants Lott and Cleland, gave a display of aerobatics and formation flying.

In June the Squadron carried out Annual Air Firing Practices at Sutton Bridge. The top scorers this year were Sergeant Cleland with 83.33% and Flying Officer Lindley with 78.33%.

A.C.2 Aircrafthand L.O. Boughey recalls;

"I went with the Squadron to Sutton Bridge. The Squadron before us had suffered severe damage when one of the old hangars collapsed. Our CO decided that our planes should be picketed out on the grass. They were all lined up with regimental precision, when it was discovered that a Skylarks nest with young, was right between the wheels of one of the 'kites. The CO ordered a complete move of 50 yards to the right and a marker flag placed near the nest for a taxi-ing warning. My swearing vocabulary was broadened that evening".

Four aircraft piloted by Flight Lieutenant J.S.L. Adams, Flying Officer Lindley and Sergeants Lott and Cleland gave a display of aerobatics and formation flying at the Norwich Aero Club Annual Flying Display. Four days later Sergeant Lott gave a demonstration of aerobatics to the Officers Training Corps during their Annual Camp at Stensal.

For the Annual ADGB Air Exercises 1930 in August, the Squadron operated from Bircham Newton. During October Sergeant Cleland won the Brooke-Popham Cup for Best Fliers for 1930 with 90% marks. The cup is held by the unit for one year.

Warrant Officer 2 Williams (the Squadron's Sergeant Major) was presented with the Long Service and Good Conduct Medal by Wing Commander N.C. Spratt, O.B.E., at the RAF Station, Duxford, at the parade held in observance of Armistice Day, 11th November.

On the 2nd December, as a result of his machine striking a tree whilst taking off from a forced landing at Broxted, near Saffron Walden, Essex, Pilot Officer J.S. Hamilton was seriously injured and admitted to hospital.

1931

In March, "C" Flight were placed 5th in the preliminary heats of the Map Reading Competition for the Sir Philip Sassoon Cup, held at Henley.

Pilot Officer B.W.E.R. Bonsey was admitted to Chelmsford Hospital, as a result of injuries received in a flying accident at Witham, Near Chelmsford on the 2nd April.

During May the Squadron took part in the Fighting Area Preliminary Tactical Exercises at North Weald. The following month they were at Sutton Bridge for the Annual Air Firing Practices. The top scorers were Flight Lieutenant Lart with 82.2% and Sergeant Lott with 66.9%.

Sergeant G. Lott was sent to Filton on the 3rd June, to collect one of the first two Bulldogs to be allocated to the Squadron. He had been flying Siskins for three years and was impressed with the improved handling and flying characteristics of the Bulldog.

During July the Squadron took part in the Fighting Area Advanced Tactical Exercises, operating from the RAF Station, Northolt. Followed by a visit for two weeks of No. 35 (Bomber) Squadron of Bircham Newton carried out affiliation exercises with the Squadron at Duxford. Later the squadron returned to Northolt in connection with the Command Air Exercises.

On the 25th July Squadron Leader A.C. Sanderson, D.F.C., took over command of the Squadron.

In September the Squadron re-equipped with the Bristol Bulldog IIa. Built in Britain as a fighter in 1929, it was powered by a Bristol Jupiter VIIF 9-cylinder air-cooled engine, giving it a maximum speed of 174mph. During this month Flight Lieutenant E.C. de V. Lart and Sergeant Lott took part in the Competition for the Brooke-Popham Cup – Best Firers. Flight Lieutenant Lart was placed 5th with marks of 73.7%.

On the 16th October the Air Officer Commanding Fighting Area carried out the annual Inspection of the Squadron.

1932

19 Squadron. Duxford 1932

In February the Squadron crest was devised. This crest was approved by the AOC-in-Chief, ADGB and is now carried by all aircraft in the Squadron. The crest is a Dolphin with laurel leaves on either side and Squadron markings underneath.

During April "A" Flight commanded by Flight Lieutenant E.C. de V. Lart with Flying Officer Lock, Pilot Officers Burleigh, Foster and Jarman, took part in the Affiliation Exercises with No. 608 (B) AAF Squadron at Thornaby, Yorks. By this time four aircraft are now fitted with R.T.

In May the Squadron carried out Affiliation Exercises at Duxford, with No. 35 (B)

Squadron of Bircham Newton, and then moved to Sutton Bridge and carried out the Annual Air Firing and Bombing Practices. The Squadron came 1st in the Fighting Area with 10.4%. Sixteen pilots fired.

On the 3rd June Flying Officer J.B.W. Pugh (Met. Flight) was awarded the Air Force Cross for exceptional work carried out whilst in charge of Meteorological Flight.

From 17th to 30th June "C" Flight of the Squadron, commanded by Flight Lieutenant H.W. Pearson-Rogers, with Flying Officers Vincent and Brown, Pilot Officer Belchem and Sergeant Rye, took part in Affiliation Exercises at Renfrew, Scotland, with No. 602 (B) Squadron, AAF.

The following month saw the Squadron operating from RAF Station, Northolt, took part in the Command Exercises. The Squadron used R/T in these operations for the first time. The Squadron flew past after inspection by the Chief of the Air Staff, Air Chief Marshal Sir John M. Salmond, C.C.B., C.M.G., C.V.O., D.S.O., LL.D.

In September the Squadron's motto was adopted – "POSSUNT QUIA POSSE VIDENTUR" – "They can because they think they can".

The official result of Squadron Averages in the Air Firing at Sutton Bridge was received. In the Fighting Area, No. 19 (F) Squadron were 1st with 10.4%. Sixteen pilots fired.

During October the Squadron took part in the Sir Philip Sassoon Pin Pointing competition – Preliminary heats, held at North Weald and Upavon. The Squadron competed at Upavon with 23, 29, 41, 54, 56 and 111 Squadrons, and were placed 1st.

RAF Duxford won the Wakefield Boxing Trophy – The following personnel of 19 (F) Squadron fought:- LAC McGrath, AC2 Dunn, LAC Wier, AC1 Evans and AC1 Brightwell.

Flight Lieutenant Lart and Flying Officer Matson competed in the Brooke-Popham Cup Competition at Sutton Bridge. Flight Lieutenant Lart was placed 4th with 18.75%. The Squadron now has six aircraft with R/T.

1933

By March 1933, the Squadron had eight aircraft fitted with R/T. "C" Flight represented the Squadron in the Sir Philip Sassoon Flight Attack Competition. The following pilots comprised the team which was placed 3rd in their heat. Flight Lieutenant Pearson-Rogers, Flying Officer Brown, Sergeant Lott and Reserve Sergeant Rye.

During April the following team took part in the Sir Philip Sassoon Map Reading Competition and was placed 3rd in their heat. Flight Lieutenant Pearson-Rogers, Sergeant Lott and Sergeant Parr. "B" flight flew to Thornaby for Affiliation Exercise with No. 608 (B) Squadron from the 6th to the 18th, and, "A" flight flew to Abbotsinch for Affiliation Exercise with 602 (B) Squadron from the 19th to the 2nd May.

On the 29th May the AOC-in-Chief Air Marshal Sir Robert Brooke-Popham, K.C.B., C.M.G., D.S.O., A.F.C., psc. visited the Squadron, accompanied by the AOC Fighting Area, Air Vice Marshal F.W. Bowhill, C.M.G., D.S.O., the AOC-in-Chief taking over command of ADGB vice the late Air Marshal Sir G. Salmond, K.C.B., K.C.M.G., D.S.O., psc.

From 29th May to 2nd June the Squadron team shot at Bisley for the Brooke-Popham-Steele Challenge RAF RA cup, which they won. First time a unit in Fighting Area had won this Trophy. Flight Sergeant Cresswell won the "Halahan" Cup for the best shot in the RAF with pistol.

During June the Squadron carried out numerous rehearsals for the Air Display at Hendon and flew there in preparation on the 21st. The display took place on the 24th and the Squadron took part in "Set Piece" with 54 (F) Squadron from Hornchurch, 99 (B) Squadron from Upper Heyford, 207 (B) Squadron from Bircham Newton and 503 (B) Squadron from Waddington.

The Squadron's Bulldogs were to defend the airfield from attack by the Bomber Squadrons. The Bulldogs were painted a ghastly reddish orange colour and during the attack on the Sidestrand bomber were all deemed to have been shot down. This meant that they could not land at Hendon and so the aircraft flew back to Duxford. Somewhere between Baldock and Royston the exuberant young pilots decided to fire off the remainder of their blank ammunition. It caused something of a panic to the unsuspecting residents living along the route below, who quickly telephoned the police that some strangely painted foreign fighters, without national markings, were shooting up the towns and villages of Hertfordshire.

During July the Squadron flew to Donibristle via Thornaby for Affiliation Exercises with No. 100 (B) Squadron for two weeks and then took part in Air Exercises at Duxford, on night operations, with Nos. 1 (F) and 43 (F) Squadrons.

On the 18th September the Squadron moved to Sutton Bridge – No. 3 ATC for Annual Armament and Air Firing. At the same time took part in the Mobilization Exercises 1933. Squadron Mobilized – with complement of transport and Reservists personnel. Squadron forms part of the Expeditionary Force. Returned to Duxford on the 16th October.

From the 19th to 21st October Flying Officer Burleigh and Sergeant Parr, who obtained best score at Sutton Bridge proceeded to No. 3 ATC and competed in the Brooke-Popham Cup. Flying Officer Burleigh was placed 4th in Fighting Area.

Spin recovery problems were still occurring with the Bulldogs. One such occurrence was in November, concerning K2160. The Bulldog went into a flat spin from which the pilot baled out (Pilot Officer D. Scorgie of "B" Flight).

Later that month the AOC – ADGB Air Marshal Sir R. Brooke-Popham, K.C.B., C.M.G., D.S.O., A.F.C., visited the Squadron, followed in December by the Under Secretary of State for Air, Sir Philip A.G.D. Sassoon, Bart., G.B.E., C.M.G., M.P.

1934

On the 8th February Squadron Leader J.R. Cassidy assumed command of the Squadron.

In April the Squadron moved to Northolt to attend the final heats of the Pin-Pointing and Flight Attack Competition, having one flight in each competition.

The 24th May was Empire Air Day. For the first Empire Air Day the Squadron was open to the public during the afternoon and normal flying was carried out including individual and flight aerobatics and practice bombing and attacks on other aircraft.

At the Annual RAF Display at Hendon on the 30th June, five Bulldogs from the Squadron, led by Flight Lieutenant H. Broadhurst (later to become Sir Harry Broadhurst) with Flying Officer S.F. Godden, Sergeant Pilots J.S.W. Bignal, R. Parr and W.J. Rye, performed various aerobatics and evolutions in formation with smoke. Their final and most spectacular was the 'Lovers Knot', in which the five aircraft would fly line abreast diving across the aerodrome, with Bignal and Rye out on each wing, and Godden, Broadhurst and Parr in the middle. The inner three would then go up into a tight loop belching red, white and blue smoke trails, as the two wingmen fanned out into an exaggerated winnow, smoke on, up and through the loop from each side in perfect timing. As Rye and Bignal passed each other they would count 'one, two, three – smoke off', thus leaving the five ribbon strands of the nuptial knot for all to admire.

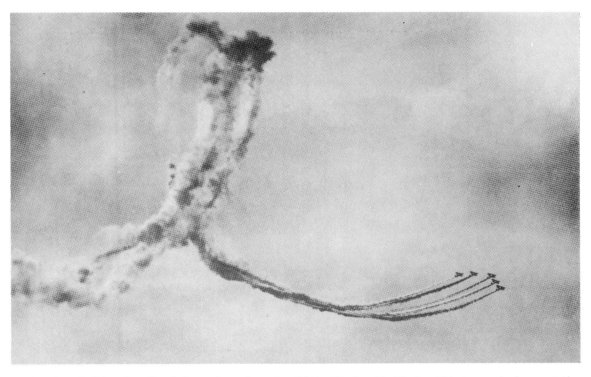

19 Squadron Bulldogs from Duxford complete a loop at a thirties Hendon Air Display. This team gained a reputation for smoke trailing and formation aerobatics.

The Squadron were the first to perform synchronised flight formation aerobatics with smoke. Other squadrons had performed smoke evolutions, but not in flight formation. The smoke had to be pumped into the exhaust and came out on each side of the aircraft, just ahead of the cockpit, so that when the pilot landed he was beautifully stained red, white or blue, depending which colour he had been operating.

In October the AOC-in-Chief, Air Marshal Sir Robert Brooke-Popham, K.C.B., C.M.G., D.S.O., A.F.C., visited the Station and Squadron.

1935

During February the Squadron flew service trials on an aircraft which, from May onwards, it was to pioneer into service; this was the Gloster Gauntlet I, which became one of the most successful biplane fighters.

On the 25th May began the re-equipment of the Squadron, when two Gloster Gauntlets were received.

Two flights of the Squadron gave demonstration on Empire Air Day, "A" Flight at Hornchurch, Fen Ditton and Henlow. "B" flight at Bircham Newton. One aircraft of "C" Flight visited Turnhouse.

Gauntlets at Duxford whilst hangars are built.

(Crown Copyright – MOD – AHB)

On the 3rd June the Squadron won the Sir Philip Sassoon Flight Attack competition at Northolt. Then on the 11th the Squadron was moved (temporarily) to Henlow in view of the Royal Review taking place at Duxford and Mildenhall.

On the 26th the Squadron moved to Hendon in connection with the RAF Display and on the 29th the Squadron was selected to carry out the Air Drill event at the RAF Display at Hendon.

From 1st to 6th July 1935 the Squadron moved to Mildenhall for the period in connection with the Royal Review. HM The King inspected the Squadron at Mildenhall on the 6th together with other RAF Units. The Squadron took part in the largest fly past the world had ever seen – 182 aircraft – at Duxford in the presence of HM The King, who took the salute from the dias of the covered pavilion. The Squadrons Gauntlets were the only machines to break away from the main body of aircraft to give a demonstration of 'Squadron Air Drill'.

The following is a copy of a message received from His Majesty the King, by Secretary of State for Air:-

"I warmly congratulate all ranks of the Royal Air Force on the magnificent display which I have had the pleasure of seeing today. I was greatly impressed both by their smartness on the ground and their efficiency in the air which leave no doubt that they will prove fully equal to any task which they may be called upon to fulfil. Please express to all ranks my appreciation of their labours in making the Review such an unqualified success together with my best wishes for the future welfare of the Royal Air Force".

Signed GEORGE R, I.

The Squadron took part in a display on the occasion of the opening of the Leicester Municipal Aerodrome, Braunstone on the 13th July. The Squadron returned to its parent station (Duxford) on the 20th, on completion of the clearing of the aerodrome after the Royal Review and then took part in Air Exercises operating from Duxford from the 22nd to the 26th..

From 9th to 19th September, Squadron moved to Sutton Bridge to carry out annual Air Firing practices. Flight Lieutenant H. Broadhurst won the Brooke-Popham Air Firing competition trophy.

In December a Gauntlet, piloted by Sergeant Rye, took part in a demonstration at Old Sarum in connection with Higher Commanders' Course. The Squadron flew to Northolt on the 17th and gave a demonstration of Air Drill and Flight Aerobatics in connection with the visit of the Turkish delegation.

1936

On the 6th January Squadron Leader J.W. Turton Jones assumed command of the Squadron.

In February the Squadron re-organised on two-flight basis owning to shortage of fitters and riggers.

From 18th to 25th April "C" Flight carried out affiliation exercises with No. 13 (AC) Squadron at Old Sarum.

In May, "A" Flight won the Sir Philip Sassoon Flight Attack competition at Northolt and then carried out affiliation exercises with No. 605 (B) Squadron at Castle Bromwich.

The 23rd May was Empire Air Day. The station at Duxford was open to the public. Normal training was demonstrated and flight attacks and flight aerobatics carried out.

In June the Squadron attended the opening ceremony at Gatwick Civil Airport on the 6th and flight aerobatics were carried out.

On the 13th June "A" Flight attended the International Air Rally and opening ceremony at Shoreham Civil Airport and carried out flight aerobatics.Followed on the 27th at the RAF Display at Hendon, when Flight Lieutenant H. Broadhurst gave the advanced flying demonstration and "A" Flight carried out the flight aerobatics event.

In July "A" Flight gave a demonstration of flight aerobatics during the tour of certain RAF Stations by HM The King. This was done at His Majesty's special request.

"A" Flight gave a display of flight aerobatics at Lympne during the International Air Rally on the 29th August. From 24th August to 11th September the Squadron moved to Sutton Bridge for annual air firing practices, during which the Sassoon air Firing Trophy was won.

Sergeant G.C. Unwin (Wing Commander D.S.O., D.F.M.) recalls:

"I joined 19 in August 1936 and the years before the war were very routine. The Squadron was regarded as one of the best fighter squadrons and repeatedly won the Sassoon Trophies for shooting, flight attack and pin pointing (map reading and navigation). The outstanding feature of those days was the 'tied together' aerobatic team".

The 14th to 17th September Flight Lieutenant Broadhurst and Pilot Officer D.W. Balden representing the Squadron in the Brooke-Popham Air Firing Competition at Sutton Bridge. Flight Lieutenant H. Broadhurst won the trophy with a score of 887. In September the Squadron began to re-equip with the Gloster Gauntlet II. This differed considerably from the Mark I in methods of construction as a result of the merger of Gloster with Hawker Siddeley. Two hundred and four were completed in two lots.

Gauntlets

On the 3rd December Air Marshal Sir Hugh C.T. Dowding, K.C.B., C.M.G., visited the Station to present the Squadron Badge to No. 19 (Fighter) Squadron.

1937

In May the Squadron was at No 3 ATC Sutton Bridge for annual Air Firing Practices followed by Empire Air Day on the 29th when "A" Flight proceeded to Donibristle and "B" Flight to Unsworth for demonstration of Flight attacks and synchronised aerobatics.

On the 26th June Squadron took part in mass Fly Past of 250 aircraft at Hendon Air Display.

From 9th to 11th August Combined Training Exercises. 19, 66 and 80 Squadrons operated on sector patrol. Exercises completed satisfactorily. Hampered slightly by weather conditions. All Gauntlet aircraft were fitted with modified flying wires by the 21st September.

In October "B" Flight took part in preliminary round of Sassoon Map Reading competition at Hucknall. They were placed first in 12 (F) Group and qualified to meet 11 (F) Group in the finals at Northolt. "A" Flight represented the squadron in preliminary round of the Flight Attack competition at Hucknall and were placed second. "B" Flight competed in Map Reading finals at Northolt and were placed second. Annual Inspection of the Station by AOC 12 (F) Group (Group Captain Probyn). 19 squadron took the fly past.

The first two weeks of December the Squadron engaged on affiliation exercises with No. 206 (GR) Squadron, Bircham Newton. Only four days flying were possible, however, owing to inclement weather. *On the 21st December Squadron Leader H.I. Cozens posted to the Squadron to take command.*

LEFT TO RIGHT: BACK ROW: *Pete Gordon, John Banham, Hiffe Cozens, Gordon Sinclair, MIDDLE ROW: George Ball, James Coward, Wilfred Clouston, Thomas Pace, FRONT ROW: Ian Robinson, Carr Withal, Mike Mee, Eric Thomas.*

(James Coward)

LEFT TO RIGHT: F/Off Pace, Robinson, Clouston, Banham and Ball. SEATED Thomas.

(James Coward)

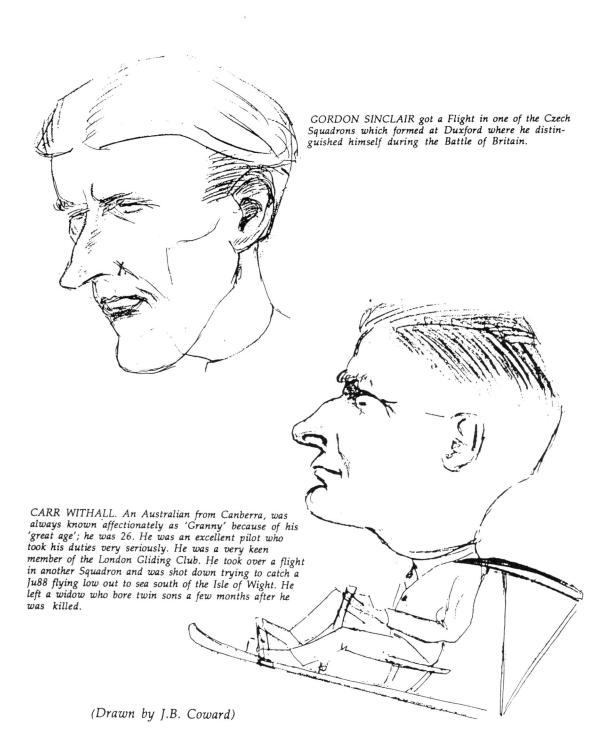

GORDON SINCLAIR got a Flight in one of the Czech Squadrons which formed at Duxford where he distinguished himself during the Battle of Britain.

CARR WITHALL. An Australian from Canberra, was always known affectionately as 'Granny' because of his 'great age'; he was 26. He was an excellent pilot who took his duties very seriously. He was a very keen member of the London Gliding Club. He took over a flight in another Squadron and was shot down trying to catch a Ju88 flying low out to sea south of the Isle of Wight. He left a widow who bore twin sons a few months after he was killed.

(Drawn by J.B. Coward)

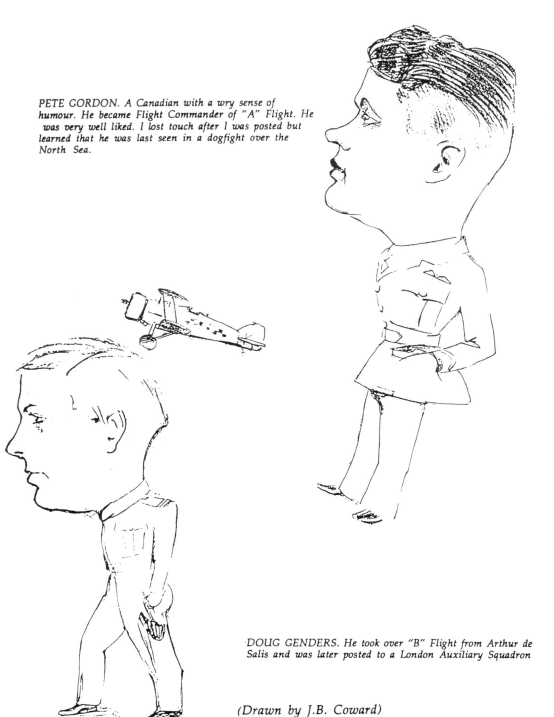

PETE GORDON. *A Canadian with a wry sense of humour. He became Flight Commander of "A" Flight. He was very well liked. I lost touch after I was posted but learned that he was last seen in a dogfight over the North Sea.*

DOUG GENDERS. *He took over "B" Flight from Arthur de Salis and was later posted to a London Auxiliary Squadron*

(Drawn by J.B. Coward)

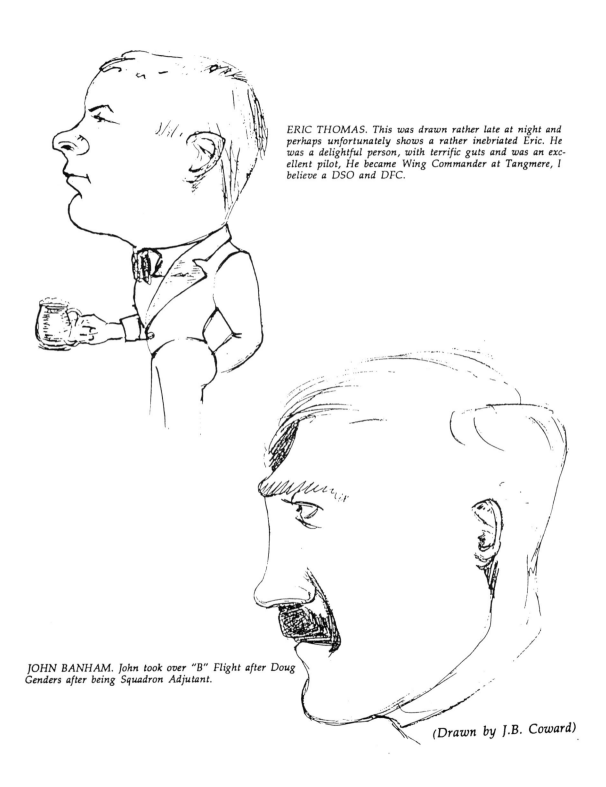

ERIC THOMAS. This was drawn rather late at night and perhaps unfortunately shows a rather inebriated Eric. He was a delightful person, with terrific guts and was an excellent pilot, He became Wing Commander at Tangmere, I believe a DSO and DFC.

JOHN BANHAM. John took over "B" Flight after Doug Genders after being Squadron Adjutant.

(Drawn by J.B. Coward)

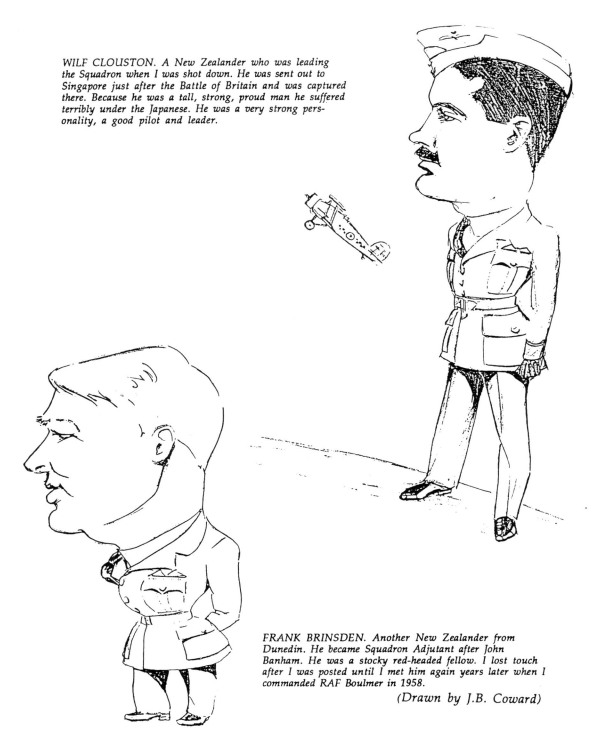

WILF CLOUSTON. *A New Zealander who was leading the Squadron when I was shot down. He was sent out to Singapore just after the Battle of Britain and was captured there. Because he was a tall, strong, proud man he suffered terribly under the Japanese. He was a very strong personality, a good pilot and leader.*

FRANK BRINSDEN. *Another New Zealander from Dunedin. He became Squadron Adjutant after John Banham. He was a stocky red-headed fellow. I lost touch after I was posted until I met him again years later when I commanded RAF Boulmer in 1958.*

(Drawn by J.B. Coward)

CHRISTMAS CARD 1937. S.L Turton-Jones, F/O J. Banham (adj), F/Lt A. de Salis, Flt Cmdr 'B' Flt, F/O P. Gordon, F/O D. Genders, F/O E. Thomas, F.O W. Clouston, F/O 'Ace' Pace, P/O C. Withall, P/O J. Coward (artist)

(Drawn by J.B. Coward)

CHRISTMAS CARD 1938. L TO R: F/O J.B. Coward, P/O Pace, F/O Genders, F/O Withall, F/O Mee, S/L H.I. Cozens, F/O Clouston, F.O Thomas, F/Lt Banham, F/Lt Gordon.

On the 6th January Informal Inspection by the Air Officer Commanding, Air Commodore T.L. Leigh–Mallory D.S.O.

From 23rd May to 18th June the Squadron moved to Sutton Bridge for annual Air Firing Practices. Pilot Officer A.I. Robinson won Air Firing Cup for highest aggregate.

On the 28th May, Empire Air Day, Squadron led by Squadron Leader Cozens, gave display of Air Drill at Sutton Bridge and Wyton.

On the 11th June the Squadron detached to Catterick for five days in connection with 12 (F) Group Tactical Exercises and during August the Squadron co-operated with Searchlight units.

On the 4th August, the Squadron secured a place in aviation history, of the first Squadron to be equipped with the Spitfire, when K9789 landed at Duxford.

The first Spitfire K9789 delivered to 19 Squadron
(Crown Copyright – Sqdn Album)

Squadron carried out night flying patrols and interceptions. Squadron co–operated with AA Units on the 9th and 10th.

On the 25th Captain Balfour, Under Secretary of State for Air, inspected station and flew Spitfire.

Pilot Officer Frank Brinsden (Wing Commander) recalls; "My first impression of the squadron when I joined it at Duxford in October 1938, was that every officer had a dog, except James Coward who had a cat. After the first working parade in the morning, the race was on to get to the crew room before the dogs took over the few easy chairs. I struck it lucky when I was made Squadron Adjutant and had an office and a chair of my own. We had an aeroplane each, a Corporal and two airmen to look after it and could take it away for the weekend if we had a reasonable cause to do so. Squadron fellowship was good and moral high. After all we were the chosen Squadron. The working pace was easy, Wednesday afternoon was for recreation and work finished about 4 o'clock each day. The Messes were run at a high standard, we all had private rooms in the officers mess, shared an efficient batman and dined in Mess Kit four nights a week. We had a mass of Squadron silver, which I believe was "souveneered" by some unprincipled so and so during the war. And we were all permanently broke.

155

Come the first Hitler scare in early 1939, all was changed. Aeroplanes were armed, camouflaged and dispersed on the other side of the airfield, our personal movements were restricted, war reservists began to arrive and all accomodation had to be shared. Squadrons were placed upon a war footing and assumed various relaxed states of preparedness. Our idyllic existence was in the past."

On the 26th September all pilots recalled from leave. Squadron remained at available at two hours notice until Germany had entered Sudetan areas.

Pilot Officer James Coward was the only pilot in the squadron at the time who admitted to being able to draw. He was therefore detailed to paint the squadrons crest on the tails of all the Gauntlets. He had just finished the last one the day before the Munich crisis. On returning to the mess that night, he was told to get into uniform and report to the hangar immediately. He arrived there to find everyone madly painting over all his hard weeks of work with camouflage.

During October despite this revolutionary new type, the squadron was at "2 hours available" during the Munich crisis. By the outbreak of World War II the squadron was fully operational.

19 Squadron's Spitfires were not delivered in time for Empire Air Day 1938, but they made their public debut at the opening of Marshall's new Cambridge Airport on the 8th October.

Squadron won first round of Sir Philip Sassoon Flight Attack trophy at Digby.

On the 22nd the Squadron sighted its first enemy aircraft whilst on convoy patrol. These patrols provided most of the squadron's operations during the "phoney" war. "B" Flight qualified to compete in final of Sassoon Trophy Map Reading Competition by winning 12 (F) Group competition.

In November the Squadron carried out affiliation exercises with No. 206 (GR) Squadron, Bircham Newton and competed in finals of both Sassoon Map Reading and Flight Attack competitions at North Weald.

Squadron carried out affiliation exercises with No. 115 (B) Squadron at Marham.

1939

On the 17th January "B" Flight flew the last three Gauntlets to Shawbury, returning the same day in a "borrowed" Oxford. During January and February the Squadron operated from Digby in Group Exercises.

On the 19th May the Squadron proceeded to Digby to take part in Group Mass Formation Flight round Midlands.

The 20th May was Empire Air Day. Squadron carried out Squadron Air Drill. "A: Flight carried out Flight Attack. "B" Flight did air drill on R/T orders from the ground.

The last of the Empire Air Days. It was by far the most ambitious. Hendon gave its first display on the 12th May 1911 and it was designed to show the military potential of the aeroplane. The show was put on for the Parliamentary Air Defence Committee but there was a high public attendance. Thereafter, Hendon air displays took place regularly, including such crowd drawing items as looping the loop and parachute drops. In the thirties 19 Squadron built up a reputation for formation aerobatics with a team led by Flight Lieutenant Harry Broadhurst. They progressed from smoke trailing Bristol Bulldogs to tied together Gloster Gauntlets.

For the next year or so 19 Squadron's aerobatic team was, like the Red Arrows today, in demand at all major aeronautical occasions.

Pilots of the Gauntlet Tied Together Team, from left to right: F/O. T. MacLachlan, F/Lt Broadhurst, P/O B.G. Morris

Formation of 19 Squadron Gauntlet with wings tied. The display team using what was the RAF's fastest fighter performed at many major events throughout the country.

On this the last Empire Air Day, a spectacular but unscheduled item, was a wheels up landing by a 19 Squadron Spitfire whose pilot (Sergeant J. Potter) forgot to lower his undercarriage.

On the 8th June Squadron Leader H.I. Cozens, was awarded Air Force Cross by HM The King.

In July Squadron carried out Night Flying maintaining Operational Patrols for Searchlight Corps training and in August took part in Annual Home Defence Exercises. Squadron maintained further Night Flying Patrols for Searchlight Corps training. Co–operating French Bomber aircraft were reported flying North and were intercepted by the squadron over Birmingham.

On the 24th August, owing to growing disturbances in Europe the Squadron was brought up to a War footing. Personnel on leave and courses were recalled; a Battle Flight being maintained at half–an–hours notice.

By the 29th August the Europe situation was becoming more critical and Reservists called up commenced reporting for duty.

SPITFIRE 1

(Crown Copyright – MOD – IWM)

THE SPITFIRE

4th August 1938

The Squadron secured a place in aviation history on this date, as the first Squadron to be equipped with the Spitfire, when K9789 landed at Duxford.

No 19 became the service test squadron for this, probably the most famous fighter of all time. Intensive flying trials began on the Spitfire, and the squadron completed 300 flying hours within a short period. It was then returned to Supermarine for stripping down and detailed examination. A small number of obvious defects were dealt with, one being the notorious undercarriage pump lever. The "Spitfire knuckle" was a painful complaint caused by the clenched fist striking against the cockpit side when working the long handle. During this operation the Spitfire could be seen to wobble erratically until the undercarriage was fully up or down. It was not long before powered retraction was introduced, much to the relief of the knuckle sore pilots.

"K9795"

(Crown Copyright – Sqdn Album)

Production slowly increased and the squadron received one Spitfire per week and it was not until the end of the year that the last of sixteen aircraft, K9811, was delivered on the 11th November.

Squadron Leader H.I. Cozens, (later Air Commodore, C.B., A.F.C,) who was the Commanding Officer at this time recalls;

"I joined 19 Squadron in December, 1937, at which time they had Gauntlets. These were slow and out of date machines.

The night Hitler made his speech in the Sports Palace in Berlin, I invited several officers to my room to listen to my radio. I also invited Flight Lieutenant Heath of 66 Squadron, as he could speak German. When Hitler said "This is the last territorial claim I have to make in Europe," everyone cheered. Later, as everyone was leaving, I said to Pete Gordon, the Senior Flight Commander, "Just a minute Pete. You don't want a war, I don't want a war, but we are a Fighter Squadron. Why do we all cheer when we feel there is to be no war?" He replied "We are not fast enough to run away".

It was then that I decided that I would do all I could to get the Spitfire that was at this time coming into production. The fact that I was a Cambridge Graduate in Engineering certainly helped my cause but I used all means available, and the nearness of Duxford to Fighter Command to secure the Spitfire for 19 Squadron.

The Spitfire arrived and we did a number of Service Trials, the most important was the intensive flying trials of 400 hours on the same aircraft. As to the flying characteristics of the Spitfire – It was like flying a lorry at low levels and low speeds. Once you had reached 10,000 feet the true characteristics became apparent and it was delightful to fly. We did trials with different airscrews, the wooden two bladed fixed pitch; the De Havilland three bladed, two speed; and so on. The Rotol airscrew was the eventual answer. The intensive flying trials were supposed to be up to 400 flying hours. We had completed over 200 when I asked my good friend Squadron Leader Fullergood of 66 Squadron, "What do we not know now at 200 hours, that we will know at 400?" He replied "Nothing". The probability of the Spitfire lasting 400 hours in war were remote. It would either be shot down or the war would be over. We decided to submit an interim report, with a comment that this would most probably be unaltered at 400 hours.

Shortly after, I was seated in my office, when the Station Commander telephoned and asked "Why are you not in the hangar at the conference?" I replied "What conference?" I went down to the hangar, to find people with sheets of paper crawling all over the Spitfires. I peeped over a shoulder at the sheet of paper – It was the report Squadron Leader Fullergood and I had submitted. I took a Rolls Royce Engineer to the tail of a Spitfire and pointed to a pool of oil round the tail wheel. I asked him if he knew where that had come from. He shook his head. I told him "Out of your engine". Rolls Royce thought their parts were machined so perfectly that when tightened up they would not leak. It was standard procedure for engines to be run up for five minutes until the oil was warm. I remarked to a Rolls Royce Engineer that "The Germans will not wait until we have warmed our engines up". So cold start trials were then carried out on the engines. A Spitfire was left outside all night for several weeks. We had a roster in which the pilots would get up at dawn and start the engine. It was getting into the winter months, so it was very cold. The engine would be started up and given full throttle for five minutes. After many weeks of subjecting the engine to this treatment, Rolls Royce stripped it down to see what damage had been done. They found no damage at all, so the warming up recommendation was found to be nonsense.

The Spitfire had airbrakes operated by a chrome plated tab on the dash which you pulled down and the airbrakes came down. One of the Spitfire Test Pilots asked me if I thought that the flaps were too big I told him they were, but keep them as they are for the extra weight which will be added in the future with armament and bombs.

The undercarriage had to be raised by a hand operated pump until such time as an engine driven pump became available. You set the throttle lever, changed hands on the stick and pumped with your right hand. This caused the aircraft to porpoise until you got the knack.

The Squadron had a visit from Air Chief Marshal H.C.T. Dowding. He said to me "I want to ask you a question and I want a straight answer. Can an average pilot fly a Spitfire without dual instruction and a period of training?" I answered "Yes". He said "Thank you, that's all I want to know because if the average pilot cannot fly a Spitfire, he cannot take on the Me109".

It would be an exaggeration to suggest that the Spitfire 'won the war' but it was the only aircraft we had that could seriously take on an Me109. So without the Spitfire we would probably not have gained and maintained air superiority over Britain.

The fact that I was an Engineer then backfired on me and I was posted from the Squadron to Designing and Producting Motor Transport in January, 1940. During my tour of duty, there were no casualties in the Squadron."

Pilot Officer F.N. Brinsden, (Wing Commander) writes "A few Spitfires had arrived before I did and joined the residue of the Gauntlets with which the squadron had been equipped. We also had a Miles Magister which was our monoplane conversion trainer pre Spitfire. I am not sure of this but I think we scored the Spitfires because our Squadron Commander, Henry Iliffe Cozens was a Cambridge University Graduate in engineering and of course a lot of service development work had to be done with such an innovative aircraft. For instance we conducted intensive and continuous flying programmes so as to establish component wastage rates and servicing cycles, engine performance and propellor compatibility, and so on.

From the outset the Spitfire was a delightful aeroplane to fly and I can recall only two idiosyncrises. The first was that the torque of the original two bladed fixed pitch propellor was such that the relatively small fin and rudder could not stop the aeroplane from swinging through about 45 degrees if the throttle was opened too viciously at take off. This was not of course a real problem once the idiosyncracy was understood, but made formation take offs a trap for the unwary. The second was the approach at night when the original pattern exhausts which stuck out like platforms glowed red, almost totally blanked out forward vision of the old goose neck landing flares. These did not light up the landing strip but gave only a reference marker. The Mark 1 had flat sided cockpit windows so you couldn't cock your head to one side to get a better view forward. The trick was to approach at night on a sort of curve of pursuit peering around the incandescant exhaust stubbs. Fortunately Duxford was a grass airfield at that time so it didn't matter too much if you didn't land straight down the runway. Later 'blinkers' were fitted over the exhausts and so the problem was eleviated a bit, and still later the exhausts stubbs were modified to reduce the glow.

These and a host of other recommendations for improvement or modification cropped up during this service evaluation period which then expanded to developing tactics for formation attacks against bomber formations, Wellington and Blenheims in our case, and our mass attacks allowed them to evolve defensive formations against co-ordinated fighter attacks.

I remember being elated when we received the first cannon Spitfires, then bitterly disappointed when they proved unreliable under combat stresses. I got myself into several good astern firing positions only to find that my guns jammed."

Pilot Officer J.B. Coward (Air Commodore A.F.C.), writes, "We were the first Squadron to be equipped with the single wooden bladed airscrews, and were fitted with tail parachutes as they had not been spun. Incidently, I was the first pilot to spin a Spitfire (by accident doing a stalled turn) and got it out quite normally without thinking of the tail parachute."

Sergeant D.G.S.R. Cox (Wing Commander D.F.C.) writes:'

"My opinion of the Spitfire – a great aeroplane, lovely to throw about and fight in. Quite a match for the Me109 in the Battle of Britain, except above 28,000 feet, when the 109 was superior in rate of climb and speed. I was fortunate to do all my operational flying in Spitfires, right up to August 1945 in Burma".

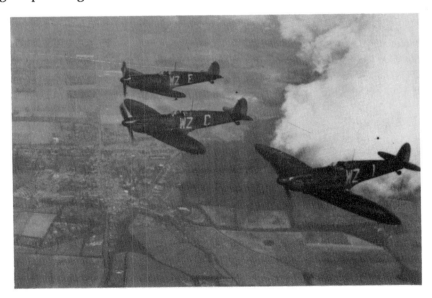

Three Spitfires over Royston

(James Coward)

163

WORLD WAR II

1st September 1939

General Mobilization of the British Forces was ordered at 0100 hours and at 1000 hours information was received that Polish towns had been bombed at 0530 hours without warning. By this time the Squadron was ready for any eventuality.

(Signed H.I. Cozens, Squadron Leader Commanding 19 (F) Squadron)

3rd September 1939

Due to the partial Mobilization completed during the preceding few days, declaration of War against Germany at 1100 hours, found the Squadron almost on a war footing and ready for any eventuality.

Squadron Leader H.I. Cozens AFC, was in command, with Pilot Officer F. N. Brinsden as Adjutant, Flight Lieutenant L.C. Withall commanding "A" Flight and Flight Lieutenant A.J. Banham commanding "B" Flight. Flying Officers W.G. Clouston; T.G. Pace; J.B. Coward; A.I. Robinson; G.C. Matheson: Pilot Officers G.L. Sinclair; G.E. Ball; A.J.A. Llewellin; G.W. Petre; L. Marples; M.D. Lyne; L.A. Haines; J.H. Bowring: Flight Sergeant H. Steere: Sergeants J.A. Coleman; G.C. Unwin; J.H. Potter; P.S. Gunning; T. Boyd; A.E.A. Bruce (RAFWR) comprised the remainder of the flying personnel, the majority of whom were quite conversant with the characteristics of the Spitfire I with which the squadron had been fully equipped for almost a year.

LEFT TO RIGHT
BACK ROW: Sgt. J.A. Coleman, F/Sgt. H. Steere, Sgt. P.S. Gunning, Sgt. G.C. Unwin, Sgt. J.H. Potter.

CENTRE: - - - - - - - - - - - -, F/O T.G. Pace, P/O G.E. Ball, F/O G.C. Matheson, P/O G.W. Petre, P/O A.J.A. Llewellin, P/O L. Marples, - - - - - - - - - - - - - -

FRONT: P/O F.N. Brinsden, F/O A.I. Robinson, F/Lt. C. Withall, F/Lt. P. Gordon, Sqdn. Ldr. H.I. Cozens, F/Lt. W.G. Clouston, F/O J.B. Coward, P/O G.L. Sinclair

NB (This photograph was taken about two months before the war broke out. P/O's M.D. Lyne, L.A. Haines and J.H. Bowring joined the Squadron just before the war and are not on this photograph)

Despite the declaration of war, there was no major entry in the record until nearly five weeks later.

6th October 1939

Flying accident to two Spitfires, K9854 & K9821. These two aircraft were flying from Watton to Duxford. Pilot Officer G.E. Ball, flying K9821 collided with the tail unit of K9854 flown by Flight Lieutenant W.G. Clouston causing him to crash at Newmarket aerodrome. Both pilots were uninjured.

"Gone are the days of standing up to your arse in plywood and saying – Sorry Sir"
Flight Lieutenant W.G. Clouston with K9854

(Crown Copyright – Sqdn Album)

8th October 1939

Two Spitfires collect from Aston Down, Nos. L1027 & L1089, to Command Reserve of 19 Squadron.

17th October 1939

The squadron was ordered to be ready to move to Turnhouse to be in the vicinity of enemy aircraft raids. From the 17th inst to the 19th inst, the weather was very stormy and overcast, and the squadron did not move.

20th October 1939

Squadron Leader Cozens in command of 19 Squadron, Flight Lieutenant Lane in command of "A" Flight, Flight Lieutenant Clouston in command of "B" Flight and 10 Officer Pilots flew to Catterick instead of Turnhouse on being posted for temporary duty. Together with seven Sergeant Pilots and 57 airmen.

21st October 1939

At 0958 hours a raid F appeared on the Plotting Table and at 1009 hours, Blue Section (Flight Lieutenant Clouston, Flying Officer Sinclair and Flight Sergeant Steere) were ordered to proceed to Scarborough at 10,000 feet. At 1015 hours, raid F was renumbered X40 and Blue Section was ordered to investigate. At 1024 hours the Section was ordered to patrol Whitby and 1031 hours to Flamborough Head and 5 miles East. At 1107 hours, Group ordered the Section to land. Nothing seen by the Section.

At 1424 hours, Blue Section (Flight Lieutenant Clouston, Pilot Officer Petre, & Flight Sergeant Steere) was ordered to intercept Raid X3, approaching Flamborough Head. Only three plots of this raid were received. At 1457 hours the Section was ordered to patrol 10 miles out to sea off Flamborough Head, and at 1500 hours an enemy aircraft was sighted. Owing to heavy AA fire from ships in convoy, Blue Section were unable to carry out attacks and when the firing ceased the target was no longer in sight. Blue Sections comments of the Senior Service were neither respectful nor complimentary.

At 1515 hours, "A" Flight (Flight Lieutenant Lane, Sergeant Unwin & Flying Officer Matheson) were ordered to patrol 10 miles East of Flamborough Head at 14,000 feet. Raid X4 appeared about 50 miles east of Flamborough Head proceeding West and when twelve miles from the coast turned North. At 1612 hours, "A" Flight were ordered to land by Group.

22nd October 1939

At 1039 hours, Red Section (Flight Lieutenant Lane & Sergeant Potter), were ordered to patrol Flamborough Head at 1,000 feet. Raid X13 appeared approximately 60 miles out to sea and then again appeared about 5 miles South of Flamborough Head. At 1042, Red Section were ordered to proceed to Hartlepool at 1,000 feet. At 1052 they were ordered to land by Group.

At 1105 hours, Yellow Section (Flying Officer Robinson & Pilot Officer Brinsden) were ordered to investigate aircraft flying between Seaham Harbour and Blyth, 10 miles east of the coast. At 1137 hours, Yellow Section reported that they had seen an Anson flying round a convoy 5 miles east of Hartlepool. At 1200 hours, Instructions received on 'I' Line from Group to investigate aircraft flying very high over Middlesbrough. At 1221 ordered to land.

At 1440 hours, Red Section (Flight Lieutenant Lane, Flight Sergeant Unwin & Sergeant Jennings) were ordered to patrol 10 miles east of Seaham Harbour at 10,000 feet. They were ordered to land at 1501 having observed five Gladiators.

1st November 1939

A new type of Spitfire fitted with a rotol constant speed airscrew was collected by Squadron Leader Cozens who began to carry out intensive flying and reliability trials with this aircraft.

8th November 1939

During the afternoon, six aircraft went to Sutton Bridge where air firing practice was carried out.

26th November 1939

Night flying was practiced by several members of the squadron. Three pilots carrying out their first solo's successfully.

27th November 1939
The squadron carried out night flying en-mass, a bright full moon assisting considerably.

30th November 1939
The month has been very quiet with no offensive or defensive patrols against the enemy aircraft being ordered. The monotony of life in this sector was eleviated by night flying practices, squadron formation air drill, affiliation exercises carried out against various bomber units and day flights made to an advance aerodrome at Horsham St Faith. In addition to low flying attacks were practiced in order to test the ground defences at Marshalls Aerodrome, Cambridge.

December 1939
The month has been very quiet generally with only one offensive patrol being ordered. Three aircraft of 'B' Flight were detailed to intercept what proved to be a friendly aircraft. The usual practice ground attacks were carried out against defences at Marshalls aerodrome, Cambridge. All night flying programmes during the month had to be cancelled owing to the unfavourable weather conditions.

1st January 1940
Squadron Leader G.D. Stevenson assumed command of the squadron.

1st February 1940
The beginning of the month found the aerodrome under snow and no flying took place, with the exception of the runway service test by Flight Lieutenant W.G. Clouston on the 2nd, until the 10th, when convoy patrols were resumed.

7th February 1940
Over eight years after his horrific accident in a Bulldog, Flying Officer Douglas Bader was posted back again to a fighter squadron. The Commanding Officer, Squadron Leader G. Stephenson was Bader's old aerobatic partner from 23 squadron and Cranwell contemporary.

28th February 1940
Three Wellington's from Bassingbourn co–operated with "A" Flight fighter attacks three and four, and deflection shooting with the cine guns were successfully carried out.

29th February 1940
Pilot Officer Trenchard was killed whilst carrying out local night flying training.

2nd March 1940
Blue Section took place in several false alarms, no enemy aircraft seen. On the second a Wellington was intercepted and on the third a friendly Blenheim was met.

16th March 1940
The squadron relieved 46 Squadron for the day. Leaving Duxford at 0950 hours they flew to North Coates. Sections of two machines carried out several convoy patrols. The squadron returned to Duxford at 1900 hours. No enemy aircraft seen throughout the day.

31st March 1940
Flying Officer Bader, whilst taking off in a Spitfire (K9858) from Horsham St Faith on a

routine mission, left the aircrew control lever in coarse pitch instead of fine, the necessary setting for take-off. The Spitfire hadn't enough speed to get airborne, and so ploughed into the boundary fence at the end of the field.

17th April 1940
Squadron moved to Horsham St Faith.

5th May 1940
At 1130 hours, Blue section was sent off to intercept a raid but no enemy aircraft were seen.

11th May 1940
Three Spitfires went on patrol at 1200 hours, and were investigating successively Raids N5 and N6, which later became Raid No. 71. The enemy aircraft was sighted some 20 miles ahead at 26,000 feet, 10 miles east of East Dudgeon Lightship.

Flight Lieutenant Clouston (Blue 1) leading, ordered the section to re-form and carried out a stern chase. The enemy aircraft was identified as a Junkers 88, which turned east on sighting the Spitfires. Flight Lieutenant Clouston instructed Flight Sergeant Steere (Blue 2) to turn east and head off the enemy aircraft which dived almost vertically to cloud layer at 9,000 feet. Flight Sergeant Steere by this time was in a better position to attack and Flight Lieutenant Clouston waited until he had got in one burst. Flight Lieutenant Clouston then opened fire with almost full deflection at 450 yards, a short burst of 2 seconds, followed by two fairly long bursts but observed no result during the whole of the attack. He dived from 26,000 feet to the cloud layer at 400 mph, and commenced flying in cloud. Flight Lieutenant Clouston and Flight Sergeant Steere stayed above the cloud and Flying Officer Petre (Blue 3) proceeded below the cloud. The enemy aircraft appeared above the cloud only once and Flight Lieutenant Clouston got in a short burst at 300 yards.

Flight Sergeant Steere (Blue 2) opened fire from 500 yards and the enemy aircraft turned towards land. He followed, getting in a burst from astern, when the enemy aircraft turned back out towards the sea. He got a final burst of 5 seconds when his ammunition expired. The enemy fire was from the top turret only and tracers passed beneath Flight Sergeant Steere's port mainplane.

Flying Officer Petre (Blue 3) closed with the enemy aircraft and a chase ensued below, in and above the cloud at 9,000 feet. The enemy aircraft was emitting black smoke on emerging from cloud and diving towards sea level. He had to use the boost cut out to overhaul the enemy aircraft which commenced evasive tactics. He opened fire at 400 yards closing to 150 yards giving in all 6 bursts. Return fire was seen coming from the top turret. On arrival back at base, Flying Officer Petre found he had no oil pressure – his oil tank and both tyres had been punctured in the combat.

The Junkers 88 later crashed into the sea and the crew were picked up.

16th May 1940
Squadron moved back to Duxford.

18th to 25th May 1940
Flying training was carried out by the whole squadron and no patrols were done. Air Vice Marshal Leigh–Mallory visited the squadron twice. It had been definitely decided that the Squadron were being moved to France but the German advance put a stop to that.

25th May 1940
The squadron moved to Hornchurch.

COPY

OPERATIONAL MESSAGE FORM.

Form "D"

Operational : Message received ~~~~~~~~~ by { Group Operations Officer / Sector Operations "B" }

| (A) 1300 | Date (B) 17/5/40 | From/To (C) 12 Grp/Duxford | Serial No: (D) 124/6 |

Information (E)

REMARKS
(for use of unit receiving only)

TO OFFICER COMMANDING 19 SQN

HEARTIEST CONGRATULATIONS TO 19 BLUE

ON GETTING THE SQDN'S FIRST "HUN" ON

MAY THE 11TH 1940

T. LEIGH-MALLORY. A.V.M.

COMMANDING 12 GRP.

R.1314

w/o.   R.A.F. Form 1149.

169

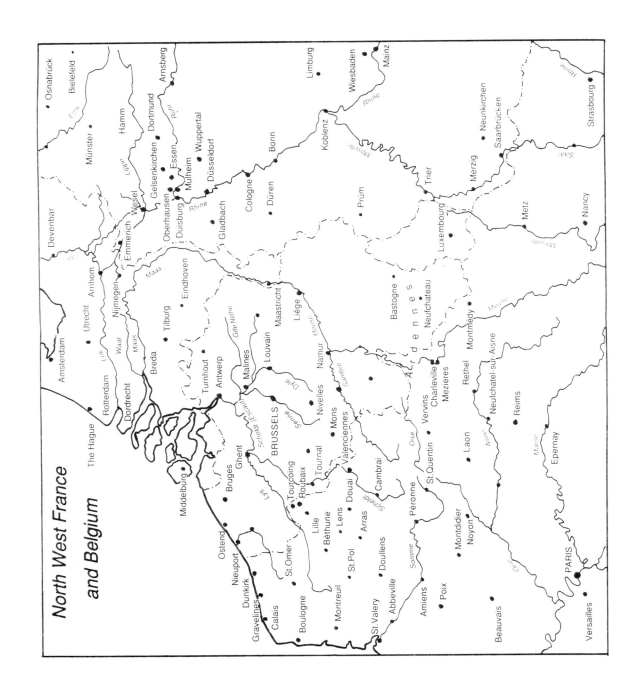

North West France and Belgium

DUNKIRK

During fierce action over Dunkirk (the squadron claimed 13 enemy aircraft for a loss of 4).

The squadron were patrolling the Calais–Dunkirk area at 0915 hours when they found a formation of Junkers 87s at 10,000 feet.

Pilot Officer M. Lyne (Red 2) followed Red Leader into the Junkers 87's and saw Squadron Leader Stevenson fire at one which turned over and went down. Pilot Officer Lyne went for the extreme right tail of the formation, selected his Ju87 and shot it down. (Confirmed by Yellow Leader). He made another brief attack at an Ju87 and then went to look for the fighters. At this time he saw a Spitfire hit by a cannon shell near the cockpit on the port side and another Spitfire going gently down with Glycol vapour pouring from the starboard side of the engine. Pilot Officer Lyne then saw about ten Junkers 87 coming in from the sea to attack Calais. He made a head on attack at one, closing to 50 yards, and then attacked an Me109 as it climbed slowly, giving it a two second burst from 100 yards. During the combat, Pilot Officer Lyne's Spitfire had received a bullet through the leading edge and punctured his right tyre.

Flight Lieutenant Lane (Yellow 1) was leading the section when the enemy aircraft were sighted. Red section attacked the starboard side and Blue section the port. Flight Lieutenant Lane followed Red section and selected an enemy aircraft turning left out of the formation. He fired one burst at 400 yards from below and astern, watching the tracers enter the enemy aircraft as it climbed and stalled. He fired again from 200 yards and the enemy aircraft then went into a dive. By this time the escorting Me109s were attacking, and Flight Lieutenant Lane was forced to break away, but sighted the Junkers 87 diving towards the sea, apparently out of control. As he looked round he saw an Me109 attacking a Spitfire which was hit forward of the cockpit by a shell from the enemy aircraft. The Spitfire went into a steep dive and he subsequently observed a parachute in the sea about half a mile off Calais. A dog fight now ensued in which Flight Lieutenant Lane managed to fire bursts at several enemy aircraft, mostly deflection shots. Three enemy aircraft attached themselves to his tail, two doing astern attacks, whilst the third attacked from the beam. He turned towards this enemy aircraft and fired a good burst in a front quarter deflection attack, which then disappeared and was probably shot down. He still had the two enemy aircraft on his tail, was down to sea level and taking violent evasive action, but gradually drew away using the 12 lb boost which gave him an air speed of 300 mph.

Flying Officer F.N. Brinsden (Yellow 2) encountered 2 separate formations of Junkers 87s, 21 in all and further off about 30 Me109s. Whilst preparing to attack he saw Flight Lieutenant Clouston fire at one Junkers 87 which crashed into the sea. Flying Officer Brinsden then selected his Junkers 87 and closing to about 200-150 yards fired a short burst. The enemy aircraft immediately went down out of control.

Sergeant J.A. Potter (Yellow 3) in line astern when the attack started, selected an Me109 which was attacking Flight Sergeant Unwin. He gave it a short burst which did not hit the enemy aircraft but caused it to change its mind and break off the attack. Sergeant Potter soon discovered that the Me109's fought in pairs or three's. It was impossible to get one without being fired upon by one or more of his friends. However, he did actually find one on the outskirts of the fight and fired a short burst from 400 yards. The enemy aircraft climbed immediately and at the top of his climb, did a stall turn to the left which exposed the whole of his aeroplane whilst he was not moving at more than 100 mph. Sergeant Potter lined his sights up and opened fire from 400 yards closing to 150 yards . He saw the bullets enter the cockpit of the Me109 which fell out of its turn, out of control and crash into the sea. During the course of the fight, he had seen a Spitfire hit by a HE Cannon shell which caused a big burst of flame from its starboard side. He thought the Spitfire was on fire but the flames died out and the aircraft dropped its nose and dived vertically towards the sea. At 3,000 feet, he was surprised to see a parachute open and the pilot appeared to be safe. He later decided it was Pilot Officer Watson as he was wearing black overalls and Squadron Leader Stevenson was wearing white. He saw the Squadron Leader's aircraft in a straight glide over the land going west, with a thin stream of blue smoke trailing behind it.

Me109

(Crown Copyright – MOD – AHB)

Flying Officer G.W. Petre became separated from his section and engaged five Me 109s with four other Spitfires. He got onto the tail of one Me109 and opened fire at 250 yards, closing to 100 yards. Pieces were becoming detached from the enemy aircraft and he carried out no evasive tactics except to pull up in a gradual climb. He broke off the attack and did not see the enemy aircraft again.

Flight Sergeant H. Steere carried out one attack echelon starboard with blue section before the escort fighters arrived. The Junkers 87s maintained their formation and cross fire was experienced by Flight Sergeant Steere. Preparing for his second attacked, one Junkers 87 was climbing slowly and steeply out of the breaking formation. He closed and gave the enemy aircraft a long burst of eight seconds while it was in a practically stalled position. The Ju87 dropped his port wing and spiralled down in flames.

Flying Officer G.E. Ball (Green 1) had been detailed as the look–out section for enemy escort fighters. He positioned himself in the best position to search for the enemy aircraft and eventually spotted a large formation of Me109s. He warned the squadron that a large formation of Me109s were preparing to attack, and then joined in the terrific dogfight that ensued. At no period of this fight was there less than three Me109 whirling round. He managed to get onto the tail of one and fired at a range of 100 yards until the Me109 went into a spiral dive with smoke pouring out from the engine. Pilot Officer Ball sustained injuries in the head and arm. "I thought I was dead, then I saw some more tracer coming past me, so I came to the conclusion I must still be alive".

Flying Officer Sinclair (Green 2) was with his leader as the combat commenced. He looked in his mirror and saw an Me109 on his tail, slightly to port and diving. He throttled back and turned hard to port, to meet the Me109, which passed him and climbed. As the enemy aircraft climbed he appeared in Flying Officer Sinclair's sights at a range of 100 yards. Flying Officer Sinclair fired a long burst and the Me109 burst into flames. He noticed that the Me109's worked in pairs, apparently covering each others attacks. Their method of attack being a steep dive from above, a short gun burst, followed by a steep climb up again.

172

Squadron Leader Stevenson (N3200) – is missing.

Pilot Officer Watson (N3237) – is missing.

At 1600 hours in the Dunkirk area the Squadron led by Flight Lieutenant Lane sighted eight Me109s at 10,000 feet, diving in ragged formation to attack.

Flight Lieutenant Lane gave the command to break formation and saw one Me109 preparing to attack Flying Officer Sinclair who disappeared into cloud. The enemy aircraft pulled out of his dive above the cloud and headed for France. Flight Lieutenant Lane chased this aircraft and delivered a climbing attack from astern firing a burst of 4-5 seconds at 300-200 yards. The Me109 lurched onto its side and fell into a vertical dive. He followed it down and pulled out at 2,500 feet when the enemy aircraft was well below him.

Flying Officer G. Sinclair (Green 1) as the formation broke, noticed (Green 2) spinning down with a Me109 on his tail. He climbed after the enemy aircraft and as the enemy aircraft did a stall turn, he presented a plan view of his aircraft. Flying Officer Sinclair fired a long burst and the Me109 immediately started to spin down out of control, he then watched him for several thousand feet, and manoeuvred onto the tail of another enemy aircraft and opened fire. He had to break off this attack as two enemy aircraft were on his tail, so he dived for cloud cover. When he climbed up again, all enemy aircraft had disappeared.

Flying Officer G.W. Petre (Blue 3) was following Blue Leader when he saw an Me109 with a Spitfire on its tail, with an Me109 on the Spitfires tail. He broke formation to go to the aid of this Spitfire which rolled slowly onto its back and dived through the clouds at 1,200 feet. Flying Officer Petre got onto the tail of the second Me109 and opened fire at 200 yards closing to 50 yards. Smoke poured out of the enemy aircraft which turned slowly over on its back and dived vertically into the sea.

Pilot Officer M. Lyne landed on the beach near Deal with engine failure and a bullet in his leg.

Sergeant Irwin (P9305) – is missing.

27th May 1940

Two patrols were carried out in the morning over Dunkirk, led by Flight Lieutenant Lane. One Heinkel 111 was attacked by the second patrol.

The squadron went up again at 1900 hours to patrol the Dunkirk area and soon split up. Flight Lieutenant Lane, Flying Officer Brinsden and Flight Sergeant Unwin sighted a Henschel 126 and chased the enemy aircraft inland as far as Ypres. Although the enemy aircraft was far slower, he used his manoeuvrability to escape the Spitfire's fire and fought them off magnificently. Flight Lieutenant Lane called the section to reform and return to the Dunkirk beaches. The enemy aircraft saw Flight Lieutenant Lane and Flying Officer Brinsden reform and turn away. Thinking he was safe he resumed his normal flight, when Sergeant Unwin dived on him out of the sun. The Hs126 burst into flames and crashed into a field.

The rest of the squadron sighted several single Dorniers 215s and Henschel 126s, between 10,000 and 20,000 feet.

Flight Lieutenant Clouston was leading the section of three Spitfires and sighted a Dornier 215 at 14,000 feet. The enemy aircraft dived and Flight Lieutenant Clouston leading in line astern, made a quarter attack from above, firing two 4 second bursts. He did not see that enemy aircraft again but encountered another Do215 at 20,000 feet. He made a surprise attack from the sun and the Dornier did not see him coming. He attacked from quarter changing to astern attack and the enemy aircraft burst into flames and dropped to the sea on its back. Flight Sergeant Steere was No. 2 in the section and followed his leader into the attack on the Dornier 215. The enemy aircraft flattened out after the leaders attack and Flight Sergeant

173

Steere made a dead astern attack, firing a five second burst and the enemy aircraft return fire ceased. He made a similar second attack after Flying Officer Petre (No 3) and followed this with a third. By this time he had expended all his ammunition, the enemy aircraft was in a vertical dive and he "black–out" when breaking away. He did not consider the Do215 could have recovered.

Flying Officer Petre attacked this Do215 with an eight second burst from dead astern. He closed well in and passed the enemy aircraft before he broke away. He did not see the enemy aircraft again.

Sergeant Jennings encountered some scattered Do215's. He attacked and chased one out to sea, firing two very short bursts into it from above. After pulling out of his dive he "blacked out" and on recovering, could not find the enemy aircraft. He then saw a large splash in the sea but this may have been a bomb burst.

Flying Officer Sinclair on the Dunkirk patrol line sighted Heinkel 111s at 4,000 feet bombing from cloud level. He became split from the squadron when he came below the cloud and spotted a He111 flying towards him. He opened fire with full deflection and the port engine caught fire, the turret gun ceased to fire and the enemy aircraft appeared to be descending. He then saw 20 enemy aircraft approaching which he identified as Do215s and attacked one which had turned inland, firing in long bursts from astern. The port engine was flaming hard and the enemy aircraft losing height fast. He closed to 40 yards and tracer was all around him. He had only 20 gallons left so he broke off the attack.

28th May 1940

The Squadron was patrolling the Dunkirk area at 1000 hours at 16,000 feet when they became engaged with a large formation of Me109s.

Flight Sergeant Steere saw one Me109 well below and carried out a stern attack, firing in short bursts. As he broke away, the enemy aircraft burst into flames and fell towards the ground.

Flight Sergeant Unwin attacked one Me109 opening from the beam with a full deflection and swinging in astern. He fired three short one second bursts from 250 to 150 yards. The enemy aircraft was last seen spinning down towards the ground from 8,000 to 3,000 feet.

31st May 1940

The new CO, Squadron Leader Pinkham flew down from Sutton Bridge in a Hurricane.

1st June 1940

The squadron led by Flight Lieutenant Lane, was on patrol at 0540 hours, two miles north–east of Dunkirk at 4,000 feet, when 12 Me110s and 12 Me109s were sighted. The Me109s dived from the clouds in front of squadron, which immediately went into line astern. Four Me110s then appeared from over the land followed by many more.

Flight Lieutenant Lane (Red 1) attacked one enemy aircraft and observed the port engine stop, the starboard engine omitted a large quantity of white vapour. The enemy aircraft dived towards the ground and at 50 feet had still failed to pull out. He then attacked another head–on and burst appeared to enter the nose of the enemy aircraft which passed below him to avoid a collision. During the combat he saw two enemy aircraft crash, one into the sea, the other into flames on the beach.

Sergeant Potter (Red 2) fired at several enemy aircraft without visible effect. He then attacked one which had just begun a steep diving turn to the left. He had a full plan view of the top of the enemy aircraft and opened fire at 400 yards. He held his fire for eight seconds

Sergeant Potter
(Peter Howard-Williams)

and could see his bullets going into the fuselage. At 150 yards he ran out of ammunition and broke off the engagement. He turned for home, when he felt a metallic "bang" and saw a hole in his port mainplane 8" x 2" which destroyed his oil cooler. His engine started to run rough, with oil and glycol smoke appearing, and eventually seized up 15 miles from land at 4,000 feet. He decided to stay with the aircraft as the sea was calm and there was a small boat below alongside which he would 'land'. He inflated his life jacket, removed his Sutton harness and RT plug from its socket. He circled the boat, kept his flaps up, straightened out and touched down. The Spitfire skimmed off the surface and as it touched down again, dug its nose into the sea. He was flung forward and his forehead and nose met the reflector sight. The Spitfire sank within 10 seconds. As he tried to get out his parachute caught on the sliding hood and he went down with the aircraft. He managed to free himself and as he did so was struck by the tail plane as it went past him. Eventually he reached the surface and was only 50 yards from the boat which turned out to be a French fishing boat, the "Jolie Mascotte" on its way to Dunkirk.

He was given dry clothes, food and drink. They picked up survivors at Dunkirk from the Destroyer "Basilisk", which had been bombed and was sinking, and returned to Dover.

Flight Sergeant Unwin (Red 3) climbed underneath one enemy aircraft and gave a burst of five seconds from an opening range of 150 yards. It blew up over his head. He then chased another who turned and climbed, giving it a long burst. The enemy aircraft's engine stopped and threw out oil and smoke. Flight Sergeant Unwin carried on the attack until within 100 yards and had to dive under him to avoid a collision. Flight Lieutenant Clouston (Blue 1) was attacking a Me110 when an Me109 came out of cloud approximately 100 yards ahead. He turned to attack with Flight Sergeant Sterne and saw his tracers enter the enemy aircraft, which pulled into a steep climb and then fell away into a glide. Flight Sergeant Steere (Blue 2) then attacked and the enemy aircraft's engine stopped. The enemy aircraft was last sighted going down obviously out of control in a spiral dive. Flight Lieutenant Clouston then climbed up to cloud base and sighted another Me109 which he attacked. Closing to 50 yards when the enemy aircraft stalled, and it went into a spin with its engine stopped. As the engagement stopped at 1,500 feet it was impossible for the enemy aircraft to recover.

Flight Sergeant Steere (Blue 2) followed his leader into the attack on an Me109 firing a 5 second burst. The enemy aircraft's engine was definitely disabled, because of his speed of closing suddenly increased. The enemy aircraft then turned over and downwards. He was then forced to make a violent manoeuvre to escape from a falling Me110 which crashed into the

175

dunes and burst into a sheet of flame. (This was probably shot down by Flying Officer Sinclair). Consequently he did not see his Me109 hit the ground, but Blue Leader confirmed it was out of control.

Pilot Officer Haines (Blue 3) delivered a deflection attack on an Me109 and saw it dive vertically into the ground.

Flying Officer Sinclair (Green 1) attacked the Me110 in line astern. He engaged one, its port engine caught fire and side slipped into the ground bursting into flames. He then turned onto an Me110 flying inland, together with another Spitfire which was above him and to port. They chased the Me110 for 2 miles inland at 50 feet, with a lot of tracer return fire, but this stopped when the Spitfires opened fire. The enemy aircraft then dived into the ground and burst into flames.

Pilot Officer H.C. Baker (Green 2), saw an Me110 to his left about 1,000 feet above and he decided to attack this aircraft. He fired a fairly long deflection shot into the Me110 and broke away to avoid colliding with it. He did not see the final result but the Me110 was waffling badly. Two minutes later, he got a similar long burst into a second Me110. As he broke away from that attack, he saw another Me110 coming head on towards him, firing. Pilot Officer Baker had just time to shoot at this aircraft before it passed beneath him, with both engines throwing out white smoke. He turned as quickly as he could onto the tail of this Me110 and gave it another burst. It then burst into flames. He attacked some other Me110s going round in a circle, when some Me109s appeared. Getting short of both petrol and ammunition, he took refuge in a cloud and headed home.

Sergeant Jennings (Green 3) opened fire on an Me110 from below, climbing to the left and finished his attack when he saw it catch fire and go into a spin. One parachute came out of this enemy aircraft and landed about a mile inland. Sergeant Jennings then attacked another from below and saw his tracers going into its fuselage. The enemy aircraft pulled violently and stalled. He didn't see what happened because he had to take action to avoid a collision, but it was probably the one Flight Lieutenant Lane saw dive into the sea.

Summary of the 1st June patrol
9 certs and 2 probables.

Flight Lieutenant Lane	1	Me110
Flight Sergeant Unwin	1	Me110
Flight Lieutenant Clouston	1 + ½	Me109
Flight Sergeant Steere	½	Me109
Pilot Officer Haines	1	Me109
Flying Officer Sinclair	2	Me110
Pilot Officer Baker	1	Me110
Sergeant Jennings	1	Me110

The squadron of eight aircraft on patrol again over Dunkirk at 0955 hours saw 20 Do215s and 12 He111s at 3,000 feet, bombing three ships off Dunkirk from cloud level. Due to the number of enemy aircraft and the fact that they climbed into a cloud at 4,000 feet, the sections broke up.

Sergeant Jennings (Red 2) after searching the clouds found a Do215, did a climbing attack from slightly ahead with nearly full deflection. He believed it caught fire, but owing to lack of fuel had to break off and return.

Flight Sergeant Unwin (Red 3) saw two He111s and gave chase. He was joined by some aircraft of No. 222 Squadron. As he started his attack from 400 yards, he experienced return fire from the rear gunner, which suddenly ceased. He closed to 100 yards and used the rest of his ammunition, by which time the starboard engine had stopped. He then left him to the fellow of 222.

Pilot Officer Haines (Blue 3) did a climbing attack from the port quarter, opening fire at 200 yards at a He111. The port engine burst into flames almost directly and he followed through his attack closing to within 50 yards, meeting no return fire and finishing up dead astern. The enemy aircraft glided steeply towards the sea with the engine still blazing fiercely.

Flight Sergeant Steere (Blue 2) pursued an He111 in and out of cloud. As he broke cloud he found himself in the middle of a formation of twenty Do215s. He immediately fired a five second burst at one, closing to 50 yards and was forced to break away downwards through the formation. The enemy aircraft's port engine gave out dense black smoke and it turned on its back and spiralled down. Flight Sergeant Steere was under heavy cross fire and also fire from behind. The enemy aircraft fire was effective. Flight Sergeant Steere's Spitfire was hit from three different directions.

Flying Officer Sinclair (Green 1) descended below the clouds alone and saw a Heinkel 111 flying towards him. He opened fire with full deflection until the port engine burst into flames. The machine then seemed to be losing height. He followed this with another attack on a formation of Dornier 215s. This enemy aircraft engine also burst into flames and when he broke off the attack, the enemy aircraft was steadily descending.

5th June 1940

The squadron returned to Duxford from Hornchurch. During its stay since the 25th May, the squadron had succeeded in destroying 28 enemy aircraft, with nine probables. Also there was the loss of Squadron Leader Stephenson (Prisoner of War), two pilots killed Pilot Officer Watson and Sergeant Irwin, and one wounded, Pilot Officer Lyne.

19th June 1940

The squadron turned its attention to the early night raiders over the UK and on 19th destroyed 2 Heinkel He111s at night.

At 0020 hours, five aircraft were ordered up individually. Flight Sergeant Steere met no enemy aircraft. Flying Officer Petre, Flight Lieutenant Clouston, Flying Officer Ball and Pilot Officer Lawson were all ordered to investigate a raid near Mildenhall.

Flying Officer Petre sighted the enemy aircraft first near Newmarket and shadowed it in the direction of Bury St Edmunds. He was about to open fire when he saw a Blenhiem in the way. He had to sheer off to one side and made a quarter attack allowing deflection. He saw his tracer hit one engine which poured out volumes of black smoke. At this moment, he was caught in a searchlight, and an exploding bullet from the rear gunner of the enemy aircraft hit his petrol tank. He was forced to jump from his blazing Spitfire. He landed safely, but was badly burned about the face and hands. The Heinkel crashed in flames near the Newmarket – Royston Road. Three prisoners were taken from the enemy aircraft, the fourth being dead as he failed to use his parachute.

Flight Lieutenant Clouston was ordered to return.

Flying Officer Ball was instructed to investigate a raid over Newmarket. He found the enemy aircraft illuminated by searchlights and recognised it to be a Heinkel 111. Over Colchester he attacked from dead astern, closing from 200 yards to 50 yards. He broke away and repeated his attack by which time the enemy aircraft was enveloped in clouds of smoke and loosing height. Immediately afterwards the searchlights lost the enemy aircraft and he returned to base. The enemy aircraft crashed at Margate, with all the crew being killed.

From :-   R.A.F. Station, Duxford, Cambs.    SECRET

To :-   Headquarters, No. 12 Group.

Date :-   20th June, 1940.   COPY

Ref :-   Dux/S.311/4/Int.

Report of Night Combat on Night of
18/19th June, 1940.

1.   This morning I visited Flying Officer G.W.Petre of
No. 19 Squadron, in the General Hospital, Bury St. Edmonds, and
obtained the following combat report which is forwarded for your
information:

2.   "Whilst on patrol between Ely and Newmarket an
enemy aircraft was sighted in the vicinity of Newmarket.   F/O
Petre shadowed it and, when between Newmarket and Bury St.
Edmonds, he was just about to fire when he saw a Blenheim in the
way.   He then sheered off to one side and came in on the quarter
of the enemy aircraft firing a burst in a deflection shot.   He
saw his tracer going into the enemy and immediately afterwards
one engine poured out volumes of black smoke where his tracer was
going into it.   At this moment our searchlights caught and held
F/O Petre with the result that the enemy gunner had an
illuminated target and opened fire.   The Spitfire was hit by
what is thought to be an explosive bullet and caught fire.   The
enemy aircraft caught fire immediately afterwards and came down
in flames near the Duxford - Newmarket road, about 1 mile east of
Six Mile Bottom.

3.   F/O Petre jumped by parachute after being badly
burned about the face and hands.   Flight Lt. W.G. Clouston who
was also stalking this enemy aircraft, saw another Spitfire
attack an enemy (which proved to be a Heinkel 111), and confirms
that the enemy aircraft was brought down by the Spitfire just
before he saw the Spitfire catch fire."

4.   As Flying Officer Petre is on the "Dangerously
Ill" list and it would be unwise for him to have many visitors
for some days, this report is forwarded to all concerned in lieu
of the normal Combat Report.

                    (Signed) A.B. WOODHALL,
                        Wing Commander,
                    Commanding, R.A.F. Station,
                    DUXFORD.   Cambs.

Copies to :-   Senior Intelligence Officer, Headquarters,
                        No. 12 Group.
                Senior Intelligence Officer, R.A.F. Station,
                        DUXFORD.

June 1940

At the end of the month the first cannon–armed Spitfires (Mk Ib's) joined the Squadron and it was thrown into service trails with this new weapon. The first cannon Spitfire delivered was R6762.

1st July 1940

Squadron Leader Pinkham gave a lecture on the merits and demerits of the cannon equipped Spitfire. It was evident that new attacks would have to be developed to cope with the disadvantages and make full use of the advantages of the new armament.

The Squadron was to be entirely re–equipped with the cannon Spitfires though so far we have but three.

The disadvantages at the moment;
1. Stoppages too frequent. Stoppages on one cannon make it very difficult to keep a steady sight with the other.
2. Firing period restricted to six seconds making defence against other fighter aircraft very difficult.
3. Lack of spread.

The advantages;
1. Terrific destructive power
2. High Muzzle velocity decreasing the amount of deflection necessary in deflection shooting.
3. Increased range and accuracy.

4th July 1940

Training flights carried out during the morning to form new attacks devised by the CO, as a solution to the problem of restricted firepower of the cannon Spitfire. "A" Flight dived in echelon from 2,000 ft above and to the side of three target aircraft, to dead astern, closing rapidly and gaining a very steady sight for the two cannon at high speed. Break away carried out downwards and to the side. The attack being then renewed from above and to the side again. One big advantage is that the German bombers often fly just beneath cloud base. "B" flight continued these practices in the afternoon. The new squadron formation was posted up in diagrammatic form in the dispersal hut. It is based on sections of two aircraft in line astern and is highly manoeuvrable. Group has taken a great deal of interest in it and the other squadrons are trying it out.

5th July 1940

Training flights of air firing carried out by the whole Squadron at Sutton Bridge. Experienced pilots firing cannon or machine guns at cone targets, while new pilots fired machine guns at ground targets. Stoppages feared in the cannons were all too evident. Chiefly ejection stoppages which were largely overcome by fitting of a rubber pad to the downward deflection plate which prevented the used round from rebounding and being trapped by the forward movement of the breech block. Only one cannon shell hit the cone.

LAC F.V. Roberts recalls;

"None of the armourers on the Squadron had any knowledge of the Hispano 20mm cannons at this time. Myself and an LAC from "B" Flight were sent on a weeks course on the cannons to Manby. We were expected to pass on our knowledge to all the other armament personnel when we returned. The cannon stoppages we had were numerous and unsolvable by us. The armourers suffered from these cannons, not only from the work these stoppages caused, but from the criticism we had to take from all.

Around the time of Dunkirk, while the Squadron were at Duxford, there had been erected a sand bagged protected machine gun post where the old watch tower had stood on the Station Flight Hangar. This particular morning being manned by 'Ginger' Hunt, one of the 19 Squadron's assistant armourers. In 19 Squadron's hangar stood a fully armed Spitfire, guns all loaded and cocked, hangar doors open and – coincidence – the gun sight more or less aligned on the gun post. Pickles, one of our maintenance Flight armourers, (actually he did office work,) was detailed to instruct a new member of the section, a recent boy entrant, on the lay out and maintenance procedure on Spit's. During his instructions, Pickles sat in the cockpit, the young man stood on the wing root – "To fire the guns, young lad, you turn this ring and press this button". The eight guns sounded terrific in the hangar. The armourer on the Station Flight hangar wasn't hurt but it wasn't only punctured and leaking sandbags that needed changing.

Later, one afternoon in September, we had Flight Sergeant Unwin's Spitfire up on trestles in "A" Flight blister hangar. There was a scamble call, and along with all the other pilots came Flight Sergeant Unwin, yelling and swearing for his plane. The plane was having a minor overhaul, gun panels and engine panels removed, ammo tank panels hanging down, guns unloaded and work being carried out on engine and airframe. I am sure we held the record for bringing a plane to serviceability after that. He was airborne in less than ten minutes, across wind and no engine warm up. I don't know if he caught the rest of the Squadron up or took on the Luftwaffe on his own, but it showed the courage of the man, and the confidence he placed in his groundcrew".

7th July 1940

Constant speed airscrews being fitted to all the machine gun Spitfires in turn. All the cannon Spitfires have them already on arrival. Performance now is vastly superior. Take off run shortened, flying far more rapid at a lower airspeed, petrol consumption down and surging at 2,100 revs eliminated by setting the revs above or below that figure as required.

It returned to ops, at first convoy patrols but soon it was fully into the Battle of Britain and hampered at this stage by frequent cannon stoppages on the aircraft:

9th July 1940

Red and Yellow Section ordered up on patrol at 1725 hours. Yellow section patrolled Watton at 15,000 ft. Red section were unable to take off after Red 3 taxied into Red 1. Red 3 being placed under open arrest.

Pilot Officer Peter Howard-Williams (Red 3) recalls;

"The Squadron was ordered to scramble as there were reports of enemy aircraft approaching the airfield. The twelve aircraft of 19 Squadron taxied out to form up for a typical Squadron take off. We had a grass airfield and no runways. I was due to fly Red 3, and coming up to tuck in on Red 1's left prior to take-off, I found I was taxying too fast in my enthusiasm and hit his tail. I was placed under open arrest which gave me 48 hours rest and a couple of mornings lying-in.

I subsequently appeared before Air Vice Marshal Leigh-Mallory, the A.O.C. of 12 Group, who endorsed my log book in red ink for "carelessness". Many months later, the Air Vice Marshal came to visit the Squadron, and was introduced to the pilots. When he came to me he said: 'I know you – how are you?' and we had several minutes conversation. It was obvious he knew me from somewhere, but couldn't remember where. I wasn't going to remind him!!! A few weeks later (March 1941) I was posted to help 118 Squadron at Filton, and became a Flight Commander. A classic example of it not mattering why your name is remembered – as long as it is.

George Unwin, who now lives within a few miles of me, says that this incident was the nearest he ever came to being killed during the war."

<table>
<tr><td>*10th July 1940*</td><td>## THE BATTLE OF BRITAIN</td></tr>
</table>

11th July 1940

The whole Squadron began convoy patrol in relays of sections, Red, Yellow, Blue, Green, the last finding it necessary to land at Coltishall owing to the rapid approach of darkness. Large convoy steaming north a few miles east of Ipswich.

13th July 1940

1800 hours "A" Flight orbited base at 18,000 ft for 20 minutes. After their return, Flight Sergeant Steere took up Sergeant Birch now on the point of becoming operational after sickness, for dogfighting experience. Sergeant Birch very unfortunately dived into the ground from a steep turn at 2,000 feet. His aircraft (R6688) caught fire but he had been killed outright.

14th July 1940

The whole squadron practiced Squadron Leader Pinkham's new formation of pairs line astern. At once attractive to watch and easy to manoeuvre.

22nd July 1940

"A" Flight sent to advance base at Coltishall. Red section did a patrol from there and returned to base at 0915, followed shortly afterwards by Yellow section who merely returned to base after a vain wait at Coltishall. This was part of a new policy to give the cannon Spitfires a chance to operate from the coast and prove their worth in action and also to relieve No. 66 Squadron to a certain extent.

24th July 1940

"A" Flight prepared to move from Duxford, where the squadron set up more or less permanent house. During its previous stay at Fowlmere, from the 25th June to 3rd July, two Nissan huts alone had been available for the squadron. Now established we settled down to enjoy the excellent messing facilities. Sub Lieutenant Blake became Messing Officer. The irrepressible Pilot Officer Howard-Williams restarted his excellent bar.

28th July 1940

Red Section went up for an hour and five minutes. Severe icing conditions encountered. Sub Lieutenant Blake sighted a Junkers 88 flying in the opposite direction. The section gave chase but lost the enemy aircraft in the cloud and found it again, whereupon the Junkers pilot executed violent turns, doubtless to verify the rear gunners excited shouts, put his nose down and escaped into cloud at full boost,pouring smoke from his engines.

Sergeant Roden (Yellow 3) crashed on landing, he overturned at the end of his landing run, but was uninjured.

31st July 1940

Flight Lieutenant B.J.E. Lane was awarded the Distinguished Flying Cross and the squadron celebrated in the appropriate manner.

2nd August 1940

At 11.15 off the Norfolk coast. Blue section of "B" Flight led by Flight Lieutenant Clouston intercepted a Hienkel 111. Each member of the section managed a good burst at the enemy aircraft. Flight Lieutenant Clouston, who had an eight gun aircraft disabled the starboard engine and possibly killed the rear gunner. The enemy aircraft carried out evasive tactics, making full use of the cloud cover to escape.

4th August 1940

Pilot Officer Sutherland who was on an AFDU course at Northolt was today killed in a Blenheim aircraft in which he was a passenger. Little is known of the accident.

Cannon firing has been carried out and many stoppages have been experienced, most of them in the first case due to the ejection being from the side instead of from the bottom as should be the case. This is of course being caused by the cannon being placed on its side. The squadron armourers are busy working fitting deflector plates but the trouble has not yet been obviated. Undoubtedly, with careful sighting and firing at correct range amazing accuracy can be obtained but in the meantime the present stoppages must be eliminated.

11th August 1940

New Spitfires equipped with two cannons and four Browning guns delivered today. It is slightly overweight but in the general opinion is a step in the right direction. Possibly another step in the right direction would be to re-equip with the old eight gun machines.

16th August 1940

The squadron on patrol at 1735 hours, were given vectors to intercept an enemy formation, 35 miles east of Harwich, at 12,000 feet. The investigation proved to be 150 enemy aircraft consisting of bombers and fighter escorts. The enemy aircraft were flying southwards, the bombers in front and the escorts of 40 to 50 Me110s behind, stepped up and a further escort of Me109s about 1,000 to 1,500 ft above.

"A" Flight attacked in two sections of three and four respectively. Flight Sergeant Unwin (Red 3) gave a Me110 a short burst at close range, which immediately half rolled and went down vertically. He was then attacked by another Me110 and took evasive action. On turning he found himself presented with a perfect target at 100 yards and fired all his ammunition into this enemy aircraft. The Me110 fell over onto its side with bits falling off. It then went into a steep dive and the tail came off. Flight Sergeant Unwin followed it down and coming through the clouds saw the end of a splash. This was despite a stoppage in his starboard cannon.

Sergeant Potter (Yellow 3) attacked several Me110s without success before he fired at one at very short range. He saw almost the whole of the enemy aircraft's starboard engine disappear. It flicked over to port and as it did so a large section of the front cabin broke away. His ammunition exhausted, he broke off the engagement.

Pilot Officer W. Cunningham (Yellow 4) attacked a Me110 which stall turned to the right and presented its underside as a sitting target. He fired a long burst at the Me110, which rolled over and dived vertically through cloud. Confirmed by Flight Lieutenant Lane who saw this Me110 still in a vertical dive as it entered cloud at 2,500 feet, and that the base of cloud was only 1,000 feet, as being out of control. Stoppage on starboard cannon after 30 rounds.

Three were definitely shot down and one probable. All Me110s. Sergeant Roden's aircraft had several bullet holes but no other damage was incurred. The Me110s when attacked, were successful in keeping us from the bombers. Generally speaking the enemy showed little enterprise, as far as could be observed, they had no rear gunners. Six of the seven aircraft engaged had stoppages in their cannons, the results would have been doubled at least had we been equipped with either the machine gun and cannon or the eight machine guns. During the engagement the Me109s did not attack.

19th August 1940

Green Section was given a vector sending them eight miles east of Aldeburgh at 1845 hours. They sighted a Me110 at 4,000 feet. Flying Officer Haines (Green 1) leading was informed by Sergeant Cox (Green 3), that there was an enemy aircraft ahead, approximately 1,000 feet higher. He recognised the enemy aircraft as being a Me110 and ordered line astern. The Me110 headed for a cloud and was attacked by Flight Sergeant Steere (Green 2) who followed it through the cloud. Flying Officer Haines climbed above the cloud and met the enemy aircraft on the other side. The Me110 was being attacked by a machine gun Spitfire just before he attacked but no apparent damage was being done. He made an attack from dead astern, opening fire at 350 yards and closing to 150 yards, by which time his cannons had stopped firing. He noticed a piece of main plane shot away and the port engine stopped dead. He then saw Sergeant Cox (Green 3) attacking and after he had broken away, the enemy aircraft slowly burst into flames and crashed into the sea. He noticed four people bale out,

Flying Officer L.A. Haines
(Peter Howard-Williams)

apparently all from the enemy aircraft which suggests that the Me110 was a Me Jaguar.[*]

Flight Sergeant Steere (Green 2) followed the Me110 into cloud but it was fully visible all the time. He opened fire at 300 yards closing to 100 yards. Lumps flew off the port engine and the airscrew stopped dead. He made a second attack after (Green 1 and 2) and noticed a glow appear from the port engine. By the time he made his third attack, the enemy aircraft was well alight and he followed it down and watched it burst into flames on the sea. After the combat he noticed an aircraft from No 66 Squadron in difficulties and about 11 miles from the coast, it started to loose height and glycol smoke appeared. The pilot baled out. Flight

---

[*] Me Jaguar – Extensive research has failed to find this aircraft type.
Sergeant D.G.S.R. Cox (Wing Commander DFC) writes:
"There was no such aeroplane. It was one of those 'mystic' aeroplanes that never was. I am certain that we did not shoot down a Me110 but a Dornier 17Z. My reasons are that four people baled out – the Me110 only had a crew of two, and it was much larger than a Me110. I had a good view of the aircraft as it dived into the sea. The wing tips were rounded, whereas the Me110 has square wing tips. At the time I said I thought it was a Dornier but was told not to talk nonsense!! Who was I, a very junior Sergeant Pilot to argue with a very senior Flying Officer."
German sources reveal that no Me110 was shot down on this day but a Dornier Do 17Z of 7/KG2 was shot down into the sea at 8.20pm near Yarmouth.

Sergeant Steere circled and then headed for Orford Ness Lighthouse. He got them to put out a dinghy and lifeboat, directed them towards the pilot. It took 50 minutes for them to reach the pilot. By this time he was short of fuel and had to land at Wattisham.

Sergeant Cox (Green 3) saw Flight Sergeant Steere (Green 2) attack the enemy aircraft just before it entered cloud. Sergeant Cox was slightly above and dived to the line astern position, but found himself too near for a favourable sight, fired only a short burst and broke away. As he did so Flying Officer Haines (Green 1) attacked from above. Sergeant Cox then came at the enemy aircraft form underneath and astern and opened fire from 500 yards. He then noticed tracers from the enemy aircraft going past his port wing. He straightened out and was dead astern, closing to 250 yards as he opened fire for two to three seconds. As he started firing he noticed another cannon machine slightly above him and on his starboard which had just finished an attack. Whilst in the middle of his attack the enemy aircraft's port engine burst into flames. Three parachutes then left the enemy aircraft as it turned slowly over on its starboard wing and dived in flames vertically into the sea.

20th August 1940

Spitfire R6833 the first machine in the Squadron to have VHF fitted. Flight Sergeant Sydney brought the aircraft from Wittering.

24th August 1940

The Squadron scrambled at 1545 hours from Fowlmere, and with 310 and 66 Squadrons were despatched to assist 11 Group. They were vectored to a formation of 50 enemy aircraft over the Thames Estuary, where at 1610 hours they sighted an enemy formation at 15,000 feet, consisting of 40 Me110s and Do215s, and above them ten Me109s. Only 19 Squadron made contact with the enemy. "A" Flight attacked the Me110s from behind, they being on the same level as the bombers. Green section "B" Flight made contact with the Me109s above the main formation.

Flight Lieutenant B.J.E. Lane (Red 1) approached the Dornier 215s from below and almost got within range when the Me110s sighted his section and turned towards them. A dog fight ensued and he opened fire from below and astern of a Me110 but was forced to break away as tracers appeared above his head from an enemy aircraft astern of him. This tracer appeared to be hitting the enemy aircraft he had been firing at, but he observed no result. Flight Lieutenant Lane then got below another Me110 and fired with slight deflection at the port engine and observed a part of the engine or mainplane fly off. The Me110 dived down and he watched it crash in the sea. After this fight he found a lone Me110 flying east with its port engine out of action. He attacked but found he had no ammunition left.

Sergeant B.J. Jennings (Yellow 2) attacked four Me110s in loose formation. His first burst knocked the top of the starboard engine and propeller off. The Me110 went down in a vicious engine turn to starboard, and was out of control. He then attacked another Me110, firing a fairly long burst, saw a piece of his tail fall off the starboard side, complete with the starboard section of his rudder. The enemy aircraft swung round and dived away to port out of sight but must be regarded as a total loss. He then found two Me110s in front of him but as he attacked these, his port gun jammed. On his next attack, his starboard gun jammed, so he returned to base.

Three of the Me110 were shot down. Green section stopped the Me109 from diving down on the flight trying to reach the bombers. Only two aircraft were able to fire off their complete armament of cannon.

19 Squadron Pilots at Fowlmere

LEFT TO RIGHT: Sqdn Ldr Lane, Sgt Lane, Sgt Potter, Sgt Jennings, P/O Aeberhardt, F/Sgt Unwin, F/Sgt Steere, F/O Brinsden, F/Lt Lawson, F/O Haines, P/O Vokes, F/Lt Clouston, Sgt Fulford?

(Peter Howard-Williams)

29th August 1940

According to information given us this day, the German formations are now keeping much closer and stepping up their "vics" in such fashion that the fire from the rear is quite devastating. Attacks were practiced mostly from the front quarter to find if any improved method could be obtained. Passing speed in head on attack rather frightening and leaves little time for sighting.

31st August 1940

The Squadron was patrolling Duxford and Debden at 20,000 feet at 0830 hours, when they were vectored south to intercept a formation of enemy aircraft. At 0845 hours, Blue Section sighted a large formation of 60 to 100 enemy aircraft, consisting of Dornier 215s, Me110s and Me109s, south of Colchester at 12,000 feet.

Blue section led by Flight Lieutenant Clouston and Green section led by Flying Officer Coward attacked.

Sergeant Cox (Blue 3) engaged in a dog fight with the Me110s. He managed to get astern of one and gave it a burst of three seconds. The enemy aircraft turned slightly to port and dived vertically downwards, with the port engine belching thick black smoke. He was unable to watch this enemy aircraft, by having to take evasive action from other attacking enemy aircraft.

Flight Lieutenant Clouston and Flying Officer Burgoyne shared an Me110.

Flying Officer F. Brinsden was shot up, baled out but with no injuries to himself. (R6958).

Pilot Officer Aeberhardt's aircraft (R6912) was damaged during the combat and when he attempted to land, his flaps did not operate. The machine turned over and was burnt out. Pilot Officer Aeberhardt was killed.

Flying Officer J.B. Coward (Green 2) during combat just south of Duxford was wounded and baled out of his machine (X4231).

The score would definitely have been higher given eight machine gun aircraft.

Flying Officer J.B. Coward (now Air Commodore, A.F.C.) recalls:

"The Squadron was scrambled from the dispersal airfield at Fowlmere at ten past eight in the morning. Flight Lieutenant Wilfred Clouston led the Squadron climbing in the direction of Debden. I was leading Green Section in his Flight and Frank Brinsden, led 'A' Flight. I had just glimpsed Debden through the mist on the port side when I spotted them almost dead ahead. I called out 'Tallyho Bandits ahead' and Wilfred led us slightly to starboard to carry out a Fighter Command No 1 Attack, turning in forming line astern and each section forming echelon port, to come up in threes behind the Dornier 217s who were in sections of three in Vic in line astern. 'A' Flight he ordered to climb up and try and hold the German Fighters (Messerschmidt 110s). I opened fire with a slight deflection shot as I closed in on the Dornier on the right of the second German section. Just after I had opened fire, I felt a bang on my left leg (about like a kick on the shin). As I was closing fairly fast I only glanced and saw my bare foot on the rudder pedal. When I opened fire I only got off a short burst and the guns stopped firing. Presumably whatever hit me must have affected the air pressure to the guns. The aircraft went into a gentle bunt gathering speed – the control column had no effect. At the time I thought that I had hit the aircraft I was attacking for my hood tore off. It could have been from gunfire. Leading a section into a No 1 Attack one was under fire from three rear gunners of the three bombers one was attacking, plus the front gunners of the three enemy aircraft in the section slightly above and behind, apart from the enemy fighters trying to protect them, so I could have been hit by any one of them. At the time I thought it must have been AcAc fire.

When I baled out I was sucked out of my seat but my parachute got caught on the back of the cockpit, so that my arms were blown back along the side of the aircraft, my gloves blew off and my foot was painfully blowing about near my thigh. I suddenly blew clear and started to do a delayed drop to get down quickly, but could not stop falling ahead over heels so that my severed foot kept twisting most painfully, so I pulled the ripcord. I think I was at about 20,000 feet when I baled out. When the parachute opened, I found I was swinging in a big figure eight and I could see my blood, which seemed a very bright red, pulsing out in big squirts and I realised I had to do something quickly to survive. My First Aid packet was in the breast pocket of my uniform and the parachute straps were so tight over my chest that I could not get at it, so I used the radio lead from my helmet to tie a tourniquet round my thigh. I was able to reduce the bleeding to a slight drip by holding my knee up under my chin. I spent some time turning round so that I was facing the direction of drift. I floated over Duxford in the direction of Fowlmere. At about 8,000 feet the wind changed almost 180 degrees and I had to turn again. Several Spitfires circled round me giving an encouraging wave, and I came down in a field by the roundabout, just beyond the Red Lion at Whittlesford. As I was pulling the parachute up under my damaged leg to keep it out of the dirt, a young fellow of about 16 came dashing up pointing a pitchfork at me, obviously thinking I was a German. I told him to 'so and so' off and fetch me a Doctor. Luckily the first car he stopped was a Doctor from the local AcAc unit who sent his driver off to fetch the necessary. He returned in about 15 minutes saying 'I'm sorry sir, but I could not get any morphia because the orderly Corporal went on leave last night and must have taken the key of the Poisons cupboard with him'. As a matter of fact I was not suffering much pain from my damaged leg, but was in considerable pain from the burns under my arms and crutch from being soaked in petrol. How lucky the aircraft did not catch fire. Funnily enough, after three weeks in hospital and a year and a half on Mr Churchill's personal staff and some flying refresher, I was Chief Instructor at No 55 Operational Training Unit at Annan, when a student on a new course said 'Do you remember me Sir'? It turned out he was the young man who had found me when I was shot down."

3rd September, 1940

As the squadron went into battle, six out of eight aircraft had gun stoppages. This ended the experiment with the cannon and the following day it reverted to 8 machine-gun Spitfire Ia's.

Eight Spitfires of the Squadron were ordered to patrol between Duxford and Debden at 20,000 feet. Operating in pairs, all aircraft were fitted with two cannons except Green Leader which had eight machine guns. The squadron was still climbing to their height of 20,000 feet, when they were warned by sector controller of the enemy approaching from the south-east and later that they were over North Weald. On reaching 20,000 feet they saw explosions and clouds of smoke from North Weald. There were 50/60 bombers at 20,000 feet, escorted by 100 fighters stretching from 20,000 to 25,000 feet, with a single fighter ahead of and above the whole formation.

Squadron Leader Pinkham (Blue 1) led the attack at two enemy aircraft and had fired only ten rounds from each gun when they jammed.

Pilot Officer E. Burgoyne (Blue 2) took the right-hand enemy aircraft and his starboard gun jammed. He was then attacked by two Me110s, but shook them off. He then attacked another enemy aircraft and his port gun also jammed. He had fired 40 rounds from the port gun and 16 from starboard before gravity stoppages in each gun.

Flying Officer Haines (Green 1) attacked the leading fighter which was by itself in front of and above the bombers. It dived towards the bombers for protection so he broke off the attack. He then noticed two Me110's on his right and just below so he immediately closed to a range of 250 yards and opened fire on one while the other dived away. The enemy aircraft was camouflaged greyish above with black crosses on main planes and egg shell blue underneath. After a burst of 5 seconds, during which the enemy aircraft employed various evasive tactics, he noticed some smoke coming from the port engine. The Me110 dived vertically towards the Thames and he followed it down. It flattened out and headed towards Whitstable at about 50 feet off the water. When near Whitstable the Me110 turned back and headed towards the mouth of the Thames. Two lines of tracer fire coming from the rear turret were passing beneath him at the commencement of his attack. He fired the rest of his ammunition from 100 yards dead astern and noticed a piece of fabric fly off. The enemy aircraft plunged into the sea.

Pilot Officer Vokes (Green 2) stayed with Flying Officer Haines (Green 1) and prepared to attack the same enemy aircraft but when he saw it destroyed he returned to base.

Flight Sergeant G.C. Unwin (Red 1) saw the single enemy fighter in front turn towards (Blue 1) during Squadron Leader Pinkham's attack. He pursued it and closing to 100 yards, blew the port engine out of the wing. The Me110 continued to fly. He attacked it again with the port gun, his starboard having jammed after 6 rounds. The starboard engine fell off and one occupant baled out. The Me110 crashed south of Maldon near Battles Bridge.

Sergeant H.A.C. Roden (Red 2) fired at several enemy aircraft but could claim no result. He reckoned he was using too much deflection.

Sub Lieutenant Blake (Yellow 1) carried out a quarter attack from above and on port side of the formation. The enemy aircraft turned violently away and downwards. He then had to take evasive action to avoid two Me110s who were attacking him. Both his guns had stoppages. He had fired only 33 rounds from the port and 14 rounds from the starboard guns.

Pilot Officer Cunningham (Yellow 2) followed his leader into the attack, but fired only 9 from port and 4 from starboard before his guns jammed.

Sub Lieutenant Blake had a probable Me110.

The squadron were very pleased to hear from C in C that they were to be re-equipped with the eight gun Spitfires in a day. No. 611 Squadron from Digby came over to Fowlmere and stood by for the squadron for the change over.

5th September 1940

Eleven Spitfires of the Squadron led by Squadron Leader Pinkham took off at 0947 hours to patrol Hornchurch at 15,000 feet. The enemy formation of 40 Dornier 215s and 40 Me109s were sighted over the Chatham/Ashford/Medway/Maidstone quadrilateral.

Squadron Leader Pinkham (Blue 1) was seen engaging three Do215 and is a casualty.

Pilot Officer Burgoyne (Blue 2) attacked individually a rear section of three Dornier 215s. Closing from 400 to 150 yards, he met experienced fire from a single gun in the port bomber. He noticed fragments falling from the Dornier but was forced to break off the attack as he received hits himself from cannon fire from the rear. He did not see his attacker but his empenage, elevator and rudder had serious damage and the auxiliary controls were useless.

Pilot Officer W.J. Lawson (Black 1) followed Blue section to attack three Do215s. He opened fire with a two second burst from astern, which caused the enemy aircraft to lurch to the right, drop starboard wing and dive away downwards apparently out of control, with every appearance of crashing. He was then attacked from the rear, his port plane was hit. He broke away quickly and found himself on the tail of an Me109, at which he fired a short burst at 300 yards, causing the enemy aircraft to go into a vertical dive. Pilot Officer Lawson was again attacked from the rear, his tailplane and port wing were damaged so he returned to base.

Pilot Officer Dolezal (Black 2) attacked the same Dornier formation as Pilot Officer Lawson from astern. He engaged some Me109s but with indecisive results.

Flying Officer Haines (Green 1) whilst following Squadron Leader Pinkham into the enemy formation was attacked by two Me109s. He did a steep turn and as the Messerschmitt 109s dived past him, he opened up his engine and chased the second one. He waited until he was at 200 yards range opened fire. After a five second burst, the enemy aircraft's engine began passing puffs of smoke. The pilot dived for the ground and began hedge hopping. Flying Officer Haines kept within range firing the rest of his ammunition, when the enemy aircraft burst into flames. He was over the fields and approaching Ashford, when the Messerschmitt climbed up to 800 feet and the pilot baled out. He came down safely in a field, while the Me109 crashed in flames in the garden of a house.

Sergeant Plzak (Green 2) singled out one enemy diving to escape attack by another squadron and got in two bursts from rear and above at the belly of the enemy, which had turned upside down. He saw black smoke emerge but had to break away on being attacked by two other enemy aircraft. He escaped by diving and doing an Immelhank turn. (This is presumably a misinterpretation – or a 19 colloqualism of the day for 'Immelmann').

The five Spitfires of "A" Flight formed a line astern and climbed in a wide circle towards the Messerschmitt 109s at 20,000 feet. The Messerschmitts were joining up for an attack on "B" Flight, but just as "A" Flight completed its turn towards the sun the fighters vanished and were not seen again.

Squadron Leader Pinkham (P9422) – is missing.

Flight Lieutenant B.J.E. Lane promoted to Squadron Leader and assumed command of the Squadron.

THE DUXFORD WING

The Duxford Wing (glamourised as the Bader Wing in "Reach for the Sky") started as a three-squadron operation, 242 & 310 Hurricane squadrons would climb to 20,000 feet, their best operating height. The Spitfires of 19 would be positioned 4,000 to 5,000 feet above to tackle the Me109s, whilst the Hurricanes attack the bombers. After the original idea and some discussion between the Squadron COs, Bader of 242, Blackwood of 310 and Lane of 19, they flew three or four practice sorties to test out the theory. The method of operation was uncomplicated. 242 and 310 Squadron of Hurricanes took off from Duxford. At the same time, 19 Squadron took off from Fowlmere. There was no joining up over the airfield, they turned straight on course, climbing quickly, while the other squadrons took position. The Hurricanes flew in line astern together, while the Spitfires flew 3,000 to 4,000 feet above, behind and to one side. The idea was that the Spitfire, with their better performance, would guard the Hurricanes against interference by Messerschmitt 109s, while they attacked the enemy formations. If there were no enemy fighters, the Spitfires would come down on the bombers after the Hurricanes had broken them up.

Flying Officer F.N. Brindsen (now Wing Commander (Retd) writes:-

"I was never a fan of the Bader 'Balbos', considering them time wasting in assembly and cumbersome in operation. In any case the formations fragmented when battle was joined, so why waste precious time assembling them? Far the most efficient, were to 'finger' the formations which wasted no time in assembly, were flexible in the air and freed the eyes for searching. Finally, I believe there can be no doubt that a clash of personalities at Group

Squadron Leader B.J.E. Lane
(Crown Copyright – MOD – IWM)

Command level, combined with giving way to Douglas Bader on the tactical use of the Duxford Wing inhibited the skills of some first class and experienced fighter pilots."

7th September 1940

The day the Duxford Wing flew its first offensive patrol, consisting of 19,242 and 310 Squadrons.

Towards five o'clock that evening, more than 300 bombers and many hundreds of fighters headed for London. The Duxford Wing was scrambled. The eight Spitfires of 19 saw a force of 20 bombers escorted by 50 fighters flying past at 15,000 feet.

Squadron Leader Lane (Red 1) dived after a Me110 which had passed in front of him. This enemy aircraft was being attacked by two Hurricanes. He fired a short burst at it whilst other aircraft were attacking at the same time. The crew of two baled out of the Me110 but one parachute failed to open. The enemy aircraft crashed one mile east of Hornchurch.

Flight Sergeant Unwin (Red 3) followed Red leader and attacked the Me110. He found himself alone after the combat, climbed to 25,000 feet and saw a Hurricane Squadron going somewhere in a hurry. He trailed them and suddenly saw three separate formations of 30 enemy aircraft each with escorts. The Hurricanes attacked the bombers and Flight Sergeant Unwin found himself surrounded by Me109s. The usual fight ensued, during which he definitely hit at least five of them but only two were definitely shot down in flames. He then climbed to 25,000 feet for a breather and shadowed an enemy formation. This force was at 20,000 feet and being attacked accurately by AA fire which scored two decisive hits. As there didn't seem to be any of their escorts left, he dived onto the rear vic of bombers and used up the last of his ammunition. The enemy aircraft wobbled but carried on.

Pilot Officer W. Cunningham (Yellow 2) attacked an Me110 and as he broke off, 'blacked out' and lost formation. He climbed and joined up with some Hurricanes (TQ Squadron letters). They flew east and attacked an enemy formation of 24 Heinkel 111s. He singled out one Heinkel 111, attacking from astern. The enemy aircraft set ablaze, and he attacked again from below, after which it began to lose height rapidly and crashed ten miles inland from Deal or Ramsgate. He climbed again and found three He111 proceeding east. He attacked from astern and fired two bursts at the leader. Whitish smoke started to come from his tail but it did not lose height. Unable to continue the attack having run out of ammunition, he returned to base.

"B" Flight were out of range by the time they had climbed to the level of the enemy formations. Blue 1 and 2 returned to base without firing.

Pilot Officer Dolezal (Blue 3) got onto the tail of an Me110 approaching Margate. The enemy aircraft turned after a Spitfire and Pilot Officer Dolezal turned inside it and gave it a full burst. The Me110 went into a spiral dive and crashed into the sea. He then attacked three He111s, hitting one which started to omit heavy smoke from its starboard engine. Having exhausted all his ammunition he broke off the combat.

The Wing's tally for the day was; 20 destroyed, five probables and six damaged.

The Wing's losses were four destroyed, one damaged, one pilot killed.

The Squadron suffered no losses.

One Spitfire pilot said that there were so many enemy fighters layered up to 30,000 feet, it was like looking up an escalator at Piccadilly Circus.

9th September 1940

The same three squadrons scrambled at 1700 hours.

Nine Spitfires of 19 saw the enemy initially as the Luftwaffe were flying north-west.

Flight Lieutenant W.G. Clouston (Blue 1) was leading the Squadron at 1800 hours, when they encountered a large formation (hundreds) of enemy aircraft in the London area at 20,000 feet. Having been detailed to attack the fighters, he was preparing to attack seven Me110s, when two Me109s crossed his sights, so he turned onto them. He fired a short burst at the rear one, which emitted glycol and then burst into flames. He continued onto the second Me109 and finished the rest of his ammunition. He could see his shots hitting this aircraft and when his ammunition had run out, saw it go down in a left hand gliding turn 'looking rather the worse for wear'.

Flight Sergeant Steere (Blue 2) was line astern when he cut across in front of Flight Lieutenant Clouston (Blue 1) and Flight Lieutenant Burgoyne (Blue 3) to attack six Me110s. He closed in giving a full deflection shot and saw his tracers going home. The Me110 started to slip inwards in a very peculiar attitude and Flight Sergeant Steere was forced to break underneath him. This Me110 was seen by Flight Lieutenant Clouston to go down in a lefthand spiral, completely out of control. Flight Sergeant Steere then chased another Me110 half way across the channel but had to break off when the guns on the French coast looked uncomfortably close.

Flight Lieutenant Burgoyne stayed with Flight Lieutenant Clouston and so did not take part in the main attack: he preferred to protect his leader which he did successfully.

Flight Lieutenant W.J. Lawson (Red 1) sighted an Me110 on his starboard, about 2,000 feet below. He turned to starboard and dived onto his tail and got in a short burst at 300 yards. Then ensued a really enjoyable dogfight which ended by Flight Lieutenant Lawson hitting the starboard engine, causing it to stop. The Me110 started to lose height and pieces fell away from his starboard wing, as he went down in a slow spiral turn. He finally crashed five miles east of Biggin Hill.

Sub-Lieutenant Blake (Red 2) reports a total of approximately 130 enemy aircraft consisting of Me110s, Me109s, He111s and Do215s. His combat report reads –

> "In the ensuing dogfight that followed, I didn't fire a round. So having turned myself inside out, I straightened up and followed the main enemy formation out to sea. Picked out a Heinkel 111 on the port side and behind the formation. Made a shallow dive out of the sinking sun and carried out an astern attack. Saw bits flying off and as I broke off observed him to be smoking and on fire".

Pilot Officer W. Cunningham (Red 3) after attacking the main formation with no visible results, broke formation to attack some Me110s when a stray Me109 (Yellow nose) passing right in front of him. He took up position on its tail and fired two very long bursts. The Me109 burst into flames and some parts of his engine flew out. Cunningham watched the destroyed

Me109 for a while and saw its pilot make no attempt to jump. On landing he found one bullet hole in the mainspar of his port wing.

Flying Officer F.N. Brinsden (Yellow 1) attacked the fighter escort of Me109s with Blue and Red Sections. In the first attack, he saw Flight Lieutenant Clouston destroy an Me109 which disappeared out of control. Still in line astern, the sections then climbed and attacked five Me110s which had formed a circle. Flying Officer Brinsden then attacked two Me109s, giving a long burst at about 15 degree deflection with no apparent results. He then joined a Hurricane in destroying a Heinkel 111, attacking from dead astern using all his ammunition up. He last saw the Heinkel 111, with its flaps and undercarriage out and both engines stopped. It was gliding on an easterly course a little south of Detling at 1,000 feet.

Pilot Officer A.F. Vokes (Yellow 2) dived to attack six Dornier 215s. He attacked the nearest which was becoming separated from the others and had its wheels down. He fired all his ammunition into the Dornier and saw bits coming off. As he turned for home out of ammunition he saw another Spitfire attacking the Dornier. Sergeant D.G. Cox (Yellow 3) attacked some Me110s in line astern and was then attacked by Me109s. During the dog fight that ensued, he managed to get onto the tail of a Me109. He fired two bursts at the Me109 which burst into flames and dived straight down.

The results were –   19: – 6 destroyed, 1 probable, 1 damaged
                     242: – 11 destroyed, 2 probables
                     310: – 4 destroyed, 2 probables, 1 damaged
Our losses were 4 destroyed, 3 damaged, and 2 pilots killed.

11th September 1940

At 1540 hours the Squadron took off, led by Squadron Leader Lane and formed a wing of 19, 266, 74 and 611 Squadrons. They climbed to 23,000 feet over North Weald and saw AA fire south of Gravesend and a large formation of enemy aircraft.

Squadron Leader Lane (Red 1) turned south and dived in a head-on attack on the leading formation of 12 Heinkel 111s. After this first attack he turned to port and saw the enemy turning south-east over Sittingbourne. There were now only seven He111s in formation with two Me110s escorts. He went for one of the Me110s from astern and saw large pieces flying off its starboard engine which stopped. On his second astern attack the starboard engine caught fire and the Me110 was last seen in a dive. The other caught fire and the Me110 was last seen in a dive. The other Me110 opened up and left the He111s. Squadron Leader Lane then carried out head-on and beam attacks without visible results, but an astern attack on the rear He111 saw its starboard engine catch fire. He had no more ammunition left and returned to base.

Sergeant Jennings (Red 2) after the first head-on attack on a He111, turned and saw its starboard engine burning. He fired again and it went down apparently out of control. "There was so much tracer whizzing past that I didn't stay to watch him crash". Having lost the rest of his formation, Sergeant Jennings then attacked a Me110 at the rear of a formation of 15. It fell back from the rest of the formation with smoke pouring from its starboard engine. He did another attack from above and behind. The Me110 crashed in a wood somewhere between Sittingbourne and Maidstone.

Sergeant H.A.C. Roden (Red 3) made an astern attack on the rearmost machine of about 30 Me110s milling round in a large circle. He dived with the sun behind him – came up from below and gave him a five second burst. As other Me110s were coming up from behind, he broke away. Pieces of the target aircraft flew off from the port mainplane, then smoke came from his port engine and it started a shallow dive. He was unable to keep his attention on the enemy aircraft as "my position was not very healthy".

Flight Sergeant Unwin (Red 4) attacked a He111 firing an eight second burst. Bits came off both engines and it went into a steep spiral. He then immediately attacked a Dornier 215, opening fire from below at 100 yards closing to 50 yards. Flight Sergeant Unwin fired all his rounds into the Dornier but could not see any result. His windscreen and engine had been shot up by fire from its bottom gunner. He dived away with smoke pouring from his Spitfire, switched off his engine and made a forced landing with his wheels down one mile north of Brentwood.

Flying Officer Haines (Green 1), climbed to engage 40 Me110s slightly higher than the Heinkels. The enemy aircraft went into a defensive circle when he attacked. He broke off the attack and waited until he noticed one a little lower than the rest. He closed to 200 yards and opened fire. The enemy aircraft's starboard engine burst into flames and it broke formation. He followed and gave the enemy aircraft a long burst and the port engine caught fire. Lots of pieces came away from the fuselage and port main planes. He had observed no rear fire from the enemy aircraft but was continually having to evade attacks by Me109s – which were painted yellow from spinner to cockpit – which dived on him from above. After the combat, Flying Officer Haines noticed several bullet holes in both main planes, but as the Spitfire appeared quite normal in flight, he climbed and endeavoured to engage some more Me110s. They went into a defensive circle on sighting him, starting to climb and headed towards the coast. He was unable to get in an attack and had to break off over Beachy Head. He crashed on landing as both tyres being punctured during the combat. He was not hurt. (X4059)

Pilot Officer Dolezal (Green 2) attacked a Me109 which had turned after a Spitfire. He got between the Me109 and the Spitfire, giving it a three second burst in a head-on attack. Black smoke poured from the enemy aircraft and it turned away to port. He turned to follow but in doing so got a full burst from the rear. His cockpit became full of oil and he had been slightly wounded by a splinter in the right knee. He landed back at base with the undercarriage pump and trim cable shot through.

Flight Sergeant H. Steere (Blue 1) fired at two Me110s with indecisive results. Sergeant D.G. Cox (Blue 2) was attacked from the rear by a Me109 but took evasive action. He then attacked a Me110, but had to break off that engagement as a Me110 attacked him. He then spotted a Dornier 215 a little way behind the rest of the formation. He made three attacks at this Do215 by which time its starboard engine had stopped. The Dornier was losing height but he had to break off the attack having run out of ammunition.

The Wings tally for this day was: 12 destroyed, 14 probables and 7 damaged.

Our losses were 3 destroyed, 3 damaged, 1 pilot killed and 1 wounded.

12th September 1940

Eight new (to us) aircraft arrived for the Squadron today – we need them badly.

13th September 1940

At 2155 hours Sergeant Potter took off and was on night patrol for an hour and 20 minutes. No enemy aircraft seen but London's new secret weapon, a solid block of AA fire looked most formidable.

14th September 1940

At 1600 hours the Squadron scrambled to patrol the London area with 242, 310 and 611 Squadrons but made no contact.

Sergeant Marek crashed through lack of oxygen. The actual reason is not known but he called up Pilot Officer Hradil, who was the only pilot in the section with VHF, and said that he had no oxygen. Sergeant Marek was killed. (R6625)

THE DAY IN THE BATTLE OF BRITAIN

The Duxford Wing were scrambled at 1122 hours and consisted of 19, 242, 302, 310 and 611 Squadrons. 242, 302 and 310 were heading south at 25,000 feet, with 19 and 611 Spitfires stepped up behind them at 26-27,000 feet. The Wing saw the enemy 3,000 feet below and down-sun. For once the Wing had position, height and numbers.

Douglas Bader described those minutes of the attack "At one time you could see planes all over the place, and the sky seemed full of parachutes. It was sudden death that morning, for our fighters shot them to blazes".

At 1215 hours the Squadron led by Flight Lieutenant Lawson saw an enemy formation of 20 bombers with escorts at 15,000 feet in the London area.

Flight Lieutenant Lawson (Blue) delivered a head-on attack at the Dornier 17s opening fire at 400 yards. He dived past the left-hand Dornier 17 of the rear vic of the enemy. Then he turned and attacked the same aircraft from the rear, opening fire at 300 yards closing to 50 yards. He saw pieces falling from the starboard wing and his starboard engine started streaming glycol. The Do17 was waffled away from the main formation and glided down with glycol still streaming from his starboard motor. He turned and attacked the main formation again but after a short burst at a Do17 his ammunition ran out.

Squadron Leader B.J.E. Lane, Sub-Lieutenant Blake and Pilot Officer W. Cunningham were flying in one section of "A" Flight.

Pilot Officer W. Cunningham (Blue 3) broke away from his section to attack a solitary Me110. His first attack from above and right rear quarter, set the enemy aircraft's starboard engine on fire. He broke away, turned in from the left and delivered another attack from the left hand side. He considered the Me110 as good as destroyed and broke off the attack. The enemy aircraft was then attacked by two Hurricanes who more or less shot him from the sky.

Flight Sergeant Unwin (Red 3) sighted the enemy formation in vics of three when the escorts dived on them singly. He engaged one Me109 with a yellow nose giving him a burst of six seconds. The enemy aircraft burst into flames and crashed between Redhill and Westerham. The pilot had baled out.

Flight Sergeant H. Steere (Red 4) turned to attack three or four Me109s. He fired at one but broke off to attack another in a more favourable position. He opened fire at 350 yards and closed to 50 yards. Thick bluish smoke enveloped the Me109 as it spiralled steeply into the clouds. Flight Sergeant Steere chased another Me109, closed on him but found that he had no ammunition left.

Flying Officer L.A. Haines (Green 1) put his section in line astern and made towards the AA fire when two Me109s appeared on his right. He turned and attacked one of them, which half rolled and dived vertically to 12,000 feet where it straighted out. He dived after it and recommenced his attack. Flying Officer Haines was flying faster than the Me109 and had to pull away to the right to avoid a collision. The Me109 half rolled and dived vertically with black smoke coming from underneath the pilot's seat. He followed it down until it entered cloud at 6,000 feet by then going at 480mph. Flying Officer Haines eased up and came through the cloud at a reasonable speed to find the wreckage burning furiously. It was painted yellow from spinner to cockpit. He then started to climb through cloud and narrowly missed colliding with a Ju88 which was on fire and being attacked by numerous Hurricanes.

Sergeant D.G. Cox (Green 3) saw six Me109s flying in line astern just above him. They saw him and attacked. He got on the tail of one but it half rolled away and escaped. He saw four flying south, turned to find the sixth attacking him head-on. As the enemy passed above Sergeant Cox, he turned and climbed steeply and came up underneath the Me109. He opened fire with a couple of bursts, stalling as he did so. Next he saw the Me109 was in a flat glide that gradually steepened. Sergeant Cox followed him down and saw him crash five miles east of Crowborough.

The morning's tally for the Wing was 26 destroyed.

The Wing landed, refuelled and was ordered up again at 1412 hours. Fifty six aircraft had taken part in the morning's combat but only 49 were available for the afternoon.

Squadron Leader B.J.E. Lane (Red 1) was leading 19 Squadron at 1450 hours when the enemy formation were sighted between 12,000 and 30,000 feet. His estimate of the number of enemy aircraft on his Combat Report reads "Whole Luftwaffe". He climbed astern of the bomber formation to engage the fighter escorts at 30,000 feet when three Me109s dived at him. A loose dog fight ensued with more Me109s coming down. Squadron Leader Lane could not get near to any of the immediate enemy aircraft, so climbed to taken on a formation of Me110s, without result. He then sighted two Me109s just above and attacked one of them. He got on its tail and fired several bursts of two seconds. The Me109 took violent evasive action and made for cloud cover. Squadron Leader Lane managed to get another burst of five seconds, the enemy aircraft flicked over inverted, and entered a cloud in a shallow inverted dive, apparently out of control. He then flew south and attacked two further formations of thirty Do215s from astern and head-on. The enemy aircraft did not appear to like head-on attacks as they jumped about a bit as he passed through.

Flight Sergeant G.C. Unwin (Red 3) with Squadron Leader Lane sighted a large number of enemy aircraft (bombers) and above seemed thousands of Me109s. He engaged an Me109 and gave him a three second burst at close range. He immediately half rolled and dived steeply into the clouds. Flight Sergeant Unwin followed but his windscreen froze up at 6,000 feet and he lost him. He then climbed back to 25,000 feet saw two Me109s passing over his head flying south-south-east. He chased them and caught them at Lydd. The first one he fired at burst into flames and went down, maybe on land, maybe just in the sea. He attacked the other and he went vertically down and crashed into the sea. Flight Lieutenant W.G. Clouston (Blue 1) took both Blue and Green Sections into attack a formation of Dornier 17s. He set the starboard engine of one afire and it went for cloud cover. He remained above the cloud, waited, and saw it in a gap. Flight Lieutenant Clouston made a beam attack as the Dornier emerged from cover and ten feet of the bomber's port wing snapped off. One of the enemy aircraft's crew baled out over a convoy 15 miles east of Burnham. He continued his attack until it went down towards the sea, rolling over and over to port.

Flight Sergeant H. Steere (Blue 2) followed Blue Leader into the Dornier 17s and singled out one on the right. He closed from 250 to 50 yards, giving several bursts. Several lumps flew off the Dornier, and the port engine caught fire. The crew baled out and the Dornier 'waffled' into the clouds, black smoke spreading rapidly. Three bombs were jettisoned before the aircraft was abandoned.

Pilot Officer Vokes (Green 2) saw Flight Sergeant Steere attack the Dornier and the crew baled out. He was surprised by an Me110 from astern. Tracer fire flashed past the starboard wing, one bullet going through the main spar. Pilot Officer Vokes climbed steeply and after two or three minutes finished up on its tail. He then 'gave him everything I had' closing from 200 to 50 yards. The starboard engine was streaming black smoke and he dived steeply. By the time it reached cloud it seemed to be out of control.

Flying Officer Haines (Green 1) as he was preparing to attack six Dornier 17, noticed five Me109s above and to his right. He climbed to attack the Me109s and they immediately formed a defensive circle. He managed to get a burst at one which did the usual half roll and dive. Flying Officer Haines followed it down to 15,000 feet when the enemy flattened out, closed in and let him have a five second burst from 200 to 50 yards. The Me109 burst into flames and disappeared into cloud in a vertical dive. Flying Officer Haines then reclimbed to 25,000 feet and patrolled the coast near Beachy Head. After a quiet five minutes he saw a lot of bombers being attacked by Hurricanes. The bombers were escorted by numerous Me110s which circled on sighting the Spitfire. He noticed two slightly behind the others closed to 250 yards and gave one a five second burst. The Me110's starboard engine burst into flames and he dived steeply. As he closed in to 150 yards, he was meeting return fire. He used the rest of his ammunition on the Me110 and at the end of his attack noticed the rear gun draped along the fuselage. Bits were coming off his starboard wing and the enemy aircraft just reached the French coast, where it crashed in flames on the beach. Flying Officer Haines then turned for home.

Flight Lieutenant W.J. Lawson led Yellow section.

Pilot Officer W. Cunningham (Yellow 3) attacked the main enemy formation, but was attacked from behind by Me109s. Sergeant Roden was hit in this attack. After an indecisive dogfight with an Me109, Pilot Officer Cunningham had a Hurricane come up on his tail. They then attacked an enemy formation, opening fire at 300 yards on the left hand machine. The Me109 dived through the clouds on fire.

Sergeant Potter (X4070) – is missing. It was later learnt that he had been wounded and was a Prisoner of War.

The afternoon's tally was 26 destroyed.

The Wing had virtually no losses in the morning's combat but we suffered 3 destroyed, 2 damaged, 2 pilots killed or missing, 3 wounded in the afternoon.

19 Squadron Spitfire being re-armed and refuelled during the Battle of Britain.

(Crown Copyright – MOD)

7th-15th September

The five Wing patrols to date had notched up the following formidable figures against the Luftwaffe, claims made immediately after the actual battle:-

Enemy aircraft destroyed   105
Enemy aircraft probables   40
Enemy aircraft damaged   18

RAF losses
Pilots killed or missing   6
Pilots only wounded   5
Aircraft lost   14

17th September 1940

Flight Sergeant G.C. Unwin was awarded the Distinguished Flying Medal. Ten certain Huns to his credit.

18th September 1940

The squadrons were scrambled three times, at 0900, 1250, and 1616 hours. The first two occasions without success. On the third, they spotted AA bursts to the south-west of London, and found two enemy groups of about 20-30 bombers, but could see no escorts.

Flight Lieutenant W.G. Clouston (Blue 1) having seen no escort led the Squadron in to attack the bombers. He attacked the starboard machine of a vic of five. It dropped away from the formation with its starboard engine on fire. The crew baled out and the Junkers crashed behind some houses to the west of Deal. Two of the crew landed within ½ mile of the crash and were collected by what appeared to be Home Guard.

Flight Sergeant H. Steere (Blue 2) attacked a Heinkel 111 which went for the lower cloud layer at only 2,000 feet. He followed it down and saw it hit the water and sink at the mouth of the Thames. He climbed through the cloud and saw a Junkers 88 streaking down. He attacked, the starboard engine burst into flames and it disappeared vertically through the cloud. Flying Officer Haines (Green 1) had previously attacked this Junkers 88, and it crashed probably close to the Isle of Sheppey.

Flight Sergeant G.C. Unwin (Blue 3) dived on an Me110 and no rear fire was encountered. He closed to 50 yards and fired. Immediately the Me110's starboard engine caught fire, and the pilot baled out. The enemy aircraft crashed near Eastchurch. This was confirmed by a Spitfire of 66 Squadron.

Flying Officer Haines (Green 1) attacked a Junkers 88, giving it a four second burst. The starboard engine began to smoke and as he climbed for another attack he was engaged by two Me109s. He chased and attacked one of these Me109s and was surprised to observe fire coming from a single machine gun mounted laterally and seemingly just under or behind the pilot's seat. He concentrated on this Me109 and got in a good long burst at 200 – 50 yards. He half rolled and diving vertically, with black smoke pouring from his engine, disappeared into cloud and was not seen again.

Pilot Officer Dolezal (Green 2) attacked a Heinkel on the outside of the formation. After his first attack the enemy aircraft fell back with black smoke pouring from its starboard engine. The rear gunner stopped firing during his second attack. He closed in twice more firing all his ammunition and the He111 went down in a spin into the sea.

Sergeant G. Plzak (Green 3) also attacked a Heinkel which dived sharply. He attacked again closing to about 50 yards and the port engine stopped. His next attack stopped the starboard engine. He attacked again and the crew baled out but the air gunner's parachute did not open. The Heinkel crashed near Gillingham.

Flight Lieutenant Lawson (Red 1) led Red Section into an attack on nine Junkers 88s. He attacked one and could see his tracers hitting the port mainplane and engine. He then experienced rear fire from one of the other enemy aircraft and was hit in the radiator. He had to break off the attack as his cockpit was filled with glycol fumes. He made a forced landing at Eastchurch. (X4170)

Pilot Officer Cunningham (Red 2) followed Red Leader and attacked the same Junkers.

Sergeant Lloyd (Red 3) joined Pilot Officer Cunningham in the attack on the Ju88 and they both continued firing until the Junkers 88 crashed in flames at Sandwich.

The Wing's tally for the day was 29 aircraft destroyed with scarcely a scratch.

25th September 1940

Flying Officer L.A. Haines and Pilot Officer W. Cunningham were awarded the Distinguished Flying Cross.

Mark II Spitfires received with cartridge starter and extra boost.

27th September 1940

The Squadron scrambled from Duxford with 242, 310 and 616 Squadrons at 1142.

The Squadron patrolled Hornchurch at 25,000 feet and sighted the enemy formation of 80 to 100 aircraft, 10,000 feet below to the south at 1215 hours.

Flight Lieutenant D.J. Lawson (Red 1) ordered the Squadron into line astern and led an attack on a large group of Me109s. He selected out one Me109 and fired several short bursts and could see his tracers hitting it. The enemy aircraft turned south, heading for the French coast in a steep dive. Flight Lieutenant Lawson followed firing the rest of his ammunition from astern, as the enemy aircraft continued his dive. Smoke started pouring out of the enemy aircraft and it failed to pull out, crashing into the sea 10 miles out from Cap Gris Nez. Sub-Lieutenant A.G. Blake (Red 2) saw the main enemy formation below on the port side. He dived to attack when he noticed about nine Me109s up on the starboard side circling to attack his section. He drew round and managed to get his sights on an Me109. He gave it a short burst and observed white smoke pour from him. The Me109 immediately turned to make for the French coast. Sub-Lieutenant Blake followed, closed within range and fired again, pulled out to the port side and throttled back. The Me109 for some unknown reason turned right across his bows, so he just pressed the button and the enemy aircraft dived straight into the sea. He followed the enemy aircraft down to the surface of the sea and noticed three other Me109s all going as fast as they could for home. There was one just in front of him on his starboard side, so he turned and raked his beam. That Me109 also went straight into the sea.

Pilot Officer Hradil (Red 3) attacked an Me109, and saw smoke coming from it, but could not consider the result conclusive. A pair of 109s were going for Yellow Section from above.

Flight Sergeant G.C. Unwin (Yellow 1) was attacked by a pair of Me109s with yellow noses. He got on the tail of one, after about ten minutes of aerobatics during which the enemy aircraft manoeuvred nearer to France. The enemy aircraft gave up and flew straight and level. Flight Sergeant Unwin closed to 50 yards and fired a seven second burst – nothing happened. He gave it another long burst – still nothing happened. He moved to one side and fired the remainder of his ammunition in a 30 degree deflection shot. The enemy aircraft stalled and spun into the sea. Obviously now the Me109 are heavily armoured. (See also page 200.)

Sergeant B. Jennings (Yellow 2) attacked the leading Me109 of a section of five. He fired one burst and the enemy aircraft turned to starboard with white smoke coming from its engine. He followed it down and saw thick black smoke coming from the engine in place of white smoke. He couldn't see the flames for the density of white smoke. As Sergeant Jennings was watching and following the Me109 down, tracers started pouring past him from the other four Me109s who were on his tail. He turned to starboard and dived away.

Sergeant D.E. Lloyd (Yellow 4) was unable to get into the circle formed by the Me109s. He fired some rounds but without result. Flight Sergeant Steere (Green 1) took his section to engage eight Me109s who were starting to mill around. He closed to 300 yards and opened fire on the leading Me109. His tracers were going smack into the cockpit and rear part of the engine, when he had to break off as a line of Me109s were on his tail attacking. This enemy aircraft was seen going down in flames by Sergeant Plzak.

Flying Officer D. Parrot (Green 2) saw three Me109s on his port side. He broke formation and attacked one which dived vertically. The enemy aircraft pulled out of his dive over Folkestone at 10,000 feet and headed out to sea. Flying Officer Parrott fired again, thick clouds of smoke and a little flame came from the enemy aircraft. It went on its starboard side and went vertically into the sea.

LEFT TO RIGHT
BACK ROW: Sgt. Charnock, F/O Brinsden, P/O Hradil, Sgt. Fulford, Sgt Lloyd, Sgt Boswell

FRONT ROW: F/O Parrot, F/O Dolezal, F/Lt Lawson, F/Sgt. Unwin, Sgt. McGregor

Sergeant Plzak (Green 3) attacked an Me109 from above and rear, giving it three bursts. The enemy aircraft's port wing was hit, caught fire and it crashed near Sandwich. He climbed and joined another Spitfire Squadron "QJ" which was attacked by 15 Me109s. Sergeant Plzak used all his ammunition on one which went into a spin, but could not see if the enemy aircraft was hit.

Sergeant B.G. Cox (Yellow 3) was shot down wounded and is in hospital. (X4237)

Squadron Leader Lane took off later and flew separately. He saw a group of Me109s preparing to attack. He attacked two of them and pulled his stick back to climb for a second attack. His Spitfire Mark II failed to respond and he was unable to pull out of the dive until he came down as low as 3,000 feet.

Sergeant D.G.S.R. Cox (Wing Commander D.F.C.) recalls:

"On the 27th September the Squadron were the top squadron of the Duxford Wing on patrol in the Deal-Dover area.

199

It was attacked by a large number of Me109s. After the initial attack, the battle developed into the usual pattern of individual fights. I found myself between Ashford, Kent and Folkestone, in the middle of four Me109s. After several minutes of twisting and turning and taking the odd shot, without any visible effect, there was a loud bang in the cockpit. For a second or two I was dazed and after getting the aircraft under control, opened the hood, turned the Spitfire over and baled out.

I was quite high and took several minutes to come down, into a ploughed field. I was taken to an emergency hospital near Ashford. There I was operated on and seven large pieces of cannon shell taken out of my right leg, from just below the knee cap to the ankle.

I was in hospital for six weeks and returned to flying duties with 19 on the 15th December 1940."

Pilot Officer R.L. Jones

(R.L. Jones)

Pilot Officer Burgoyne (Green 4) (X4352) – is missing.

The Wing's tally for the day was 13 destroyed, but lost 5 aircraft and 3 pilots.

The Squadron had the best total for the day of 7 destroyed and a probable.

Our pilots were of the opinion that during the recent lull in operations, the German Air Force had taken the opportunity of armouring the Me109s more heavily. This was shown by the difficulties experienced in scoring vital hits except in deflection shots and by the decrease in speed of the Me109.

28th September 1940

Pilot Officer R.L. Jones, (Flight Lieutenant) writes;

"When patrolling the Tenterden area at about 29,000 feet, we were instructed to return to base – also being informed that no enemy aircraft were in the vicinity.

I was 'Arse End Charlie' and we were diving to 20,000 feet but my relaxation was suddenly interrupted, when about four feet of my starboard wing just peeled away. My immediate reaction at the time being – Poor show on a new aircraft. This was followed at once by a loud bang and a hole appeared above the under-carriage. Realising that I was being shot at by an aircraft 'up sun', I took immediate evasive action, simultaneously my engine cut out for good and I finished up in a high speed stall and spin.

My radio was also out of action so I was unable to notify the Squadron on the R/T and they subsequently returned to base unaware of the problem.

After coming out eventually from the spin at about 10,000 feet – the aircraft was not responding to the controls in a satisfactory way – I realised the hood was jammed and all efforts to open it failed. I subsequently made a crash landing on a dead engine in one of the only two fields available in a heavily wooded area just outside Hawkhurst, unfortunately landing amongst a flock of sheep and with regret, many were killed.

I was rescued by the Army and taken to the local doctor at Hawkhurst, who did first aid on a flesh wound in my leg and they took me into their Mess. They gave me lunch and then delivered me back to Fowlmere.

The aircraft P7432, apart from broken propellors and a radiator, a few holes and missing parts was hardly damaged by the forced landing."

5th October 1940

At 1550 hours the Wing on patrol again over Debden and North Weald at 25,000 feet. No enemy aircraft seen.

Pilot Officer Vokes returned from AFDU with a cannon Spitfire which had been tested thoroughly. The feed has a boost coil which helps to push the cartridge in as a spring in the magazine runs down. The feed chute has now a wider sweep and goes through one of the struts.

8th October 1940

Pilot Officer Vokes carried out some air to ground firing at Sutton Bridge trying to stop the cannon. No stoppages were experienced.

At 10.40am the Squadron led by Flight Lieutenant Clouston patrolled at 20,000 feet but no enemy aircraft seen.

Pilot Officer Vokes again tested the cannon and got no stoppages. This seems quite hopeful.

20th October 1940

Pilot Officer Vokes went to Digby to collect explosive ammunition for the cannon.

25th October 1940

Squadron patrolled again but nothing seen, except for a Wellington and a Blenheim. The Wellington touch down and finished up in the turnip field.

29th October 1940

1615 hours the Wing was on patrol again over the Kent area, and there was a considerable amount of AA fire. Squadron Leader Bader's radio was u.s. so the Wing was unable to set favourably. Some members of the Squadron saw about seven Me109s above them. They were unfortunately unable to attack them.

Sub-Lieutenant "Admiral" Blake
(Peter Howard-Williams)

Sub-Lieutenant Blake was doing search behind the Wing, and was probably attacked by the seven Me109s, as he was found near Chelmsford. (P7423).

Sergeant McGregor (P7379) made a forced landing but is safe.

5th November 1940

At 1145 hours the Squadron sighted some Me109s in the Deal area at 15,000 feet.

Sergeant Charnock (Green 1) saw three enemy aircraft circling and climbed, circled with them until he caught up on one. He opened fire from 150 yards and flames and smoke came from the engine. The other two enemy aircraft broke off.

Flight Lieutenant Lawson was at 26,000 feet doing rear search when he saw two condensation plumes heading north north west from Ramsgate. He followed over London they turned south west then south east back towards him. He was up sun from them and they didn't see him until he was 1,000 yards away. They were Me109s, first one dived south and then the other followed. He got on the tail of the last one and fired. The Me109's cockpit cover broke away and he continued in a steep dive. Flight Lieutenant Lawson gave him a second longer burst and the enemy aircraft disappeared into cloud in a vertical dive. He pulled out of his dive and did not see the Me109 crash, but believes it did into the sea 10 miles south of Dungeness.

The Squadron was patrolling the London area with 242 Squadron at 1540 hours when they sighted about 20 enemy aircraft at 28,000 feet.

Flight Lieutenant Lawson was leading, ordered line astern and engaged the Me109s. He fired at one Me109 from 200 yards with his machine guns, which turned over and went straight down. He tried to follow but could not keep up with him. He then attacked another Me109 from 100 yards with his cannons. The enemy aircraft immediately became enveloped in white and black smoke and pieces fell off in the region of the wing roots. It went slowly over, and plunged down through thick cloud. Flight Lieutenant Lawson followed and as he emerged through the cloud saw a patch of oil in the Estuary which he assumed to be the result of the crash as the Me109 was obviously out of control.

Flight Sergeant Unwin (Red 3) saw a He113 on the tail of a Spitfire and before he could attack, it had shot the Spitfire down near London. He caught the enemy aircraft, gave it a long burst, and it crashed in the sea in flames.

At 1615 hours on a Wing patrol at 26,500 feet over the Thames Estuary, "B" Flight, led by Flying Officer Haines encountered a number of Me109s 2,000 feet above them. The Flight climbed to attack.

P/Off Hradil

(R.L. Jones)

Flying Officer Haines attacked one Me109 which passed 400 yards in front of him. He closed to 200 yards and fired a short burst. The Me109 dived to 2,000 feet, where Flying Officer Haines closed again to 200 to 100 yards and "let him have a long burst". A small stream of black smoke came from underneath the engine and the Me109 slowed up considerably. He had now run out of ammunition and so formated on the right side of the Me109, when a Hurricane, piloted by Pilot Officer McKnight of 242 Squadron, attacked with a long burst from 150 yards. Bits came off the Me109's starboard wing and the engine began issuing a large stream of black smoke. The pilot baled out and landed in a tree at Birchington, Kent.

Pilot Officer Hradil was shot down and it was reported that his Spitfire was seen descending in flames.

Pilot Officer Hradil (P7545) – is missing.

8th November 1940

The Squadron patrolled at 1635 hours between Sheerness and Canterbury, led by Squadron Leader Lane. A report of some Heinkel 113s over the coastline but the targets could not be found. Squadron Leader Lane was shot down by a Hurricane bearing all British markings. He made a forced landing at Eastchurch (P7477).

15th November 1940

The Squadron was on convoy patrol, 25 miles east of Deal at 20,000 when two condensation plumes were sighted above at 35,000 feet. Blue section led by Flight Lieutenant Clouston broke off to attack the stern one, with Yellow section breaking away to cut him off. Red section proceeded after the leading enemy aircraft.

Squadron Leader Lane (Red 1) climbed after the leading enemy aircraft and when it sighted the Spitfires approaching, turned east and dived. He ordered line astern and at 8,000 feet opened fire. He then observed an object leaving the aircraft which appeared to be a piece of cowling, at the same time a stream of coolant appeared from the port engine. Squadron Leader Lane broke away and later observed the enemy aircraft's starboard engine on fire (Red 3 apparently being responsible for this). The Me110 climbed and Squadron Leader Lane attacked from starboard quarter. The Me110 turned and dived into the sea ½ mile south of Southend in the middle of the convoy.

Pilot Officer Cunningham (Red 2) saw smoke coming from the port engine of the Me110 after Red leader's attack. He then attacked firing three bursts and saw the starboard engine break into flames, and eventually crash into the sea. Pilot Officer Cunningham's windscreen was splintered by a bullet from the rear gunner.

Pilot Officer Vokes (Red 3) by the time he attacked the Me110, the port engine was smoking and the starboard engine was on fire. The enemy aircraft attempted to recover from the dive, stalled off the turn and dived into the sea. One airman baled out at 4,000 feet and landed near the convoy.

The rear Me110 was attacked by Blue and Yellow Sections.

Flight Sergeant Unwin (Yellow 1) saw he had a good chance to cut off one of the Me110s as it dived. He closed and gave it a long burst which stopped one engine. As he broke off he saw Sergeant Fulford attack and one wing fell off the enemy aircraft which crashed into the sea.

Sergeant Fulford (Yellow 2) chased one of the two Me110s, intercepted it as it dived away, he fired and saw his bullets strike the port wing which broke off.

Flying Officer Haines (Green 1) Spitfire was somewhat slower than the others. Yellow section managed to head the enemy aircraft off and it dived towards and underneath Flying Officer Haines. When he saw it coming he half rolled, closed to 150 yards and opened fire. He continued firing until the Me110 entered cloud at 10,000 feet, by which time glycol was streaming from its starboard engine and lots of pieces came off. He then broke away as his ammunition was exhausted and watched the Me110 crash into the sea. There were no survivors.

It was rather hard to say who had been most instrumental in getting him, as everyone except Flight Lieutenant Clouston had fired.

"The B——s just shouldered me out of the way," he complained. "I couldn't get near enough to fire at all!" That the Flight Commander, who was supposed to be leading the attack should be pushed aside, so to speak, by the rest of his flight, all determined to get in a burst, struck everybody as being extremely funny.

Sergeant Roden was critically injured carrying out a forced landing in bad visibility when he struck a tree. (P7420)

Flight Lieutenant Lawson awarded the Distinguished Flying Cross.

28th November 1940

At 1600 hours whilst on convoy patrol five miles east of Ramsgate, at 20,000 feet, the Squadron was attacked by four Me109s.

Flight Sergeant Steere (Green 1) was carrying out rear search when he saw four Me109 closing and informed the rest of the Squadron. Three of them overshot Flight Sergeant Steere and he closed behind one of them giving him a burst of seven seconds. The enemy aircraft half rolled, spiralled downwards straight into the sea.

Flight Sergeant Unwin (Yellow 1) immediately put his section into line astern and chased two Me109s heading south-east. The enemy aircraft dived and turned. Flight Sergeant Unwin closed to 100 yards and gave a long burst, followed by Sergeant Fulford, and then they attacked again. The Me109 dived away steeply, followed by Flight Sergeant Unwin who was shooting all the while. The enemy aircraft went straight into the sea. Sergeant Jennings (Yellow 2) attacked and chased away an Me109 which was trying to attack Flight Sergeant Unwin.

Sergeant Fulford (Yellow 3) chased an Me109 with Flight Sergeant Unwin which dived towards France. He got on its tail and fired all his ammunition from 50 yards.

Flying Officer Haines, with Sergeant Plzak (Green 2), climbed and broke away, dived at high speed, and was shot at by another Spitfire as Flying Officer Haines followed. No apparent damage was done to the Me109 as he pulled out of the dive and entered cloud, heading for the French coast. Flying Officer Haines could dimly see the Me109 and closed to 100 yards and fired the rest of his ammunition. The Me109's fuselage became completely obscured by black smoke and glycol, before it crashed into the sea off the French coast.

F/Sgt. G.C. Unwin DFM
(Crown Copyright – Sqdn Album)

6th December 1940

Flight Sergeant Unwin was decorated with the Bar to his Distinguished Flying Medal.

26th December 1940

Flight Sergeant Unwin promoted to Warrant Officer.

12th January 1941

One aircraft patrolled the base at 12,000 feet, and was recalled. Pilot Officer Howard Williams crashed on landing. (P7648).

22nd February 1941

The Squadron was brought to readiness and took off on a false alarm.
Night flying practice, Sergeant Johnson crashed after take off and was killed.

23rd February 1941

Wing practiced patrol at 23,000 feet with 310 Squadron. Sergeant Brooker unfortunately landed with his undercarriage retracted.

22nd March 1941

On a practice flight, Pilot Officer Cowley landed with his undercarriage retracted.

24th March 1941

On a practice flight, Pilot Officer Anderson (P7617) baled out after hitting Sergeant Charnock's aircraft at 3,000 feet. He landed safely.

4th April 1941

Red Section led by Pilot Officer Vokes was sent off to intercept a suspicious Wellington. The interception was made and the Wellington was forced to land at Bassingbourne. Friendly.

21st May 1941

The Squadron went to West Malling with Nos. 310 & 266 Squadrons to take part in a large offensive operation by Bomber Command. Several other fighter squadrons were involved. The roll of 19 was to patrol in company with 310 and 266 Squadrons at the south-east area of England, at 20,000 feet, to protect the bomber squadrons which raided two points in enemy occupied France from German fighters, should the later pursue the Blenheims as far as the English coast and beyond. Unfortunately, the Huns were not so ambitious. The operation as a whole was a success.

15th June 1941

Squadron Leader R.G. Dutton, D.F.C. and Bar posted to the Squadron, and Squadron Leader B.J.E. Lane, D.F.C. was posted to Headquarters 12 Group.

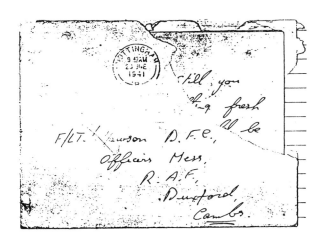

12 Group !!

22/6/41.

Dear Nineteen,

I feel I must write and thank you all for the parting gift. I about express half of what I felt in my few blushing words, but then I don't think anyone is in a position to speak coherently under such circumstances. Anyway thanks a lot.

I hope to come down ere long to discover what fate

2.

you employ !! Still you might have something fresh for me and it would be quite impossible to justify my existence at all if.)

My conscience was bothered by my conscience.

I am doing what I can about arranging something for you but it is slow work I am afraid.

Finally let me say that I had a grand time with you all & I only hope you did too. Thank you all.

Best of luck & goodbye
Brian Lane

17th June 1941

At 1955 hours the Squadron took off from West Malling to patrol the Manston – Dover – Hawinge area in support of No 11 Group who were co-operating with Bomber Command in an offensive operation over enemy occupied France. Although bandits were reported in the area, none were seen and the Squadron landed back at Fowlmere two hours later.

21st June 1941

Took off from West Malling at 1150 hours. While squadrons of 11 Group acted as close escort to a small force of bombers on an offensive operation against an objective near St Omer. The Squadron together with Nos. 266 and 65 Squadrons, patrolled just out to sea of Mardyck to cover the bombers' retreat. The Squadron patrolled at 15,000 to 18,000 feet and the Blenheims returned unmolested, although a message was received of enemy aircraft approaching, none were seen. However, as the Squadron approached the east coast coming back, there were numerous reports of enemy aircraft near Deal. The Squadron were down to 6 to 8,000 feet but no enemy aircraft were sighted. After about 50 minutes the Squadron was ordered to pancake. Due to shortage of petrol some machines of the Squadron had to land at other airfields.

23rd June 1941

Eleven aircraft took off from West Malling at 1305 hours to patrol Le Torquet – Bologne at 18,000 feet. Squadron Leader Dutton took off late owing to starter trouble and joined up with the Squadron at 1345 hours. At 1355 hours, five miles west of Le Torquet at 17,000 feet, two Me109s dived down through the Squadron formation firing at them and dived away.

Squadron Leader Dutton managed to fire at one Me109 and claims it as damaged.

Pilot Officer G.W. Scott didn't see the Me109 until he was hit on his starboard aileron by a shell. He broke away sharply to the left and as he did so was hit by a second burst on the tail unit. He went into a partial spin and the enemy aircraft passed underneath him. Pilot Officer Scott gave him a five second burst from dead astern but the enemy aircraft was travelling very fast and soon out of range.

27th June 1941

Twelve Spitfires left West Malling at 1612 hours with 266 and 65 Squadrons. They were to patrol the Hardelot – St Omer – Gravelines area at 20,000 feet. A formation of 12 Me109s was encountered. Several of these enemy aircraft dived on Pilot Officer Tucker (Yellow 2).

Sergeant Kosina (White 2) turned towards the 12 Me109s above him when he saw two below him. He dived on the two below firing at the leading Me109 from astern and slightly above, closing to 200 yards with two short bursts. He saw his bullets hitting the fuselage and cockpit. The enemy aircraft turned on its back and spiralled slowly down. He followed it down to 7,000 feet where he left it still diving steeply and spiralling slowly.

Pilot Officer Scott (Green 1) and Pilot Officer Andrews (Green 2) became separated from the Squadron. Pilot Officer Scott saw a Spitfire diving in flames and the pilot baling out. He engaged three Me109s but without any visible results. He attacked another three, one of which dived away after being hit by a short burst at 250 yards and was not seen again. He evaded the other two which chased him to the French coast.

Pilot Officer Andrews (P7379) – is missing.

The late evening patrol of ten Spitfires was over the same area with the same Squadrons. The enemy were encountered at 2140 hours. Heavy and accurate flak was experienced and the red bursts attracted five or six Me109s in line astern. The Squadron led by Flight Lieutenant Lawson was in loose formation. Flight Lieutenant Lawson (Red 1) did a climbing quarter attack at the rear enemy aircraft which pulled up and stalled. Glycol vapour poured form under wings and the enemy aircraft went into a spiral dive. After 1,000 feet smoke and flames spurted from the fuselage and the dive became steeper. He disappeared into the haze, diving vertically and on fire. Flight Lieutenant Lawson found himself alone after the combat but not for long – six Me109Fs were climbing very fast in his direction. He turned towards them and delivered a diving attack at the rear machine opening fire from slightly above at 200 yards. The Me109F fell over onto its starboard wing and went into a dive with glycol vapour streaming from his right wing root. He did not observe anything else as he was attacked by the remaining five Me109s. He thought discretion the better part of valour, took evasive action and returned to base.

Pilot Officer Vokes (Yellow 1) climbing to 24,000 feet when he saw an Me109F attacking a Spitfire. The enemy aircraft saw him, dived and attacked. Three times the enemy aircraft managed to attack him but they were not allowing for deflection. The Me109F pilot made his third attack slower and allowed Pilot Officer Vokes to turn on him. Pilot Officer Vokes saw his trail of bullets converge on the enemy aircraft and followed him down to 12,000 feet where he was lost in a vertical dive in haze.

Sergeant Plzak (White 1) delivered a stern attack on an Me109, firing two short and one long burst. He saw his bullets hitting the enemy aircraft on the engine and fuselage. Black smoke came from the engine, the enemy aircraft turned on its back and dived slowly into the haze.

Sergeant Cox (Green 2) got behind four Me109s and attacked the rear one, giving two two second bursts as he closed to 150 yards. Flames came from below and behind the pilot of the enemy aircraft which turned over and went down vertically in flames. He was about to join two Spitfires, when he saw what he thought were eight Spitfires. He was surprised to see four streams of tracers pass him on his left and his Spitfire was then hit in the glycol tank and wing. Sergeant Cox's engine failed and he glided home and crash landed two miles south-west of Lydd. (P8460)

Pilot Officer Cowley (P7813) – is missing.

21st July 1941

Twelve Spitfires took off from West Malling with 266 & 65 Squadrons at 1955 hours. The instructions were to cover the retreat of a force of bombers from the French coast. They were informed that there were enemy aircraft in the St Omer area. The Squadron were flying in loose fours when they were attacked from behind and above by Me109s.

Flight Lieutenant Cunningham (Blue 1) followed one pair of Me109s with Pilot Officer Stuart (Blue 2) and although not able to get within effective range fired one burst in their direction. Pilot Officer Stuart was then attacked by another pair of Me109s but was able to evade them. Flight Lieutenant Cunningham found himself orbiting above the Squadron and sighted six Me109s coming from the north-west. He climbed to attack and as the enemy aircraft attacked the Spitfires below, he followed firing at the last enemy aircraft from 300 yards. He saw his tracers enter the fuselage and although no apparent damage was observed, the enemy aircraft broke away and dived steeply downwards.

Sergeant Charnock (Green 1) saw tracer going past him on his port side. He throttled back and skidded violently to starboard. He was overshot by the Me109 slightly to port and below. He turned after the enemy aircraft and fired two short bursts from 250 yards and he started to climb. White glycol smoke appeared from the enemy aircraft which went into a gentle spiral. Sergeant Charnock then closed and fired three more bursts which caused black smoke to pour out followed by a sheet of flame. He fired one more burst, followed the enemy aircraft down and saw it crash five miles north of Montreuil. The pilot did not bale out.

Sergeant Brown (Green 2) turned to attack the Me109 as it went by and got in a short burst as the enemy aircraft outclimbed him. He was then attacked by other Me109 and had to take evasive action.

Sergeant Brooker (Yellow 2) was with Flying Officer Oxlin (Yellow 1) when he saw two Me109s coming from below and behind just in range. One attacked Flying Officer Oxlin and the other himself. Cannon shells were passing to his right, so he violently turned left. Bullets came through the hood and various parts of the aircraft, injuring him about the right eye. As he turned back he saw three Me109s and sprayed them with a short burst – beam attack. The hood and another piece came off the second machine but he was going too fast to see what happened. He landed at Manston slightly wounded and was detained in sick bay there.

Pilot Officer Oxlin (P7547) – is missing.

Pilot Officer Tucker (P7860) – is missing.

Squadron Leader Lawson assumed command of the Squadron.

7th August 1941

Twelve Spitfires of the Squadron took off from West Malling with 257 and 401 Squadrons at 1730 hours. Their duty was to patrol the Mardyck – St Omer area to cover the withdrawal of bombers from the Lille area. The Squadron was at 24,000 feet and sighted several formations of Me109 as they crossed the French coast. The enemy adopted its usual nibbling tactics, one or two aircraft at a time diving on a section and a general melée ensued.

Sergeant Charnock (Green 1) became separated from the Squadron during one of his turns and joined another Spitfire squadron at 25-26,000 feet. He saw four Me109Es and seven Me109s ahead, some 1,500 feet below. He dived on the last Me109 out of the sun opening fire at 350 yards. His burst hit the tail of the enemy aircraft and it turned to the right. His second burst resulted in a large piece of the enemy aircraft somewhere in the region of the cockpit, flying off followed by the whole hood which just missed Charnock's starboard wing. The Me109 turned on its back, dived vertically down from 17,000 feet and disappeared in cloud at 3,000 feet still diving vertically and clearly out of control.

Flight Lieutenant Vokes (Yellow 1) saw an Me109E attacking a Spitfire and climbed to attack. He got in several short bursts as they dived down to 8,000 feet, saw one spark in the fuselage but otherwise saw no result.

Sergeant Brooker (Yellow 2) having become separated from the Squadron was pursued by two Me109Fs across the Channel. He turned away and as they passed him fired a full deflection shot of two seconds at 150 yards. One of the enemy aircraft flew straight through his line of fire but he then lost sight of it. Sergeant Brooker was able to turn inside the Me109F, which supports the view that a Spitfire can turn quicker.

Pilot Officer Scott when also returning over the channel saw that he was being followed by an aircraft he thought to be a Spitfire. This aircraft was an Me109F which was making no attempt to overtake or attack Pilot Officer Scott. It seems that the mistake was mutual. Pilot Officer Scott noticed however, that the Me109F had a dark brown spinner which put him on his guard. He turned round to have a closer look and the Me109F dived steeply away. Pilot Officer Scott managed a quick burst at 250 yards range but observed no results.

Flight Sergeant Plzak is believed shot down by flak.

Pilot Officer Milman (P7924) crashed at Charing Hill on returning home and died later in hospital.

Flight Sergeant Plzak (P7771) – is missing.

12th August 1941

The Squadron consisting of 12 Spitfires took off from Ipswich at 1130 hours as part of 12 Group Wing on "Operation Circus 77". The function of the Wing was to act as high cover for a force of Blenheims which were attacking a target in the Ruhr. The Wing patrolled at 1220 hours in the Schouwen – Walcheren area at 1,500 feet. Twelve to 16 Me109s were engaged in a general dogfight but due to the amount of cloud no decisive results can be claimed.

Pilot Officer Cox (White 1) saw two Me109s appear from behind cloud. The first enemy aircraft dived on him, followed by the second and he skidded aside from both in turn. He turned sharply after the second enemy aircraft and gave him two bursts from 150 yards. Immediately there was glycol and grey smoke from his engine and he went from a gentle right hand turn into a vertical dive, disappearing into cloud. Pilot Officer Cox went through the cloud after him but could not find him as he came out of cloud on the other side, overland (Schouwen). Squadron Leader Lawson also got in a squirt at an Me109 which had dived on him. He chased him through two banks of cloud and got in three bursts at 300 yards but no results could be observed.

Pilot Officer Calvert (P7693) – is missing.

21st August 1941

The Squadron was re-equipped with long range Spitfire IIs, which it took over from 234 Squadron.

25th August 1941

The Squadron took off from Matlask at 1235 hours and rendezvous over Coltishall with 17 Blenheims which they were to escort to bomb a convoy off the Dutch coast. The Blenheims attacked the convoy of Ymuiden. Several direct hits were observed. The bombers were escorted back to the English coast. Two Me109s and four Me110s were seen but none of these attempted to engage our fighters.

27th August 1941

Yellow Section of Sergeant's Brooker and Davies, scrambled from Matlask at 1125 hours and after various vectors, succeeded in intercepting a reconnaissance Spitfire on his return from Holland.

28th August 1941

The Squadron took off from Matlask at 1800 hours with 12 long range Spitfires and rendezvoused with 17 Blenheims over Coltishall. The formation crossed the Dutch coast at 2,000 feet and turned towards their target the Rotterdam docks in line abreast. Very heavy flak was encountered from both the ground and ships.

Pilot Officer Marsh, Pilot Officer Stuart and Flight Sergeant Strihavka shot up a ship in the mouth of the river, south of Rotterdam.

Sergeant Charnock and Pilot Officer Edmonds each shot up a machine gun post.

Sergeant Sokol attacked a factory.

Squadron Leader Lawson and Pilot Officer Marsh had become separated from the rest of the Squadron and were coming home on the starboard side of the bombers. Fifteen miles off the Dutch coast, Pilot Officer Marsh saw his leader on the tail of an aircraft which he thought to be a Spitfire. Squadron Leader Lawson did not appear to go into action and had no enemy aircraft on his tail. Likewise there was no flak but he broke away and Pilot Officer Marsh did not see his leader again.

Squadron Leader Lawson (P7995) – is missing.

29th August 1941

Eleven Spitfires of the Squadron took off from Matlask at 0820 hours to search for Squadron Leader Lawson missing from the previous day's engagement 20 miles west of The Hague. They swept the area from sea level to 500 feet without success and were about to return to base when they encountered a formation of ten Me110s. The enemy aircraft were in line astern and they were apparently engaged in bombing practice as there was a smoke flare in the sea. The enemy aircraft attacked Blue Section first and a general dogfight ensued.

Flight Lieutenant Vokes (Red 1) ordered the Squadron into echelon formation about 2/300 yards apart and was in this formation when the enemy aircraft were sighted. He climbed into the sun above them and saw one Me110 making for a cloud. He positioned himself for a head-on attack as the enemy aircraft came out. He fired a short burst and got behind him, continued firing and saw his bullets striking the fuselage. The Me110s were then forming a defensive circle and return fire was being experienced. He broke away and attacked a single Me110 making for cloud cover, pieces came off the tail and its port engine began to smoke. The enemy aircraft made cloud cover and having fired all his ammunition returned to base.

Sergeant Watson (Red 2) climbed with his leader and followed him into the attack on an Me110. He then got on the tail of another Me110 and attacked it from astern at 150 yards range. Part of the enemy aircraft, which Sergeant Watson could not identify, flew off and he then had to break away.

Sergeant Brooker (Yellow 1) saw eight to 10 Me110s going towards Blue section on his port. The enemy aircraft then saw him and came at him line astern to attack. Sergeant Brooker turned for a head on attack and fired at the leading one. The enemy aircraft's port engine started smoking and he was seen to crash into the sea. He then attacked another Me110 but his windshield was hit with a cannon shell making it impossible to get his sights on it but he squirted a short burst at it.

Pilot Officer Marsh (Yellow 2) attacked an Me110 from 200 yards and the rear gunner of the enemy aircraft ceased firing but no other result could be observed.

Flight Sergeant Strihavka (Green 1) saw the ten Me110s attack blue section and a Spitfire break away with two on his tail. He got on the tail of the last Me110 and opened fire but did not see any result. He then saw two Me110s being chased by a Spitfire and opened fire on these two from 100 yards but had to break away to avoid them. Flight Sergeant Strihavka found himself behind another Me110 following a Spitfire. He fired from 200 yards, saw white and black smoke coming from the starboard engine which then caught fire. Having no ammunition left and an Me110 on his tail, he broke away and headed for home.

Sergeant Lysicky (Green 2) turned towards the ten Me110s, picked his one and attacked from below at 200 yards. He fired two long bursts and broke away as there was another enemy aircraft on his tail. He then attacked another Me110 with its port engine on fire, with another Me110 escorting it. He attacked the damaged aircraft from astern at 500 yards closing to 200 yards. As he broke away the enemy aircraft glided down with its port engine stopped, towards the sea. He then attacked the Me110 which had been acting as escort, from 200 yards and saw glycol coming from the port engine in a thick stream of white smoke.

Pilot Officer Stuart – is missing
Pilot Officer Edmonds – is missing
Sergeant Davies (P8255) – is missing
Sergeant Parkin – is missing.
Flight Lieutenant Vokes has since been killed in a flying accident.

7th September 1941

The Squadron was re-equipped with the Spitfire IIa.

28th September 1941

The Squadron of 14 aircraft left Matlask and went to West Raynham to take part in bumper exercises in co-operation with the Army. The exercises were to envisage an enemy landing in East Anglia. The Squadron was to represent the enemy fighter wing with two other squadrons.

3rd October 1941

Exercise "Bumper" completed and the Squadron returned to Matlask. The pilots agreed that the exercise was of great value as it showed the conditions they would have to fly under in the event of an invasion.

24th October 1941

Two Spitfires were scrambled at 1305 hours and given vectors 35/40 miles east of Matlask at 7,000 feet. At 1327 hours an aircraft was seen approaching from the north-west and they climbed up sun from which to identify and attack. The enemy aircraft was identified as a Junkers 88, but the enemy aircraft waggled its wings to make our aircraft think it was friendly.

Flight Sergeant Strihavka (Green 1) pursued and had to fly at full throttle, such was the speed of the enemy aircraft. He closed to 50 yards before opening fire, broke away so Sergeant Lysicky could attack. He followed the enemy aircraft through some cloud and attacked again. The enemy aircraft was taking evasive action by turning sharply to port and starboard. Closing from 300 to 100 yards he opened fire with several long bursts and saw the port engine smoking and pieces flying off the underneath of the fuselage. He heard strikes on his Spitfire, saw Sergeant Lysicky was ready to attack so broke off.

Sergeant Lysicky (Green 2) followed his leader and attacked after him. At this moment the enemy aircraft waggled his wings and he instinctively broke away. Thinking he might have been mistaken in his identification climbed away and saw the enemy markings on its wings. Smoke was also coming from the port engine of the Junkers 88. He attacked again after Flight Sergeant Strihavka but lost the enemy aircraft in cloud.

The enemy aircraft was heard panicking on his RT that his port engine had packed up. All the damage to Flight Sergeant Strihavka's Spitfire was from 303. In view of the formidable armament carried by the Ju88 it is considered that the pilots pressed home their attacks with resolution and if they had been flying Spitfire Vbs with which the Squadron are being equipped, it is difficult to see how the enemy aircraft could have escaped.

25th October 1941

The Squadron was re-equipped with the Spitfire Vb, the first two becoming operational during the afternoon.

27th October 1941

Two Spitfires took off at 1430 hours to patrol a convoy 30 miles off the coast, north east of Matlask. At 1500 hours they were informed of an enemy aircraft due east, they broke off and saw a Do17 approaching. The enemy aircraft went up into cloud and although the section followed under the cloud, it was not seen again. They returned to the convoy and were put under considerable peril by being fired upon by a Destroyer standing by a sinking ship and another Destroyer on the north-east side of the convoy. It is understood that an aircraft from 152 Squadron was shot down by AA fire from a convoy at approximately the same time and place. Sergeant Lysicky (Blue 1) and Pilot Officer Halford (Blue 2) saw a few Ju88s but were unable to get in any decisive attacks due to cloud cover.

6th November 1941

Two Spitfires Vb (two cannon, four mg) took off from Matlask at 0825 hours to intercept an enemy aircraft over the sea. Sergeant Sokol (White 1) RT went u.s shortly after crossing the coast, so Sergeant Watson (White 2) took the lead. At 0855 hours Sergeant Sokol sighted a Ju88 at 30 to 50 feet and was unable to attract Sergeant Watson's attention.

Sergeant Sokol dived to attack, as the enemy aircraft turned east. He gave chase closing to 300 to 400 yards and opened fire with cannon and machine guns in a high quarter attack. The enemy aircraft then disappeared into haze and Sergeant Sokol turned towards our coast, when almost at once he saw another or the same Ju88 coming from the east at sea level. He attacked the Ju88 which started weaving, closing to 200 yards astern he fired two short bursts. His first burst was cannon then machine gun only, having expended his cannon ammunition. The enemy aircraft was then lost in haze. During the combat Sergeant Sokol's Spitfire received a bullet through the mainspar which punctured his wheel, but he landed safely.

Sergeant Watson saw nothing of the combat.

Blue Section took off from the Martlesham Heath and flew at zero feet intending to make landfall at Knocke but got too far north and struck the estuary of the Flushing. The Section then turned making for Knocke and sighted a ship about a mile away which turned out to be a Destroyer. Both aircraft attacked the Destroyer opening fire with cannon and machine gun from 500 yards and flying straight over the top of the Destroyer. The cannon shells were seen exploding on the Destroyer but no damage could be noted. Sergeant Charnock (Blue 2) then broke away to the left intending to come round and attack the Destroyer again, but saw a Submarine with its conning tower above the water. He attacked the Submarine with cannon from 200 yards but had no time to observe any result. Flight Lieutenant Chadburn (Blue 1) attacked the Destroyer again until he had no ammunition left.

20th November 1941

Four Spitfires Vb took off from Matlask at 0740 hours to a point 45 miles off the Dutch coast from the Hook of Holland at zero feet. At 0810 hours Blue section saw three E boats sailing due east. Green section who were delayed in take off, failed to establish contact and took no part in the engagement.

Flight Lieutenant Chadburn (Blue 1) saw three E boats, the right hand pair being close together, the third one some distance to the left. He attacked the left hand boat from quarter to broadside on the port side. He opened fire with cannon from 400 yards and with cannon and machine gun from 300 yards, closing to point blank range. His cannon shells burst on the E boat, on the side and stern. He climbed in a left hand turn and opened fire again with cannon from 500/600 yards. When he last saw the E boat, it was well down by the stern, smoke and flames were coming just aft of amidships. The smoke was thick and heavy and was billowing out. The E boat had stopped and the other two were going round in a circle.

Sergeant Parkinson (Blue 2) climbed to 200 feet then attacked the two E boats on the right. He opened fire at 150 yards diving down on the two boats with cannon and machine gun. He closed to point blank range and could see shells bursting on the top of the deck. The two boats were so close together, he cannot say which he hit, but it was possible his fire sprayed them both. The boats were firing at him as he came in.

24th December 1941

Blue Section, Pilot Officer Vernon and Pilot Officer Hindley, took off from Coltishall at 1140 and flew at zero feet to attack the aerodrome at Khewysk. At 1210 hours the Section saw a convoy of four ships about 10 miles from the coast from Katwyk. The convoy was going south at eight to 10 knots. The Section flew over the convoy making for the Dutch coast when they noticed they were being chased by two Me109s which had been patrolling the convoy. Blue Section turned towards the enemy aircraft and got on their tails. Pilot Officer Vernon opened up on his Me109 from 300 yards with cannon and machine guns. A lot of black smoke came from the port side of the Me109 which went down towards the sea and made for the Dutch coast at high speed. He then attacked with cannon only from 400 yards but no result was observed. The enemy aircraft was pulling away from Pilot Officer Vernon as it went over the Dutch coastline, so he turned back to join up with Pilot Officer Hindley.

Pilot Officer Hindley attacked the other Me109 and gave a two second burst of cannon only from astern at 400 yards. No result could be observed. This enemy aircraft made off at high speed for the Dutch coast. The Section reformed and turned for home. They saw a sailing barge about 30 feet long, and attacked this vessel.

Pilot Officer Vernon saw bits of the mast and sails blown away as a result of his attack.

Pilot Officer Hindley attacked from broadside on, with cannon from 70 yards and hit the barge on or below the waterline.

Pilot Officer Hindley then attacked the leading ship in a convoy from stem to stern with cannon and machine guns from 100 yards to point blank range. Smoke was then seen to come from this ship by Pilot Officer Vernon. Pilot Officer Vernon then sprayed the other ships in the convoy but no results could be observed.

27th December 1941

Two Spitfires Vb scrambled from Ludham at 1010 hours and then given vectors taking them in the neighbourhood of Shipwash Lightship. At 1050 hours they saw a Ju88 approaching from the east at 9,000 feet. A Spitfire from 11 Group was seen diving to attack.

Sergeant Netopil (White 1) closed to 400 yards and opened fire from dead astern with cannon and machine gun. The enemy aircraft dived for cloud cover which was below, and as it entered, black smoke was seen coming from the starboard engine. The enemy aircraft was dodging from one cloud to another, but Sergeant Netopil was able to get in a second burst of cannon and machine gun. The enemy aircraft was last seen with smoke still coming from the starboard engine.

Sergeant Sokol (White 2) was waiting patiently behind his leader to get into a favourable position to attack. He was just about to open fire when a Spitfire from 11 Group appeared in his sights 50 yards ahead.

The enemy aircraft was chased by Spitfires from 11 Group as well as our Squadron and the result was a shared damaged Ju88.

It is understood that Y service has reported that the enemy aircraft landed at Montdidier in a damaged condition.

22nd January 1942

Four Spitfires Vb (two cannon – four machine gun) took off from Ludham at 1713 hours and patrolled over the sea east of Yarmouth. At 1725 hours they were 60 miles east of Yarmouth at zero feet when a Junkers 88 was sighted by Squadron Leader Davies approaching from the port bow at 300/400 feet.

Pilot Officer Brooker (Yellow 2) was the first to attack from a front beam position at 500 yards closing to point blank range but observed no result as he passed over the tail of the

214

enemy aircraft.

Squadron Leader Davies (Red 1) found his RT not working and so waggled his wings to attract the attention of the others. As Yellow section carried out the first attack, he turned to starboard and got onto the tail of the enemy aircraft and opened fire from 600 yards. Squadron Leader Davies experienced heavy and accurate return fire which appeared to be double tracer cannon from the dorsal gun position. The enemy aircraft disappeared into cloud and as it emerged he attacked again. Some part of the enemy aircraft was seen to fly off.

Flight Lieutenant Chadburn (Red 2) followed his leader into the second attack. The enemy aircraft was taking no evasive action but turning in a right hand circuit, it was climbing to gain cover in cloud above. Flight Lieutenant Chadburn opened fire from astern with cannon and machine gun from 600 closing to 300 yards, during which all his cannon ammunition was expended, but no result observed before the Junkers 88 disappeared into cloud.

Flight Lieutenant O'Leary (Yellow 1) was unable to get in his attack before the enemy aircraft disappeared into cloud.

1st February 1942

Wing Commander Grandy (White 1) took off from Coltishall at 1000 hours making rendezvous at 1015 hours with Pilot Officer Brooker (White 2) as White Section, flying on a vector of 120 degrees from Ludham for five minutes at sea level. Wing Commander Grandy climbed from time to time in order to make RT contact. Pilot Officer Brooker who should have remained at sea level was forced to climb as well owing to his RT functioning erratically. At 1105 hours an enemy aircraft was reported flying west at 2,000 feet, south of the Section. Wing Commander Grandy ordered Sergeant Brooker to remain at sea level whilst he climbed to cloud base, at 2,500 feet. Sergeant Brooker was not clear why Wing Commander Grandy had climbed to cloud base, climbed to 1,000 – 1,500 feet. At 1115 hours Sergeant Brooker saw a Dornier 217 approaching slightly behind him and to port at 2,000 feet. He gave a Tally-ho, turned to port and fired from 600 yards closing to 500 yards with cannon and machine guns. He was still firing as the enemy aircraft climbed into a patch of cloud was only 500 feet thick, 700 yards long and surrounded by clear sky. He returned to base. Grandy having heard the Tally-ho orbited and searched but saw nothing. He then thought he saw an aircraft crashing into the sea causing a big long white splash with a high column of water at one end. On investigation he saw a long disturbance together with black patches he thought to be oil.

Note: Y Service reported that the enemy aircraft reached its base and no claim was allowed.

2nd February 1942

Two Spitfires took off from Ludham at 1306 hours and were orbiting Haisborough Lightship. At 1325 hours at Dornier 217 was sighted.

Pilot Officer Devereux (Blue 1) saw Pilot Officer Henderson (Blue 2) climbing after the Dornier and followed. Unable to find the enemy aircraft he returned below cloud and saw two more Dornier 217s. He gave a Tally-ho but again these two enemy aircraft also disappeared into cloud.

Pilot Officer Henderson (Blue 2) saw a Dornier 217 and climbed after it as it disappeared into cloud. He then heard Pilot Officer Devereaux (Blue 1) give a Tally-ho and immediately sighted the two Dornier 217s in line astern just below cloud base. They disappeared into cloud and he followed, flying on his instruments and guessed what course at 280mph. The chase lasted 10 minutes during which time he saw one of the enemy aircraft on three occasions for a few seconds in lighter patches of cloud, 500 yards ahead. Eventually he sighted one of the enemy aircraft in a clearer patch of cloud and attacked from the stern quarter with cannon and machine gun. The enemy aircraft turned to port and Henderson attacked again. The port engine of the enemy aircraft caught fire with pieces flying off. A second fire started either in the rear cockpit or starboard engine. By the time he had expended all his ammunition, the enemy aircraft was well alight and small flickering flames were coming from the starboard engine. Two of the crew were seen to bale out as the enemy aircraft glided down towards the sea in a gentle right hand turn. Pilot Officer Henderson transmitted for a fix in case it might be possible to pick up the two airmen who had baled out.

Note: The enemy aircraft is claimed as destroyed which is most gratifying for Pilot Officer Henderson, as this is the first occasion he had been in action.

5th February 1942

Blue Section, Flight Lieutenant Chadburn and Sergeant Hutt, took off from Ludham at 0810 on convoy patrol. At 0920 whilst 20 to 30 miles east of Lowestoft the Section pulled the plug, did a steep turn and climbed after the enemy aircraft but were unable to get within range before it disappeared into cloud.

12th February 1942

The Squadron was at readiness from midday and at 1526 hours, ten aircraft led by Flight Lieutenant Chadburn took off from base to act as cover for bombers which were understood to be attacking the *Scharnhorst* and the *Gniesenau* which were coming up the channel. The Squadron flew the patrol line for 40 minutes and plenty of friendly bombers were seen, both going out and returning. There were plenty of shipping activity.

Sergeant Neotopil lost contact with the Squadron in cloud at the south end of the patrol line and with his RT u.s landed at West Malling.

Sergeant D.T.E. Reid, (AD332) a Rhodesian, became separated from the Squadron in cloud soon after the take off. His body was recovered from the sea by a trawler off Yarmouth.

17th February 1942

Red Section, Pilot Officer Brooker (Red 1) and Pilot Officer Cooper (Red 2) took off at 1310 from Ludham to patrol Great Yarmouth. At 1400 hours a Junkers 88 was sighted at 1,200 feet. Pilot Officer Brooker managed to get in an attack from long range with cannon and machine gun as the enemy aircraft flew into cloud cover. No decisive result was observed. The Section was informed by control that the enemy aircraft was still flying north and followed below the cloud. A few minutes later the enemy aircraft appeared out of cloud above Red Section. They dived down towards sea level and came up underneath the enemy aircraft and closed to within 200 yards.

Pilot Officer Brooker again opened up with cannon and machine gun fire in a three second burst. His cannon ammunition was then expended. The enemy aircraft disappeared into cloud and was not seen again.

19th February 1942

At 1145 hours, Pilot Officer Devereux when taking off on the north-south runway collided with Pilot Officer Crowcroft who was landing. Both aircraft caught fire and the pilots were killed. (AD323 and BL682).

Blue Section, Pilot Officer Henderson and Sergeant Reed, and Green Section, Sergeant Lysicky and Sergeant Parkinson, patrolled the convoy "Merit" at the north of the sector front.

Red Section, Sergeant Neotopil and Pilot Officer Cooper, with Yellow Section, Pilot Officer McKenzie and Sergeant Mills carried out a dusk sweep, 50 miles east of Great

Yarmouth. No trade.

24th March 1942

The Squadron, led by Squadron Leader Davies took off from Redhill at 1450 hours to rendezvous with 609 and 412 Spitfire Squadrons. They were escorts to six Boston Bombers whose target was the Marshalling Yards at Abbeville. On nearing the target, fifteen Fw190s were sighted approaching from inland at 10,000 feet. The enemy aircraft made repeated attacks from down sun, attempting to dive through the Spitfire Squadrons onto the bombers, but only one enemy aircraft was seen to attack a bomber and this without result. Pilot Officer Round (Yellow 2) and Sergeant Lysicky (Green 2) fired short bursts at the enemy aircraft as they dived to attack, but could not observe the results owing to the speed of the action and were unable to follow up their attacks as this would have meant breaking their formation.

Sergeant Netopil (AD307) – is missing.

Sergeant Mills (AD551) – is missing.

4th April 1942

The Squadron moved to Hutton Cranswick

26th April 1942

At 0725 hours the Squadron proceeded to West Malling for a Wing Sweep. The Squadron was accompanied by Nos 133 and 412 Squadrons led by Wing Commander Walker. The Squadrons took off at 1345 hours and rendezvous with 11 Group Wing at Eastchurch. The Wing crossed the channel at 14,000 feet from Sheerness and made landfall between Mardyk and Gravelines. They swept down the south of St Omer and made out to Toukeut. Turned to starboard in mid channel and when 10 miles off St Englement, eight Fw190s were sighted attacking five Spitfires from another squadron. The enemy aircraft were seen to dive and attack the Spitfire from behind and above.

Squadron Leader Davies led the Squadron into attack the Fw190s. He managed to get a head-on attack from 500 yards and fired a short burst before the enemy aircraft passed beneath him. He didn't observe any result although Flight Sergeant Reed saw the enemy aircraft do a half roll and was last seen in a vertical dive. At 1730 hours the Squadron again with 133 and 412 led by Wing Commander Walker took off for another Wing Sweep. The Wing crossed the French coast between Mardyk and Gravelines at 14,000 feet. They swept down by Gunibes and out at Hardelot. Heavy flak was experienced in the Gunibes area and Flight Sergeant Royer's aircraft was hit.

1st June 1942

The Squadron was released from operational duties from the 1st to 14th June inclusive, in order to proceed to Group Air Firing Practice Camp at Warmwell. The Squadron only being required to perform duties of an operational nature in case of an emergency or Wing Sweeps.

3rd June 1942

The Squadron led by Squadron Leader Davies proceed to Middle Wallop to take part in an offensive sweep. At 1500 hours the Squadron together with two other squadrons to escort Boston bombers whose objective was Cherbourg harbour. The Squadron climbed to 9,000 feet and crossed the channel, making two orbits just off Cherbourg when they sighted the bombers making their way home. No enemy aircraft seen.

18th June 1942

The weather was unfavourable and no flying of any kind was carried out.

A signal was received from the Air Ministry to the effect that Sergeant Pilot W.H. Mills, reported missing from an operational sortie on the 24th March 1942, and afterwards notified as a Prisoner of War, had arrived in the United Kingdom on the 11th June, having escaped from the French Prison Camp.

22nd June 1942

The Squadron led by Squadron Leader Davies flew to Harrow Beer to take part in a Wing Sweep. At 1830 hours the Squadron, with 310 and 234 Squadrons took off to cover wing to six Bostons on an attack on Morleix. The Wing crossed the French coast at 11,000 feet at Plesta, after making an orbit to starboard, the Bostons were seen coming out and the Squadron followed them. They recrossed the French coast at Tretustil and followed back to about six miles east of Berryhead, when three splashes were seen in the sea. Squadron Leader Davies told Flight Lieutenant Edwards to take over the Squadron, and together with his number two Sergeant Ridings went down to investigate. Pilot Officer Henderson and Flight Sergeant Royer also went down and after orbiting the scene saw three crashed aircraft in the sea.

Squadron Leader Davies then saw an Fw190 and attacked it, and claims it as damaged. Squadron Leader Davies reported the crashes and circled for 40 minutes.

Sergeant Ridings (W3644) – is missing.

30th June 1942

Following the welcome news of Sergeant Mills, news was received from the International Red Cross via the Air Ministry, quoting German information that Sergeant Netopil who was missing on the 24th March 1942 in the same operation as Sergeant Mills, was captured on that day, wounded and taken to a Field Hospital. He is classified as a Prisoner of War.

23rd July 1942

The Squadron moved to Colerne for "Fighter Night".

24th, 25th, 26th & 27th July 1942

No operational flying was carried out but extensive practice flying was done.

31st July 1942

The Squadron moved from Colerne to Perranporth. With regard to the Squadron's stay at RAF Station, Colerne, the Squadron Commander sent a communique to the Officer Commanding, Colerne. Thanks from himself and the Squadron for their most pleasant stay at their Station. Appreciation was expressed for the very fine welcome and all the help received particularly in regard to the very great assistance received from the aerodrome and control officers, and also from operations. At the same time a letter was written to the Chief Air Staff Officer at Group Headquarters, telling him of the worth of the Squadron's visit to Colerne, particularly with regard to the fact that in consequence of the pilots being able to concentrate on night flying training, the Squadron had become Moonlight Operational.

19th August 1942

The Squadron took part in "Operational Jubilee", (air support for the Dieppe Landing) making three sorties in the day.

At 0800 hours, 12 Spitfire Vbs took off and crossed the coast at Beachy Head at 3,000 feet.

They reached Dieppe at 10,000 feet as top cover. Eight Fw190s were sighted to the west of Dieppe and at first the enemy aircraft made no attempt to engage. As the Squadron passed over Dieppe the Fw190s came in to attack. The Squadron broke up into sections and several combats took place.

Pilot Officer J. Henderson (Blue 3) fired at two Fw190s which immediately dived steeply and his engine cut out as he attempted to follow. He then sighted two more Fw190s, southwest of Dieppe at 2,000 feet which were weaving. He climbed slightly above and up sun of them, he made a diving attack. Although both enemy aircraft saw him as he made his attack and both dived steeply away, he followed, fired and as a result two streams of white smoke emitted from each side of the fuselage of the enemy aircraft. It then went into a vertical dive and was last seen still smoking and in the dive at 6,000 feet. Pilot Officer Henderson was then attacked by two Fw190s and his aircraft received hits on the port mainplane, and port machine gun ammunition tank. He had to take violent evasive action but managed to land safely at his base. Pilot Officer Henderson reported seeing a Spitfire explode in the air over Dieppe.

Squadron Leader Davies, Sergeant Mundy (Red Section) made a stern attack on an Fw190 from 500 yards range and as a result the enemy aircraft immediately broke away from his leader and dived away towards land. The enemy aircraft was last seen at 500 feet in a steep dive over land. It is thought by the pilots concerned in the engagement that the enemy aircraft could not have made a safe landing, although no claim has been made.

Flight Lieutenant Bradley (Blue 1) also dived on an Fw190, with the result that the enemy aircraft flying at the time in a shallow dive, immediately went into a steep vertical dive towards the sea. He then saw a Dornier 217 about to attack two ships off Bernard Le Grande at 7,000 feet and climbed to attack. He fired a two second burst but did not observe any result.

Pilot Officer Royer attacked two Fw190s but did not observe any result. He then saw Sergeant E.R. Davies being attacked by two Fw190s and black smoke was emitting from the Spitfire.

Sergeant E.R. Davies (BM542) was later picked up in the channel having baled out from his machine. He was suffering from bullet wounds in the forehead.

At 1150 hours 12 Spitfires took off from Dieppe, crossing the English coast at Beachy Head. They arrived over Dieppe at 4,000 feet and as a turn was being made to port, four or five unidentified aircraft were sighted up sun. When the turn was completed, four Fw190s were sighted coming out of cloud but when they saw the Spitfires they turned back into the cloud. Two Dornier 217s were then seen over the rear of the main concentration of our shipping, bombs being dropped, but well wide of their target.

Flight Lieutenant Bradley (Blue 1) fired at one of the Dorniers as it was entering cloud but did not see any result.

Three of our ships appeared to be burning, one of which had the appearance of a Destroyer.

At 1615 hours, on this the third sortie in the Operation Jubilee, 12 Spitfires took off and crossed the coast at Beachy Head, at 2,000 feet under cloud. When 20 miles out, ten Fw190s were sighted at 3,000 feet coming in for a head-on attack at the Squadron. The formation broke into sections and individual combats took place.

Flight Lieutenant C.F. Bradley (Blue 1) saw ten Fw190s above and ahead in a gentle climbing turn to their starboard. He waited until all except the last one had passed overhead and turned up under its belly, firing a longish burst from below developing into an astern attack. He saw a large piece fly off the enemy aircraft which then turned on its back and dived vertically towards the sea. He was about to follow up the attack when he had a cannon stoppage and so broke off to port. As he did so he saw a splash in the sea, but could not be certain whether it was his enemy aircraft.

Sergeant J.W. Foster (Blue 2) received hits on his starboard mainplane and a cut on his right leg from a cannon splinter.

Pilot Officer J. Henderson (Blue 3) climbed and attempted to approach two Fw190s from behind and beneath. As he fired both enemy aircraft dived steeply and following them his engine cut. He then saw two more Fw190s, climbed above and up sun of them and made a diving attack. They also dived steeply and he continued his attack until he saw white smoke in two streams emitted from each side of the fuselage of one of the enemy aircraft. The last he saw of this enemy aircraft was in a vertical dive at 8,000 feet with smoke still emitting, as he was attacked from astern by another Fw190. Pilot Officer Henderson's Spitfire was hit on the port mainplane and gun ammunition tank.

Sergeant I.M. Mundy (Red 2) sighted three Fw190s passing to starboard, made a steep turn, and selected the centre one. As he attacked he saw strikes of red flashes on the starboard wing near the aileron, as his shells struck their target. Another Fw190 was behind him, so he broke away and in doing so lost sight of the enemy aircraft he had just attacked.

Sergeant E.A. Blore (EP523) – is missing.

From the combats that had taken place during the day, all pilots stated that the enemy had shown a disinclination to make a fight and if we had had a speedier plane there would have been an even greater difference in the final score.

25th August 1942

Flying Officer R.A. Watts and Pilot Officer I.M. Mundy scrambled at 1305 hours and patrolled Dodman Point. The weather closed in and Pilot Officer Mundy crashed at Carthew, northeast of St Austell on a hill. He received concussion and back injuries. The aircraft was completely wrecked (AR422).

September 1942

The Squadron got the Spitfire Vc. (For technical data see page 366.)

1st September 1942

Squadron Leader P.B.G. Davies, Flight Lieutenant R.H. Edwards and Pilot Officer J. Henderson were awarded the Distinguished Flying Cross.

6th September 1942

The Squadron flew to Tangmere to take part in an Offensive Operation. The Squadron took off from Tangmere at 1735 hours to act as a rear support for Flying Fortress's setting course for Beachy Head at 5,000 feet. Rendezvous not being made with the Biggin Hill Wing at the appointed time, the English coast was crossed and the formation climbed to 23,000 feet. When within nine miles of the French coast, 30 bombers were sighted on their way out being attacked by two Fw190s. White smoke was seen coming from the engine of one of the bombers and a single engined aircraft was seen going down issuing white smoke.

15th September 1942

The Squadron moved to Middle Wallop for an offensive operation. They took off at 1650 hours led by Squadron Leader Davies, climbing to 8,000 feet as they crossed over the Isle of Wight and reached 16,000 feet whilst 30 miles off the French coast. Several orbits were then made and heavy smoke was seen coming from Cherbourg. No enemy aircraft were seen during this operation and the Squadron returned over the Isle of Wight.

16th September 1942

The Squadron returned to Perranporth.

18th September 1942

Squadron Leader Boddington, D.F.M., assumed command of the Squadron.

23rd September 1942

White Section were patrolling 35 miles south east of Falmouth at 0945 hours.

Pilot Officer H.A. Simpson (White 1) saw a Junkers 88 flying in a south easterly direction at 8,000 feet. As he closed to 700 yards the enemy aircraft climbed for cloud. He managed to get in a short burst as it entered cloud. He received another vector from control and saw the enemy aircraft at 7,000 feet, 700 yards away. He closed to attack and the enemy aircraft went into a diving turn to starboard and jettisoned four white objects which appeared to be small parachutes. He followed, firing three long bursts from astern at 400 closing to 200 yards, expending all his ammunition. He saw red flashes on the enemy aircraft between the port engine and fuselage and black smoke poured from both engines. Pilot Officer Simpson experienced inaccurate return fire from the tail of the enemy aircraft.

Sergeant D.J. Love (White 2) waited until his leader had completed his attack, by which time the enemy aircraft was down to 1,500 feet still in a diving turn. He fired a long burst from astern slightly above closing to 100 yards. A large white puff of smoke then emitted from the bottom of the fuselage. He lost sight of the enemy aircraft at 500 feet as it disappeared into mist still in a dive.

2nd December 1942

Pilot Officer L.M.M. Ciechamowsik (EP749) was killed as the result of a flying accident when he flew into a hill at Mary Tavy, Devon.

3rd December 1942

Red Section were on an offensive patrol approximately 80 miles west of Point Duriz and sighted three Arado 196 who opened fire at them. Pilot Officer D.W. Connor (Red 2) was turning from the appointed patrol line at 1005 hours when he sighted three Arados 196s. He turned towards them and was warned by Flying Officer Watts (Red 1) that four Fw190s were approaching from behind. He turned to port and a Fw190 turned to meet him but overshot. Pilot Officer Connor made a tight turn and got on its tail, firing from 300 yards, but observed no results. He then manoeuvred onto the tail of another Fw190, closing to 200 yards. He saw cannon strikes on the port side of the tail plane, and the enemy aircraft immediately made a steep side slip to port. He was unable to follow as two Fw190s were firing at him and had to take evasive action, climbing into cloud he shook them off.

Squadron Leader V.H. Ekins assumed command of the Squadron.

15th January 1943

The Squadron led by Squadron Leader V.H. Ekins took off from Exeter at 1105 hours as support to Boston bombers on a raid of Cherbourg docks. No 234 Squadron was leading the formation of bombers, with No 19 Squadron on the left and No 13 Squadron on the right. The

English coast was crossed at Exmouth at 2,000 feet and the formation climbed to 19,000 feet. They crossed the French coast west of Cherbourg and a wide sweep was made over the peninsular, coming in over Borneville and out east of Cherbourg still maintaining the height of 19,000 feet. Heavy flak was experienced over Cherbourg, accurate by height on the bombers. Bombs were seen to burst in the target area. On the return six enemy aircraft were reported heading north near the Isle of Wight but they were not seen. The Squadron turned to port along the coast and landed at Exeter at 1250 hours.

18th January 1943

"A" Flight led by Squadron Leader V.H. Ekins made a rendezvous with three Whirlwinds[*] over the Lizard at 1350 hours. They flew at zero feet for 28 minutes turned, held course for another 14 minutes which brought them to within two miles of Ushant. Turning north they sighted four Fw190s flying at zero feet. Squadron Leader Elkins gave the order to break formation as another two Fw190s were seen 1,000 yards away to the left firing at one section. Combat then took place.

Flight Lieutenant P.H. Bell (Blue 1) was five miles north of Ushant when he sighted four Fw190s making to attack Yellow section. He broke formation and went into a head-on quarter attack on one of the enemy aircraft closing to 200 yards. He made a steep turn to port and saw two more Fw190s coming in on his right. He made a head-on attack at one of these Fw190s closing this time to 50 yards, and saw his cannon strikes on the enemy aircraft's port wing. He broke away and had to take evasive action as there was a Fw190 attacking him from the rear.

Sergeant A. Glover received many hits on his aircraft, including a large hole in his fuselage with the controls shot away. He received severe injuries in which a cannon shell passed through his armour plated seat, and exploded in his right buttock. In spite of the damage to his aircraft (EP756) and the injuries to himself, he made an excellent landing.

Sergeant W.H. Sloan (EP603) – is missing

26th January 1943

At 1450 hours the Squadron took off from Perranporth led by Wing Commander P. O'Brien, acting as medium cover on Operation "Ramrod". They crossed out over the Lizard at sea level, climbed round a large rain cloud, striking the French coast at Plouesant at a height of 12,000 feet. The Squadron went along the estuary north of Morlaix, following with a sweep to the right along to the estuary at Morlaix. The Squadron crossed out at Ile de Vatz and headed for home at 15,000 feet when they sighted two Fw190s on the port side, flying east two miles away. The Fw190s split formation as they were attacked by Flight Lieutenant Cox and Pilot Officer Mundy. No results were observed.

8th February 1943

Black section, comprising of Sergeant I. Hutchinson and Sergeant A.B. Clydsdale took off on a patrol in order to escort a convoy "Limited". They located the floating dock escorted by three Destroyers, three to four miles south west of Haslend Point, over which they patrolled over five minutes. In the course of the patrol, (Black 2) sighted a floating mine with spikes, ten miles south west of the point. He immediately informed Operations and kept a close watch on the mine, but was unable to inform the convoy as they were not fitted with VHF.

---

[*] The Westland Whirlwind was the first twin-engined single seat fighter in service with the RAF (1940). It suffered from being under-powered (Rolls Royce Peregrine) and due to its poor performance was mainly used as an escort fighter and later (1942) as a fighter bomber.

9th to 28th February 1943

No operational flying whatever was carried out. On the 11th, 20th and 23rd, a small amount of practice flying was done. On the 26th, six aircraft flew to Northolt and back for the purpose of being fitted with special drop tanks. The reason for the lack of flying was the forthcoming exercise "Spartan", in aid of which the Squadron was released from operational duty by HQ Fighter Command. The pilots were mainly occupied in the intensive instruction on the ground subjects in preparation for "Spartan".

1st March 1943

The advance party arrived at No 121 Airfield HQ for exercise "Spartan". All kit was taken from the lorries and the process of finding our site and tentage, together with the unpacking that must be done. At 1530 hours, the CO with 17 pilots arrived at Middle Wallop from Perranporth. Ten aircraft carried 90 gallon drop tanks containing petrol, six aircraft carried 90 gallon tanks containing equipment, and two aircraft were without. Immediately after landing, all pilots refuelled by themselves. Sixteen aircraft being refuelled and the drop tanks in an hour and 50 minutes.

Exercise "Spartan" was designed to obtain experience of Army Support operations and accustom the squadrons participating to the conditions which would be encountered later in Europe. It is recorded in the Squadron diary that "The experience under the composite group had proved beneficial to all, the training had been good and the life under canvas had increased the physical fitness of all".

12th March 1943

The end of exercise "Spartan".

14th March 1943

The Squadron returned back to Middle Wallop. The Officers and Senior NCOs were allowed to visit their respective messes. Words can not describe our feelings to a real meal, as a change to the usual bully beef and biscuits.

3rd April 1943

The Squadron moved to Perranporth for an offensive operation, acting as rear cover to 12 Venturas on an attack on Brest. The Squadron took off at 1510 hours and a patrol was made of the Ile de Baty, Ile Vierge area at 15,000 feet. Only seven pilots were able to complete the mission owing to the remainder having tank trouble. Three Fw190s were sighted but they made no attempt to engage.

Pilot Officer Opie and Flight Sergeant Baragwanagh whilst on patrol south of Plymouth, sighted two Fw190s and immediately engaged, damaging one.

10th April 1943

Sergeant A. Glover returned to the Squadron having fully recovered from his wounds received in action in January.

13th April 1943

The Squadron took off at 1040 hours and flew to Manston where they were refuelled and briefed. At 1150 hours the Squadron took off from Manston, acting as close escort to eight Whirly bombers, bombing the Marshalling Yards at Brugge. The weather was unsuitable for bombing as the Belgium coast was reached, so the formation returned back to base.

15th April 1943

The Squadron were escorting 12 Boston bombers attacking Poix Aerodrome, at 1700 hours. The bombers after making their attack split into two boxes of six. One box made a steep turn whilst the other six delayed their turn. The Squadron therefore split, six Spitfires escorting each box of bombers.

Flight Lieutenant Wrigley (Red 3) was escorting six bombers who had made a steep turn after their bombing attack. The bombers were then attacked by 10 Me109Fs from astern, and Flight Lieutenant Wrigley opened fire on the leading enemy aircraft which half rolled and dived away. The second Me109 was attacking a Spitfire (Pilot Officer Opie) in front of him. He opened fire on the Me109 with cannon and machine gun closing to 200 yards. This enemy aircraft side slipped, dived vertically out of sight and was observed to have white smoke pouring from it.

21st April 1943

The Squadron took part in the exercise "Welsh".

15th May 1943

At 1615 hours the Squadron took off together with Nos 132 and 602 Squadrons to act as close escort for 12 Bostons on an attack on Poix aerodrome. Rendezvous was made with the bombers over Bexhill at zero feet, flying on a course and steadily climbing to cross the French coast at Le Treport at 14,000 feet. The target was reached at 1700 hours and bomb hits were observed in the dispersal area and runways on the aerodrome. Intensive heavy flak was experienced over the target. After the attack the bombers split into two boxes of six, which also split the Squadron into six escort in each box. The formations were then subject to series of attacks by two formations of enemy aircraft, one comprising of ten Me109Fs and the other eight to 10 Me109Fs and Fw190s. Interception was made and from the ensuing combats, Flight Lieutenant Wrigley damaged one Me109F. One Spitfire was seen to be going down under control emitting white smoke. The bombers were escorted home without loss.

Pilot Officer Opie (W3432) – is missing.

16th May 1943

The Squadron took off from Tangmere to act as close escort for six Mitchell bombers on an attack on Caen aerodrome. Rendezvous was made over Selsey Bill at zero feet. They climbed and crossed the French coast south of the Siene. The target was attacked from 13,000 feet, hits being seen on the aerodrome and buildings to the northwest. No enemy aircraft were encountered, although heavy flak was experienced over the target. The Mitchells were escorted home and all aircraft of the Squadron landed at Fairlop.

24th May 1943

The Squadron, together with Nos 118 and 402 Squadrons, led by Wing Commander Rabagliati, took off from Coltishall at 1119 hours. The Squadron acted as close escort to 32 Beaufighters attacking a southbound enemy convoy off Egment. Eight cargo vessels with 12 escort vessels were attacked by torpedo and cannon by the Beaufighters. Flak was intensive and fairly accurate. One Beaufighter was seen to crash into the sea. No enemy aircraft were seen and the remaining Beaufighters were escorted safely home.

27th May 1943

This was a memorable day for the Station and the Squadron. Their Majesty's The King and Queen visited the Station. All pilots were introduced to their Majesty's. The Queen having a long chat to our Australian pilots.

Four Spitfires took off from Coltishall at 1645 hours for a shipping reconnaissance off the Dutch coast. They flew in line abreast from Great Yarmouth and at 1725 hours sighted the Dutch coast at Ijmuiden. White Section turned to port on a course of 018 degrees and Blue Section turned to starboard on 233 degrees. Flying Officer Mills (Blue 1) and Sergeant Greenfield (Blue 2) sighted two Trawler type ships thought to be minesweepers, which immediately opened fire with accurate light intense flak. Flying Officer Mills received a machine gun hit through the radiator faring and Sergeant Greenfield a cannon hit which made a large hole in the fuselage forward of the stern frame which cut the elevator trimming wires and one set of elevator control wires. Both pilots made it home. Flying Officer Mundy (White 1) and Sergeant Richie (White 2) sighted a Trawler off Egmont and opened fire, making a beam attack. Flying Officer Mundy saw his cannon strikes on the starboard stern of the vessel. No return fire was experienced.

31st May 1943

The Squadron flew down to Martlesham to take part in an offensive operation. At 1734 hours the Squadron led by Flight Lieutenant Bell took off to act as close escort for 12 Mitchells attacking the harbour at Flushing. Rendezvous was made over Clacton and the Squadron formated in line abreast to the right of the bombers. The formation began to climb, reaching 10,000 feet over Blankenberghe, with the Squadron 2,000 feet above the bombers. An orbit was made over Flushing and heavy palls of smoke were seen over the target area after the bombing. Ten Mitchells were escorted back plus one straggler, with his starboard engine emitting smoke. The Squadron orbited this disabled bomber and it was escorted safely back to the coast.

11th June 1943

The Squadron, comprising of only seven aircraft, owing to the rest being unserviceable, flew down to Martlesham for briefing. Six aircraft, plus six from No 416 Squadron took off at 1145 hours from Martlesham, to act as close escort to ten Venturas who were to attack the harbour installation at Zeebrugge. Rendezvous was made over Bradwell Bay at 1200 hours at zero feet. The bombers climbed to 12,000 feet while the Squadron maintained a height of 14,000 feet. Landfall was made south of Zeebrugge when a turn to starboard was made over the target.

Flight Lieutenant Wigley observed a direct hit on a factory. Flak was comparatively light and all the bombers were escorted safely home.

The Squadron landed at Martlesham at 1315 hours and then flew on to Coltishall where they were briefed for a further operation. Six of the Squadron plus six of No 416 Squadron took off from Coltishall at 1810 hours. Flight Lieutenant Bell led the Squadron who were to attack shipping off The Hague. The Squadron swept the area but no shipping was seen.

13th June 1943

The Squadron were up at 0430 hours having to be at Martlesham just after dawn. Nine aircraft took off from Martlesham at 0835 hours to act as close escort to 12 Mitchells attacking the docks at Flushing. Rendezvous was made over Bradwell Bay and the formation started to climb. The bombers climbed to 12,000 feet while the Squadron was 4,000 feet above. The bombers attacked the target from this height and heavy intense flak was experienced over Flushing, accurate for height and direction. One Spitfire was seen to go down emitting smoke. One bomber was seen to be hit in the starboard engine but it was however, escorted safely home.

Flying Officer Mundy came back one hour after the Squadron had landed. He had spun out of formation in the turn over Flushing and in doing so lost sight of the Squadron. He was fired at by two Fw190s but returned unscathed.

Another operation was called for later in the evening and at 2120 hours, the Squadron led by Wing Commander Rabagliate took off to act as close escort to 11 torpedo plus 18 antiflak Beaufighters. Their target was an enemy convoy off Peten, south of Denhelder. Rendezvous was made with the Beaufighters over Coltishall at 1,000 feet. The English coast was crossed at Minterton and a course set for the convoy, which was sighted 33 minutes later. The convoy consisted of one 6,000 ton vessel and several escort vessels of smaller tonnage. The Squadron flew outside and parallel to the convoy whilst the Beaufighters made their attack. Three small ships were seen to be hit and one other listing, but observation was difficult owing to the poor light and haze in the area. One Beaufighter was seen to be on fire.

9th July 1943

The Squadron was on readiness for an early morning "show" and took off in the following order, to act as close escort to 12 Mitchells detailed to attack the Marshalling Yards at St Omer.

Blue Section – Flight Lieutenant Bell, Sergeant Vass, Flying Officer Foster and Flight Sergeant Ripon.

Red Section – Squadron Leader Ekins, Pilot Officer Baragwanath, Flight Sergeant Wass and Sergeant Biggs.

Yellow Section – Flight Lieutenant Wigley, Sergeant Carson, Flying Officer Mundy and Flight Sergeant Cooper.

Take off was at 0715 hours and rendezvous was made at zero feet. The Squadron formated on the bombers, Blue Section on the left, Red and Yellow Sections on the right and set course for Letouquet climbing all the way to a height of 11,000 feet. On reaching the French coast the formation turned for St Omer and Yellow Section moved to behind the bombers. Blue and Red Sections remained in their positions. The Mitchells bombed the target, turned left and recrossed the French coast at Gravelines. Pilots' reports show the bombing to be inaccurate as bursts were seen in residential areas. Light flak was encountered from coastal areas but none was observed over the target.

Although the sortie was without incidence whilst over enemy occupied territory, the enthusiasm of the Squadron which earlier was at a high peak, because it was once again playing its part in an offensive operation after so many disappointments, was marred by an unfortunate accident which happened in the circuit while the aircraft were spreading out to land. While leading Blue Section in a break away Flight Lieutenant Bell and the CO collided rendering both their aircraft uncontrollable. Squadron Leader Ekins baled out immediately and effected a safe landing, bruising his legs and cutting his hands. Flight Lieutenant P.H. Bell was not so fortunate, his aircraft (BL852) headed straight towards the ground from 1,500 feet, where the collision occurred. He baled out but his parachute failed to open in time to save him.

10th July 1943

The Squadron took off at 0615 hours to act as top cover for 12 Venturas on a bombing raid of St Omer. The Squadron was to co-operate with No 132 Squadron also acting as top cover and rendezvous was made over Sandwich with the bombers at 500 feet. Course was set for Mardyke climbing all the way from the English coast to a height of 14,500 feet, 4,000 feet above the Venturas. A course was set from Mardyke to St Omer, and the target attacked. The formation then turned left and recrossed the French coast at Gravelines. Bombing was excellent and numerous strikes were seen on the target which was the Marshalling Yards. No enemy aircraft were seen although 30 plus were reported to the south of the target heading north.

14th July 1943

At 0830 hours the Squadron took off with No 132 Squadron to act as escort cover to 18 Bostons, detailed to bomb Abbeville aerodrome. Rendezvous was made with the Bostons flying in three boxes of six. The formation climbed all the way to the French coast to 13,000 feet. Bombs were seen to fall in the dispersal areas and building around the airfield. No enemy aircraft were seen and flak was very light.

15th July 1943

At 1600 hours, the Squadron led by Wing Commander Bird-Wilson, took off from base to escort 12 Bostons to bomb Poix airfield. The formation climbed to 14,000 feet and the Bostons attacked the airfield from 10,000 feet. The Bostons then turned left and immediately 20 plus enemy aircraft were reported and seen to be climbing up behind the formation. They attacked the bombers from out of the sun and the escorting fighters broke away to engage. Many combats ensued and various sections of the Squadron became separated. Three pilots, Flight Lieutenant Wigley, Flying Officer Foster and Flight Sergeant Clydsdale attacked enemy aircraft but no claim has been made, while Flight Sergeant Hutchinson's aircraft was hit badly by cannon shell. Flight Lieutenant Wigley and Flight Sergeant Rippon were also hit, the latter by flak, but both returned safely. Intense and accurate flak was experienced over the target area and all the way back to the French coast. One bomber was damaged by enemy aircraft but reached friendly shores safely. The rest of the month the Squadron acted as close escort on many bombing missions, without any notable incident.

4th August 1943

The Squadron took off at 1845 hours to act as close escort to 36 Marauders detailed to bomb the docks and shipyards at Letrait. The Squadron rendezvoused with the bombers at 12,000 feet over Beachy Head and set course for the target. Bombing was good and bursts were seen in the shipyard and submarine pens. The formation flew between two layers of cloud on the return. A number of enemy aircraft were seen but they did not attack.

15th August 1943

The Squadron led by Group Captain Rankin, D.S.O., D.F.C., was airborne at 0925 hours escorting Marauders to bomb St Omer aerodrome. The Wing, 132, 602 and 19, rendezvoused with 36 bombers and set course for Gravelines. The target was bombed and flak was experienced over the target and back to Calais.

The Squadron took off again at 1905 to escort 21 Marauders to bomb the Marshalling Yards at Abbeville. This was in the nature of a diversion for very large numbers of Fortresses bombing various French aerodromes. A small amount of accurate flak was experienced over the target. No enemy aircraft were sighted.

17th August 1943

The Squadron took off at 1140 hours. They rendezvoused with six Mitchells and set course for the French coast. The bombers attacked the Marshalling Yards at Calais.

At 1555 the Squadron was airborne again to escort 36 Marauders bombing Poix aerodrome but the mission was cancelled due to the weather.

18th August 1943

On returning from an escort sortie the pilots were informed that they were to move that afternoon to No 122 Airfield, Gravesend. They also received the very welcome information that they were to be re-equipped with the Spitfire IXs immediately. This type was powered by a Rolls Royce Merlin 61 12-cylinder V liquid cooled 1,515hp engine, giving it a maximum speed of 408mph, a ceiling of 44,000 feet and a range of 434 miles. It was armed with two x 20mm cannons and four machine guns.

19th August 1943

Today the pilots were busy examining and getting the gen on the Spitfire Mark IX. They were given a talk by Wing Commander Bird-Wilson D.F.C., and he told them of various points in connection with the handling of the new aircraft. The day was spent practice flying and generally becoming accustomed to the kite.

20th August 1943

More new Spitfire IXs arrived today and these had to be tested. Practice flying, air firing, aerobatics and dogfighting. Everyone approved of the aircraft and the Squadron were looking forward to many successes with them.

27th August 1943

The Squadron were airborne at 0935 hours to act as top cover to 18 Mitchells bombing Berway aerodrome. The formation climbed rapidly with the Squadron at 25,000 feet. The bombers turned back at the French coast due to adverse weather conditions but the Squadron carried out a sweep along the coast towards Caen.

At 1850 hours, 12 aircraft were airborne to act as high cover to 60 Fortresses detailed to bomb the ammunition dump just north of St Omer. A rapid climb was carried out to 25,000 feet over St Pol at which height a number of sweeps were carried out from there to the target area. The Squadron became split into sections of four. Enemy aircraft were in the vicinity but none of the Squadron had combats.

2nd September 1943

At 1805 hours the Squadron took off to act as high cover for Marauders, Mitchells and Venturas' bombing the ammunition dumps in Hesdin Wood. The Squadron carried out sweeps for 25 minutes whilst the bombers attacked their target. The bombers experienced severe flak but the bombing was seen to be good. No enemy aircraft were seen.

3rd September 1943

The Squadron were airborne at 0820 hours to act as high cover to Marauders bombing Beauvaislille aerodrome.

At 1250 hours they were again acting as high cover to Venturas bombing ammunition dumps and oil storage tanks in woods ten miles north of St Omer. While ten miles inland, Sergeant Ritchies (Green 4) aircraft (MA833) developed engine trouble and finally packed up altogether. He headed out towards the coast and was losing height rapidly. He was forced to bale out six miles north of Gravelines at 4,000 feet. Flying Officer Ross (Green 3) escorted him until he baled out and saw him picked up by an enemy Air-Sea Rescue boat from the French coast.

6th September 1943

At 0650 hours the Squadron was airborne to act as top cover to Marauders bombing Rouen Marshalling Yards.

At 1125 hours the Squadron took off to cover the withdrawal of Fortresses which had bombed targets in southern Germany. The Squadron rendezvoused with the Fortresses over Bernay and swept behind the main force until they were clear of the coast.

At 1710 hours the Squadron were again airborne to act as high cover to 72 Marauders bombing the Marshalling Yards at Serqueamp. Many enemy aircraft were reported in the area. The Squadron swept but only one sighting of the Hun, which were not engaged. An air-Sea Rescue search was carried out for a Fortresses crew in the drink. White 3 and 4 saw three dinghies with 50 men in them and gave mayday for them and plotted their position.

9th September 1943

At 0430 hours, pilots were reporting to the briefing room to hear the gen on an important operation which was to take place this day. It was rumoured that there would be an intensive air operation against the Hun in France and the Squadron was still seeking its hundredth victory. The gen was that a large ambitious exercise was to take place in the channel made to appear like an invasion fleet approaching Bologne, so drawing the Luftwaffe, in force, into the air. The Squadron was on readiness all morning. At 0750 hours, 12 aircraft were airborne to patrol the Bologne area between 16 to 18,000 feet for 40 minutes. The patrol was carried out whilst Marauders, Mitchells and Venturas bombed Bologne continuously, but no enemy aircraft were drawn to the vicinity.

16th September 1943

The Squadron took off at 1650 hours to act as top cover to 72 Marauders bombing Beaumont le Roger. Several gaggles of enemy aircraft were seen and during the ensuing shambles the Squadron was split up. Flying Officer Page and Sergeant Biggs had combats and Pilot Officer Baragwanath fired at several Fw190s but is making no claim.

18th September 1943

The Squadron took off at 0920 hours to act as top cover to 12 Mitchells bombing Rouen Marshalling Yards. Many enemy aircraft were plotted and the Squadron was vectored south of the target. Sweeps of the area were carried out but no contact was made. The Squadron returned to the coastal area at St Valery. As the formation was about to leave for home, 20 plus enemy aircraft were sighted 200 feet below, about ten miles to the south. The sections broke up to engage but the enemy aircraft dived towards the land and no combats took place.

21st September 1943

At 0850 hours the Squadron took off to act as cover for Mitchells bombing the coke ovens at Leus. The Squadron did large sweeps over Douai and Amiens. Over Amiens, Green Section dived on two Fw190s and Flight Lieutenant Wigley fired all his cannons at one, which dived away and may have been damaged.

24th September 1943

At 1055 hours the Squadron was airborne as top cover to 72 Marauders bombing Eureux aerodrome. Flight Lieutenant Wigley saw three Fw190s below and broke away to attack. He jumped them with his section and fired a long burst at one. He saw no result until it rolled on its back and went down.

3rd November 1943

The Squadron took off at 0945 hours to act as high cover to 72 Marauders detailed to bomb St Andre de L'eure aerodrome.

At 1325 hours they again acted as high cover to the Marauders this time bombing Schipol aerodrome (Amsterdam).

No enemy aircraft seen.

5th November 1943

The morning was spent doing practice flying and cine gun exercises. At 1300 hours the Squadron took off to act as top cover to 280 Marauders bombing Calais constructional works. Huns were plotted but none sighted.

7th November 1943

The Squadron took off at 0925 hours to act as top cover to 72 Marauders bombing Montidier. No enemy aircraft were seen.

Flight Sergeant Prebble developed engine trouble ten miles inside the French coast and turned for home. Flight Sergeant Hutchinson returned with him, but owing to a head wind, he reached about ten miles off the Dieppe coast when he was down to 4,000 feet. He called up and said he as going to bale out. Flight Sergeant Hutchinson followed him down to 3,000 feet where he lost sight of the aircraft momentarily. When he next sighted the aircraft, it appeared to stall and then hit the water. He circled the area for about 15 minutes without seeing any sign of the pilot or parachute. The sea was very choppy and Air-Sea Rescue could find no trace of the pilot. Flight Sergeant Prebble is thought to have been unable to abandon his aircraft.

Flight Sergeant F.G.D. Prebble (MJ215) – is missing.

11th November 1943

Today was a red letter day in the Squadron's history. It was a clear fine morning and we were briefed at 1115 hours. Our roll was a fighter sweep in the St Pol area as a diversion for Marauders bombing a construction works on the Cherbourg peninsular. The Squadron was airborne at 1155 hours. They had been over France for about 30 minutes, when 122 Squadron who were on our port side, were jumped by about 14 or 16 Huns. They turned towards the enemy aircraft when a Fw190 broke away and dived down. Flight Lieutenant Drinkwater who's chase was seen by Wing Commander Bird-Wilson reports;

"I was leading White Section of 19 Squadron, flying east at 17,000 feet near St Pol, when I saw Fw190's and Me109's mixing it with 122 Squadron. On flying nearer to the scrapping, I spotted an Fw190 break away and dive rapidly west. I turned and used full boost and revs, chased him down from 18,000 feet and got in a couple of bursts from dead astern. The Fw190 pulled out at about 2,000 feet and I turned to starboard with him and got in several deflection bursts at an angle of 10 degrees at a range of 150-200 yards. I saw cannon strikes but could not say what part of the enemy aircraft I hit as my windscreen was fogged up. I had to pull over and across the top of the Fw190 to avoid collision. We were less than 1,000 feet. I pulled up to

3,000 feet and on looking down I saw the Fw190 hit the ground and burst into flames".

This was confirmed and was the Squadron's hundredth victory.

The Squadron landed at 1335 hours and were told there was an other briefing at 14.30 hours.

At 1505 hours the Squadron was again airborne to sweep the same area. This time the Marauders were attacking construction works at Calais.

In the evening, we all adjourned to the local, where we drank the health of Flight Lieutenant Drinkwater and the Squadron's hundredth victory.

Flt/Lt Drinkwater cuts the "Hundreth Hun" Cake

(Crown Copyright – Sqdn Album)

23rd November 1943

The Squadron took off at 1140 hours to act as high cover to 72 Marauders bombing Lille/Vendevilie aerodrome.

26th November 1943

The Squadron was airborne at 0920 hours to escort 120 Fortresses as far as Le Teilleirs. The Squadron then did a sweep of the Rouen area but no enemy aircraft were seen. It was very cold.

At 1255 hours this time escorting Marauders bombing Rosiere aerodrome.

5th December 1943

At 1220 hours took over acting as a fighter umbrella for Marauders and Mitchells bombing the Le Touquet area.

27th December 1943

Squadron Leader V.H. Ekins D.F.C., handed over command to Squadron Leader N.J. Durrant. Flight Lieutenant Drinkwater returned from an American airfield where he had been learning to fly the new Mustang III, which the Squadron hopes to be equipped with shortly.

6th January 1944

The pilots were briefed at 1945 hours, their roll being a fighter umbrella to various bombers attacking 'No Ball' targets in the Poix area. The Squadron took off at 1125 hours and climbed to 17,000 feet and crossed over into France. Huns were reported north east of Rouen and White Section spotted four enemy aircraft coming in from the port, at 1,000 feet below, and went in to attack. As White Section went in, the rest of the Huns poured in from out of the sun, but they had missed their moment and there was a free-for-all battle, in which both us and the Huns were split up. The Squadron returned home in ones and twos. Flight Sergeant Hutchinson shot a Fw190 down, which crashed in a field, and damaged two others. Other pilots who were in the combat but made no claim were, Squadron Leader Durrant, Pilot Officer Wass, Flight Sergeant Carson, and Flying Officer Page. Flight Sergeant Vassiliades attempted to fire but there was no response to the firing button.

7th January 1944

The Squadron took off from Gravesend at 1228 hours with the role of withdrawal cover to Fortresses and Liberators of 5th, 6th, 7th and 8th Combat Wings. The first box passed out at Cambrai and Arras escorted by four Thunderbolts. In the St Pol/Doullens area eight Fw190s attacked the Fortresses in fours line astern. Flight Lieutenant Drinkwater (White 1) saw the Fw190s coming out of the sun. The enemy aircraft broke away in disorder when they saw the Spitfires. He picked on one and started to fire at 400 yards and it went into a vertical dive and was lost in cloud. He did not see any strikes but claims it as damaged on assessment of Combat Film No TAF184.

12th January 1944

There was no flying this day, but the pilots went in relays to No 65 Squadron dispersal to learn the cockpit check on a Mustang.

13th January 1944

All pilots attended a lecture on escape and evasion in Germany.

21st January 1944

The Squadron commenced practice flying on the Mustang IIIs and also some formation flying with the Spitfires.

At 1200 hours the Squadron took off on a fighter sweep of the Bayeux – Cambrai area. They climbed to 18,000 feet and an Me210 was sighted by Wing Commander Grant, who gave chase and opened fire, scoring several hits. Both squadrons 'queued up' for attacks and many strikes were seen. Those who fired were: Flight Lieutenant Wigley, Warrant Officer Woodward, Flight Sergeant Chisham, and Flying Officer Page. Squadron Leader Durrant and Flight Sergeant Hutchinson became separated from the Squadron on the way out and were bounced by four Me109s. Their aircraft sustained slight damage but both returned safely.

During the afternoon the Squadron returned to practice flying in the Mustangs. Flying Officer D.A. Page was killed when he crashed in a Mustang on a practice flight a few miles from base, the causes are yet unknown.

24th January 1944

The Squadron took off at 0900 hours on a fighter sweep of the Le Touquet area. They climbed to 22,000 feet, and were then instructed to act as a fighter umbrella over Pas de Calais whilst it was being bombed by Marauders. No enemy aircraft were seen.

Immediately on landing, the Squadron was briefed to act as withdrawal support to five combat wings of Fortresses returning from the south west of Germany. The Squadron took off at 1145 hours and commenced climbing to 28,000 feet. Eventually the bombers were found, with formations of Thunderbolts slightly above and smoking. One section of which came down as though to attack, but they recognised us and continued on their course.

25th January 1944

Six Spitfires were flown to Detling and were being replaced with Mustangs. Practice flying in the Mustangs was carried out in the morning. In the evening a Squadron party was held in Gravesend, the groundcrew being the guests of the pilots.

Mustang 111

(Crown Copyright – MOD – IWM)

30th January 1944

An exercise was carried out in which the Squadron attacked ground targets and troops. The navigation was good and targets detailed were suitably attacked, although the umpires criticism was that many of our aircraft were exposing themselves unnecessarily to attack from light flak, especially in the get away after the attack. This was mainly due to inexperience and new aircraft, and with practice will undoubtably be improved.

14th February 1944

The Squadron became operational with the Mustangs. Its new task involved long-range bomber escorts and dive-bombing, the greater range of the Mustang enabling the Squadron to reach farther into Germany. Armed recces were also popular that summer and enabled the Squadron's pilots to have a go at German aircraft again.

15th February 1944

This morning the Squadron made its debut with the Mustang IIIs. The pilots were briefed for a fighter sweep over Holland and Northern France at 25,000 feet and took off at 0950 hours.

White Section – Flight Lieutenant Drinkwater, Flight Sergeant Biggs, Flying Officer Wass, Flight Sergeant Vassiliades;

Dick Section* – Squadron Leader Durrant, Flight Sergeant Redgate, Flight Lieutenant Ross, Flight Sergeant Carson;

Green Section – Flight Lieutenant Wigley, Flying Officer Cooper, Flight Lieutenant Lamb, Flight Sergeant Chisham:

The Squadron swept the Antwerp, Brussels, Cambrai area and returned over Bologne, without any enemy intervention. Although uneventful, everyone was happy with our new kites.

The Squadron was airborne again at 1530 hours to do another fighter sweep across Holland to within two miles of the German border.

White Section – Flight Lieutenant Drinkwater, Flight Sergeant Fellows, Flight Sergeant Vassiliades, Flight Sergeant Redgate;

Dick Section – Squadron Leader Durrant, Flight Sergeant Chesham, Flying Officer Wass, Flight Sergeant Wells;

Green Section – Flight Lieutenant Wigley, Flight Sergeant King, Flying Officer Cooper, Flying Officer Paton:

20th February 1944

The Squadron was airborne at 0940 hours on a fighter sweep to Bergen, north of Venlo, on the German border in support of Marauders bombing Eindhaven and Fortresses going to Germany. They crossed at zero feet and ten minutes from the Dutch coast started to climb and crossed the same at 9,000 feet. Accurate and intense flak was experienced.

At 1335 hours the Squadron acted as withdrawal support to Fortresses and Liberators returning from Germany.

2nd March 1944

At 1030 hours the Squadron took off to escort Fortresses going to Frankfurt. The Squadron escorted them as far as the River Meuse, where Thunderbolts took over. No enemy aircraft seen.

---

* Not a cock-up by the Editor; they actually used that identification.

4th March 1944

Today was the first show to be done with Mustangs with long range tanks. The Squadron was airborne at 1210 hours to rendezvous with Fortresses that had bombed Berlin, 90 miles south west at Leipzig, 450 miles from base. Very bad weather conditions were encountered, climbing through cloud at 12,000 feet and not reaching the top until at 26,000 feet.

Flight Sergeant Redgate (White 2) was never seen again after entering cloud but it is believed he had engine trouble.

Flight Sergeant T.H. Redgate (FX188) – is missing.

6th March 1944

The Squadron was airborne at 1140 hours to act as withdrawal support to 660 Fortresses which had been bombing Berlin. Rendezvous was made with the bombers 110 miles west of the target and escorted them back without engaging any enemy aircraft.

7th March 1944

The Squadron flew to Coltishall. Taking off again at 1455 hours to escort 30 Beaufighters to attack shipping in the Heligoland Bight.

8th March 1944

The Squadron took off at 1255 hours to act as withdrawal support for Fortresses and Liberators bombing Brunswick. No enemy aircraft seen.

9th March 1944

At 1135 hours the Squadron was airborne to act as fighter cover to Fortresses bombing Berlin. Rendezvous was made at Celle, near Hanover. No enemy aircraft seen.

Flying Officer Saville was hit by flak. He called up to say that his oil pressure had gone and that he was baling out.

Flying Officer D.E. Saville (FZ133) – is missing.

18th March 1944

The Squadron provided escort to 12 Mosquitoes at Electrical Equipment Factory at Hengels at low level. They took off at 1500 hours.

24th March 1944

Three aircraft escorted Fortresses to Schweinfurt, the rest returned to base because of tank trouble. Flight Lieutenant Wigley (Dick 1) was shot up by flak and baled out on a local golf course a few miles from base. He was flying FZ139.

29th March 1944

The Squadron took off at 1520 hours to escort 27 Beaufighters on a shipping strike off the Hook of Holland. The formation flew at zero feet across the North Sea and the convoy was sighted. A highly successful attack was carried out as 18 Beaufighter went in first as anti-flak, followed by nine torpedo carriers. Two ships were claimed as sunk and several others as severely damaged. One Beaufighter was lost.

8th April 1944

The Squadron took off at 1210 hours to do a Ranger to the Brunswick area in support of Fortresses and Liberators bombing in that area. No enemy aircraft were seen on the way in but

Warrant Officer Sima and Flight Lieutenant Ross sustained light damage from flak. On the return trip, the Squadron went down to zero feet and shot up ground targets, before climbing up again to cross the coast.

9th April 1944

Today was the Squadron's turn for practice bombing and in all 29 sorties were flown. Cloud prevented dive bombing, so low level attacks were carried out.

10th April 1944

The Squadron took off at 0910 hours to act as fighter umbrella over Le Havre whilst Marauders were bombing targets in that vicinity. The area was swept without incident.

At 1720 hours they acted as close escort to Beaufighters on a shipping strike off the Frisian Islands. The only shipping found were small vessels which were not attacked.

11th April 1944

At 0930 hours the Squadron took off to act as withdrawal support for 900 Fortresses and Liberators bombing an aircraft factory in the Magdeburg area. Flak was experienced both on the way in and during the withdrawal. Flight Lieutenant Ross and Pilot Officer Chisham sustained light damage. The Squadron covered the second group of Liberators leaving the target but no enemy aircraft were intercepted.

It was announced that evening that Flight Lieutenant Drinkwater had been promoted to Squadron Leader and will take over as Commanding Officer of No 122 Squadron.

12th April 1944

Flying commenced this morning with dive bombing practice at 1035 hours.

22nd April 1944

The Squadron took off at 1625 hours with No 65 Squadron to do a fighter sweep in the Strasbourg – Nancy area. 19 Squadron was acting as top cover to the other squadron.

Wing Commander G.R.A. Mc G. Johnson D.F.C. sighted 14 Me109s at 16,000 feet, south of Leon at 1730 hours. They were 400 yards below and turning to port, half rolled and dived. He followed one down, lost him but continued to dive and flattened out at zero feet. He then saw five Me109s on his port side, showing black smoke. He chased these, caught the last one and opened fire. Petrol then sprayed out from its drop tank as he overshot him and got on the tail of two other Me109s. He fired from dead astern at the rear enemy aircraft and saw his strikes. The enemy aircraft then took him through some high tension cables which interrupted his firing. The Me109 was incredibly low and either his engine stopped or he throttled back. Wing Commander Johnson put down 20 degree flaps and closed in firing as he did so. Light smoke streamed out, his nose dropped and the Me109 hit the side of a small valley and blew up. Flight Sergeant Vassiliades also destroyed a Me109.

Pilot Officer Chisham was attacked and hit. He was heard to say that he was force landing.

Pilot Officer W.A Chisham (FX990) – is missing.

23rd April 1944

The Squadron took off in the afternoon and swept the Bois and Metz area, without success at zero feet. On the way out just before climbing to cross the coast, Flight Lieutenant Ross was hit by flak which was seen by Flight Sergeant Pearce (Green 4). A few seconds later, it was observed that his machine was on fire and he was seen to turn on his back and hit the deck from 200 feet. The aircraft immediately burst into flames.

Flight Lieutenant D.C. Ross (FZ158) – is missing.

25th April 1944

The Squadron took off at 0815 hours acting as fighter cover for Fortresses which had been bombing Frankfurt. No enemy aircraft were seen.

26th April 1944

The Squadron took off before dawn to do a fighter sweep in the Rheims – Koblenz area. The sweep was uneventful.

That evening at 1740 hours the Squadron acted as close escort to 30 Beaufighters attacking shipping off the Frisian Islands. An enemy convoy was sighted at 2050 hours and the Beaufighters attacked with cannon and torpedos. One ship was set on fire and blew up and several others were severely damaged. One Beaufighter is missing.

28th April 1944

Flight Sergeant B. Vassiliades (White 1) was at zero feet at 1540 hours in the Liagle area leading White section when Flight Sergeant Fellows reported an unidentified aircraft at 100 feet.

Flight Sergeants Warren (White 3) and Flight Sergeant Fellows (White 4) broke towards it and Flight Sergeant Vassiliades followed and came up line astern, but was unable to identify it. He flew line abreast, identified it as a Arado 96, turned and attacked. After several attacks he saw strikes in the cockpit.

Flight Sergeant Warren (White 3) opened fire from 150 yards astern and saw his strikes on the fuselage. The enemy aircraft was taking violent evasive action as White section attacked in turn. His next attack was from 150 yards astern again, the enemy aircraft stalled off, glided down over some high tension cables and crash landed in a field. He attacked again and the enemy aircraft burst into flames.

Flight Sergeant Fellows (White 4) got in long bursts from 400 closing to 100 yards in a head-on attack, whilst the others of White section attacked from astern and portside.

4th May 1944

The Squadron participated in large scale invasion exercises on the south coast, by supplying fighter cover over the beaches.

6th May 1944

Flying Officer Germain with two aircraft from No 122 Squadron carried out a ranger over to Denmark at zero feet. The three aircraft flew over the North Sea at zero feet and round the Frisian Islands. After successfully beating up an aerodrome where each pilot claims a damaged, the section was bounced by four Fw190s. Flying Officer Germain was shot down. His aircraft was seen to burst into flames and was last seen diving vertically on fire.

Flying Officer E.L. Germain (FX955) – is missing.

8th May 1944

The Wing was released today for dive bombing and at 1935 hours, the Squadron took off for a target in Northern France but cloud was over the target. An alternative target of Mardyke aerodrome was successfully attacked. Many hits being scored in the dispersal areas.

At 1700 hours the Squadron took off again to attack the Marshalling Yards north of St Quentin. Excellent results were observed as the Squadron attacked from 10,000 feet.

11th May 1944

The Squadron took off at 1100 hours to bomb the Marshalling Yards at Charleroi. The attack was highly successful in spite of hazy conditions.

At 1820 hours they attacked the same target. This time the haze made it difficult to find the target and the bombing was disappointing.

12th May 1944

The Squadron flew to Southend for a bombing and gunnery course lasting one week. This provided the pilots and groundcrew with a respite from the intense operational activity which this "pre-invasion" period brought. When this brief spell was over, the Squadron proceeded to Funtington.

20th May 1944

The Squadron moved to Funtington.

At 1505 hours the Squadron took off to bomb the marshalling yard at Verberie. Hits were observed. Dive bombing became one of the regular duties of the Squadron from this time.

21st May 1944

Eight Mustangs of the Squadron together with two Mosquitos of 418 Squadron set course at 1400 hours from Coltishall at zero feet. Landfall was made east of Lildstrand where the Red and Blue Sections, with one Mosquito flew to the north of Aalborg and White and Green Section with the other Mosquito flew south of Aalborg, intending to meet again at Hobro.

Flight Lieutenant Shirreff (White 1) sighted a Leo 45 flying south at 2,000 feet and the Mosquito gave chase. At this moment an Me109 came in towards Flight Lieutenant Bird (Green 1) who pulled up in a climbing turn and met the enemy aircraft head-on. The enemy aircraft opened fire and Flight Lieutenant Bird's aircraft burst into flames and disintegrated. Flight Lieutenant Shirreff then saw the Mosquito open fire at the Leo 45 and bits fell off it. The section reformed and continued south. Another Leo 45 was seen at 1,000 feet. The Mosquito turned to starboard, followed by White Section and Green 2, closing in from dead astern. The Mosquito fired and broke away. Flight Lieutenant Shirreff then attacked from dead astern, opening fire at 400 yards and closing to 150 yards and saw his strikes all over the enemy aircraft. Pieces fell off, the enemy aircraft burst into flames, disintegrated and fell to earth.

Warrant Officer Bell (White 2) was ahead and above the section and put down some flap. He saw the Mosquito attacking the Leo 45 and he opened fire from 400 yards closing to 150 yards. The enemy aircraft stuck her nose down which brought Warrant Officer Bell into line astern and he continued firing. He saw his strikes on the port engine, which blew up and the port wing fell off. The enemy aircraft then fell in flames.

Warrant Officer Woodward (Green 2) was in line astern with the Mosquito and Flight Lieutenant Shirreff. After they had attacked, he opened fire from 300 closing to 75 yards and saw his strikes all along the fuselage. He broke away and next saw the enemy aircraft burning on the ground.

Flight Lieutenant A.G. Bird, D.F.C. (FX999) – is missing.

Flight Sergeant W.T. Warren (FB198) – is missing.

23rd May 1944

The Squadron took off at 0720 to carry out a fighter sweep in the Koblenz – Metz – Nancy areas. Considerable heavy and accurate flak was experienced. Three aircraft were slightly damaged during the sortie – Flight Sergeant Vassiliades, Flying Officer Smith and Warrant Officer Sima.

24th May 1944

The Squadron became airborne at 1049 to dive bomb railway junctions and stations at Buchy, Northern France. No flak was encountered and the bombing was carried out with excellent results. It was generally agreed to have been the best bombing done to date.

28th May 1944

The Squadron took off at 1340 hours to give withdrawal support to Fortresses and Liberators bombing targets in the Magdeburg area.

29th May 1944

Squadron Leader Gilmour took command of the Squadron.

30th May 1944

The Squadron took off at 0900 hours to escort bombers attacking the airfields at Oldenburg south west of Bremen. Heavy flak was encountered but the attack was pressed home.

3rd June 1944

The Squadron took off at 1410 hours to dive bomb a petrol dump, north of Paris. The target was located and bombed from 8,000 feet. Bombs dropped in the target area but no direct hits were scored.

'D' DAY – 6TH JUNE 1944

The Squadron operating under the 2nd Tactical Air Force, acted as close support for the landing of airborne troops behind enemy lines; in conjunction with this task an army reconnaissance of the beach-head was made. Subsequently the Squadron flew many armed reconnaissance sorties over the battle area. Bombing and straffing of enemy communications, roads, railways, bridges, transport and armoured fighting vehicles took place with excellent results.

The Squadron took off at 2030 hours to do an armed reconnaissance over the beach head. In conjunction with the reconnaissance sortie, the Squadron acted as close escort to an Airborne Division namely the 5th Landing Brigade, who were landing behind the enemy lines. The operation was successful and there was no interference from enemy aircraft.

7th June 1944

At 0755 hours the Squadron took off for an armed reconnaissance with 500lb bombs. The weather was very bad, the cloud being down to 1,000 feet in places. Bombing was impossible.

At 1200 they tried again and patrolled south of Caen, bombing enemy motor transport and armoured vehicles. During the bombing Pilot Officer Wendt was hit by flak and baled out. Unfortunately he appeared to land in the burning wreckage of his own aircraft.

Pilot Officer W.D. Wendt (FZ141) – is missing.

Western France

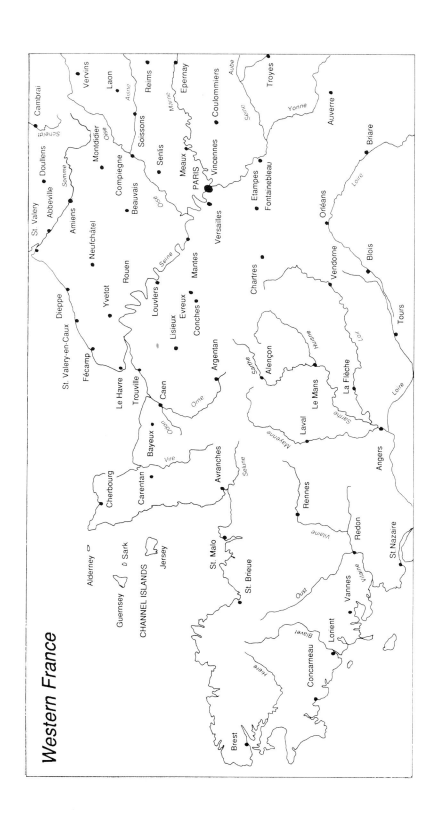

The third sortie of the day was at 1815 hours but again the weather prevented bombing.

8th June 1944

The Squadron took off at 0535 hours for an armed reconnaissance over the battle area. Enemy motor transport and marshalling yards were attacked with considerable success.

Again at 0950 hours they took off on another successful armed reconnaissance.

The third sortie was at 1930 hours but the weather was very bad over the battle area.

10th June 1944

Six Mustangs led by Flight Lieutenant Lamb on an armed recce in the Argentan area, were vectored to a wood south of Caen, at 1920 hours. Ground attacks were being made on Military Targets in the Thury Harcourt area.

Flight Lieutenant Lamb reports "We had just finished straffing some Motor Transport vehicles when I sighted two Me109s flying across us at 2,000 feet about one mile away. I ordered the section to jettison bombs, open up and chase. I picked the right hand one and gave him a five second burst from line astern from 400 to 200 yards. I saw numerous strikes on his starboard wing and he then went into thin cloud and I overshot. There was a general melee and I picked him up again dodging in and out of cloud. I chased him for about 15 minutes and finally I got close to his tail only to find that I was out of ammunition."

Flight Sergeant Carson straffed some trucks and climbed to 2,500 feet when his leader reported two Me109. He got in behind the enemy aircraft on the left and opened fire from 450 yards. The enemy aircraft went into a gentle turn and he could see his strikes on the cowling. He continued to close, saw more strikes, when the enemy aircraft turned on its back at 500 feet, and crashed into the ground blowing up as it did so.

Warrant Officer Sima after straffing the ground targets sighted two Me109s flying in line abreast. As he closed in, the port enemy aircraft flew into cloud, so he flew left and waited for it to reappear. It did so, in the opposite direction. He chased and closed to 300 yards, fired and saw his strikes all over the enemy aircraft. The enemy aircraft started to emit white smoke, went into a slight dive, hit the ground and burst into flames.

Warrant Officer Holmes attacked the ground targets and then shared the Me109 with Warrant Officer Sima. He followed the Me109 into cloud. He chased him through broken cloud firing six to eight bursts and observed numerous strikes on the starboard wing. He then lost him in the cloud.

12th June 1944

The Squadron took off at 1930 hours on an armed reconnaissance. Enemy ground targets were attacked with considerable success.

At 1930 hours they were escorts to Bostons and Mitchells bombing targets south of Caen. Once again many enemy ground targets were attacked.

14th June 1944

The Squadron took off at 0520 on an armed reconnaissance. Whilst bombing and straffing an enemy road convoy, Flight Sergeant Kairton's aircraft blew up and went straight in. It is believed that he flew too low and was caught in the blast of his own bombs.

Flight Sergeant D.B. Kairton (FX882) – is missing.

The second sortie at 1140 hours, the Squadron was on a bombing attack on the marshalling yards at Rambouillet but due to cloud cover over the target, the attack could not be carried out. When returning three Me109s were seen at 2,000 feet, 10 miles south east of Dreux.

Flying Officer Paton (Green 1) jettisoned his bombs and dived down on one of the Me109s. As he closed the enemy aircraft broke hard to port and dived towards the ground. Flying Officer Paton followed at ground level and opened fire at 400 yards closing to 300 yards. He saw strikes behind the cockpit and the aircraft hit a tree and pulled up steeply. He fired again and saw more strikes on the wings. The undercarriage fell down, and the enemy aircraft fell to the ground and blew up.

Warrant Officer Sima (Green 2) attacked after his leader and fired about six bursts seeing strikes from a four second burst at 350 yards, when the Me109 flew through his line of fire.

Flight Sergeant Wells also attacked the same Me109 and saw his strikes when his starboard guns stopped firing.

Pilot Officer Schofield (White 1) opened fire on his Me109 from 300 yards and saw his shells hit.

The Me109 destroyed was shared by the four pilots.

Warrant Officer Bell (White 2) was at 5,000 feet, 30 miles west of Paris when it was reported that there were three Me109s at zero feet. He saw an Me109 flying away south-east and gave chase. He overhauled so slowly that he opened fire at 800 yards. The enemy aircraft turned to port and Warrant Officer Bell followed, his bombs dropping off in the turn. The Me109 was weaving and turning and Warrant Officer Bell was having difficulties in getting his sights on him. The enemy aircraft straightened out and he got in a burst from line astern. The Me109 did a shallow dive into a ploughed field. Warrant Officer Bell circled and made an attack at the wreckage which burst into flames.

15th June 1944

The Squadron moved to Ford. On the third armed reconnaissance at 2120 hours, enemy motor transport was reported moving up the road south east of Falaise, but no movement could be observed. As an alternative, bridges were attacked and the Mezidan – Lisieux railway line.

16th June 1944

The Squadron took off on an armed reconnaissance at 1355 hours. Convoys bombed in the Vire – Vimoutiers area, with several direct hits.

The second sortie at 2100 hours and attacked the railway embankment at Mantleaux.

17th June 1944

On an armed reconnaissance at 1735 hours, bombing was difficult due to cloud cover. Flight Sergeant Vassiliades and Flying Officer Maynard bombed a small convoy and were bounced by eight Me109s but got away. Flight Sergeant Vassiliades's machine was hit on starboard wing and landed on the beachhead to ascertain the damage. He returned to base OK.

A sortie later that day on the same railway line scored a direct hit and the line was severed.

20th June 1944

The Squadron was detailed for a bombing attack on Railway Line near Rambouillet. At 1630 hours ten miles from the target, 12 Fw190s were sighted climbing to attack the Squadron.

Squadron Leader Gilmour D.F.C., D.F.M., "Bombs were jettisoned smartly and a merry battle ensued. I got behind a Fw190 and started firing from about 300 yards. I saw strikes. The Fw190 started for cloud and I followed closing to astern still firing. I hit him squarely just before entering cloud. I came through to see a Fw190 spinning down to crash in a pall of flame near some woods behind a village. (Confirmed). I climbed again and closed on another Fw190. I had to break after this attack but my No 2 Pilot Officer Staples, saw strikes on this aircraft and saw it going down."

Flight Sergeant Carson saw four Fw190s coming up from 5 o'clock below. He immediately broke and his No 1 spun off his trim and was lost sight of. There was a big mix up and he attacked four or five aircraft. Flight Sergeant Carson saw strikes on one but it broke down and he lost it. He got strikes on another and saw smoke coming from it. He had to break away but the enemy aircraft appeared to be badly hit and was going down smoking. He attacked some other aircraft until his ammunition ran out.

Flight Lieutenant Lamb was leading Green section when the Fw190s attacked. He ordered "Jettison bombs and engage". The German showed considerable inclination to stay and dogfight but was obviously inexperienced as it was quite easy to outfight him, though at first we were outnumbered by three to one. He engaged two Fw190s with short burst and saw one spin with pieces chipped off him. Later, he bounced another and closed in seeing many strikes, a bright explosion from the fuselage and large pieces drop off. He saw the enemy aircraft spin in and explode on the ground.

Pilot Officer Davies (Green 2) kept with his leader to guard his tail during the dogfight. Whilst on the tail of a Fw190 he had an opportunity to have a squirt from 200 yards. He saw a bright flash and strikes all over the fuselage with pieces falling off. His leader did most of the shooting whilst Davies watched his tail. The Fw190 dived through cloud and crashed.

Flying Officer Plumridge (Green 3) saw his No 2 unable to get rid of his bombs and spin off in a turn. He was following Flight Lieutenant Lamb and Pilot Officer Davies when he saw a Fw190 about to attack Pilot Officer Davies. He opened up from 3-400 yards, saw no strikes. Closed to less than 200 yards and saw strikes on the fuselage and starboard wing. An Fw190 was about to attack him, so he had to break away. Both enemy aircraft then disappeared into cloud.

Flight Lieutenant Collyns was leading White section. He attacked a Fw190 from 200 yards and fired just as he started to zoom and turn. His first burst missed, so he altered deflection and saw numerous strikes on and around the cockpit and pieces falling off. At that moment, Collyns was hit by a cannon shell in the starboard wing and had to break off combat with the Fw190 as it started to roll away.

Pilot Officer F.D. Schofield (FB223) – is missing.

21st June 1944

At 1840 hours the Squadron was dive bombing a bridge over Conches.

Flight Lieutenant Lamb (Green 1) with his section was acting as cover whilst the rest of the squadron dive bombed the bridge, when 10 to 15 Me109s arrived. He ordered his section to jettison bombs and attack. "We had a wizard dog fight, one Me109 turning with me for a while until eventually he threw in the sponge and broke it off. I closed in on his tail and gave him everything until I ran out of ammo and he was pouring smoke. I watched him go down and crash in a field."

Flying Officer Paton (Green 3) attacked an Me109 and gave it a very short burst. He saw his strikes on the cockpit and the pilot baled out. He then attacked two Me109s on the deck chasing a Mustang which was firing at a 109. They broke away as he overshot and pulled up.

Warrant Officer Sima attacked a Me109 and saw strikes on the fuselage and a bit of white smoke come from it.

Flight Sergeant Vassiliades (White 1) after his bombing run broke left into sun and saw 15 to 20 Me109s. He climbed hard and tried to engage the last one, but had to break violently as he found two Me109s firing at him. He then saw a Me109 diving and followed it down to the deck giving it several bursts. He saw some strikes and the engine stop. The enemy aircraft glided for about 2,000 feet and crashed into a little forest and caught fire.

Flight Lieutenant R. Haywood put up a splendid show when, having been hit in both legs by a Me109, he stayed and fought, until he had shot down the aircraft which had attacked him. He then returned to base and made a splendid landing, in spite of his injuries. He was admitted to hospital. Fortunately his wounds are only flesh ones and he is well on the way to recovery.

22nd June 1944

At 1210 hours the Squadron took off to strafe enemy troops and motor transport in the Cherbourg peninsular. They dived from 15,000 feet to zero feet, and the whole wing straffed in line abreast, attacking anything of military importance on the ground. Flight Lieutenant Collyns (FB105) was hit and sustained a glycol leak. He pulled up to 6,000 feet and baled out safely.

At 1750 and 1930 six aircraft took off on armed reconnaissance and attacked ground targets.

24th June 1944

The Squadron was airborne at 0605 hours on an armed reconnaissance in the Druix area. About 20 Me109s were sighted and engaged. A good fight ensued during which the Squadron shot down four and damaged one. Flight Sergeant Vassiliades – two Me109s destroyed, Flying Officer Maynard – one Me109 destroyed, Warrant Officer Bell – one Me109 destroyed, and Warrant Officer Holmes – one Me109 destroyed.

25th June 1944

In the morning, the Squadron, together with the rest of No 122 Wing, moved to an airstrip in France only about five miles from the front line – Martrigny. This move obviously gave the Squadron a great advantage by cutting out the two-way journey across the English Channel, so that the pilots could spend much more time over the battle area.

26th June 1944

After a day of putting up tents and digging slit trenches, the weather clamped down. The day was spent sitting in leaky tents and playing cards.

27th June 1944

The armed reconnaissance at 0705 and 1615 hours were made difficult due to the weather. On the second sortie, Flying Officer Paton saw two enemy aircraft, had a squirt but without any luck. In the evening a few sorties were made to Bayeux and the town was clobbered in suitable 19 style.

28th June 1944

The Squadron took off at 1520 hours to dive bomb bridges south west of Caen, in the hope of impeding the withdrawal of the enemy's Panzers in that area. Some heavy and accurate flak on the way to the target. Flight Sergeant Pearce and Flying Officer MacNiel were hit but not severely damaged. Several near misses were obtained. Just after lunch, the aerodrome was straffed by eight Fw190s. Everybody dived smartly to earth and no damage was done. Two of the Huns were shot down by our light flak.

Mustang being repaired in Normandy

(Crown Copyright – MOD – IWM)

29th June 1944

The previous day's target was attacked at 0845 hours. Bombing was excellent and bursts were seen all round the bridge, although no one was lucky enough to breech it.

30th June 1944

Due to the weather, the Squadron were unable to take off until 1735 hours to dive bomb the crossroads at Villers – Bocage area. Bombing results were good and no enemy aircraft were seen.

Flying Officer Cameron was seen to go into a spin after pulling out of his dive, and went straight in for reasons unknown.

Flying Officer M.L. Cameron (FZ181) – is missing.

3rd July 1944

The target today was a bridge on the River Orne. The Squadron took off at 1915 hours and attacked the bridge, although there were several near misses, no direct hit was scored. Flak in the area was intense and concentrated, Flying Officer Cooper's machine being hit but he landed safely.

6th July 1944

The Squadron took off 0800 hours for an armed reconnaissance in the Flers – Argenten – Bernay area. There were junctions and marshalling yards south east of Argenten, which were attacked with considerable success and several direct hits were scored.

8th July 1944

Airborne at 0615 hours on an armed reconnaissance, without bombs, in the Caen, Bernay, Dreux, Argenten, Caen areas. Flying Officer Cooper took Green Section down and straffed a goods train standing in the sidings west of Vernouil and strikes were observed throughout the whole length of the train. Intense light flak was encountered during the attack, but the Section dived beneath the cordon of fire and got away successfully.

Jamjar Section attacked some buses loaded with enemy troops.

At 1000 hours the Squadron took off on another armed reconnaissance west of the previous sector. On the Caen – Villiers road, Green Section went down to attack Motor transport. Flying Officer Cooper scored many strikes on two lorries.

Jamjar Section consisting of Flight Lieutenant Lamb, Flying Officer Maynard and Flight Sergeant Vassiliades, at 1945 near Alencon, were staffing military targets. They then saw two Me109s flying east and gave chase. During the chase, both enemy aircraft were first damaged and then destroyed as they struck the ground and blew up. One enemy aircraft pilot baled out.

10th July 1944

At 0750 the Squadron took off to dive bomb a German Headquarters south west of Caen. Two direct hits were scored. The Squadron said farewell to Flight Lieutenant Lamb, on his promotion to Squadron Leader and he leaves to take command of No 65 Squadron.

(Whilst CO of 65, he was shot down over Holland on the 9th September, and was fired at by the Hun pilot as he descended in his parachute. He took evasive action by pulling the cords, and was not hit, but the violent motion whipped off his shoes, which vanished into the blue. His eyes and leg had been burnt before he left the aircraft, so his one mile sprint to shelter was not enjoyable. He was hidden by the Dutch and his injuries were attended to by a Dutch doctor. At the end of three days he could see properly again, and almost the first thing his eyes alighted upon was a policeman arriving with his shoes, beautifully polished. He was chased by the Gestapo, complete with hounds, but was back with his Squadron ten days after being shot down.)

12th July 1944

Squadron Leader Gilmour, D.F.C., D.F.M., was leading the Squadron on an armed recce in the Le Mans area. When flying on course south east of Caen at 12,000 feet, his section was bounced by eight Me109s, the section broke and a general melee ensued. He saw a further eight Me109s circling above with a Fw190. He had a few squirts before picking on a definite enemy aircraft. He manœuvred to get astern and the enemy aircraft saw him, half rolled and dived. Squadron Leader Gilmour followed in an almost vertical dive, through cloud to 3,000 feet, when he started to pull out. At this moment, the Me109s port wing snapped off and the aircraft flicked violently straight into the ground. He looked at his ASI and it was showing over 600mph. He blacked out pulling out of the dive. When Squadron Leader Gilmour came to, he was at 12,000 feet. There were no enemy aircraft about so he went down again to pinpoint his enemy aircraft and saw another Me109 which had made a heavy forced landing (wings broken off and fuselage snapped) burning in a field.

Flying Officer Paton broke left when attacked by the Me109s. At 9,000 feet he saw an Me109 on its own. He dived to attack closing to 100 yards and saw numerous strikes on the starboard wing root and starboard side cockpit and engine covers. He overshot the enemy aircraft and pulled up steeply. The Me109 was pouring columns of black smoke and diving into cloud. It looked as though he had no power.

(Intelligence Officer's Note:- "This ties up with the one Squadron Leader Gilmour saw burning on the ground and therefore Flying Officer Paton claims an Me109 destroyed.")

Flying Officer Staples was behind his No 1 Flight Sergeant Wells who was chasing an Me109. A Fw190 came up behind Flight Sergeant Wells and in front of Flying Officer Staples. He fired at the Fw190, which then broke down and he followed. Firing again, he saw numerous strikes on the engine cowling. The enemy aircraft did a wing over and went down vertically with black smoke and occasional jets of flame coming from the engine. He followed the enemy aircraft down in a vertical dive at 580mph, he was going even faster and it entered cloud at 3,000 feet still having made no effort to pull out. Flying Officer Staples eased out of the dive just recovering at 800 feet, searched for wreckage without success.

Flying Officer Davies heard the shout of 'break' as he saw eight Me109s diving to attack. He broke to starboard and pulled back up in a zoom. He saw a Me109 just above him so got astern and fired. A big puff of black smoke came from the enemy aircraft which half rolled and disappeared into cloud.

Flying Officer Heath turned with his No 1 Flight Lieutenant Collyns towards the fight. An Me109 came at Flight Lieutenant Collyns and he held his fire until 250 yards. He saw strikes on the tail and wing root of the Me109. As the enemy aircraft pulled up he fired another long burst, again noting strikes on tail and wing root. The Me109 smoked slightly, rolled over and spun down slowly. Flying Officer Heath broke his attack to meet the attack of another Me109.

Warrant Officer Carson broke right, into the attacking Me109s. He climbed up after two and gave the port side one three bursts, closing to 200 yards. He saw his strikes on the port side forward of the cockpit, and white smoke came from the engine. He also had to break away as another Me109 came into attack.

Flying Officer Maynard sustained slight head injuries but landed safely at base.

Flight Sergeant P. Donkin (FB113) crash landed on the airfield with a dead engine.

The claims for this day were:-

Squadron Leader Gilmour	–	1 Me109 destroyed
Flying Officer Paton	–	1 Me109 destroyed
Flying Officer Staples	–	1 Fw190 damaged
Flying Officer Davies	–	1 Me109 damaged
Flying Officer Heath	–	1 Me109 damaged
Warrant Officer Carson	–	1 Me109 damaged

13th July 1944

The Squadron was airborne at 1705 hours to act as escort to Nos 65 and 122 Squadrons who were bombing Marshalling Yards south of Paris. No Huns were seen. The bombing was good and a couple of directs were obtained.

14th July 1944

The Squadron took off at 1010 hours on an armed reconnaissance of the Alencon – Chartres area. Cloud made reconnaissance difficult but enemy motor transport was successfully attacked.

15th July 1944

The Squadron moved to Ellon.

16th July 1944

At 0300 hours the Huns artillery opened up with extremely accurate fire on the airfield. This continued intermittently until 0400 hours by which time everybody was considerably shaken, especially as nobody had had time to dig slit trenches. Several of the tents were damaged by shrapnel but no pilots were damaged. Three groundcrew were killed (L.A.C. R.C. Tebby, Cpl. G.J. Sloman and Cpl. J.D. Ellis) and several others injured. When dawn came, the Squadron had only four serviceable aircraft left. The Squadron was released this day from operations to allow for maintenance to start repairing the damage and the pilots to get some sleep. Needless to say we changed our sleeping site to a much more pleasant and healthy spot some three miles from the drome.

Flight Lieutenant "Jock" Taylor recalls;

"The night of the merciless shelling. We had just arrived at Ellon, Normandy, which was about three to four miles from the front lines. Naturally, the good old Wermacht had it well taped and easily saw the Mustangs take up residence. We went into our tents, happily listening to shells from a nearby artillery winging their way to the German lines. However, around 3.00am we weren't quite so happy when a two way traffic began! The Germans had moved one or two of their noted 88mm guns up as close as possible, under cover of darkness and proceeded to give the place a good going over with anti-personnel shells. They left a shallow mark upon hitting and showered plenty of shrapnel forward. 65 Squadron was dispersed on one side of the runway and 19 and 122 on the other, and the Germans didn't waste anything. 65 Squadron had the benefit of the first session, then after half time they neatly switched over and gave 19 and 122 Squadron the benefit. Twenty one aircraft damaged by shrapnel and a bowser set alight".

18th July 1944

The Squadron took off at 0930 hours to give close army support by bombing the village of Garcelles. The trip was a very successful one and the target was duly pranged. The squadrons aircraft flew to Lantheuil for the night as a precaution against the shelling.

19th July 1944

The Squadron took off at 1445 hours to act as escort to Mitchells bombing oil and petrol dumps near Orleans. Rendezvous was made with the bombers, the target area was clear and the Mitchells carried out their bombing uninterrupted by flak or enemy aircraft.

25th July 1944

At 0615 hours, the Squadron was airborne to attack a village, St Sylvain, south east of Caen. Cloud cover made pin pointing over the target impossible, so an alternative crossroads south of Villiers Bocage was attacked with considerable success and several direct hits being scored.

The second sortie at 1035 hours was an armed reconnaissance and fighter sweep south of Paris. The Squadron's target was the railway tunnel west of Mantes Gassicourt, which was well and truly pranged. At least 15 direct hits being scored. The Squadron climbed up again and in the vicinity of Dreux, about 40 Fw190 and Me109s were seen. The Squadron climbed hard to intercept but failed to make contact.

The third sortie was to attack a train east of Dreux. At 1615 hours east of Lisieux, at 10,000 feet, after chasing two Me109s south east of Cherbourg, Warrant Officer Carson (Green 1) and Pilot Officer Simon (Green 2), had to break away as they were being attacked by two more aircraft which turned out to be Mustangs. He and Pilot Officer Simon rejoined the Squadron when they sighted four Fw190s with long range tanks. The enemy aircraft passed on the right and he broke round and followed them. Warrant Officer Carson attacked the Fw190 on the right, followed it down, firing as he closed to 200 yards. Strikes were seen forward of the cockpit and at 1,500 feet the enemy aircraft's pilot baled out.

Warrant Officer Bell selected the left hand Fw190, following it down to the deck as he overhauled it slowly. He opened fire at 400 yards and the enemy aircraft broke violently as strikes were observed on the port wing. "A wizard dog fight ensued, during which the enemy aircraft did a series of steep turns and aerobatics". He saw no strikes. The Fw190 then did some very low flying and Warrant Officer Bell got in a short burst from dead astern. The enemy aircraft pulled up and as he overshot it saw the pilot jettison the hood and bale out at 1,000 feet.

26th July 1944
The first sortie was at 0655 hours on an armed reconnaissance in the Evreux – Mantes area. Trucks were attacked in the Mantes – Gassicourt, and two direct hits were scored, with one truck being left in flames.

Flight Sergeant Vassiliades awarded the Distinguished Flying Medal.

This was the Squadron's first "gong" for over 18 months.

30th July 1944
The Squadron was briefed to dive bomb with 1,000lb bombs on Cahagnes, but at 0920 hours the mission was cancelled due to the Army advancing ahead of schedule. The Squadron then took off at 1145 hours, led by Flight Lieutenant Collyns, with 1,000lbs. The target being Coulvain and on the crossroads. In the words of Flight Lieutenant Collyns "The crossroads were well and truly plastered".

31st July 1944
At 1001 hours the Squadron was airborne on an armed reconnaissance of the Alencon – Chartres – Forges area. Ten railway trucks were attacked with bombs, in sidings in Illiers L'Eveque.

1st August 1944
The Squadron was airborne at 2015 hours to act as escort to 24 Mosquitos bombing objectives in Poitiers. The escort went uneventful but Flight Sergeant Fellows went down and shot up some trucks on the Alencon – Dom front road, leaving one smoking and damaging another.

Flight Sergeant A.J. Fellows (FZ140) – is missing.

4th August 1944
Again the barges on the River Seine were attacked.

5th August 1944
At 1825 hours the Squadron renewed its attack on the barges on the River Seine. Three barges were sunk and many damaged. Warrant Officer Woodward called up to say that his engine had stopped and was going to force land some place south of Louviers.

Warrant Officer L.T. Woodward (FB105) – is missing.

This morning the Squadron received the good news that Flight Sergeant Fellow's plane had been found just north of Caen, and that he was in the 6th Canadian General Hospital, at La Deliverande, with wounds in the hand and thigh. It is understood that after bombing the barges, he saw a staff car preceded and followed by escorting motor cyclists. He went down to strafe it and when banking to observe the results, was hit by something in the throttle control box.

6th August 1944

The objectives again were the barges on the River Seine. Two barges at Caudebec and four at Quillebeuf and one at De la Rouque being attacked.

7th August 1944

The Squadron took off at 1325 hours, led by Wing Commander Johnstone. Twelve aircraft each carrying 1,000lb bombs for the Seine. One tug towing a barge was blown round 90 degrees and a barge was blown onto its side. Several direct hits were scored on the jetty. Flying Officer Hart who had joined the Squadron on the 6th August, his aircraft was seen to explode in mid-air.

Flying Officer D.F. Hart (FB166) – is missing.

8th August 1944

Squadron Leader W.W.J. Loud D.F.C., was leading on an armed reconnaissance at 1820 hours in the Etampes-Chartres area and had dropped their bombs on barges on the Seine. Flight Sergeant Vassiliades (White 1) spotted a lorry beneath and was sent down to straffe, whereupon he called to say that he could see two Me190s at zero feet. White section engaged one of them and the rest of the squadron did turn abouts above. Squadron Leader Loud then saw 13 Fw190s approaching from the south, carrying tanks. The Squadron gained height and when doing so noticed 12 Me109s also approaching from the south. The Fw190s jettisoned their tanks and dived down to the deck, as the Squadron closed on the Me109s. Squadron Leader Loud saw a Me109 diving towards the deck and gave chase and caught him up. The enemy aircraft was flying extremely low – at times beneath wires – and Squadron Leader Loud had great difficulty in getting a bead on him. He gave it a burst from 600 yards dead astern and pieces were seen to fly off. The Me109 pulled up, turned over onto its back and half rolled to the ground, exploding immediately on contact. As Squadron Leader Loud broke away he saw another enemy aircraft crash and catch fire, having been shot down by Flying Officers Scott and Glanville (White 2 & 3).

Flight Sergeant W.G. Abbott was with Squadron Leader Loud throughout the combat. He saw the Me109 pull up into a loop with pieces falling off, from which it did not recover and dived into a cornfield where it burst into flames. The pilot however, managed to bale out at a height not greater than 800 feet and appeared to land safely.

Flight Sergeant Vassiliades D.F.M., (White 1) spotted two Me109s about 500 yards behind. He turned, engaged one, and with his third burst saw several hits on the cockpit apparently killing the pilot because the enemy aircraft went into a shallow dive, striking the ground and completely disintegrating. He then saw several other Me109s at his height, 200 feet. He selected one on the outside and chased at full power, but could not gain on it. He opened fire from 1,000 yards hoping the enemy aircraft would weave or turn. He chased it for 20 minutes when suddenly the enemy aircraft broke right. On the turn Flight Sergeant Vassiliades closed to 400 yards, fired and secured hits on the engine and saw glycol stream from it. The engine cut and the enemy aircraft made a forced landing in a field near Gien. He turned and opened fire again on the enemy aircraft whilst it was on the ground observing several hits.

Flying Officer P.T. Glanville (White 2) whilst turning to port to attack a lorry, saw the two Me109s at zero feet. White leader engaged one and he dived to attack the second, with White 3. As he closed, the Me109 lost considerable speed and he was in danger of overshooting. Flying Officer Glanville lowered his flaps, reducing speed to 150mph attempting to get inside the Me109. The enemy aircraft made a 360 degree port turn straightened up and attempted to fly off. He caught up and again the enemy aircraft went into a tight steep turn. He gave the enemy aircraft several bursts and saw the strikes on the wing and the ground around it. Unable to get a satisfactory burst he zoomed up and saw Flying Officer Scott attack the strikes being made. Flying Officer Glanville then closed for another attack during which the Me109 rolled on its back and struck the ground and exploded.

Flying Officer J.A. Scott was straffing the truck when he saw the two Me109s. He followed Flying Officer Glanville and manoeuvred to secure a favourable position to attack, whilst the enemy aircraft and Flying Officer Glanville were on tight turns. He dived between them and fired a five second burst from 400 yards closing to 250 yards. He did not see any strikes and finding he could not hold his turn, climbed to 1,000 feet. He saw Flying Officer Glanville attack again but observed no strikes. The enemy aircraft flicked onto its back, dived into the deck and burst into flames.

9th August 1944

At 0181 hours the squadron took off for their regular target on the Seine. One very large barge was clobbered. On the way home some transport was straffed, resulting in two flamers and three damaged. One armoured fighting vehicle was also damaged.

The next mission at 1222 hours, again for the barges on the Seine. Twelve barges were located at Caudebec and the Squadron sent down twenty 500lb's on them.

On the third sortie the Squadron was on an armed reconnaissance of the Chartres – Dreux area subsequent to having bombed Barge Concentrations on the River Seine when at 1800 hours two Fw190s were seen.

Flight Lieutenant Collyns (White 1) dived down with his section and intercepted one of the enemy aircraft. He attacked at ground level from 300 yards, and the enemy aircraft pulled up and stall turned. He fired whilst the Fw190 was turning and saw strikes. Followed him round, still firing and saw more strikes. The Fw190s pulled up into a stall turn for the second time and Flight Lieutenant Collyns got in a good burst from 75 yards. The enemy aircraft turned on its back and exploded as it hit the ground.

The Squadron reformed and headed for home when three minutes later, the CO reported two enemy aircraft passing underneath us.

Flight Lieutenant Collyns turned and dived to attack and saw six Fw190s in line abreast. He selected the second from the starboard side, closed to 100 yards firing. The hood together with other pieces flew off the enemy aircraft and it started to smoke. Flight Lieutenant Collyns flew abreast of the enemy aircraft and saw the pilot preparing to bale out, as Warrant Officer Larsen (White 2) attacked him. The pilot baled out and the enemy aircraft crashed in flames.

Warrant Officer Larsen (White 2) followed Flight Lieutenant Collyns into the attack on the second Fw190, giving three second burst at very close range. He was forced to break almost immediately in order to avoid crashing into the Fw190, and saw a parachute open beneath him.

Flying Officer Plumridge (Green 3) spotted a Fw190 on its own when the Squadron dived on two others. He registered strikes with intermittent burst and coming in line astern, saw the hood fly off with his next burst. Several other bits flew off the enemy aircraft and at this moment Flying Officer Plumridge's guns jammed. He pulled level with the Fw190 and saw the pilot slumped sideways in the cockpit. The enemy aircraft then nose-dived into a wood and burst into flames.

Flying Officer Clayton was following his No 1 in a turn to starboard, when an enemy aircraft appeared from below and crossed between them. Stopping his turn he came out in line astern of the Fw190 at 150 yards. Opening fire he held his burst until there was a large flash on the enemy aircraft and black smoke billowed out. He then lost sight of the Fw190, which was seen by Flying Officer Maynard, to be pouring glycol and oil. It then turned on its back at 100 feet and went straight into the ground.

10th August 1944

The Squadron carried out three missions during the day and all were directed at the barges on the River Seine. It was a day of good bombing for the Squadron.

11th August 1944

The Squadron took off at 1119 hours, again bound for the Seine on which two barges were bombed. On the way home while straffing some motor transport, Flight Sergeant Vassiliades was hit by flak and forced to bale out. He was heard to say on the RT that he had been hit and was forced to do the big bale.

Flight Sergeant B.M. Vassiliades (FB116) – is missing.

At 1525 hours five barges were attacked with 18 500lbs and two direct hits were scored. Pilot Officer Davies's aircraft was seen to blow up prior to bombing. As a direct result of this incident of Pilot Officer Davies, the Wing is not carrying 500lb bombs again until an enquiry has been made.

Pilot Officer E.R. Davies (FB168) – is missing.

12th August 1944

An armed reconnaissance at Bernay – Les Andelys – Dreux area at 1126 hours. Scattered motor transport was seen and attacked. A total of six were left smoking or burning. At 1135 hours in the Lisieux area, the Squadron was attacked by 12 to 16 Lightnings. Fortunately, no one was hurt or even hit.

The next mission was an armed reconnaissance of the Sees – Falaise – Evreux – Mortagne area, the object to pin point our forward troops. The squadron took off at 1735 hours and American tanks were seen in Sees. The Squadron was vectored onto some bandits late in the reconnaissance but some Spitfires had arrived first and there was nothing left for 19 when they arrived on the scene.

13th August 1944

The Squadron took off at 1410 hours on an armed reconnaissance in the Bernay – Mantes – Gassicourt – Dreux area. Movement was seen on the road in the area but was not attacked as it could not be recognised as hostile.

14th August 1944

The Squadron was first airborne at 1508 hours on an armed reconnaissance of the Dreux – Mantes – Gassicourt – Louviers – Bernay areas. Some motor transport was seen and attacked.

At 1845 hours, once more the Yanks had a swipe at 19 with no ill results to the Squadron. Some motor transport was shot up leaving one in flames and two smoking.

15th August 1944

Squadron Leader Loud was leading on an armed reconnaissance of the Lisieux – Bernay – Dreux areas. At 0800 hours they were flying at 4,500 feet in the vicinity of Laigle when they saw eighty to hundred Fw190s and Me109s flying towards them. The Squadron climbed and got into the sun above the enemy formation, and dived to attack. As they did so, Squadron Leader Loud spotted another seventy or more Fw190s and Me109s carrying long range tanks. Squadron Leader Loud's section attacked the first formation of eighty to hundred enemy aircraft. Green section attacked the second formation of seventy plus enemy aircraft and White Section climbed to engage the top of the second formation.

Squadron Leader Loud got onto the tail of an Me109 and opened fire closing to 200 yards from dead astern. A lot of pieces fell off the tail of the Me109 and a few seconds later it began to smoke and flames were coming from beneath it. By this time the enemy aircraft was at zero feet and was seen falling into a wood by Flying Officer Connor. Squadron Leader Loud turned away to attack an Fw190. He got on its tail and all his guns jammed.

Flight Lieutenant Collyns (White 1)attacked the formation of seventy aircraft and in the general melee that followed got his sights on an Fw190. He saw strikes on the port side of the enemy aircraft and smoke coming from it. As it violently pulled up, he looked back to see another enemy aircraft attacking him. Flight Lieutenant Collyns broke away and with his No 2 flew straight through ten to fifteen Fw190s and milled around with them rapidly loosing height. He fired at an Fw190 and saw a few strikes but had to break away because of another enemy aircraft on his tail.

Flying Officer Glanville (White 3) singled out four enemy aircraft and fired a short burst at the second Me109 from the left. He saw strikes on the port wing root but was forced off his attack by twelve Fw190s diving on him. He got on the tail of one long nosed Fw190 but again was forced to break off as six enemy aircraft were preparing to attack him.

Pilot Officer Sima saw three Fw190s diving towards the deck and he gave chase. One broke right, one left and Sima followed the middle one flat out. He fired from 400 yards and saw strikes on the tailend of the fuselage. Black smoke then came from it and he fired until he had expended all his ammunition.

At 1240 hours on an armed recce and sweep of the Dreux – Mantes – Gassicourt – Bernay area, the leader of 122 Squadron called up and said he was mixed up with some Me109s at 12,000 feet over Dreux aerodrome. The Squadron climbed hard and a dog fight ensued.

Flight Lieutenant Collyns saw an Me109 which dived off in a south easterly direction at a very high speed with emergency boost smoke pouring from his ports. He dived after this enemy aircraft but found he was not overtaking it, so fired a burst from 800 yards. He saw an explosion that looked like the enemy aircraft blowing up but did not see this enemy aircraft strike the ground.

In spite of the overwhelming odds the Squadron suffered no losses during this combat and only two aircraft were slightly damaged.

The Squadron were back up again on an armed reconnaissance of the Dreux – Louvres – Bernay area at 1144 hours. One staff car was left smoking and four motor transport damaged, including one flamer. Three Me109s were met north of Dreux and one was probably destroyed by Flight Lieutenant Collyns.

The third and final sortie took off at 1533 hours for an armed reconnaissance east of the River Seine.

17th August 1944

At 1232 hours the Squadron were bound for the well known route of Lisieux – Bernay – Vernon – Mantes – Gassicourt. Mechanised enemy transport was seen on various roads and duly straffed, leaving three smoking and three damaged. The Squadron took off again at 1715 hours on the same route. This time two three ton lorries were left in flames and one motor cyclist chased off his bike. American tanks with cerise markings were seen just south west of Bersailles. Paris next stop, we hope.

18th August 1944

The first two missions of the day were with 500lb bombs for the barges on the River Seine.

At 1515 hours the Squadron went on its greatest mechanised enemy transport staffing expedition. The long awaited chance had arrived, the German transport was pulling out of the Vimoutiers area, and 19, like all the other squadrons in Normandy sailed in and dealt the Von Kluger's elements a mortal blow. A total of 21 MET destroyed and 17 damaged was obtained on this one sortie.

Flying Officer Connor was thought to have been hit, he lost height and crashed into a house. Flying Officer Glanville went off into a cloud on his own and has not been seen since.

Flying Officer P.T. Glanville (FZ112) – is missing.

Flying Officer D.W. Connor (HB827) – is missing.

From 1710 hours until dusk, the Squadron went out in pairs or fours to bash the retreating Hun, and ended the day with 38 Mechanised Enemy Transport destroyed, 11 smoking and 42 damaged.

19th August 1944

The orders for the day were "Continue destroying the German Army" with this in mind the Squadron was airborne at 0905 hours. At 0945 hours north west of Bernay, Squadron Leader Loud was leading on an armed reconnaissance in the Lisieux – Bernay area, when thirty plus Fw190s and Me109s were seen. The Me109s immediately dropped their long range tanks and zoomed aloft, while the Fw190s showed willing.

Warrant Officer Bell (White 3) was climbing to attack Me109s in the sun when he was warned of Fw190s diving on him from astern. White section broke to port and Warrant Officer Bell selected one Fw190 which went into a steep climbing turn to port. He fired from 200 yards closing to 130 yards and saw strikes on the starboard wing. His next burst saw the cockpit burst into flames and the hood fly off. The enemy aircraft spiral dived in flames and crashed.

Flight Lieutenant Wood damaged one Fw190.

At 1138 hours the Squadron was airborne and shot up seven mechanised enemy transport and one was left flaming. Two of the Squadron's aircraft were hit by flak. Flight Lieutenant Wood was seen to bale out and land safely, but did not move and its thought he must have been hit. Flying Officer Clayton also baled out but landed in our territory and returned to the Squadron later in the day. He was flying FB159.

Flight Lieutenant N.W. Wood (FB122) – is missing.

Sections of four aircraft were sent up to attack mechanised enemy transport with the total for the day of 27; three flamers, 12 smokers and 12 damaged.

20th August 1944

The Squadron was on an Operation Fighter Sweep, east of Paris at 6,000 feet, when at 1920 hours two formations of four and six Fw190s were sighted.

Wing Commander R. Johnston was leading the Wing on a Fighter Sweep and led his section in pursuit of four Fw190s. Opening fire on the left hand one, saw one strike and the enemy aircraft pulled up and entered a small cloud at 5,000 feet. An amusing but rather ineffective hunt started in and out of cloud which he had to terminate when he heard another leader in trouble.

Flight Lieutenant J.H. Taylor followed Wing Commander Johnston and waited until an

Fw190 appeared out of cloud, closed to 300 yards and opened fire from dead astern. Closing to 50 yards the enemy aircraft went into cloud again but he continued to fire until he lost sight of it. As he came out into clear sky saw the enemy aircraft and attacked again from 300 yards and saw pieces fly off it. He saw him again briefly and noticed something approximately four feet long hanging beneath the fuselage. The enemy aircraft disappeared into cloud.

Flying Officer J.E. Staples D.F.M., (White 2) selected the starboard enemy aircraft of the formation of four. The enemy aircraft dived to zero feet and he fired from 1,000 yards as the Fw190 began to weave. He steadily closed the range to 400 yards, opened fire and saw his strikes on the ground below the enemy aircraft. The Fw190 made a climbing turn to port as he fired again at 350 yards. He saw no strikes but the Fw190 jettisoned his hood and baled out. He followed taking photographs until the Fw190 hit the ground and burst into flames. Bullets then hit the ground in front of Flying Officer Staples as he was bounced by another Fw190. He broke hard to starboard towards the enemy aircraft and started a turning match at 500 feet. The enemy aircraft eventually broke away and took violent evasive action as Flying Officer Staples closed firing from 500 to 300 yards. Again he saw no strikes but the enemy aircraft pilot baled out.

Flying Officer Staples saw his Leader Flight Lieutenant Collyns (White 1) engaging a Fw190 from line astern. This Fw190 was close behind Flying Officer Staples and above him. So to protect himself he kept a close watch on the Fw190 as Flight Lieutenant Collyns was attacking. He then saw the Fw190 do a steep dive and go straight into the ground and explode.

Flight Sergeant Abbott (White 4) received instructions to dive and make individual attacks on the Fw190s. He selected a Fw190 and approached from dead astern, closing to 400 yards before he opened fire. He continued firing until he was within 200 yards during which time the enemy aircraft turned to port and he saw numerous strikes on the fuselage from the engine to the tail plane. At this moment the section was instructed to break as more Fw190s were coming in behind us. He pulled up to port and saw the burning scattered remains immediately beneath him, although he did not see the actual impact with the ground.

Flight Sergeant C.R. Wells (White 3) with his section bounced four Fw190s and he saw two crash and burst into flames. He then looked behind and saw an Fw190 coming at him. He broke and did one and a half turns and got onto its tail. The enemy aircraft dived to the ground and Flight Sergeant Wells got a burst in as it was doing so. He saw strikes just behind and below the cockpit with further strikes at the wing root. Another Fw190 got behind Flight Sergeant Wells, so he had to break off. He then sighted a Fw190 diving down and heading away from the scene of combat. He followed and gave it four bursts from extreme range. He didn't see any strikes because his incendiary ammunition had run out, but the enemy aircraft went through some trees along a road and crashed in flames in a field.

Warrant Officer Carson followed two Fw190s opening fire at one of them but observed no strikes. One enemy aircraft broke to port, the other climbed towards cloud. He chased the latter into cloud firing intermittent bursts and saw strikes on the starboard side of the fuselage. He had to break off when the wing was ordered to reform.

Flight Lieutenant B.G. Collyns (FB194) – is missing.

21st August 1944

The rain kept the whole wing on the ground and some welcome rest was obtained.

Flight Lieutenant Glanville arrived back with the Squadron late last night. He had spent an unpleasant 48 hours in the Huns lines.

25th August 1944

At 0722 hours the Squadron took off on an armed reconnaissance of the Rouen – Neufchatel – Amiens area. In the vicinity of Epinay an engine drawing eight coaches was spotted. The Squadron went into the attack and the whole train blew up. It was an ammunition train. In addition, the engine was straffed and damaged. Four mechanised enemy transport were attacked and left burning or smoking.

At 1355 hours the Squadron was airborne again in the Amiens – Beuvais – Gisors area. Flying Officer I. Mundy, flying with the Squadron for the first time after a rest from operations, was hit by flak in the area of St Saens. He was unable to recover form the hit and was seen to crash. The Squadron bagged seven Jerry vehicles on this trip, two in flames and five damaged.

Flying Officer I.M. Mundy (FB201) – is missing.

At 1745 hours off Dieppe, in the Somme – Amiens area, it was another mechanised enemy transport attack. One left burning, three smoking and one damaged.

26th August 1944

The very useful total of 12 MET was shot up on an armed reconnaissance in the Rouen – Neufchatel – Amien – Gisors area at 1412 hours. Three being left in flames.

A repeat reconnaissance at 1926 hours of the same area but no movement was seen.

27th August 1944

Flight Lieutenant Hughes was leading the Squadron on an armed recce and sweep of the Rouen – Neufchatel – Abbeville – Amiens area when they were warned of enemy aircraft at 16,000 feet, east of Rouen. At 1450 hours the Squadron sighted 12 Me109, with another eight Me109s stepped up behind the first formation.

Flight Lieutenant Hughes attacked the starboard section of four Me109s, closing to 200 yards. The enemy aircraft broke starboard, half rolled, jettisoned the hood and the pilot baled out. He had seen no strikes on this enemy aircraft. He then attacked another Me109 which was heading towards Green Section. He closed and fired at the second Me109 which turned and dived. Flight Lieutenant Hughes followed it down and used the remainder of his ammunition. Pieces fell away from the port mainplane and an object, he thought was the hood, came off the fuselage. The Me109 was streaming black smoke and diving vertically. At 4,000 feet he had to break off as another Me109 came in to attack.

Flying Officer Wheeler met the Me109s head on and after climbing and turning got behind two enemy aircraft. The Me109s went through various manoeuvres – steep turns – a slow roll and half rolls diving away. He fired several bursts closing to 250 yards but saw no hits. He again closed to 75 yards but again saw no results. Closing to 50 yards and this time saw hits around the cockpit. They were at 4,000 feet and the enemy aircraft half rolled, the pilot baled out and he watched the parachute open and descend.

Flying Officer Staples led his section underneath the starboard four Me109s in a gentle dive to have plenty of speed then zoomed up in a climbing turn and got behind the starboard enemy aircraft. It weaved as if undecided which way to turn and then half rolled starboard. He saw the enemy aircraft use "Ha – Ha" boost and glycol started puffing from exhausts, which must have been the result of Flight Lieutenant McLeod's attack. Flying Officer Staples opened fire from 250 yards and saw hits behind the cockpit. The Me109 went down in a vertical dive with glycol pouring from both sides of the engine. At 10,000 feet the hood was jettisoned and the pilot baled out. Flying Officer Staples saw the enemy aircraft hit the deck and explode south east of Rouen.

Flight Lieutenant McLeod followed Flying Officer Staples and came up below and behind the enemy aircraft. He fired from 150 yards and held the burst, seeing hits and then glycol streaming from underneath. The Me109 turned starboard on its back and went down vertically.

Flight Lieutenant MacNeil was attacked by an Me109 and saw a few hits on his machine. He broke away and took evasive action and in doing so found he was on his own. He then spotted a lone Me109 and attacked, getting it several bursts from 800 to 100 yards during the five minutes he chased it. He was only firing with one gun, the other having been damaged by the first Me109, but saw several hits on the fuselage. He was forced to discontinue the chase when his ammunition ran out.

28th August 1944

The Squadron were airborne at 1003 hours on an armed reconnaissance of the Neufchatel – Poix – Amiens area. One Diesel engine, one steam engine and two trucks were attacked and damaged.

31st August 1944

The Squadron was not airborne until late hour of 1810 hours. The swiftly changing bomb line and the thrusting spearheads of the UK and American Armies made the accepting and rejection of targets the order of the day. The task was an armed reconnaissance which proved uneventful.

1st September 1944

The Squadron took off on an armed reconnaissance at 1250 hours in the St Omer – Haxebrouck area. They attacked some mechanised enemy transport and left four in flames. With the swiftly changing bomb line, the identification of transport becomes increasingly difficult.

2nd September 1944

The Squadron flew to its new roost at St Andre in the early hours of the morning and took off on its first mission at 1105 hours, an armed reconnaissance of the Ypres – Courtrai – Tournai area. Uneventful.

3rd September 1944

The Hun were rapidly moving out of straffing range, necessitates that again we must move, this time to Beauvais Nivilliers.

At 1825 hours the Squadron did a fighter sweep of the Givet – Brugge – St Omer area. Mechanised enemy transport was attacked totalling four flamers, one smoker and six damaged.

4th September 1944

A further patrol of the forward areas during which mechanised enemy transport was attacked and enemy movements reported.

5th September 1944

The war had passed beyond the reach of No 122 Wing and with it 19 Squadron. All squadrons were released until further notice.

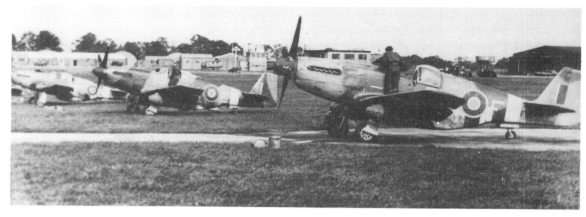

Mustangs. Sept '44

(Crown Copyright – Sqdn Album)

6th September 1944

With the Hun fleeing across Belgium, operating from Beauvais Nivilliers recedes still further, so Paris became everybody's mecca.

9th September 1944

The Squadron arrived at Grimbergen, north of Brussels to join "A" Flight who had arrived the day before. Just three days after the Bosche had left. The Squadron was airborne at 1256 hours on an armed reconnaissance of the Arnhem – Zwolle – Lingen area. The object of the mission was to seek out and destroy locomotives. The Squadron shot up and badly damaged three engines in the area. Warrant Officer Bell and Flight Sergeant Abbott were hit by intense light flak, south of Apeldoorn.

Warrant Officer Bell was heard to say that he was going to bale out.

Warrant Officer M.H. Bell (FX887) – is missing.

Flight Sergeant W.G. Abbott (FB148) – is missing.

10th September 1944

The Squadron was early off the mark this morning at 0721 hours on an armed reconnaissance of the Zwolle – Lingen – Arnhem area, seeking out locomotives. They did extremely well, eight were severely damaged, three damaged and several carriages and trucks were straffed. All these were shot up in the Nijmegen area.

At 1237 hours airborne again in the Roermond – Geldern – Zwolle – Anerafoort area. The results were five trains severely damaged, and one slightly damaged.

The third reconnaissance at 1724 hours was in the Munchen – Bocholt – Nijmegen area. Five engines severely damaged, one damaged, and 20 coaches and 15 trucks were well straffed.

11th September 1944

The first reconnaissance of the day at 1337 hours in the Arnhem – Zwolle – Lingfen – Muster area. Five trains damaged and one river launch damaged.

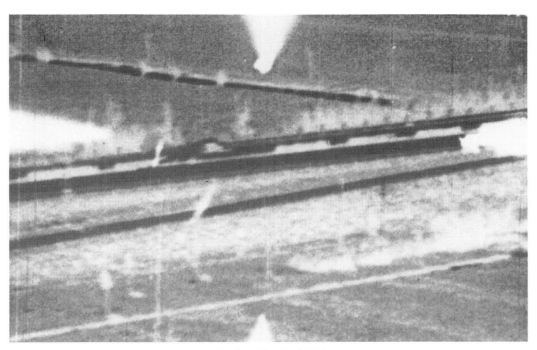

Combat Film No 12126
Flying Officer Webster attacking ground target. 1330 hours 12/9/44

Combat Film No 12125 (Negative)
Flying Officer Staples attacking ground targets. 1330 hours 12/9/44

12th September 1944

The Squadron resumed the engine hunt in Holland. The 1247 hours reconnaissance was extremely successful with six engines being severely damaged, and one damaged. Two vehicles were also attacked. One left in flames and the other smoking. The 1716 hours reconnaissance resulted in one barge being damaged and a truck set on fire.

13th September 1944

The Squadron was airborne at 0735 hours continuing to seek and destroy enemy transport. The result was one engine severely damaged, one engine destroyed, three coaches damaged. Two tugs were attacked in the Zwolle Dieppe. One left smoking and the other damaged. Two armed launches and two barges on the Zeider Zee. Airborne again at 1350 hours in the Hook of Holland and Einhoven area. The Squadron was advised that Huns were approaching Einhoven from the south, so the Squadron climbed and turned towards the Hun but could not find them.

ARNHEM

17th September 1944

The Squadron was airborne at 1532 hours to patrol the Arnhem area to cover a great Allied Airborne Operation. Landings were being made in the Arnhem, and Nijmegen area by British, American, Polish and Dutch troops. The Wing's task was to keep Huns out of the area.

The eight Mustangs of the Squadron had just been relieved on patrol and were leaving the area on an armed reconnaissance of the road east of Emmerich when they were informed of enemy aircraft approaching from the east. They climbed to 12,000 feet and sighted three large gaggles of Fw190s, totalling 50 to 60 aircraft at 1700 hours. As the enemy aircraft closed the range to 600 to 800 yards, the Squadron broke hard to starboard into them.

Flight Lieutenant Hughes saw the Fw190s immediately in front of him at close range and he opened fire. The Fw190 disappeared under his nose and as he turned he saw it spinning down with white smoke streaming from it, the hood came off and the pilot baled out.

Flying Officer Staples turned into the Fw190s and his section split up into pairs. He and Flying Officer Slee got above the dogfight and dived on two Fw190s. Flying Officer Staples got behind the port one and Flying Officer Slee was firing at the other. He closed to 300 yards and saw two or three strikes behind the cockpit. They were then attacked by fifteen Fw190s and continued turning with eight while another seven kept diving on them and zooming back up again. During the turning match Flying Officer Staples managed to fire at one Fw190 and saw a few strikes on its tail fin, which caused the enemy aircraft to spin down, but he did not see it hit the deck. Flying Officer Staples's aircraft was very badly hit by a Fw190 which had got between him and Flying Officer Slee. He last saw Flying Officer Slee being attacked by five enemy aircraft, whilst he was being attacked by eleven. Flying Officer Staples received a hit in the radio and eventually both tanks were hit, so he dived down towards the deck. The enemy aircraft let him go, thinking he was out of control. He had no compass or radio, but was attacked no more and managed to return to base.

Flying Officer Maynard saw a Me109 about 1,000 yards in front of him and gave it a burst at 800 yards but did not see any strikes. The enemy aircraft slowed down considerably and he saw some white vapour appear from under its engine. The enemy aircraft started to turn towards him and he fired a long burst closing from 200 to 50 yards. He didn't see any strikes as it disappeared under his nose and he pulled up to avoid it. Flying Officer Maynard saw white vapour still coming from him, when Flying Officer Webster attacked.

Flying Officer Webster broke to starboard and the Hun did the same, so they came in on our tails. He found himself alone except for Jerries and kept turning. He attacked an Fw190 but saw no result and found three Fw190s on his tail. He broke away and saw Flying Officer Maynard attacking a Me109 and vapour come from the enemy aircraft. He closed from 500 to 50 yards on the Me109, with only one gun firing. The enemy aircraft was by then doing a gentle turn, travelling very slowly and taking no evasive action. Something came off its port wing and he lost sight of it as he passed.

Flying Officer Scott was attacked by a number of Fw190s and Me109s. Eventually he got on the tail of an Fw190 which took evasive action by pulling up vertically, during which he got in a burst. The enemy aircraft went into a stall turn, flicked on its back and dived right down to the deck. Flying Officer Scott followed him down and fired several bursts from astern. The enemy aircraft levelled out and he fired again. Warrant Officer Beckett, who was following, saw a large piece come off the enemy aircraft. Flying Officer Scott's guns ceased to fire so he broke away and let Warrant Officer Beckett have a go. At this moment he sighted some enemy aircraft diving to attack them, so they broke off the attack.

Flying Officer R.A.B. Slee (SR437) – is missing.

18th September 1944

The Squadron was unable to take off before 1150 hours due to the weather being 'clampers'. They patrolled the Arnhem area. White Section, Flying Officer Scott and Flying Officer Bibby, lost the Squadron over base, so flew a northerly course intending to strike east over Rotterdam and join the Squadron in the Arnhem area. Just south east of Rotterdam they were bounced by twelve Fw190s. Flying Officer Scott by turns, tight and otherwise, clouds and what have you, returned safely to base but his aircraft was badly shot up.

Flying Officer C.O. Bibby (FZ195) – is missing.

19th September 1944

No flying due to the weather.

20th September 1944

A memo was received from Rear Headquarters, 83 Group, saying that the wreckage of Flying Officer Hart's aircraft (missing on the 7th August) had been found. Flying Officer Hart was dead and had been buried by the Germans in a place unknown.

The order of the day was to patrol the Arnhem area and keep the Huns out of the sky. Bad weather prevented an early start and 19 Squadron was the first airborne at 1235 hours. The Arnhem area was patrolled but was uneventful.

At 1637 hours the Squadron with No 122 Squadron were airborne on a fighter sweep of the Winter Wyk – Munchen Gladbach – West Cologne. The Squadron was led by Wing Commander Operations, Wing Commander W.W. Loud, D.F.C., who was promoted to this position from Commanding Officer of 19 Squadron on the 18th September.

21st September 1944

The Squadron took off to patrol the Arnhem area at 0922 hours, to keep the Hun away from the Airborne Division which had been dropped at Arnhem. The best the Squadron could do was to patrol above cloud. Two rocket trials were seen, one with its base in the Munchen Gladbach area and the other in the vicinity of Bocholt. The trails were of a great height and were possibly V2s.

At 1255 hours the Squadron took off again to patrol Arnhem. Flight Lieutenant R. A. Haywood was flying for the first time with the Squadron, since he was shot up by a Me109 on June 21st – Bob was shot up but the 109 was shot down – by him.

LEFT TO RIGHT: TOP ROW: W/O Larsen, F/O Owen (ADJ), Cpls. Faulkner, Stanley, Crisp. SECOND ROW: P/O Holmes, F/Lt. McLeod, F/Lt. Webster, F/Lt. Clayton, F/Lt. Haywood, P/O Carson, Sgt. Kay, F/Sgt. Brenner. BOTTOM: W/O Natta.

(Crown Copyright – Sqdn Album)

22nd & 23rd September 1944

The weather was duff and what patrols could be made were uneventful.

24th September 1944

The Squadron were roused from bed at the very early hour of 0500 hours and at 0627 hours were airborne in the Arnhem area. An engine was attacked and severely damaged. Seeing 19 swooping down the engine driver crammed on his brakes and hey presto! another engine drawing wagons came round the bend and sailed into the engine braking. It ploughed through it and five wagons were derailed. The engines and wagons were then cheerfully shot up. The weather commenced to deteriorate but the Squadron were airborne again at 1300 hours on a repeat patrol.

26th September 1944

Three sorties were done this day but the weather was not good and no Huns were seen.

27th September 1944

Again three sorties were flown, and the weather was not good, cloudy with rainstorms. Patrols were flown in support of our troops at Arnhem.

The first patrol at 0625 hours shot up two trains.

The second patrol at 1125 hours and two more trains were found, attacked and severely damaged.

On the third patrol, the Squadron was patrolling the Arnhem area at 19,000 feet when bandits were reported approaching from the east. At 1630 hours twenty Fw190s were sighted.

Flight Lieutenant Paton engaged the enemy aircraft which dived for cloud. He followed them through the cloud and came out on the tail of a Fw190. He closed to 800 yards and opened fire. He saw strikes just as the enemy aircraft entered cloud again. He chased the Fw190 firing whenever the enemy aircraft broke cloud cover and saw several hits and a piece fly off. He last saw the Fw190 entering cloud streaming volumes of black smoke. Flight Lieutenant Paton flew under cloud base waiting but the chase had taken him over the Ruhr. He became subject to intense accurate flak and was forced to climb and so lost the Fw190.

Flying Officer Webster turned after the Fw190 which had made a head-on attack at them. He got on its tail and opened fire at the left hand one of the three Fw190s. The normal high boost trail from the enemy aircraft changed to thick black smoke, although he had seen no strikes. The Fw190 disappeared into cloud and he was not catching up, broke off.

28th September 1944

The Squadron's tour on the continent with the 2nd Tactical Air Force came to an end when they returned to Matlask. This move brought about a change in their role, from tactical to long range escorts to our strategic heavy bombers of Lancasters and Halifax's carrying out raids by daylight on the Ruhr.

From August 1943 to this day, the Squadron had operated under the control of No. 122 Wing, with Nos. 65 and 122 Squadrons.

"A MESSAGE FROM THE COMMANDING OFFICER

I have received many signals of congratulation on the magnificent part played by No.122 Wing in the battles which have led to the final defeat of Germany. You have every reason to be proud of the fact that this Wing has the finest record of successes over the enemy since D Day, of any Wing in the Tactical Air Force. Since the Wing landed in Normandy it has been in the forefront of the battle, and has frequently operated within shelling distance of the enemy. In the race through France, Belgium and Holland, and again in the swift advance across Germany, the Wing remained operational throughout, and indeed achieved some of its most outstanding successes while on the move. This fine record could not have been achieved without the hard work, enthusiasm and determination of every man, and I wish to thank you all for the tremendous efforts you have made to earn such a great reputation for the Wing."

P.G. JAMESON D.S.O., D.F.C.
Group Captain
Schleswigland, November 1945.

29th September 1944

No flying today, everyone 'brassed'.

5th October 1944

The Squadron took off at 0915 hours from Matlask to escort Lancasters to Wilhelmshaven. No enemy aircraft seen.

6th October 1944

Another escort to Lancasters to the Ruhr. Airborne at 1530 hours, led by Flight Lieutenant Hughes. While on patrol several aircraft believed to be a jet were observed at great heights but they made no effort to interfere with us or the bombers.

7th October 1944

Cleve and Emmerich were the targets for the Lancasters and Halifax's. The Squadron took off at 1238 hours as the escort. Excellent bombing was observed but once again 'Schickelgruber's' fighters were conspicuous only by their absence. The flak was very intense and the bomber boys had a very uncomfortable time.

11th October 1944

After two days foul weather in which no flying was done, the Squadron took off in equally foul weather or worse. Despite this the intrepid '19 Pursuit', led by Wing Commander Loud were airborne at 1537 hours as target cover for Lancaster's at Henrik. Very accurate bombing was observed but once again no enemy fighter attempted to interfere.

Earlier this morning Pilot Officer R.A. Hutchinson, a second tour pilot, who had just returned to us, had a bad smash on the edge of the aerodrome and sustained bad injuries.

14th October 1944

The Squadron moved to Andrews Field, whence similar missions were flown, mostly against targets in the Ruhr.

The powers that be suddenly produced an early show just to facilitate our move. After a mad rush of packing, briefing and breakfast (for some) the Squadron was airborne at 0745 hours to escort a thousand Lancasters and Halifax's to Duisberg. Hopes ran high when 'jet jobs' were reported but they turned out to be friendly Mosquitos.

18th October 1944

The Squadron was airborne at 0930 hours to escort the Lancasters to Bonn. The Wing led by Wing Commander Loud observed excellent bombing results. A fair amount of twitch was experienced when the flak became decidedly personal.

21st October 1944

No operational activity but lovely weather, so the powers that be decided to see how fast the Wing could land. Practice flying was the order of the day. Masses of aircraft were observed, belting at the runway at the same time and Flying Control very nearly produced foreign bodies on several occasions. However, all our aircraft returned safely and retired to the bar to recover their shattered nerves.

25th October 1944

The Squadron escorted Lancasters to Essen. A certain amount of dicing on the way out, as the Squadron had to climb through a stream of bombers, estimated to be 40 miles long. One bomber was seen to blow up.

26th October 1944

Leverkeusen was the target for the Lancasters this day. The Squadron was led by Squadron Leader Wright. The trip was uneventful, except that Squadron Leader Wright had to make a forced landing in a field about 30 miles south of Brussels. He had engine failure and was seen to walk away from his aircraft (FZ162).

28th October 1944

The squadron, together with Nos 65 and 122 Squadrons, patrolled Cologne during a bombing attack by 600 Lancasters and Halifax's.

30th October 1944

The Squadron was airborne at 1035 hours on a Lancaster escort to Vesseling.

31st October 1944

The Squadron was airborne at 1305 hours to escort 100 Lancasters to Bottrop.

1st November 1944

The Squadron took off at 1730 hours, led as a Wing by Wing Commander Loud. Escorting Lancasters to their target of Hamburg.

4th November 1944

The Squadron this day were escorting Lancasters to Solingen at 1225 hours.

5th November 1944

One hundred and eighty Lancasters were escorted at 1125 hours, to bomb the same target as the day before, Solingen. Two aircraft believed to be hostile jet planes were seen but did not engage.

6th November 1944

Again escort to Lancasters at 1300 to bomb Geilenkirchen. Intense heavy flak was met in and around the target area. Two bombers were seen to go down having been hit.

8th November 1944

At 0910 hours the Squadron was airborne on a Fighter Sweep with 65 and 122 Squadrons. The area of Munster, Hamm, Paderborn was swept at 12,000 feet. Some enemy aircraft were sighted at 5,000 feet in a shallow dive and the Mustangs dived to attack. They closed to 600 yards and opened fire but no strikes were seen. The enemy aircraft were then at 1,000 feet and probably intended to land on an airfield at Dummer Lake. After being fired upon the enemy aircraft pulled away straight and level, and trails were being observed from the jets.

9th November 1944

Two hundred and thirty Lancasters were escorted at 0920 hours. The target was Wanna Eickel.

11th November 1944

The Squadron took off at 0930 hours to escort Lancasters bombing Kastroprauxel. Flak was quite intense and rather personal, being directed at the fighters.

15th November 1944

Again fighter escort at 1345 hours to Lancasters bombing Dortmund.

16th November 1944

At 1400 hours the Squadron took off as fighter escort to 418 Lancasters bombing Duren.

18th November 1944

The Squadron took off at 1335 hours to escort 400 Lancasters bombing Munster.

21st November 1944

The Squadron was airborne at 1320 hours on a Fighter Sweep with 65 Squadron, led by Wing Commander Loud. While the Wing was over Knocke a report was received that 40 to 50 Fw190s were flying from Antwerp to Aachan. Speed was increased but no enemy aircraft were observed.

22nd November 1944

The Squadron took off at 1400 hours as escort to 160 Lancasters bombing Geilenkirchen. One bomber was seen to blow up and disintegrate in the air.

26th November 1944

The Squadron took off at 0940 hours to escort 75 Lancasters bombing Fulda.

27th November 1944

The Squadron took off at 1335 hours to escort 150 bombers to Cologne.

29th November 1944

The Squadron took off at 1325 hours to escort 270 Lancasters bombing Dortmund.

30th November 1944

A Fighter Sweep at 1135 hours with 65 and 122 Squadrons of the area Hilversum, Munster, Gutersloh and Dummer Lake.

2nd December 1944

The Squadron escorted 90 Lancasters bombing Dortmund.

4th December 1944

The Squadron were escorts to Lancasters bombing Oberhausen.

5th December 1944

Today escorted 100 Lancasters bombing Hamm.

8th December 1944

Escort to 220 Lancasters bombing Heinbach.

11th December 1944

Escorted 150 Lancasters to Essen.

12th December 1944

Escort to 150 Lancasters bombing Witten. When approaching the target area at 26,000 feet, 14 to 16 Me109s were sighted, the Wing immediately split and combat ensued. The Squadron saw four Me109s but these dived for cloud before they could be engaged. Flight Lieutenant Paton suddenly and mysteriously left the formation and spiralled down through the bombers.

Flight Lieutenant J. Paton (SR433) – is missing.

13th to 17 December 1944
Fog bound.

18th December 1944
The Squadron was on a Fighter Sweep at 1344 hours round Dummer Lake.

23rd December 1944
The Squadron escorted 27 Lancasters and three Mosquitos to Cologne.

24th December 1944
The Squadron was airborne at 1253 hours to escort 168 Halifax's to a German Air Force Station at Essen. Many fires were seen in the target area. The Squadron landed at Bradwell Bay and were conveyed by truck to base.

25th December 1944
The Squadron was up early to the sound of much groaning, briefed and into the trucks to Bradwell Bay. On arrival we found that the bombers were not going after all. Hoping to fly back to base to enjoy what was left of Christmas, Group decided to send the Squadron on Fighter Sweeps of the Frankfurt area. Landing again at Bradwell Bay because base was clamped, and home by truck.

27th December 1944
Up early once more and off to Bradwell Bay. The show was close escort to 150 Lancasters bombing Cologne.

29th December 1944
Today the target for the Lancasters was Koblenz.

31st December 1944
One hundred and fifty Lancasters were escorted to Vohwinkel.

1st January 1945
At 0845 hours the Squadron took off to escort 100 Lancasters bombing Dortmund – Ems canal. The bombing results were good.

2nd January 1945
At 1335 hours for a Fighter Sweep with 65 and 122 Squadrons, led by Wing Commander Loud of the Rhine, Dummer Lake area.

3rd January 1945
At 1120 hours to escort 50 Lancaster bombing Castrop – Rauxel.

5th January 1945
At 1250 hours to escort 150 Lancasters bombing Ludwigshaven.

14th January 1945
The Squadron was airborne at 1245 hours to escort a 100 Halifax's over Saarbrucken. Hostile aircraft were reported but not seen.

15th January 1945

At 1300 hours the Squadron took off to escort 75 Lancasters to Langendreen. Flight Lieutenant D.B. MacNiel collided with an aircraft of No 234 Squadron and was last seen spiralling down in the area south east of Nijmegen. One parachute was seen.

Flight Lieutenant D.B. MacNiel (FB131) – is missing.

28th January 1945

The squadron took off at 1230 hours on a Fighter Sweep of the Frankfurt – Munster area. The sweep was cut short due to the adverse weather conditions.

29th January 1945

The Squadron was airborne at 1220 hours to escort 150 Lancasters bombing Krefeld.

1st February 1945

At 1445 hours the Squadron took off to escort 160 Lancasters bombing Munchengladbach.

3rd February 1945

The Wing was briefed for a Fighter Sweep of the Frankfurt area, with permission to strafe east of the Rhine. The Wing split up owing to the bad weather and the Squadron found two small marshalling yards at Stockheim and Lahnstein, which they attacked and shot up 12 wagons there. We have at last fired our guns in anger again, after an all too long lapse.

5th February 1945

The Squadron had a general sortie to St Ann's Castle, reputed the oldest pub in the district and a very pleasant evening was had by all.

13th February 1945

The Squadron flew north to Peterhead where it flew as escort to Coastal Command Beaufighter and Mosquito strikes, attacking shipping off the Norwegian and Dutch coast. These operations occasionally provided the Squadron with an opportunity to engage the enemy and in this fashion it saw the War in Europe out.

17th February 1945

The Squadron did a few sector reconnaissances to familiarise themselves with the area, when there was a much hurried recall at 1615 hours and the pilots returned to find the much talked about 'Scotch Mist' over the 'drome. However, after several attempts everyone got down alright.

20th February 1945

The Squadron decided to fly to Dallachy, the Beaufighter station, for tea and a talk with them. As the Squadron was coming in to land, Flight Lieutenant Hussey, D.F.C., D.F.M., spun in on the approach and was killed.

Flight Lieutenant Hussey, D.F.C., D.F.M. (FB199).

3rd March 1945

After waiting all morning, a show finally came off and the Squadron was airborne at 1415 hours to escort 20 Mosquitos to Norway, between Bergen and Stavanger. No shipping was seen so the strike was aborted.

7th March 1945

Twelve aircraft took off at 1947 hours to escort 44 Mosquitos on a shipping strike between Sweden and Denmark, and down into the Kattegat. Course was set for Denmark. A convoy of eight ships was sighted in the Kattegat which was successfully pranged by the Mosquitos. Strikes were seen on the four centre ships and left smoking. One was listing and stopped. We then set course for base and in spite of our expectations, no more Huns were sighted.

12th March 1945

The Squadron rendezvous with 44 Mosquitos of Banff Strike Wing at 1320 hours. Acting as escort to a shipping sweep in the Skagerrak area and on the return journey they flew from the mouth of Oslo Fiord to Kristianland, keeping about 10 miles out from the coast. No shipping was seen and the formation set course for base. They were passing Lista to the south, when Flight Lieutenant Butler leading White Section, saw some aircraft passing him head on. The visibility was bad down on the sea, making it hard to identify the aircraft. They turned out to be ten Me109s. Green and Tonic Section was then bounced by three other Me109s. A dogfight ensued.

Squadron Leader Hearne gave the orders to drop tanks and turned starboard across the Mosquitos climbing to 3,000 feet in the direction of the attack. He saw two Me109s amongst Green Section turning in tight circles, one with both his wheels down. This did not seem to cramp the Me109s style, however, as he was turning as tightly as some of the Mustangs, and firing repeatedly. Squadron Leader Hearne got onto this enemy aircraft's tail following it round the same three tight orbits to starboard, firing two short bursts from 150 yards and saw his strikes on the starboard wing root on the second burst, until it straightened out temporarily. Just as the enemy aircraft was going into another steep turn to starboard, he got in a good one and a half second burst from 300 yards. Black smoke came from the Me109's engine and it went immediately into a steep dive straight into the sea. The enemy pilot jettisoned the hood but he did not bale out.

Flight Lieutenant Butler was leading White Section and did a steep climbing turn as the enemy aircraft passed. A dogfight commenced, and he was compelled to do a series of climbing turns to the left and eventually managed to get on the tail of a Me109. He fired closing to 200 yards, after which clouds of white smoke began to pour out of the starboard side. He then saw his No 2, Squadron Leader Hill attack this same Me109, still with white smoke coming from it. It then went into a very steep dive and Flight Lieutenant Butler followed it down to 1,000 feet where he gave it another burst. The enemy aircraft continued to dive but Flight Lieutenant Butler was forced to break away as five Me109s came down on his tail from above. He took violent evasive action and went down to zero feet, fire from the enemy aircraft hitting the sea off his starboard wing. He then saw an aircraft behind him go into the sea, which he thought must have been Squadron Leader Hill.

Pilot Officer Avery's aircraft was hit five times by 20 and 13mm cannon and he himself received cannon splinters in the back.

Squadron Leader M.R. Hill (KH444) – is missing.

13th March 1945

Flight Lieutenant R. Haywood was doing an air test when he ran into some bad weather and hit the ground. He was killed instantly.

20th March 1945

The Squadron took off at 1420 hours and the ten Mustangs were escorted by one Mosquito, on a Ranger to Aalborg and Lista. The sortie was uneventful.

23rd March 1945

The Squadron, led by Squadron Leader Hearne was airborne at 1520 hours as escort to Mosquitos of Banff Strike Wing, to the Stadtlandet area. The Mosquitos split up, one section going north the other south, when the Stadtlandet area was reached. The northern section found and attacked a 3,000 ton off Kvam, scoring many hits. One Mosquito was hit by intense light flak from the island and crashed into the sea. The southern section found and attacked a 2,000 vessel south of Stadtlandet and scored many hits. The Mosquito leader was hit by flak from the ship and exploded in mid air.

25th March 1945

Eight Mustangs were airborne at 1320 hours to escort 15 Mosquitos to Strandlandit area. A 2,000 ton vessel was seen against a steep cliff face. Bombing was attempted but no hits scored.

30th March 1945

The Squadron led by Squadron Leader Hearne was airborne at 1325 hours to escort Mosquitos from Banff Strike Wing to Portsgrund. Three Motor Vessels of 2,000 tons were seen and attacked. The Mosquitos scoring many dry and wet hits. The Mosquito Leader was seen to go down in flames.

2nd April 1945

Practice flying and night flying for the whole Squadron in the Mustang IVs which we have nearly re-equipped with.

4th April 1945

The Squadron escorted Beaufighters at 1700 hours on a dusk strike to Aadals Fiord. The Beaufighters went up the Sogal Fiord and found a 3,000 ton motor vessel which they attacked and hit.

5th April 1945

The Squadron escorted 34 Mosquitos to the Kattegat at 1435 hours. They crossed the Danish coast at zero feet and sighted five motor vessels of 800 to 2,000 tons in the Kattegat. Three were left burning furiously and the other two were left smoking. On the way back over the Danish coast some scattered small light arms fire was encountered and just as the Squadron was crossing out, Flight Lieutenant Butler, who was leading White Section, was seen to pull up, burst into flames and go straight into the sea 100 yards off the coast.

Flight Lieutenant Butler (KM137) – is missing.

11th April 1945

At 1340 hours the squadron of 12 Mustangs, led by Squadron Leader Hearne took off from Peterhead. They escorted 20 Beaufighters of Dallachy Strike Wing on a shipping sweep and reached landfall west of Lindesnes, turning north west. A minesweeper was seen in the Fede Fiord but better targets were seen and attacked. The Squadron could not observe the results due to clouds of smoke and steam from the targets. After the attack the force turned north west and then set course for base. The Beaufighters crossed out 10 miles north of Lista.

Squadron Leader Hearne observed Lista on his port side and upon close scrutiny of the area he saw at least ten to fifteen enemy aircraft orbiting Lista at heights stepped up from zero to

9,000 feet. He immediately turned to port towards Lista, calling White Section to follow. Green Section wisely followed his previous orders and gave close escort to the Beaufighters. He entered the circuit of Lista in a left hand turn at 8,000 feet from the north and would undoubtably have been mistaken for another formation of Me109s, had he not been unlucky enough to cross 2,000 yards in front of a formation of four Me109s. These Me109s obviously did not suspect him but he could not afford to take this chance. He turned to port towards them and they split up into pairs. Two of them dived down over the aerodrome but the other two stopped to give combat. In the ensuing fight which consisted of a series of tight climbing turns, his No 2 spun out, his No 3 broke off because he had no gunsight, leaving Squadron Leader Hearne and his No 4 against the two Me109s. After about five turns it was obvious that the Me109s had bettered their positions and gained some height. All this while he had been turning on the point of stall with 10 degree flaps. Consequently he order his section to break off the fight, rolled over on his back and made for home followed by his No 4 and White Section.

Attack on shipping from Beaufighters

(A.S. Doley)

Some 20 miles from Lista he reversed their direction and went back at 5,000 feet. As he neared Lista he spotted two Me109s going north doing a right hand circuit of Lista with their wheels down. As Hearnes closed on them, they broke port, jettisoned their tanks and partially retracted their undercarriage. He turned with one whilst his No 2 Flying Officer May chased the other one away and returned to give him cover. Instead of trying to turn with the Me109, who was obviously an experienced pilot, he continually reversed the direction of his turn to get partial head on attack, in which it could not fire at him. Squadron Leader Hearne succeeded in first damaging it from astern and finally hit him squarely in the cockpit at 200 yards range. The enemy aircraft went straight into the water three miles from his aerodrome.

On arrival at base, Wing Commander Davenport of 13 Group HQ rang up to say that the Beaufighters wished to congratulate the Squadron on their very excellent escort for which they were extremely thankful.

14th April 1945

The Squadron were airborne at 1325 hours in a very miscellaneous order as they had to wait at the end of the runway for a long time and numerous aircraft boiled over. Ten minutes later they joined up with the 21 Beaufighters to escort them to a Submarine Depot Ship in the Josing Fiord. The Squadron had orders to patrol Lista after the attack while 65 Squadron brought the Beaufighters back.

Squadron Leader Hearne led the Squadron and after seeing the last of the Beaufighters out over the coast from Josing Fiord turned eastwards to sweep around Lista. White Section of four Mustangs flew straight to Lista at 5,000 feet, while the Squadron Leader's section, with Green Section, a total of five Mustangs flew inland at 5,000 feet until he came to Fede Fiord. They then descended to zero feet, flew down the fiord as low as possible with Lista Aerodrome in full view on his left. Squadron Leader Hearne saw one aircraft airborne over Lista flying very low and was in fact beating up the aerodrome, because he pulled up to 400 feet over his base, turned very steeply right and headed due north for the hill just north of Lista. Here the enemy aircraft turned to port and put his wheels down intending to come straight in to land. The enemy aircraft had to cross out to sea in this orbit and Squadron Leader Hearne intercepted it about one and a half miles off shore of its base. As he turned to port to intercept, climbing to 500 feet a heavy five gun battery from the shore placed five very accurate flak bursts just in front of him. He attacked from the port quarter and the Me109, once aware of the situation, pulled his wheels up and gave an amazing display of combat flying, which had it been luckier, might have ended disastrously for one or even two of our aircraft. Although heavily outnumbered and with a reasonably good chance of bridging the one and a half miles of sea and seeking the protection of his heavily defended base, he chose to fight it out, firing on every single occasion he could bring his guns to bear. Squadron Leader Hearne damaged the Me109 slightly with his second burst as a thin trail of white smoke began to issue from its port wing root. He then broke off while the other Mustangs, eager to kill, pounced on the Me109. None of them could get sufficient deflection on it until, choosing an appropriate opportunity, Squadron Leader Hearne came down on it in a tight turn to port and fired a short burst from 200 yards. Squadron Leader Hearne saw a red glow appear in the cockpit of the Me109 as it rolled gently over and went vertically into the sea, no more than a mile and a half from its base and in full view, no doubt, of flying control, he had been beating up a few moments before in so spectacular a manner.

26th April 1945

The Squadron escorted 21 Beaufighters to Fede Fiord. The Beaufighters found their target and attacked. As it was so near Lista, Huns were almost certain to come up, and sure enough, as the Beaufighters were leaving the target, their leader reported six enemy aircraft going across the front of him.

Flight Lieutenant Shirreff who was leading the Squadron saw some enemy aircraft under him going inland. He was about to attack when he saw some more enemy aircraft waiting inland, hoping he would be drawn away. He decided to keep the Squadron together and close to the Beaufighter and wait for the Me109s to attack. Although the enemy aircraft were a good 25 plus stronger having failed to draw any of the escort away, did not attack. Three Beaufighters were lost but none through enemy fighters.

29th April 1945
Filthy weather with snow and sleet showers. In the afternoon, the Squadron watched a film on how to try and ditch a Mustang. Which finally convinced everyone of its impossibility, since no one has yet come out alive to tell the tale.

2nd May 1945
The Squadron was up 0415 hours and with 65 Squadron were airborne at 0615 hours led by Wing Commander Wickham. Escorting 22 Mosquitos to the Kattegat. Some submarines were sighted 15 miles off the east coast of Denmark and two were attacked by the Mosquitos and probably sunk. A Minesweeper was next attacked and was left stopped and sinking. No enemy aircraft seen.

3rd May 1945
The Squadron was airborne at 1700 hours to escort 35 Beaufighters to the Jutland area. They crossed over the Danish coast and two Beaufighters were badly shot up. Two ships were eventually pranged between Fyn Island and Denmark.

4th May 1945
Six aircraft with 234 Squadron took off at 1315 hours to escort 48 Mosquitos to Fyn Island and Denmark. An E Boat was attacked to the north east of Denmark and then attacked a convoy of five ships in the Kattegat. All the ships were left smoking. On the way out a small motor vessel was attacked. The force then crossed out over Denmark and during this crossing 234 Squadron lost an aircraft. Flying Officer Schofield and Flight Lieutenant Yearwood were both hit fairly badly by light flak but luckily little serious damage was done.

Just after the Mosquitos had made their first attack, Flight Lieutenant Davidson (Tonic 3) and Pilot Officer Natta (Tonic 4) collided and crashed into the sea. No sign of them was seen in the water.

Flight Lieutenant J. Davidson (KH818) – is missing.
Pilot Officer B.M. Natta (KH674) – is missing.

A Section of the Squadron was airborne at 1545 hours with 65 Squadron to escort Beaufighters. Several of the Squadron had tank trouble, leaving three Mustangs to do the escort. The weather was impossible over the target area, so the formation turned back. After turning back a train was sighted which was pranged by Flying Officer Maynard and Flight Lieutenant Seed. On returning it was found Denmark and North Germany were surrendering the next day.

6th May 1945
Many rumours of Norway's Armistice, so perhaps the Squadron has done its last show over Europe.

7th May 1945
Bad weather, so the Squadron was released. Many went into Peterhead and on return found a big party going on in the Mess and heard that VE Day was to be on the next day. There was a terrific party that sailed over to the NAAFI and back again.

The day started quietly with the Squadron on 30 minutes readiness. At 3.00pm everyone heard Mr Winston Churchill broadcasting the cessation of hostilities in Europe which were to officially end at 2400 hours that night. That night there was a big party in the Mess and also an All Ranks Dance in the Concert Hall.

The Squadron accounted for 145½ enemy aircraft destroyed, 24 probable and 57 damaged.

The Following Decorations and Awards were made to Officers for duties carried out while serving with the Squadron

Flight Sergeant G.C. Unwin	D.F.M. and Bar
Sergeant B.J. Jennings	Distinguished Flying Medal
Flight Lieutenant W.J. Lawson	Distinguished Flying Cross
Sergeant H.W. Charnock	Distinguished Flying Medal
Flight Sergeant M.L. Swanson	Distinguished Flying Medal
Flight Sergeant K.E. Crosby	Distinguished Flying Medal
Squadron Leader P.B.G. Davies	Distinguished Flying Cross
Flight Lieutenant I.H. Edwards	Distinguished Flying Cross
Flying Officer J. Henderson	Distinguished Flying Cross
Flight Lieutenant D.P. Lamb	Distinguished Flying Cross
Flight Sergeant B. Vassiliades	Distinguished Flying Medal
Flight Lieutenant B.G. Collyns	Distinguished Flying Medal
Warrant Officer L.H. Bell	Distinguished Flying Cross
Squadron Leader W.W.J. Loud	Bar to Distinguished Flying Cross
Flight Lieutenant L.J. Wright	Distinguished Flying Cross
Flight Lieutenant E.S. Hughes	Distinguished Flying Cross
Pilot Officer T.A. Carson	Distinguished Flying Cross
Squadron Leader P.J. Hearne	Distinguished Flying Cross

ENEMY AIRCRAFT

Date	Destroyed	Probable	Damaged
11.5.40	1 – Ju88		
26.5.40	6 – Ju87	1 – Ju87	
	6 – Me109	1 – Me109	
27.5.40	1 – Do215	2 – Do215	
	1 – Hs126		
28.5.40	2 – Me109		
1.6.40	6 – Me110	1 – He111	2 – Me110
	3 – Me109		
	2 – Do215		
	1 – He111		
19.6.40	2 – He111		
2.8.40			1 – He111
16.8.40	2 – Me110	2 – Me110	
19.8.40	1 – Me110		
24.8.40	3 – Me110		
31.8.40	2 – Me110		
3.9.40	2 – Me110		1 – Me110
5.9.40	1 – Me110	1 – Do215	2 – Do215
	1 – Me109	1 – Me109	
7.9.40	2 – Me110		1 – He111
	1 – He111		
	2 – Me109		
9.9.40	1 – He111	1 – He111	
	1 – Me110		
	1 – Me109		
11.9.40	4 – Me110	1 – Do215	
	1 – He111	1 – He111	
	1 – Me109		
15.9.40	8 – Me109	2 – Me109	1 – Do17
	2½ – Me110	1 – Me110	
	2 – Do17	1 – Do215	
	½ – He111		
18.9.40	3½ – Ju88	1 – Me109	
	2 – He111		
	1 – Me110		
27.9.40	7 – Me109		1 – Me109
5.11.40	2 – Me109	1 – Me109	
	1 – He113		
15.11.40	2 – Me110		
28.11.40	3 – Me109		
23.6.41			2 – Me109
27.6.41	2 – Me109	1 – Me109	2 – Me109

21.7.41	1 – Me109		2 – Me109
7.8.41	1 – Me109		1 – Me109
12.8.41			1 – Me109
29.8.41	2 – Me110		2 – Me110
24.10.41			1 – Ju88
27.12.41			1 – Ju88
22.1.42			1 – Ju88
1.2.42		1 – Do217	
19.8.42	1 – Fw190		2 – Fw190
18.1.43			1 – Fw190
4.4.43			1 – Fw190
15.5.43			1 – Me109
11.11.43	1 – Fw190		
6.1.44	1 – Fw190		2 – Fw190
22.4.44	1 – Me109		
28.4.44	1 – Ar96		
21.5.44	½ – Leo45		
10.6.44	2 – Me109		1 – Me109
14.6.44	2 – Fw190	1 – Fw190	5 – Fw190
20.6.44	2 – Me109		
21.6.44	4 – Me109		1 – Me109
23.6.44	4 – Me109		1 – Me109
8.7.44	2 – Me109		
12.7.44	2 – Me109		3 – Me109
			1 – Fw190
25.7.44	2 – Fw190		
8.8.44	4 – Me109		
9.8.44	4 – Fw190		
15.8.44	1 – Me109	1 – Me109	4 – Fw190
19.8.44	1 – Fw190		1 – Fw190
20.8.44	5 – Fw190		4 – Fw190
27.8.44	3 – Me109	1 – Me109	1 – Me109
17.9.44	1 – Fw190		3 – Fw190
			1 – Me109
27.9.44			2 – Fw190
12.3.45	1 – Me109	1 – Me109	
11.4.45	1 – Me109		
14.4.45	1 – Me109		

145½ destroyed: 24 probables: 57 damaged

THE IMMEDIATE POST WAR YEARS
1945 – 1946

1945

On the 13th May, the Squadron was briefed with 122 Squadron to escort six Mosquitos to Oslo to do a Fly Past. The Squadrons were led by Wing Commander Wickham, who however had to turn back early, and the formation was taken over by Squadron Leader Hearne. The Mustangs were then ordered to turn back due to very bad weather. However, Green Section – Flight Sergeant Speed, Flight Lieutenant McLeod, and Flight Sergeant Edwards, led by Flight Lieutenant Shirreff, whose RT was u.s., went on with the Mosquitos and clear weather was run into over Oslo. The force 'beat up' Oslo for about 20 minutes and then returned.

Sunday 20th May. A day off duty for everyone. The peacetime Sunday once more being recognised. The weather was fine and a few of the squadron led by Squadron Leader Hearne, made a sortie to Cruden Bay in the afternoon and achieved some success, returning with an outsize lobster and a fine collection of winkles.

Three days later the Squadron moved to Acklington, where it was welcomed by Wing Commander G.W. "Gordon Willie" Petre, the Station Commander, who had been a pilot of 19 Squadron in 1940.

During the afternoon of 12th June, both flights did practice interception but the weather was not too good, with a lot of low cloud. Flight Lieutenant Clayton and Flight Lieutenant Young were doing interception. They had to descend through cloud at one point, and on coming through it, Flight Lieutenant Clayton found he was by himself. Flight Lieutenant Young was never seen again and after pairs searching the sea for most of the evening, a Norwegian ship reported having seen an aircraft dive into the sea and exploding, at approximately the same place and time. This was assumed to be Flight Lieutenant Young.

On the 20th June the weather was bad, with low cloud. Flight Lieutenant Shirreff with a section of three, took off and went north to look at the weather. The cloud got lower and Flight Lieutenant Shirreff ordered the section to climb up through it. However, Flight Lieutenant Robson stayed below the cloud and hit a railway embankment. The aircraft broke up immediately and Flight Lieutenant Robson was killed.

At the end of the month, the Squadron had an exercise with the Navy in which six Mustangs went and straffed HMS Glasgow, to give the AA gunner practice. It was a most enjoyable exercise and a novel experience being allowed to 'beat-up' one of His Majesty's Ships without being fired upon.

In July a day was taken up with the new pilots doing local flying. There was a visit from Air Marshall Rob to the Squadron.

The following day the 5th, in the afternoon, 12 Group laid on a Fly Past of five Squadrons, over Group led by Wing Commander Storrer. The Squadron mustered nine aircraft, led by Squadron Leader Hearne, and rendezvous was made over Kirton Lindsay. The Fly Past went by successfully.

Flight Lieutenant Yearwood and Flying Officer Maynard were awarded with the Crois de Guerre.

On the 13th August the Squadron moved to Bradwell Bay.

In the evening of the 14th there was a fairly large gathering of the boys in the *Green Man*, one of the local pubs. At midnight, the Prime Minister, Mr Atlee broadcast to the nation and we were told that Japan had surrendered. A bonfire was lit on the sleeping site and those in bed were pulled out. In the end, quite a decent fire was got going. Luckily, nothing important found its way into the blaze.

VJ DAY – 15th August the Station Commander came over the tannoy and informed us we had two days off to celebrate VJ Day.

There was a Squadron gathering in the *Cricketer's Arms* in the evening of the 17th, to discuss the formation of a '19 Squadron Club' to include all ex-19 Squadron Pilots. It was voted that Flight Lieutenant Shirreff and Flying Officer Maynard should be Secretary and Vice Secretary to get the club formed.

The rest of the month was spent in practice air to ground firing and bombing.

On the 7th September the Squadron moved to Molesworth and began to re-equip with the Spitfire XVI.

The Squadron had two commitments in the afternoon of the 10th, a Fly Past for the Brazilian Ambassador and a rendezvous with the Horsham St Faith Mustangs for the Battle of Britain Fly Past on the 15th.

Molesworth
BACK ROW: W/O Foes, W/O Elliss, F/Sgt. Morrison, Sgt. Handford, W/O Bennett, Sgt. Maurice, Sgt. Willis. MIDDLE ROW: W/O Hughes, F/Lt. Jack May, F/O Slidy Knight, F/Lt. Ellis, F/O Bartholemew, F/O   , F/Lt Wilson, F/O Williamson, F/Lt. Mutter, W/O Vine, W/O Speed. FRONT ROW: F/Lt Wass, F/Lt. Clayton, F/Lt Doley, S/Lr. Hearne, F/Lt. Miller, F/Lt. Taylor, F/Lt. Mowatt.

A full scale rehearsal for the Battle of Britain parade began on the 11th. The whole thing was a shambles with wings out of order, late and off track, but 19 flew some nice formation.

The following day a revised system was tried for the big show. This was better but a lot of polishing is needed, and many practices were threatened. The day after was a horrible shambles in the morning, just as the Squadron was about to take off they were told to stop. They hastened back and after 20 minutes were told to go up on the original times. After cutting corners the Squadron just made it but only seven out of the 28 did.

In the afternoon they tried again with better results, except that the Squadron was diverted to Andrews Field in various stages of undress. The next day again the big practice in the morning. The weather was not good but the practice went off very well.

On the 15th at 1119 hours the Squadron set course for Horsham in perfect formation for the big parade. It all went very well, although the weather was not good. In spite of all the bumps, the Squadron kept good formation for nearly two hours travelling all over London and arrived back dead on time. Then in a cloud of dust – everyone went on weekend.

On the 5th October Squadron Leader J.R. Broughton AFC, took command of the Squadron.

On the 15th the day dawned bright and clear with the Commanding Officer's Colour hoisting Parade. The spectacle was watched with interest by all taking part, most of whom had not been up so early nor been on parade for some years.

11th November the Armistice Parade was held and all personnel were present.

The rest of the month and most of December, the Squadron fought to keep the Mustangs serviceable. With modifications and engine changes, on one day only three Mustangs were available.

1946

On the 2nd January the Squadron took to the air and concentrated on cine-gun fighter tactical exercises, formation and low flying in the area.

Visibility was so poor on the 7th that there was very little flying. However the highlight of the day came after lunch, someone arranged a truck to take us to Huntingdon Brewery. The Chief Brewer showed us around and after some quick orbits round the vats and fermenting vessels, a crafty look at the girls in the bottling section, we were vectored to a room where we tasted 74% proof whisky. The boys investigated many bottle wines and spirits and there was a strong tendency for being last man out when we left. However, we remained an honourable crowd, the tasting room was the last and most important objective. Our host very kindly gave us a free hand which lasted for two hours.

During March the Squadron did low level cross country, and the 19th was the last day of Mustangs' flights. The Spitfires' replacements arrived on the morning of the 20th.

The first seven Spitfires were airborne three days later in the morning, one went on its nose but otherwise OK.

The rest of the month and early April, the pilots were familiarising themselves with the Spitfires.

On the 10th April, Squadron Balbo to ranges at Nordhorn, Germany. Six aircraft set off at 0830 hours to Manston where they were led by Wing Commander Bond to Einhoven, Holland. The ranges were not manned and we had to return with our ammunition.

During the month more dear friends depart as we say farewell to our beloved Mustangs. We flew them down to Llandow today and say farewell to a fine aircraft.

On the 25th, Squadron Leader C.I.R. Arthur D.F.C. and Bar, assumed command of the Squadron.

The Squadron flew to Lubeck, Germany, via Manston and Einhoven on the 2nd May. On arrival at Lubeck at 1830 hours, the Squadron were greeted by Group Captain Dwyer and Wing Commander Harris, D.S.O., D.F.C. The groundcrew had arrived four hours earlier in Dakotas.

On the 6th the Squadron started off on a full eight week flying program, air to air, air to ground and dive bombing. Things were going very well until Wing Commander Daly pranged a wing tip on landing (SL601).

The next day was another good day's work on the ranges. The boys are beginning to get their eye in and the scores are looking better. Flight Sergeant Denton turned off the perimeter track and tipped up on his nose.

The 9th was a wizard day for flying and the Squadron had another good day on the ranges.

On the 17th the weather was not very good so the air to air was cancelled but we continued with the air to ground and bombing. Flight Lieutenant Venables ran into some light flak over the air to ground target and collected a .5 round in his radiator, presumed to be one of his own. He got back to base with very little glycol left and rather a warm engine.

By the 3rd June close support and combined ops part of the program commenced. Rain stopped flying in the morning. During the afternoon, one sortie was flown.

VE DAY – *8th June*
The day's celebrations started with a full Station Parade, the Band of the Welsh Guards supplying the music. The month continued with the exercises.

On the 19th June Flying Officer Russell-Grant was killed in a Jeep.

The Squadron set course for England at 1400 hours on the 28th and arrived back at Wittering at 1900 hours.

The following day the Dakotas arrived with the Groundcrew and equipment.

From the 6th to 15th July the Squadron was on leave.

The Squadron seemed to have settled down to the regular events of leave and weekends.
The 26th was used for practice in preparation for a Fly Past over the American Embassy on the 1st August, six aircraft had a close formation trip over 12 Group Headquarters.

On the 1st August a quiet morning was had cleaning the aircraft and at 1645 hours the formation took off for London. The flight went very well although it was rather bumpy over London. The formation was Squadron Leader Arthur, Warrant Officer Vine, Flight Sergeant Morris, Flying Officer Langham, Flight Lieutenant Furneaux, Flight Lieutenant Mowatt, Warrant Officer Denton, Warrant Officer Daley and Flight Sergeant Haywood.

By September the Battle of Britain Fly Past was on the immediate horizon and some of the Squadron were a little disgruntled that they were to be led by a Fleet Air Arm Squadron. The team was selected; Squadron Leader Arthur, Flight Sergeant Inglis, Warrant Officer Haywood, Flight Lieutenant Furneaux, Flight Lieutenant Mowatt, Flying Officer Langham, Warrant Officer Daley, Warrant Officer Vine, Flight Lieutenant Williams, Flying Officer Smith, Warrant Officer Hughes and Flight Lieutenant Caruana.

On the 11th at Biggin Hill, practice for the whole Squadron. The weather was pretty duff and as they were forced low over the sea, Warrant Officer Hughes and Warrant Officer Haywood found themselves in quite a dicey spot during the protracted turn to port. However, all arrived safely home. And on the 14th at the very last moment, our wing was scrubbed out of the Fly Past because we gather that the weather could have left us in a very poor position. However, while all the other squadrons were juggling with sticks, rudders and throttles sweating and cursing each other, we had a pleasant morning posing for the press.

The next day was the same. The glamour was laid on thick in the afternoon when the Squadron did a Fly Past for a Television Program and a scramble for the Universal News.

In October the recent call to arms from the Farmers enticed a large number of our airmen, some pilots and our ranks are sadly depleted.

THE HORNET YEARS
1946 – 1951

1946

On the 4th October when other squadrons were thinking of jet equipment, No 19 became the second unit to receive the long range DH Hornet fighter, the fastest piston-engined fighter in the RAF. Three aircraft arrived for our new establishment. The next day the first Spitfire to be allotted away, was flown to Horsham St Faith.

On the morning of the 9th, the first of our number, Warrant Officer Vine, diced merrily off in a Hornet. Although he cautiously maintained that a first flight was insufficient experience on which to base an opinion, the Squadron gathered that he quite approved of the aircraft.

The following day, Warrant Officer Hughes and Warrant Officer Whyte followed in Arthur Vine's slipstream and they successfully completed their first sortie in a Hornet.

On the 26th November the eighth Hornet arrived from Linton-on-Ouse. The weather was perfect for a change, having been 'clampers' all month, except for the cross wind which made landing and take offs a matter for extra care. Flight Lieutenant Williams, Warrant Officer Haywood, Warrant Officer Whyte and Flight Sergeant Inglis all did high climbs. Warrant Officer Haywood attained an altitude of 37,500 feet in 23 minutes.

All pilots reported that the Hornet handled very satisfactory at high altitude.

By the end of the month the Squadron found to their pleasant surprise that they had done much better than the other Hornet Squadrons in the present trying circumstances, even with an added disadvantage of lack of experience.

During December the Squadron took part in an exercise supported by two other (imaginary) Hornet squadrons in which they were engaged in an armed recce over 'enemy occupied territory'. During the sweep they were bounced by 'enemy aircraft' (Meteors), and a free for all ensued. Judging from our pilots' reports when they landed, they acquitted themselves well and were very favourably impressed with the handling of our new aircraft against the jets. Needless to say the 'Line Book and the Kitty Box' benefitted from the exercise.

During the month a Mosquito was being used to train the pilots for conversion to the twin engined Hornet.

1947

January, February and March
    The second 'ice age' is upon us, with snow and frost. Very little flying done at all.

On the 18th April the Squadron took part in Operation 'Rufus II', a demonstration flight over Halton, for the benefit of the Chief of Air Staff and various members of the Cabinet, including the Prime Minister. The Squadron flew past with four aircraft in vic formation, one in the box, led by Squadron Leader Arthur, with Flight Lieutenant Higson, Warrant Officer Haywood and Warrant Officer Whyte.

On the 23rd April the Squadron moved to Church Fenton.

Operation 'Webb Foot' was carried out on the 28th and 29th with four aircraft led by Squadron Leader Arthur, Flight Lieutenant Donaldson, Flight Lieutenant Higson and Warrant Officer Haywood.

In May, Operation 'Webb Foot II' at Coltishall under Eastern Sector. The Squadron supplied four aircraft of which Flight Lieutenant Donaldson and Warrant Officer Haywood were top cover, Flying Officer Smith doing the recce and Flight Lieutenant Higson as reserve. The Ground Controllers had the top cover above the wrong ship and consequently the exercise from our point of view was unsuccessful.

In May and June the main object of the flying being to complete two continental cross countries per pilot, the training required for the squadron's coming trip to the Middle East.

There were three cases of engine failure during the month of June in which two Hornets force landed, Flight Lieutenant Donaldson at base and Warrant Officer Whyte at Spilsby. The third being partial engine failure in the Mosquito.

July was a fluctuating month as regards the Squadrons' flying activities. The weather was good, bad and indifferent. Towards the end of the month, aircraft were suddenly grounded for inspection of the engine bearings. Several of the aircraft were found to be faulty and serviceability reached a new low. Despite these drawbacks, a reasonable months' flying programme was carried out, consisting mainly of aerobatics, formation and navigation trips.
One of the chief features of the month was a Fleet Exercise on the 30th, for which purpose the Squadron spent two days down at Chivenor, Devon. To make up the required nine aircraft, the Squadron was compelled to borrow from 64 & 65 Squadrons. The object of the exercise was to provide escort patrols over the Home Fleet off Lands End in the English Channel and to intercept any bomber aircraft of the opposing force.

During the first part of August, priority was given to practice GCA approaches at Bassingbourne (Cambridge), the nearest Station thus equipped. All pilots managed to get in at least two practices in the Hornets. When returning from one of these practices, Flight Lieutenant Donaldson developed engine trouble, upon attempting to land at base on one engine, one of his flaps did not lower. He managed to go round again and made a successful flapless, single engine landing.

A Fly Past by three Hornets was carried out on the 15th, during the inspection of the Squadron by the AOC No 12 Group. Pilot Officer Haywood was detailed to do a solo aerobatic display but his perspex hood burst, injuring him in the ear before he could commence his display. He did a good landing without further incident.

All Hornets were grounded at the beginning of September for a Special Technical Instruction No 8 and modifications. These were all completed by the 10th and flying could begin again. This consisted of routine air tests and formation practices. The Squadron's first attempt at 'Pressure Pattern' (single heading flight method of navigation). Several successful flights to Falmouth and back were made using this technique.

During the week commencing the 15th, preparations were made for getting the aircraft and pilots on top line for the navigational practice cross country to Fayid, in the Suez Canal Zone.

This exercise commenced on the 22nd. Six aircraft with two reserves flew down to Manston on the 21st with the object of getting an early start the following day. The Section being as follows:-

Busride –	Red One	– Squadron Leader Arthur
	Red Two	– Flying Officer Smith
	Blue One	– Flight Lieutenant Donaldson
	Blue Two	– Flight Lieutenant Ransley
	Yellow One	– Flight Lieutenant Lord
	Yellow Two	– Pilot Officer Haywood

These three sections set off at intervals in the morning from Manston on the morning of the 22nd and on arrival at Istres, a high surface wind of 55mph was blowing, namely Mistral. Luckily the wind was blowing straight down the runway and all six aircraft landing and taxied in without any real anxiety. Yellow Section carried out a single heading pressure flight on this leg with an error of 15 miles at Istres. When the wind had dropped to 10mph, they were allowed to proceed to Cagliari (Elmas). At Elmas, Yellow One's aircraft went u.s. due to a defective cooling pump and was forced to stay behind while Red and Blue Sections reached Castle Benito for a night stop.

The accommodation in the transit mess at Castel Benito being very satisfactory. Blue Leader's aircraft was found to have a very badly worn tyre but a spare Hornet wheel and tyre was unearthed. The crews working overnight to make an early start on the 23rd possible.

Lunch was taken at El Adem, refuelling and on to Fayid which was reached a good two hours before sundown. A sound night's stop at Fayid, was followed by a reasonably early start on the 24th on the first homeward leg to El Adem. After landing at El Adem, Red 1 and Red 2's aircraft went unserviceable. The engine bearing bolts on both aircraft being found loose and they were unable to proceed until the following morning. Meantime Blue Section carried on to Castel Benito and then Elmas for a night stop, finding Yellow Section still awaiting a new cooling pump. On Thursday morning, Blue Section set course from Elmas and reached Church Fenton without further incident the same afternoon. Red Section after getting away from El Adem on the Thursday morning, were, upon reaching Elmas, compelled to remain there for two days due to unfavourable conditions at Istres and did not get back to Church Fenton until Saturday afternoon the 27th, having left Elmas that morning.

On the 20th Church Fenton was open to the public. A very large crowd turned up to see the RAF at work and the flying display by the Squadron, doing formation Fly Past with three aircraft and another doing aerobatics. Also intercepting three Lancasters in view of the public.

Flying during October was mainly of navigational nature, the first of which being a continental cross country exercise on the 1st, which took the three aircraft doing it to the limit of their endurance.

On the 8th six pilots flew their Hornets down to Coltishall, preliminary to an exercise with Bomber Command the following day. The exercise being very successful from our point of view, our role being to escort 16 Lancasters and Lincolns at 18,000 feet around the south coast of England and then northwards, to protect them from attacks by Meteors from Tangmere and Horsham St Faith. Our main problem was how best to keep with the bombers with our 100 mile an hour overtaking speed. This however was solved by doing 'S' turns in sections above and behind the bombers.

A number of low level cross countries were carried out on routes laid down by 12 Group Headquarters and all pilots completed at least one practice. The most interesting route being across the Lake District to Northern Ireland and back via Scotland.

In November flying was mostly of a tactical nature. Further exercises on daylight bomber escorts being carried out.

On the 10th the Squadron flew four aircraft down to Stradishall, along with two from 65 Squadron, for experience with low level and high level escorts. The first practice was carried out on the 11th, and after the bombing run at 7,000 feet, the escorts carried out practice quarter and astern attacks. During an astern attack Pilot Officer Steedman collided with a Lancaster bomber. Our pilot and seven of the eight occupants of the Lancaster were killed. The only survivor was the pilot of the Lancaster.

Another exercise on the 25th, when 24 bombers were escorted by 12 Hornets from 64, 65 and 19. Attacks by Meteors and Spitfires being made and once again, in our opinion, we had the measure of the jets.

On the 25th, Pilot Officer Turner, in attempting to overshoot on one engine, lost control at 150 feet and was killed.

1948

January – At last the Squadron's aircraft are fitted with gun sights and although of a temporary nature, this month has seen them in great use. The Squadron obtained the air to ground range at Holbeach for a week.

Two pilots in conjunction with 64 and 65 Squadron took part in a bomber interception exercise on the 20th.

Towards the latter end of the month, most pilots managed to do camera gun exercises.

Two continental cross countries were carried out successfully, and also five low level cross countries, as well as other navigational sorties.

All in all it was a very good month from the training point of view.

During February training was continued, mainly on cine camera gun exercises. A number of single engine flying practices were carried out and some single engine landing practice.

On the 12th of March, four aircraft took part in an interception under GCI control on American B29 aircraft at a height of 20,000 feet. The exercise was successful and all pilots managed to get in four cine camera gun attacks.

On the 22nd the first Hornet III was collected, with another three the following day and one more the day after that.

April has been a very successful flying month for all pilots. At the beginning of the month endurance tests were carried out on the Hornet III. This consisted of several four hour flights at 2,000 and 10,000 feet over this country and the continent. The fuel consumption figures obtained compare favourably with those of the manufacturers.

From the 12th to the 16th, training was devoted to air to ground firing at Paston Ranges near Colitshall. All pilots carried out several successful sorties.

Exercises were again carried out during the month on interception of American B29s. On the 23rd a similar exercise was carried out against naval aircraft.

Several pilots carried out 'Homing Exercises' on the new talking beacon at Linton on Ouse. Results were fair.

During May the first fortnight was confined to air to air cine camera gun exercises followed by air to air firing on the ranges. Results so far have been well up to standard and each pilot is getting plenty of practice.

The majority of the flying in June was confined to air to air and air to ground firing.
On the 20th, three Hornets piloted by Flight Lieutenant S. Donaldson, Flying Officer Smith and Pilot Officer Sharples gave a demonstration of close formation flying for the benefit of members of the Royal Observer Corp at RAF Acklington. The single engine formation was well received and demonstrated the capabilities of the Hornet aircraft.

Hornets at Church Fenton, 12th May '50

("Flight")

On the 24th July, Squadron Leader Arthur, Flight Lieutenant Mills, Flying Officer Smith and Pilot Officer Haywood, flew down to West Malling to take part in exercises with the Royal Observer Corp on the following day. The exercises consisted of short-legged cross country covering the south of England.

During the first ten days of August, a large number of sorties of air to sea firing was carried out at Paston Ranges and also high altitude firing of guns over the North Sea, with subsequent timing checks on quick re-arming and refuelling afterwards.

Further stress has been made on single engine flying and landings as a priority over the month.

On the 18th Squadron Leader Woodward assumed command of the Squadron.

Towards the latter end of the month, mostly individual exercises were carried out such as cine camera gun, aerobatics and instrument flying. The remainder being battle and close formation, also practices in single engine close formation.

A Fly Past on the 17th was done for the benefit of the Air Officer Commanding, Air Vice Marshal T.C. Traill, C.B., O.B.E., D.F.C., on his annual inspection.

Flying commenced on the 3rd of September with Exercise 'Dagger'. On the first day two interceptions were made, B29s at 31,000 feet and Mosquitos at 25,000 feet. The second day, the Squadron was brought to readiness at 1300 hours and scrambled to intercept six B29s at 25,000 feet, successfully. All three sections were airborne from the time the very cartridge was fired at one minute 45 seconds, which was very fast going. The third day was busier with the Squadron intercepting five Mosquitos, after which two more sections tail chased ten B29s a 100 miles over the North Sea and intercepted them at 28,000 feet. No sooner had these two sections refuelled then they were airborne again to intercept more Mosquitos. Throughout the

286

exercise our serviceability remained at 100 per cent, the controlling was very good and all squadron pilots had at least two successful interceptions. The exercise has been carried out in cooperation with the United States Air Force B29s, practicing various methods of attack.

The Squadron had three aircraft taking part in the Battle of Britain Fly Past over London on the 15th.

On the Battle of Britain Open Day, Squadron Leader Woodward, Flight Lieutenant Donaldson and Flying Officer Smith gave a very pleasing display of close formation flying to a large crowd, including attacks on Lincoln bombers and also demonstrating the capabilities of the Hornet in single engine close formation. Individual air displays were carried out by Flying Officer Starkings, Pilot Officers Haywood and Taylor at Horsham St Faith, Leeming and Finningley.

The Squadron reached an all time high much to the credit of our Groundcrews who have maintained a high standard of serviceability throughout the whole of October.

Interceptions and practicing attacks with the cooperation of the B29s.

On the 24th, four pilots took part in an exercise with the Royal Observer Corp in 'Operation Hedgehop'. This consisted of low level cross countries.

The flying during November was sadly curtailed by the extremely bad weather, fogbound.

In December flying practice and training syllabus were well up to standard and well covered.

The Squadron were attached to the RNAS Culdrose from the 8th to 12th for participation in Exercise 'Sunrise'. Needless to say the sun did not rise and apart from one false scramble the weather conditions prohibited operations. Nevertheless, benefit was derived from the liaison with the Royal Navy which was 100 per cent.

1949

January started with exercises which were long range navigational to Fayid. The pilots were Squadron Leader Woodward, Flying Officer Starkings, Pilot Officer Haywood and Pilot Officer Taylor. Squadron Leader Woodward and Pilot Officer Haywood completed the exercise without many difficulties but Flying Officer Starkings was forced to make a single engine landing at El Adem due to a u.s. cooling pump. Pilot Officer Taylor made a successful forced landing in Sicily, brought about by a series of events, weather, RT and finally fuel shortage. Nevertheless, all four aircraft left Malta on the 18th and arrived together at Church Fenton the same day.

In February the Squadron reached its flying target this month, great credit being due to the Groundcrews who worked a considerable amount of overtime to combat a high rate of unserviceability.

During March the aircraft strength was further reduced to a total of six aircraft when Flying Officer Barley hit a tree in making a low level attack on Abbotsinch airfield during the Forth Clyde exercises. The aircraft was flown back to base safely. The exercise as a whole was greatly appreciated by all pilots taking part in it, as it gave them simulated operational experience and a chance to prove the effectiveness of a Hornet aircraft at low level intruder attacks.

During April the Squadron obtained a replacement Mosquito and two replacement Hornets, which brings us up to full establishment again.

More than half the flying training for May was carried out at APC Acklington. The Squadron's averages on air to ground firing were showing a progressive improvement when unfortunately, all aircraft were grounded for air firing, by a defect in the front gun beam mounting.

On the 29th, Flight Lieutenant Mills and Flying Officer Varley flew to Acklington, where Flight Lieutenant Mills gave an aerobatic display for the Royal Observer Corp.

During June & July the Squadron participated in exercise 'Foil'. The Squadron was detached to Sector Headquarters at Linton on Ouse and shared a hangar and office accommodation with No 64 Squadron. The exercise was divided into three phases and lasted ten days, providing an invaluable introduction into intruder tactics for both experienced and inexperienced pilots. Apart from one sortie by four aircraft in a wing formation simulating an attack on London at 25,000 feet, all sorties were carried out at zero feet. Such a role demanded a high standard of low level navigation and map reading in order to achieve the briefed time over the target. Targets were normally aerodromes and radar stations in the eastern and southern counties. The detachment was a constructive success and augurs well for the Hornet as a penetration intruder, due solely to the 100 per cent serviceability made possible by the keenness, enthusiasm and hard work of the Squadron's Groundcrew.

Sqdn Ldr Woodward and Pilots – Church Fenton 1950

(Crown Copyright – Sqdn Album)

As the 15th September approached, rehearsals for the Fly Past over London became more intense. The actual Fly Past which included four aircraft from the Squadron, flown by Squadron Leader Woodward, Flight Lieutenant Mills, Pilot Officer Czerwinski and Pilot Officer Tresize was very well timed and the formation flying excellent in spite of bad

288

weather conditions over London. The AOC recorded the quality of flying in a message to all that took part.

The 17th, Church Fenton held its 'At Home' day to 12,000 members of the public. The Squadron led by the CO opened the flying programme with formation drill, which included a very impressive formation fly past with each aircraft on one engine only. Flight Lieutenant Mills gave a demonstration at Horsham St Faith and Flying Officer Varley showed off the Hornet at Turnhouse.

On the 20th, the Squadron moved to Linton on Ouse to take part in the Operation 'Bulldog'. The first two days were marred by fog and low stratus, which hung low over the whole country. During this time the Squadron flew 11 low level intruder sorties, successfully attacking aerodromes and radar installations. On the 26th, seven more intruder sorties were flown successfully. The serviceability of the aircraft was extremely well maintained during the exercise, in spite of additional work caused through the failure of components, such as cooling pumps and in one case a propeller.

In October the weather restricted the flying during the earlier part of the month. Two accidents during the month.

Pilot Officer Tresize had to make a force landing at Manby with a radiator punctured by air to ground ricochets.

Flying Officer Varley made a heavy landing on a single engine approach which collapsed the port undercarriage.

1950

In exercise 'New Year', during January, the squadron put up ten sorties against various targets in Crossland and although visibility at the base was very poor throughout the day, no sorties were aborted. Apart from the exercise 'New Year, the squadron concentrated on low level tactical formation drill and each pilot carried out at least one level cross country over the continent.

February saw the continuation of Yorkshire Sector's 'war' against Eastern Sectors in the form of exercise 'Pancake'. Once again this gives the squadron's pilots practice in intruder missions. A total of twelve sorties were flown and in every case, the pilots found and attacked their targets successfully. Night flying this month saw all pilots, with the exception of the two most recent additions, are now fully qualified by day and night.

The weekly pay parade has again been instituted after a lapse of nearly ten years. The general impression is that it is welcome by the airmen.

The squadron started April at Acklington in continuation of Armament Practice Camp. After setting a high showing of marksmanship on the air to ground range with a squadron average of 36.18%. (The Commanding Officer, Squadron Leader V.C. Woodward obtained the highest individual average of 60.5%.) The squadron turned to air to air practice hoping to achieve a similar standard. The result was an excellent squadron average of 10.2%. The honours this time went to Flying Officer Starkings, the squadron's PIA with an average of 17.4%.

The first part of July was devoted to practice for the RAF Display at Farnborough, and to the display itself, for which the squadron were detached to West Malling from the 4th to the 8th.

During August, the first few days were spent getting the aircraft into a full state of serviceability, preparatory to the squadron's move to Sylt, APS. The squadron flew to Sylt on the 10th, the groundcrew and freight followed on the 11th. The detachment was a great success, both on and off duty. The shooting results, with the exception of air to air, were good. The squadron's first introduction to rocket firing and low level bombing produced to some satisfactory low errors. The results would have been better had the pilots been able to stay up at any one exercise for several days as at previous APS's.

The squadron returned from Sylt on the 1st of September after a very pleasant APS attachment. The results were good, the squadron's order of merit being 1st in bombing, 2nd in air to air and air to ground and 3rd in R/P.

The first half of the month was devoted to preparations for the Battle of Britain Open Day and the Fly Past.

The flying programme on Open Day was carried out successfully despite very poor weather. The squadron's aircraft visited many other Stations. Pilot Officer Mitchell gave a very impressive aerobatic display at Church Fenton, which included a Fly Past with both propellers feathered.

Squadron Leader B.L. Duckenfield assumed command of the squadron.

The first week of October was occupied in warming up exercises for Exercise 'Emperor' which commenced on the 7th. The squadron carried out some very successful sorties during the first part of the exercise, but our aircraft were intercepted more frequently during the last two days. This was caused by having several targets for each sortie and by unrealistic routing which gave the defending forces a chance. Lessons learned from 'Emperor:-
1. That the guns should be fully depressed to allow for a shallowed dive in air to ground attacks.
2. That the Meteor is easier to evade than the Vampire.
3. That the defending fighters seemed reluctant to press home their attacks at very low levels.

Sergeant Moxon hit a tree at low level after getting into the slipstream of a Meteor, during the Exercise 'Emperor'. The aircraft was considerably damaged but Sergeant Moxon brought it back to base safely.

During December the squadron learned with some disappointment of the change of roll from intruder to interceptor. This feeling was relieved to some extent with the realisation that the Hornet is obsolete as an intruder and by the fact that the squadron is to be re-equipped with the Meteor Mark 8. (Preceded by training on the MK4.)

THE METEOR YEARS
1951 – 1956

1951

In January training for the new roll of the intercepter has continued. The emphasis being on such exercises as giro gun sight, formation, high level QGH and GCA on interception exercises. The latter not particularly successful due to the inexperienced controllers. As far as Meteor conversion is concerned, all pilots but one have now flown the Meteor Mark 4, and most have about five hours on the type.

During March the conversion of all pilots to Meteor 4 aircraft is now complete, except for one or two minor exercises. The weekly high level interception exercises at Linton on Ouse continues. The squadron realising that both they and the controllers need much practice. On the 20th, all Meteors were grounded for aileron modifications and remained so for the rest of the month.

On the 16th of April, the first four Meteor F8s arrived at Church Fenton and from this time things began to improve. By the end of the month, the squadron had eight Meteor 8s serviceable and flying.

Pilot Officer C.N.C. Mitchell in a Meteor 4 landed a few yards short of the runway, collapsing the undercarriage.

Flight Sergeant Campel in a Meteor 4 on a practice single engine landing, landed with his undercarriage up.

Neither pilot was hurt.

Meteor F8's

(Crown Copyright – Sqdn Album)

291

The month of May has been very successful. The squadron received a further eight Meteor F8s and a Mark 7. Serviceability has been good, the number of aircraft flying being restricted more by a lack of skilled groundcrew. The new aircraft have been painted up with the squadron markings, the Squadron Commander's aircraft having markings on the fin in addition to the fuselage. It is expected that the squadron will shortly divide into two flights.

June was considered to be a success, serviceability was good apart from a spate of cracked windscreens. Pilots are becoming more accustomed to the new squadron role brought about by the conversion to Meteor F8s, and the standard of high level flying is improving steadily. Whenever possible, Wednesday mornings have been devoted to formation fly past of as many aircraft as it is possible to put in the air. The most ambitious formation was one consisting of sixteen aircraft. The squadron put up eight aircraft and flew as a wing with No 616 Squadron, Royal Auxiliary Air Force, who are at present training on the station. This was the first attempt at a wing formation but nevertheless was encouragingly successful.

In August the squadron practiced interceptions, particularly with Patrington GCI. All our returns were sent to Patrington after each practiced interception, giving details and the pilots comments. Practice interceptions were showing improvement but the fighter was seldom brought into a favourable position to attack. During the early part of the month the squadron was visited by five fighter controllers from Patrington, who were flown on practiced interceptions in the Mark 7. This gave them an idea of interception from the pilot's point of view. On the 14th, the squadron carried out a maximum effort, flying through from 0830 to midnight. At the end of the month, 'A' flight commenced formation aerobatics practice and are hoping to have a team of four ready for 'Open Day' on the 15th September.

The squadron has now split into two flights and second line servicing echelon, under a new Engineering Officer, Flight Lieutenant Buckingham.

Exercise 'Pinnacle' – 29th September to 7th October
During the exercise the squadron's scramble time was much improved, finally being cut down to two minutes for the twelve aircraft. Practice interceptions were made and the squadron encountered 'window and jamming'.

On the 18th October twelve aircraft flew to Soesterberg, Holland, on a goodwill mission to the Royal Netherlands Air Force.

November – The Squadron now has more pilots than at any time since the end of the last war. The first line servicing sections are fairly well up to establishment but the second line servicing section is well below establishment. Much credit is due to the Engineering Officer, Flight Lieutenant J.O. Shackleton and his second line personnel for enabling the squadron to reach its target during this month.

1952

On the 10th January an aircraft following another in a stream landing, struck a jeep and the Runway Controller's Caravan, killing one airmen and injured an Officer. The aircraft landed on its belly with the pilot unhurt.

On the 20th, during a Command Exercise, two aircraft collided while attacking the same Lincoln bomber. Both aircraft crashed near Linton on Ouse. Sergeant J.R. Richmond was killed and Flight Lieutenant G.M. Smith was seriously injured.

The resurfacing of the runway and perimeter tracks from the 22nd to the 31st necessitated the closing of the airfield.

All the squadron's living-in ground personnel have now been moved into one barrack block and are consequently much happier.

On the 11th of February, the squadron moved to Acklington, for the annual shoot. The syllabus was completed in three weeks on flag and glider targets.

On the 1st of April, the squadron's aircraft was inspected by the AOC No 12 Group and later in the day, twelve aircraft carried out a fly past over the airfield.

Night flying was carried out during the month, consisting of circuits and landing, high level cross countrys and sector reconnaissances.

On the 25th, Meteor F8 (WB105) had a turbine failure in the air and Flying Officer Morris made a successful single engine landing.

There were two accidents in May and on both occasions the aircraft struck the airfield boundary fence whilst coming in to land.

On the 1st, Sergeant Marlow (WH275) and Flying Officer Williams (WE856) on the 23rd whilst doing night flying.

On the 29th June, a Royal Observer Corp exercise was held and the squadron participated by doing medium and low level cross country flights, providing trade for the Observers all over Yorkshire.

A welcome part of July's flying has been the detachment to RAF Coningsby, for bomber affiliation.

Air firing played a large part in this month's flying, the squadron was able to use the 'Hinderwell Staithes and Skipsea' Air to Air Firing Ranges for six days. The squadron's averages for the month increased to 9.9%. Flying Officer Harrison had the highest score of the month with 32.6%.

In August two weekend ROC exercises were held during the month. The first being navigation exercise and gave some 'trade' to the Royal Observer Corp. The second exercise, two or four Meteors were scrambled and vectored to low flying RATS (Royal Auxiliary Vampires) by means of ROC pilots. The squadron was brought to standby three times, before any scramble was given, but eventually six Vampires were intercepted. Of these four were intercepted on position reports and the other two opportunity targets. This was a most exciting sport requiring concentration and a high degree of skill on the part of the pilots. During the afternoon, two of the squadron's aircraft flew as RATS and found that their position was being transmitted with only a few seconds delay.

Several bomber and Sabre affiliations were flown.

Flight Lieutenant Steven led the squadron aerobatic team in practices for the coming Battle of Britain Display. Flying Officer Harnett, Sergeant Mercer and Sergeant Marlow were the other members of the team. Flying Officer Phipps, Flying Officer Harrison and Sergeant Logan are giving individual aerobatic displays.

There were three accidents during the month. One was caused by skidding into an obstruction whilst taxi-ing, one by overshooting the runway and one by collision with a bird in flight.

Flying Officer Phipps (WE855) on the 7th.
Flying Officer Harnett (WH275) on the 10th.
Flying Officer Harrison (WE962) on the 28th.

Flying during September was more intensive than during recent months, this was because of increased serviceability towards the end of the month. Also the pilots' strength is now the highest it has been for several years. Exercises included bomber affiliation on two days, one night's flying programme and air firing on four days. A large part of the flying done during the first three weeks of the month was practice for the Battle of Britain Flying Display. Four squadron pilots took part in the Battle of Britain Fly Past over London on the 15th. The display on the 20th was hampered by the weather but the advertised programme was carried through. The squadron's contribution was an individual and formation aerobatics, a mock attack on a ground target by four aircraft.

In October the Squadron took part in exercise 'Ardent'. On the 4th, the squadron flew 53 sorties of bomber interception and convoy escort patrols. The exercise continued until the 12th.

Several facts were brought out as a result of the exercise:

a. Scramble times have reached three to four minutes for twelve aircraft from dispersal. This shows an improvement from Exercise 'Pinnacle' when the dispersal was nearer to the runway in use.

b. The join up of the Wing after take off is now quite good having improved a lot this summer during practices with 609 and 606 Squadrons. Join up generally completed by 15,000 to 20,000 feet depending on the number of aircraft. However, a few aircraft have unaccountably become underpowered and are quite unable to keep up with the formation during the climb. Whenever possible, these aircraft are being fitted with the large intakes.

c. There was a lack of target information from the controllers. Although the squadron was scrambled long before the target came within radar coverage, necessitating long patrolling. Although on one occasion the target Lincolns were over base as the squadron was scrambled, the squadron was then vectored 100 miles out to sea before a reciprocal vector was given. Target height information was non existent or very inaccurate. The controllers transmitting techniques were often bad, leading to confusion and cluttering up of the RT with repeated transmissions.

There were five accidents during the month.

Flight Lieutenant Partridge (WA984) on the 5th.

(WA758) on the 9th, no pilot.

Sergeant Couttes (WE855) on the 17th.

Flying Officer Turgoose (WE962) on the 17th.

Pilot Officer Mann (WA969) on the 17th.

There were two main sector exercises during November. On 16th an interception was made over The Wash with USAF Sabres of the Bentwaters Wing. Great benefit was derived from the ensuing combat; we should like many more of such exercises to be laid on. The Eighty-Sixes were intercepted by eight Meteors at 25,000 feet and in the mêlée that followed, descended to 10,000 feet and below. In turns below 15-20,000 feet we were able to track the Sabres successfully and several assessable films were brought back. The Sabres only out-distanced us at high mach numbers in prolonged dives. On Sunday 23rd, the Squadron participated in a 'Rat and Terrier' exercise which lasted throughout the day. The targets were low flying F84's, F86's, Vampires, Invaders and Lancasters of Coastal Command. The ROC plotting system enabled the slower flying targets to be intercepted.

In January the accent was on air firing. Forty-eight effective sorties were flown giving a squadron average of 13.4%. Flying Officer Jenkins achieved the record score to date with 63.7%. A sector exercise against RCAF Sabres was carried out on 15th. All the four Sabres were contacted and the encounter was inconclusive as they were reluctant to attack our aircraft while we could not close with them. Twelve aircraft flew to RAF Fassberg on the German Eastern border on 26th on a short visit to the second TAF. The visit was a very welcome one and all too short; it was the squadron's first overseas flight since Autumn 1951.

A varied training programme was carried out in March. The emphasis this month was on air firing in preparation for the APS attachment and on similar attacks on flags towed at 18,000 feet. For an overseas flight to Malta, four aircraft were fitted with full tankage and left on the 9th March. Bad weather at Malta prevented the aircraft from continuing past Istres but the two day trip was nevertheless appreciated. The squadron aerobatic team consisting of Flying Officer Harnett, Flight Lieutenant Stephen, Flying Officer Jenkins and Flying Officer Mann, gave a display for Marshal Tito at RAF Duxford on 18th March. Two aircraft unfortunately collided during the display involving Flying Officer Harnett (WK858) and Pilot Officer Mann (WH351). Both pilots were killed and the aircraft were scrapped.

The squadron spent all but two days of April on attachment to APS. Results were gratifying with a final Squadron average of 19.6%. The highest grade during the attachment was 47.5% achieved by the commanding officer. Air firing with the giro site, flag targets were towed between 15-18,000 feet. The Squadron had not fired at these altitudes previously. Squadron moral was very high during the attachment and a very successful Squadron party was attended by all flying and ground personnel at the end of the attachment in addition to an inter-Squadron party with 72 Squadron who will be joining us at Church Fenton this month. One unavoidable accident when Flight Lieutenant Steven's aircraft (WH350) on air-ground firing, receiving a bullet ricochet.

On return from APS a sector exercise was held on the 25th April in the course of which GCI control produced no targets except friendly fighters. On the following day the Squadron took part in a full scale 'Rat and Terrier' exercise when 27 sorties were flown. The radar control of low flying targets compared very unfavourably with the ROC Broadcast used on previous exercises. Venoms, Meteors, Neptunes and A26's, were intercepted mainly as opportunity targets.

During May an average of 14.7% was recorded by the Squadron over 40 effective air firing sorties, the highest individual score for the month was 35% and was achieved by Flight Lieutenant C.R.G. Neville. The average was 53% over 102 effective shots, this being an improvement on the 51% attained during March the last month of normal Squadron training.

On the 22nd a turn round exercise was carried out by the Squadron. This consisted of scramble take off, high altitude air to sea firing and a complete re-fuel on the isle on landing with sections coming into readiness again as soon as possible. Bomber affiliation exercises were carried out on the 1st with B50's and Lincoln's on the 15th. On the 1st an affiliation with F86 aircraft proved to be both interesting and instructive. Reasonable results were achieved by the Squadron on a 'Rat and Terrier' exercise on the 13th with Meteor F11's acting as target aircraft. A night flying programme was carried out on the 9th and 28th. As it is several months since the Squadron has had the opportunity to night fly, most of the exercises were set to reconnaissances and cross country navigational trips.

Pilot Officer Thompson (WB109) at altitude had centre bearing failure in the port engine. He managed to land on a single engine without further damage.

On the 1st June nine aircraft were detached to Cottishall for exercise "Tartar" over the period of the Coronation. The Squadron was detached to North Weald on the 23rd June with 13 Meteor 8's for the RAF review Fly Past practices. Weather prevented practice on the first few days but four were done by the end of the month.

The Squadron's flying at North Weald during the first two weeks of July was concentrated mainly on rehearsal for the RAF Review Fly Past, while unserviceability limited other flying. This included more high level PI's for preparation for exercise "Momentum". For the Fly Past rehearsal, nine or more aircraft were used according to serviceability. Twelve took part in the full scale rehearsal, the only set back was constant cancellation of practice due to low cloud base. Fourteen aircraft were serviceable for the Fly Past itself, and the Squadron returned to Church Fenton the following day after a farewell party had been held at North Weald.

A 'Rat and Terrier' exercise was carried out on the 23rd, while it was once again found that close control by radar for low level targets does not produce results. All the hostile Canberra's and RCAF Sabres that were seen were attacked as opportunity targets. We should welcome back the ROC broadcast system for these exercises.

Pilot Officer Boulton on his first trip on the Squadron had a flame extinction in both engines at height. He managed to re-light both engines.

During August Sections were detached to Cottishall to act as targets on high level interceptions and to Duffield to act as reinforcements for 'Rat and Terrier' operations.

Exercise "Momentum" itself resulted in many patrols at 40,000 feet for long periods with little excitement. It was thought that many of the Canberra targets were descending from this height to very low levels, which was between the coverage of the long range radar and that of the normal equipment, and thus were lost sight of by GCI stations, more than 100 miles from the coast. However, there was considerably more activity during the second and third phases of the exercise including two low level raids at this airfield by F84's on the final Sunday.

Altogether the Squadron claims 22 hostiles destroyed including 2 Canberra's, 1 B45, 2 B29's, 1 B50, 1 PR Mosquito, 12 F84's, 2 F86's and 1 Vampire. All were high level targets except for the F86's and the Mosquito which were at 20,000 feet. Similar results were very good during the exercise the GGS Mk 3 recorder has made a big all round improvement in this respect.

The ground crews, now much reduced in numbers since centralised servicing was introduced at Church Fenton, again proved their willingness to work hard over the long periods and consistently rapid turn rounds were achieved.

Following exercise "Momentum", three days of intensive air firing was carried out. These were very successful as the average over 44 effective shoots, well above Squadron average, was 24% and the average for the top 12 shoots was 32%. One flag containing 143 bullet holes, was captured by a party of 12 Group Staff Officers for their OC's inspection. The following day a congratulatory signal was received from the AOC by the four pilots concerned. These sharp shooting gentlemen were Flying Officer Cresswell, Pilot Officer Hopkins, Flying Officer Goadby and Pilot Officer Hanson.

There was one fatal accident during the month involving Pilot Officer G.M.J. Yeilding (WA758).

On the 19th September, the Squadron's formation aerobatic team flew to Newton to perform on the RAF "At home" at Newton on the Battle of Britain day.

During October the GCA installation completed its calibration tests and became available for general use in the latter half of the month. As this is the first time that GCA has been available for two years on this station, every opportunity was taken to provide the pilots with practice, for some it was the first time they had used this approach aid.

Army sector exercise took place on the 27th. The first phase consisted of fighter aircraft from Church Fenton intercepting formations of Meteor 8's and NF11's attacking this country from the North Sea. On the whole the interceptions were successful. In the second phase numbers 19 and 72 Squadron's played the role of the attackers.

Pilot Officer P.R. Boulton (WE856) was performing aerobatics when his aircraft broke up in the air. The pilot was killed.

The month of November started with air to air firing which took place on the 2nd, 3rd, 4th and 6th. Twenty-nine effective sorties produced a Squadron average of 24.1%, the most outstanding score being, that of Sergeant Logan, who obtained no less then 77 hits out of 120 rounds fired, giving a score of 64.2%.

Two interception exercises involving 19 Squadron took place. The first a high level interception exercise was on the 10th, the second over the weekend of the 28th and 29th. In these weekends exercises the Squadron flew alternately as attackers and interceptors. The controlling for the interception was found to be of a rather low standard.

Eleven of the aircraft in the Squadron are now fitted with a Martin Baker automatic ejector seat and an explanatory lecture on them was given by Wing Commander Jewel on the 12th.

1954

Flying for the month of January commenced on the 4th with the normal battle formation training sorties and a period of night flying from 16-1700 hours.

Squadron Pilots 1953/54

(*Squadron Leader B. Beard*)

297

On the following day, pairs of aircraft flew on a sector early morning exercise, consisting of a low level flight from pre-determined points over the North Sea. An air firing programme was carried out on the same day with the remaining aircraft.

12 aircraft of the Squadron were due to take off at 0900 hours for a day liaison visit to RAF Jever on the 11th, but owing to weather conditions on the Continent, the take off was put back hourly until the clearance came at 1300 hours departure. The 12 aircraft took off in fours at ten minute intervals and set course for Jever. When approximately 100 miles from Jever, all aircraft were diverted to Alhorn the home of Nos 96 and 256 NF 11 squadrons. After the controlled let down over Alhorn, all aircraft eventually arrived in the circuit with a 200 feet cloud base. All landed without incident and 12 grateful pilots were heard blessing a most efficient control officer. (Take a bow Officer Priestley!)

From the take off at Alhorn, Flying Officer Harrison's hood blew off but he landed back without further incident and a new hood was flown in from another station in Germany and he was able to proceed to Jever the following day.

On the 23rd January, a new system of flying was started whereby four sorties were flown per day with a complete break over the lunch period. This was necessary owing to the shortage of ground crews and the longer time for turn round with the introduction of the new F700E. This system has proved to be far more efficient than a whole day's flying without a break.

There was one accident during February. Flying Officer Hanson in (WL117). The starboard tyre tread stripped off on take off and severed the starboard brake air line. On landing the pilot was unable to prevent the aircraft from running into the overshoot area due to the lack of brake pressure.

Exercise "Magna Flux" took place over the first five days of March except for Wednesday the 3rd when the weather was very poor. Although the weather was good on the remaining four days there was very little activity in the Northern Sector and little flying was done.

On the evening of Friday 26th a night flying programme was carried out and the newer pilots were able to have their first sight of the local area at dusk. The remainder of the Squadron flew night cross-country trips. Training of the more recent arrivals of the Squadron has been continued on every possible occasion during the month.

On the last day of May a Dacre trophy was presented to the Squadron by Air Commodore G.B. Dacre CBE., DSO. Among the official guests present were Mrs Dacre, Air Marshal Sir Dermott Boyle, KCBO, KBE, CB, CBE, AFC, CNC Fighter Command and Lady Boyle; Air Vice-Marshal Crisham CB, CBE, AOC Number 12 Group; Air Commodore Stephenson CBE Commandant of CFE;[*] and Air Commodore Bowling CBE Northern Sector Commander.

The first few days of July saw the completion of the training programme at APS and the Squadron returned to base. There followed a period of practice for the annual exercise "Dividend". The emphasis during this period was on the high altitude PI's a good investment as the majority of the work on exercise "Dividend" did, in fact, consist of higher altitude interceptions.

There was one aircraft accident during the month when Sergeant Jennings (WB107) where the aircraft ran off the end of the runway during a braking test. The pilot was uninjured.

---

[*]   A previous CO of 19 Squadron, shot down over Dunkirk in 1940; later to be killed in an F100 accident in the USA.

September – The Squadron now has 35 pilots all of whom have current instrument ratings but it is being found increasingly difficult to renew all ratings with a single Meteor 7 which suffers long periods of unserviceability. On the 18th of the month the station was "At home" for the Battle of Britain day. Aircraft from the Squadron took park in the wing Fly Past and mock attacks on the Lincoln.

During November the position in the authorisation of low level flights was clarified. The Squadron took full advantage of this and on the 4th November Squadron aircraft did a low level interception on 12 aircraft from DFLS.

Throughout the month individual aircraft were sent to do low level cross-countries in low flying areas. The Squadron engaged in several interception exercises during the month using Broadcast Control and DME. A high interception rate was achieved. Many ordinary high altitude PI's were also carried out, the Squadron flying 66 hours on this type of exercise.

Now that unauthorised 'bouncing' has been quashed, most formation sorties include a tail chase and a single aircraft is regularly authorised to 'bounce' a particular section of aircraft engaged in battle formation. In this way the Squadron in endeavouring to keep its pilots familiar with combat handling of an aircraft and also ensure that a continual look-out is maintained.

1955

January saw the introduction of a new type "flying training return". This took a little getting used to but it was found that no change was necessitated in our actual flying programme or matters of flying. Flights are now authorised by numbers representing specific exercises instead of writing out the exercises in words.

On the last three days of March pilots were engaged in an exercise in which for the first time they operated against B36's. It was generally agreed that this exercise was of value to the fighter pilots if only to give them experience of making attacks on aircraft of this size.

Squadron Leader B. Beard recalls:-

"I had a happy and busy tour, during which time I am pleased to say that we managed to win both Fighter Command Trophies, the Dacre Trophy for air firing and the Duncan Trophy for poor weather and night flying reinforcement flights.

I always thought that our "Squadron Taxi", which was a genuine London taxi suitably camouflaged, drew a number of laughs when it led a convoy of cars to local towns and villages. One had to approach fairly close to read the one inch red letters on the rear door which read: "Don't laugh Mother, your daughter may be inside". It also contributed to the Squadrons Fund, as we loaned this useful vehicle, at the "going rate" to 72 and 609 Squadrons, who completed the Church Fenton Wing."

In April Squadron Leader D.J. Fowler, AFC assumed command of the Squadron

During May the shortage of Meteor spares is becoming more and more apparent and AOG priorities more and more customary. This causes speculation as to whether the aircraft will outlast in service the spare backing. It would be easier to judge if there were any sign of new equipment. It looks, at the moment, as if this Squadron may have the doubtful distinction of being the last to fly Meteors operationally.

Squadron Taxi

In June exercise "Fabulous" was sprung upon us which necessitated keeping some aircraft permanently on the ground from the 18th to the 22nd for operational scrambles. The visit of the Air Officer commanding No.13 Group on the 23rd meant further non flying periods for parade rehearsals and general training.

There was one accident during July when Flying Officer Paynes' port tyre burst on landing and the aircraft struck a brick wall and was destroyed. Flying Officer Payne was unhurt.

During August there were two accidents. Pilot Officer L. Hook (WL172) the tyre cover stripped during take off damaging the mud guard and the underside of the main plane. The aircraft landed without further damage. The second accident was Flying Officer P.C. Kenrick (WH249). The aircraft struck Cleveland Hills in cloud and the pilot was killed.

The routine flying practice for September was broken by two factors one the Battle of Britain day and two, the summer exercise "Beware". On the Battle of Britain day the Squadron took part in formation Fly Past over Thornaby, Catterick and Church Fenton. A demonstration of attacks on tail flag targets was also carried out by four aircraft over Church Fenton. Individual aerobatic displays were given at Binbrook, Turnhouse and Thornaby.
    The Squadron moved to Ouston between the 21st and 23rd to take part in "Beware". News has now been received of the re-armouring of the Squadron with a Hunter Mk 4 aircraft on the 4th of November. This is welcome news as it is serving as a stimulus to the whole Squadron.

The first two days of October were taken up with the last phase of "Beware". The Squadron returned to Church Fenton on the 3rd October.
    Twelve aircraft were detached to Leuchars for "Running Tide" between the 11th and 13th.

This exercise provided a fair amount of activity probably due to the absence of Hunter support.

The Squadron also took part in exercise "Phoenix", a DRW exercise and a turn round exercise.

During November eight Squadron aircraft carrying long range tanks acted as targets in an inter-sector PI trial. The aircraft landed at Kinloss, unfortunately only seven returned due to a taxi-ing accident when one struck a hangar after brake failure. The long range tanks and two aircraft were retained and enabled the majority of Squadron pilots to carry out long range flying.

Squadron aircraft strength was further reduced on the 25th when an aircraft was completely burnt out after catching fire in the ASF hangar. Aircraft strength is therefore now 18.

On the 30th of the month the establishment changes to that of a Hunter Squadron. There is, however, no sign of a Hunter and no word of explanation as to the delay or postponements.

1956

There was one accident in January. Pilot Officer L. Hook stalled into the undershoot area whilst making an approach during poor weather and fortunately he managed to get airborne again and landed safely.

The Squadron has now been informed that re-equipment with the Hunter 4 will not now take place. Headquarters 13 Group have verbally agreed that aircraft strength is brought up again to 22 Meteor 8's and the agreement of Headquarter Fighter Command to this policy has been requested. In the meantime 5 Meteor 8's have been transferred from No.72 Squadron and authority has been requested for this. The return to the Squadron after the repair of WL107 damaged in Pilot Officer Hook's accident will bring the strength to 22.

A feature of March was a series of exercises designed to test the effectiveness of an autonomous control system from a Master GCI plus a sub-GCI against single targets on a hard front. During two of these exercises first six then twelve aircraft operated from Acklington. Successful interceptions were made against Meteor 11's from Alhorn but less success was achieved against Canberra targets.

The battle flight system of having a pair of aircraft available for "Ad hoc" interceptions seemed to work quite well and the interceptions were carried out on the Canberra's with a few Valiant's sometimes available.

During the month, notification was received that the Squadron standard was ready for collection. It was collected from Hobson's in London by Flying Officer J.T.C. Long. Preparations are now going ahead for the presentation which it is hoped will take place late in June or early July.

On the 26th of May, B Flight plus the officers of A Flight left for the attachment to Horsham St Faith for exercise "Fabulous".

There were two accidents in June. Flight Lieutenant A. Neale had a flame out in his starboard engine while turning down wind, and carried out a successful force landing. The pilot was unhurt. Flying Officer B. Fletcher hit a bird with his starboard main plane immediately after take off. The starboard main plane was damaged, and Flying Officer B. Fletcher carried out an ordinary landing.

Meteor F8 "WK691" "T"

Flown here by Flight Lieutenant Bennett. This was the Authors favourite aircraft which he serviced during his tour. The Squadron markings on the engine cowlings and wing tips were done by him.

(F/Lt. T. Shepherd)

THE PRESENTATION AND CONSECRATION OF THE SQUADRON STANDARD

The original use of a symbol by the Armed Forces is lost in antiquity. It is known that the Assyrians, Egyptians, Greeks and the Romans all had ensigns and standards which were regarded with the greatest veneration.

They have been in use by the British Forces for many centuries. It is probable that their original purpose was to be the rallying point during a confused battle. Enshrined on them are the battle honours recording the proud traditions of the unit concerned and constituting a memorial to those who have gone before and have contributed to these traditions. Above all, a colour or standard is a symbol of a Sovereign's trust in the unit concerned.

The practise of consecrating the colours is of very long standing and because they have this religious significance, they become not only an outward sign of unity, loyalty and achievement, but also a symbol of fellowship with God. The combination of these factors places a deep significance on every Colour or Standard in the Royal Air Force. Each is to be honoured as a symbol of trust which the Sovereign reposes in the Royal Air Force, and is an emblem of its achievements, the shrine of our Service traditions, a reminder of the devotion and sacrifices of our predecessors, and an inspiration to those who serve in the Royal Air Force.

THE STANDARD

"The Squadron Standard" was created by His late Majesty King George VI to mark the twenty-fifth anniversary of the Royal Air Force in 1943. It is awarded only to Squadrons of twenty-five years' standing, or with a history of special outstanding operations.

Her Majesty The Queen affirmed her father's decision and gives personal approval to each standard created.

The Standard consists of a fringed and tasselled silken banner mounted on a pike crowned by a golden eagle. Eight selected battle honours in scroll surround the Squadron Badge, and the decorative border contains the rose, leek, thistle and shamrock, beautifully embroidered.

BATTLE HONOURS

*Western Front 1916-1918
 Arras
 Somme 1918
 Amiens
*Dunkirk
*Battle of Britain 1940
 Dieppe
*Normandy 1944
 France and Germany 1944-1945

*Somme 1916
*Ypres 1917
 Lys
 Hindenburg Line
 Home Defence 1940-1942
 Channel & North Sea 1941-1942
*Fortress Europe 1942-1944
*Arnhem

*Denotes Honours emblazoned on Standard.

On the 11th July, in glorious weather, the Air Chief-Marshal, Sir Donald Hardman, G.B.E., K.C.B., D.F.C., made the presentation in a striking and memorable ceremony. The Standard bearer is Flying Officer M.A. Telford.

(Yorkshire Evening Post)

Officers and airmen on the Presentation Parade

(Crown Copyright – Sqdn Album)

The first of August found the Squadron at Horsham St Faith taking part in exercise "Fabulous". On the 21st to the 24th the Squadron took part in exercise "Fawn" an exchange visit with number 350 Squadron Belgian Air Force, Beauvechain.

Normal Squadron training was interrupted during September for the Battle of Britain day preparations and exercise "Strong-Hold". Exercises taken part in this month were two sector exercises, two DFLS routes for 'Rat and Terrier' exercises and exercise "Strong-Hold". Exercise "Strong-Hold" was a two phase exercise, phase one from the 19th to the 23rd, and the second from the 26th to the 28th.

Activity was at a reasonable level with the majority of scrambles resulting in a number of successful interceptions. On the Battle of Britain day the Squadron carried out a Fly Past over Dishforth, Thornaby and Ouston finishing with a mock attack on the air field. Set piece aerobatics were carried out over Hendon Holton by Sergeant J.C. Knox.

The Squadron is due to re-equip on the 20th October with Hunter F6 aircraft.

There was one accident in October which was unfortunately fatal. Flying Officer C. Pearson's Meteor 8 dived into the ground at high speed near Worksop.

Hunter F6

(Crown Copyright – Sqdn Album)

THE HUNTER YEARS
1956 – 1962

1956

The mid 1950s were exciting days in the RAF for those whose thoughts were centred mainly on the thrill of flying and the places throughout the world where such a pleasurable occupation might be fulfilled. A fighter crew-room then was no place for talking of pensions, careers in industry or even house mortgages, and anyone who did so would be seen at best as eccentric, more suited to a tour on the "Kipper Fleet".

The world still beckoned; Germany, Cyprus and the Mediterranean bases. The Gulf, Aden, Singapore and numerous staging bases across Europe, Africa, the Middle and Far East. To add to the promise of attractive postings, a new generation of aircraft were coming into service to boost the fighter element of the RAF, previously starved in favour of the Bomber force.

Indeed, the British aircraft industry was in its hey day. Rival companies had produced both the Swift and the Hunter to meet the day-fighter role and the DH110 and the Javelin for night all/weather. The infamous Sandys Defence White Paper which forecast the replacement of manned fighters by SAM did not emerge until 1957 to be followed by the even more traumatic cancellation of projects in Denis Healeys' 1966 White Paper.

The Hunter versus the Swift competition was firmly decided in favour of the Hunter with the Swift enjoying only a brief and difficult in-service career in the PR role. The Javelin joined the Hunter in the front line inventory at the expense of the DH110 which went on to become an effective carrier-borne aircraft as the Sea Vixen FAW.

But whatever the politics and the wider Defence issues, 19 Squadron was delighted to see the arrival of their first Hunter F6 in October 1956.

The fulfilment of the re-equipment date has proved a great moral builder for all ranks. A Vampire T11 trainer has also been received, this is to replace the Meteor T7.

November saw the beginning of Hunter conversion on the Squadron.

Flying in the Hunters commenced on the 8th of the month after a 3 day period of ground instruction. Because of the degree of supervision required, the amount of flying carried out was small at first but has increased in volume throughout the month as permitted by aircraft serviceability. Flight Lieutenant E. Richards is supervising the basic conversion, he being the only experienced Hunter pilot on the Squadron. By the end of the month, ten pilots were fully converted and five at various stages. Since the Squadron is required to provide an operational detachment at Horsham St Faith of the 28th December, it will not be possible to take on any more further conversions and all further effort will be devoted to reaching operational standard with those converted or now converting.

Serviceability has been a major problem. Only ten Hunters have been delivered and the other six being at modification centre. Considerable trouble has been experienced with the ancillary equipment, particularly the oxygen system.

It has been just possible to reach operational standard with the twelve pilots detached to Horsham St Faith on the 29th December. Bad serviceability had dogged the Squadron and the shortage of spares is chronic. There are practically no spare parts readily available and cannibalisation has been resorted in order to provide six serviceable aircraft to go to Horsham.

Two more aircraft have arrived during the month bringing the total to fourteen, it is hoped to have the remaining two soon. Conversion of the remaining Pilots will proceed during January. It is hoped that the Squadron will be fully operational by the end of the coming month.

1957

On the 1st of January, a detachment of the Squadron were at Horsham St Faith for exercise 'Fabulous'. On the 2nd, whilst at Horsham, the Squadron were honoured with a visit by the Air Office Commanding in Chief, Fighter Command, who was visiting the Station that day. The Squadron returned to Church Fenton on the 4th. The Hunter conversion program was then restarted, with approximately half the Squadron to convert. By the end of the month all but two pilots had completed the program and a more operational type of training was being done. There were two incidents during the month – Flying Officer T.H. Sheppard and Flying Officer M.A. Telford had bird strikes whilst taking off from Horsham St Faith. In both cases minor damage was done.

On the 18th February the Squadron became fully operational and all pilots but one, delayed by sickness, had converted to the type. The end of the month saw the Squadron air firing on the flag for the first time. It was found that by operating singly instead of in pairs, that no time was lost, and that four aircraft could still fire on one flag, and the whole exercise was easier on the pilots and the turnround teams. There were two accidents during the month – Flying Officer T.H. Sheppard had hydraulic failure, resulting in a manual landing on nose wheel and starboard main wheel. The pilot was not injured. Flying Officer P.A. Clee landed with a burst tyre but no great damage was done.

Sqdn Leader D.J. Fowler and Pilots 1957

March was devoted mainly to weapons training, i.e., cine and air to air firing. Night flying was carried out once this month. On the 16th April, the Air Officer Commanding paid his annual visit. "A" Flight, under Flight Lieutenant E. Richards comprising of eleven pilots and eight Hunters were detached to RAF Wattisham on the 17th to 25th on exercise 'Fabulous'. There was one incident during April, when Flight Lieutenant A.L. Bennett lost the rear half of the starboard link connector. In spite of the heavy vibration, a safe landing was made.

During May, the Squadron participated in Fighter Command exercise "Vigilant". On this the first occasion in which they have used the Hunters on a major exercise, the records give the following information; From Church Fenton – 36 scrambles, 23 kills, 4 contacts. At 0415 hours on the morning of the last day of the exercise, six aircraft were sent up to operate from Turnhouse and from 9 scrambles the pilot achieved six kills. There was one accident this month – Flying Officer J.T.C. Long experienced brake failure on his Hunter which finished in the overshoot. There was fortunately no damage to Flying Officer Long.

In June the flying task was devoted to air firing. All pilots had several shoots and some good scores were obtained. At the end of the period there was a general feeling that we were finally getting the measure of the Hunter F6 as a gun platform. The last week of the month saw an exchange visit between "A" Flight led by Squadron Leader Fowler and a similar formation from No. 7 Squadron, Belgium Air Force. There were two accidents during the month when on the 16th, Flying Officer A.G. Bridges was throttling back some minutes after becoming airborne when the rear half of his starboard link collector came adrift and lodged over his starboard intake. A check by his leader showed no further damage and a safe landing was made. On the 19th, Flight Lieutenant P.F. Mollan, after a session of aerobatics and the practiced emergencies was coming in for a manual circuit when he had a complex hydraulic failure. A safe manual landing was carried out.

July again was mainly devoted to air firing and by the end of the period the majority of the pilots had completed their Dacre Trophy shoots. There was some improvement on the last month but we were still not fully satisfied with our results. The last week of the month saw "B" Flight (under the command of Flight Lieutenant M.M. Foster,) at Wattisham on Exercise "Fabulous". There were two near misses during the month when on the 15th, Pilot Officer A. Tyldesley had a sticking altimeter above 8/8th cloud, but came down in formation and landed safely. On the 18th, Flight Lieutenant P.F. Mollan had another unbriefed manual landing when he had to use his emergency undercarriage button after his port main wheel stuck partially down after take off. A normal manual landing was made.

In August, Major R.G. Newell (U.S.A.F) assumed command of the Squadron (an event thought to be unique in Fighter Command – if not RAF – history, of a Squadron being commanded by appointment of other than an RAF officer.) The second week of the month was devoted to high altitude cine and the aircraft servicing preparations for the following weeks detachments. This began on the 12th, when eight aircraft left for the Royal Dutch Air Force Station, Leeuwarden. A similar formation of No. 324 Squadron, Dutch Air Force came to Church Fenton. There were two incidents, when on the 15th, Flying Officer Bond, aborted take off at Leeuwarden in a Hunter and ended up in the overshoot. The following day, Flying Officer Smith was landing a Hunter at Acklington, when fumes in the cockpit caused him to land a little fast. He too finished up in the overshoot area. Neither Flying Officer Smith or the Hunter suffered any damage.

The Squadron Team selected to compete in the Dacre Trophy put in extensive practice during

September in high level cine and air to air firing. For the Battle of Britain day, the Squadron provided a Flypast of six Hunters led by Major Newell and an individual low level aerobatics by Flight Lieutenant T.H. Sheppard. The formation flew over Norton, Leconfield, Thornaby and Dishforth. The NATO exercise "Strikeback" required six Hunters on state from 0600 hours to 1900 hours for ten days – 19th to the 28th inclusive. During this period the Squadron intercepted aircraft of Bomber Command returning from strikes on the US Fleet and Norway. Flying Officer Tyldesley allowed a Hunter to stall on landing. Slight damage was caused to the tail cone.

Major R.G. Newell (USAF)
Hunter and Squadron Taxi.

(Crown Copyright – Sqdn Album)

The Squadron was placed second overall in the competition for the Dacre Trophy. At the end of the cine stage of the competition the Squadron were about 100 points behind No. 63 Squadron, but after the air firing finished only eleven points behind. From the 15th October to 5th November, the Squadron attached eight Hunters and twelve pilots to Aldergrove. This detachment proved good Squadron training, mostly in practice interceptions.

November was devoted to weapons training. During the last few days of the month a number of 'Battle Fours' were flown giving much needed practice in tactical flying. In December, cine quarter attacks at 20,000 and 30,000 feet were practiced as well as the 'Battle Fours'.

During January the Squadron carried out normal training in accordance with the new 12 Group syllabus. This syllabus put the emphasis on tactical intercept training. On the 7th February, there was a near miss in a snowstorm when Flying Officer C.P. Field and Flight Lieutenant A.W. Gleadon were unable to land at base due to very reduced visibility. They were both fortunate and skilful in landing with very little fuel left at Acaster Malvis and Sherburn in Elmet respectively.

On the 20th March the Squadron took part in Kingpin/Adex exercise against Valiants and Canberras. This exercise was directed at targets in the 13 Group area and so the Squadron was reinforced with 17 Hunters from Nos. 56, 63 and 74 Squadrons. Six Hunters from the Squadron were used and a good number of interceptions were made.

During April a fairly successful fortnight of air firing was carried out, the first week at high level and the second week at low level. Flying Officer A. Park had the best individual score of 45%. Eight aircraft were not fitted with radar ranging apparatus which is extremely valuable in all cine exercises.

On the 1st May was the A.O.C.'s annual inspection of the Squadron. From the 5th to the 16th, the Squadron carried out intensive high level air firing. There was incident during the month when Flying Officer McCord had a tyre burst on landing and the other burst when he skidded sideways down the runway. There was no damage to the pilot.

The big feature of the month of June had been the conversion of all but three of the aircraft to long range specifications by the fitting of two 100 gallon inboard tanks. This has enormously increased range, endurance and amount of training which can be accomplished each sortie. There was one incident this month when Flight Lieutenant Sheppard found himself in a cloud which extended down to 500 feet during a QGH/GCA with a jammed RT button in the 'in' position. Without RT therefore, Flight Lieutenant Sheppard competently extracted himself from the delicate situation by overshooting and map reading his way to Driffield where he landed safely.

On the 14th July "B" Flight went to RNAF, Woensdrecht on exercise "Fawn". The detachment was very successful in that a large number of PI's were carried out on Hunters, F84's, F100's and F86's, giving very realistic training.

On the morning of the 25th August, ten aircraft flew to Duxford with a further two to follow, to rehearse the Flypast for the Battle of Britain. A total of 45 Hunters from Nos. 1, 19, 56, 63 and 65 Squadrons were airborne on rehearsal, 19 being led by Major Newell, with Flight Lieutenant Mumford and Flight Lieutenant Sheppard as Flight Leaders.

The 1st September was Technical and Press Day at the SBAC Farnborough Show. The Squadron flying from Duxford put up twelve Hunters each day of the week. On the 7th the Squadron returned to Church Fenton and Flying Officer G.K. Moore was killed when his aircraft crashed after take off from RAF Duxford. Flying Officer Moore's aircraft was seen to cross under his leader and apparently enter a stall from which the aircraft entered, what appeared to be an uncontrollable roll. The aircraft struck the ground in a nose down and right wing low position. On the 20th, RAF Church Fenton was opened again for the Battle of Britain Day.

1959

At the beginning of April, the Squadron took part in exercise "Topbait". The exercise being very successful with the Squadron having plenty of 'kills'. Air firing was done for a few days in the month with Flying Officer A.J. Park again achieving best score with 70%.

From the 4th to the 6th May, the Squadron were detached to Horsham St Faith for a low level 'Rat and Terrier' exercise. On the 25th, nine pilots and eight aircraft went on a "Fawn Beta" exchange with pilots of No. 8 Squadron of the Belgium Air Force at Chievres. It was the first time the Squadron had taken part in a ten day exchange instead of five.

On the afternoon of the 12th June, the Squadron departed to Acklington for a fortnight's concentrated air firing. This proved to be very beneficial, the overall Squadron average being 16.7%. Flying Officer Park was the top scorer with 78%.

After twelve years at Church Fenton, the Squadron moved to Leconfield on the 26th June.

In July, Squadron Leader L.W. Phipps AFC, assumed command of the Squadron. On the 19th August, six Hunters were detached to Wattisham for a night exercise. Unfortunately Flying Officer S.A. Edwards suffered port brake failure on landing and disappeared past his leader into a corn field. Luckily neither pilot nor aircraft suffered any damage. The Hunter was repaired and flown back to Leconfield. A few days later, the same aircraft had brake failure again, ran off the runway and into a ditch. This time the pilot was Flying Officer G.B. Pickering. Flying Officer A.J. Park was a member of the Fighter Command Air Firing Team which went to Paris to compete in the NATO competition. He did very well and helped the team into second place behind the Canadians.

On the 11th November the Squadron took off for Nicosia, Cyprus. Flying Officer S.A. Edwards suffered bird strike which necessitated an engine change at El Aden. On arrival at Nicosia it did not take long before a full flying programme was under way. For the first time in two weeks this entailed doing Battle Flights and PI's, the standard of which was very high. An RN/RAF exercise with HMS Defender was participated in and the last part of the month was air to ground firing and rocketing.

In December the Squadron moved to Akrotiri for the remainder of the stay in Cyprus. Soon after arriving in Akrotiri there were a couple of mishaps when Flight Lieutenant G.N.M Pickersgill, playing for the Squadron in a Hockey tournament, fell over and fractured his arm. Squadron Leader L.W. Phipps managed to break his ankle.

1960

The Squadron began the return to the UK on the 13th January. March was a good operational month for intensive training with the emphasis on the air defence role.

In June a detachment of Six Hunters flew to Stradishall to take part in Her Majesty the

Queen's birthday Flypast. The highlight of July was the detachment of the Squadron to the armament practice station at Sylt. Some good scores were achieved, the highest being 58% by Squadron Leader Phipps and Flying Officer P.P.W. Taylor.

During August the training was interesting and varied, between long navigational trips, low level navigational trips and high-low-high exercises all with drop tanks fitted. Air to ground firing on Cowden Range and Army Co-operation exercises.

During the first week of September, the Squadron participated in an Army Co-operation exercise, a chance to put into operation the lessons learnt during the training in the previous month. With the Battle of Britain "At Home" Day drawing nearer, the Squadron as well as maintaining training in the air defence role, began practicing for the flying displays. The two individual aerobatics pilots, Squadron Leader L.W. Phipps and Flying Officer J.R. Hawke began their practice in earnest. On the 18th, the Squadron flew to RDAF Skrydstrup where they took part in the NATO exercise "Flashback" for eight days.

1961

The New Year began with a detachment to RAF Sylt, Germany for a five week period of air firing. The Squadron achieved an average of 29.7%, an improvement on our last detachment. It was pleasing to see that the individual pilot averages were nearer the mean rather than the usual big difference between top and bottom averages.

On the 9th to the 15th May, the Squadron took part in exercise "Matador". Immediately after the exercise the Squadron had the misfortune to lose an aircraft when Flying Officer P.A. Bacon had to eject. A helicopter from 228 Squadron was scrambled and he was back on the station within minutes being only slightly injured.

On the 22nd June, six Hunters were employed on exercise "Doris". The object of the exercise was to provide realistic air defence training to No. 11 Group by intercepting aircraft which approached from outside domestic radar cover and at the same time to provide air defence training targets for the Royal Norwegian Air Force. To achieve this, the six Hunters went to Norway and landed at Rygge, having been intercepted by Norwegian fighter on the way. After lunch, the Hunters returned to Leconfield, simulating an attacking bomber force which aircraft of No. 11 Group intercepted. Lightning courses for groundcrew are progressing according to schedule and with the disbandment of our sister Squadron No. 72 of the 30th June, we were due to receive from them a large proportion of their highly skilled tradesmen. A big change of pilots is at present taking place but by the end of August the situation should have stabilised and the Squadron should be in the form that we will see in the Lightning.

Squadron Leader L.W. Phipps (Air Vice Marshal, AFC) recalls:-
"In mid-1959, shortly after re-arming with the Hunter F6, No 19 Squadron moved from Church Fenton to Leconfield. If someone had to invent a fighter station they would have placed it in pleasant countryside just outside a fine small market town. They would give the station classic late 1930s buildings in a tasteful layout, including a good officer's mess, and set the whole establishment amidst mature trees and shrubs looked after by caring gardeners. The station would be close to ranges, low flying areas and other training airspace and there would be a predictable weather factor. And the best people in the Air force would be posted there. That was Leconfield, near Beverley, East Riding of Yorkshire, 1959.

Shortly after 19 Squadron had happily settled in, its role as a fighter squadron was extended. Until now the Fighter Command Hunter force had been day interceptors. Endless high level practice interceptions (not very exciting), some air to air firing (good news), and day QRA (a UK defence necessity). In September 1959 the force was given the day fighter/ground attack role and the squadrons began training, at low level. Tactical navigation, simulated attacks and the real business of pointing the aeroplane towards the ground with the accuracy to achieve good scores with bullets and rockets. The bullets were of course 30mm Aden and results were immediately good. But the old three inch rockets needed more range practice before results were acceptable.

F.O. NICHOLLS F.O. CURETON ....LL F.O. BACON (B.ROW)
F.O. OUSTON F.O. JOHNSON F.O. FULLER F.O. PICKERING (C.ROW)
F.O. TURBIN F.O. PARK
F.L. WHITE F.L. CHRISTIE S.L. PHIPPS F.L. PICKERSGILL
CPT. BJORKLUND 'SHANDY' (F.ROW)

(Crown Copyright – Sqdn Album)

In late November 1959, the Squadron deployed to Cyprus for what was known as Exercise "Quicktrain". One of the Fighter Command Squadrons, usually a Hunter Squadron, was always on deployment there in the air defence role, flying out of Nicosia, then a joint user RAF/Civil airport. For 19 Squadron, "Quicktrain" was a special opportunity for pilots and groundcrew alike to round off and consolidate the work up started in UK. Lots of flying, lots of high morale and lots of Cyprus social life, all of which then continued at Akrotiri for the second half of the detachment. The only thing that went wrong was that the Squadron Commander broke his ankle during mess games and was casevaced home, meeting up with the rest of the Squadron again when they returned from Akrotiri in mid-January 1960.

By now the Squadron had established a precise working and operating style which several of its pilot members were to emulate when they later became senior officers. For example, at precisely 0700 every working day at Akrotiri those assembled in the Canberra Operations Briefing Room would set their watches by the noise of four Hunters rolling down the runway. So what! Well, it *was* precisely 0700B and it *was* every day – without fail! Several years later one of the occupants of the Hunters made his mark as Station Commander at Lossiemouth when morning assembly used his entry and not the clock on the wall for the morning time check.

The continued precision of the next 18 months owed much to the two people who led the Squadron aircraft engineering team. Flying Officer Mike McDowell (not a S Eng O, not a J Eng O but THE Eng O), was a trainee racing driver/engineer with Jaguars before joining the Royal Air Force. His excellence as an engineer and manager was matched by Warrant Officer Mac McLean who had all of the qualities which engender immense respect in warrant rank in the Service. These two helped keep the Squadron on a 'high' throughout the routine of home base, throughout more overseas detachments (including two Armament Practice Camps on the German holiday island of Sylt) and throughout complex engineering/personal/ political situations: like when a Hunter with brake failure rolled out beyond the end of the runway at Leconfield, across a road, putting its nose and canopy into an immense dung heap in the next field. Which was more important? To rescue the pilot, placate the landowner or minimise recovery aircraft damage!

Flying Officer G.B. Pickering parks his Hunter in the dung heap.
(Crown Copyright – Sqdn Album)

The pilot in this case later left the RAF to make a name for himself flying Mosquitos, Mitchells, Flying Fortresses, and many others, in aviation films. Remember "633 Squadron"? Other pilots went on to other successes: from the 19 Squadron of the time have come three air vice-marshals, two air commodores, two group captains and a Brigadier-General. The latter was a US Marine Captain on exchange with 19 in 1960-61.

The Hunter era at Leconfield was a very happy one."

On the 4th July, Squadron Leader R.M. Raw, AFC, assumed command of the Squadron.

From the 7th to the 15th September, the Squadron was detached to RAF Skrydstrup, Denmark for the NATO exercise "Checkmate". The exercise was to test the defence and flexibility of the NATO Forces and the Squadron was used in the low level interception role. On the 12th, Flying Officer D.M. Nicholls whilst flying a low level patrol mission at 1500 feet, was seen to roll and hit the ground. He was killed.

On the 10th and 11th October, the Squadron did a total of 21 operational turnrounds, these gave the groundcrew practice in re-fuelling and re-arming a number of aircraft as quickly as possible in as near to operational atmosphere as is possible in peacetime as well as giving the pilots an opportunity to fire four guns at altitude. From the 12th to the 19th, the Squadron was on exercise "Halyard", during which they continued with the high level practice interceptions and competition cine.

The Squadron was honoured on the 23rd October by an official visit from Her Majesty the Queen Mother, who spent the afternoon at Leconfield. A number of Officers, NCO's and Airmen were presented to Her Majesty in the Squadron coffee bar.

1962

On the 19th June, Air Vice-Marshal Clayton, Officer Commanding No. 11 Group, visited Leconfield for the annual inspection. The Squadron's Standard was paraded in the morning and six aircraft flew operational turnround in the afternoon. On the 22nd, Flying Officer Van Wyk returned with the victorious RAF team, from RNAF, Leeuwarden, having won the Guynemer Trophy in the Air Gunnery competition.

HIGH FLIGHT

Oh, I have slipped the surly bonds of earth,
And danced the skies on laughter-silvered wings
Sunward I've climbed, and joined the tumbling mirth
Of sun-split clouds and done a hundred things
You have not dreamed of: wheeled and soared and swung
High in the sunlit silence. Hov'ring there,
I've chased the shouting wind along, and flung
My eager craft through footless halls of air.
Up, up the long delirious, burning blue
I've topped the windswept heights with easy grace
Where never lark, or even eagle flew,
And, while with silent, lifting mind I've trod
The high untrespassed sanctity of space,
Put out my hand, and touched the Face of God.

by John Gillespie Magee, Jr.

THE LIGHTNING YEARS
1962 to 1977

1962

With the possible exception of the change from the piston Hornet to the jet Meteor, no bunch of 19 Squadron pilots ever faced a more demanding (albeit exciting) conversion than Mick Raws' men did in 1962/63 with the arrival of the Lightning.

Apart from the enormous increase in sheer performance on two engines, the pilots now had to master the Airborne Intercept radar which effectively gave them a genuine night all-weather capability with air to air missiles in the style of the USAF F102 and F106. Naturally, the specialist night/all-weather Javelin crews disputed that the single-seat Lightning could ever do their job as effectively as a dual-place aircraft – but that argument is outside the scope of this history.

What is without question is that the Lightning guys were seen as being a bit special – and they saw themselves that way too. Indeed, "High Flight", the piece of poetry reproduced opposite might well have been written by a Lightning jock.

On the 11th October, the Squadrons first Lightning T4 (XM988) arrived, followed by the second (XM994) on the 6th November.

The first Lightning F2 arrives

(Crown Copyright – Sqdn Album)

In December the squadron was the first to be equipped with Lightning F2s. These aircraft were exclusive to Nos 19 and 92 squadrons, which became known as the Leconfield Wing. Only 44 were built of which 31 were later converted to the F2a, re-entering service in 1968. The first

Lightning 2A (XN775) arrived on the 17th and was a vast improvement on the FIA, with improved re-heat system, longer range, and more advanced electronic equipment.

1963

By February, the Lightning F2's had been arriving steadily during the month. Most of the pilots have had at least one trip. March saw the commencement of the operational conversion of the pilots onto the Lightning F2, and the Squadron received the last of its 12 Lightning F2s.

During March, Flight Lieutenant K.W. Hayr was awarded the A.F.C.

At the end of June, the Squadron was declared partially operational and it should not be long before all the pilots complete the operational conversion.

On the 25th July, Squadron Leader W.F. Page assumed command of the Squadron.

On the 1st August the Squadron became fully operational on the Lightning F2.

(Crown Copyright – Sqdn Album)

During October, Flight Lieutenant David Jones had an exciting sortie, when he had the nose wheel of his Lightning F2 stuck in the 'up' position. He handled the situation superbly and did very little damage to the aircraft upon landing.

Early in February, inflight refuelling training commenced and 55 sorties were flown on tankers (then Valiants).

The beginning of June saw the Engineers on the modification program to prepare the aircraft for the visit to Cyprus. On the 20th, the Squadron flew out to Cyprus. All aircraft arrived safely, apart from Flight Lieutenants Farrer and Johnson, who had to divert to Luqa. They arrived at Akrotiri on the 23rd. The Squadron then took part in exercise "Choctaw". This entailed three aircraft flying to Bahrain.

On the 17th August, four aircraft led by Squadron Leader Page "fawned" to Rheims, France for three days. The following week four Vautour aircraft of 3/30 Squadron at Rheims reciprocated the visit.

From the 8th December onwards, the Squadron concentrated on supersonic PI's, interspersed with profit and radax for our NCR pilots. On the 17th, they commenced low level intercepts.

1965

During January, the Squadron participated in the State Funeral of Sir Winston Churchill. The Squadron formed part of the formation flypast and provided one Officer, Flight Lieutenant W.A.N. Lane, to 'Keep the Vigil' during the Lying in State.
    The Squadron was then chosen to take part in the trials with the Victor K1 flight refuelling tankers with the object of increasing the Lightning's on station duration and enhance their overseas deployment capabilities.

On the 24th March, Flight Lieutenants Manning and Scott flew the Squadrons first Victor tanker IFR. On the 31st the Squadron received the Dacre Trophy from Mrs Dacre at a parade. The Squadrons Standard was paraded and Air Marshal Sir Douglas Morris took the salute. The Squadron also retained the Aberporth Trophy for being the most efficient Squadron at the annual missile practice camp at RAF Valley.

Squadron Leader W.F. Page (now Group Captain, OBE. AFC. FBIM) recalls:-
    "On arrival, the Squadron were getting over the shock of having just converted from the Mach 1 Hunter to the Mach 2 Lightning. The Squadron had a full complement of twelve Mark 2s and one T. Mark 4, plus one Hunter T. Mark 7. In the next few months the Squadron pilots broadened their experience on the aircraft and explored the full performance envelope of the new aircraft. One thing that sticks in mind very clearly, is the Squadron system of the planned flying/servicing. We quickly dropped into a routine of flying our required target of 300 hours per month.
    May 1964 saw the first Missile Firing detachment to Valley in Wales. All five Firestreak missiles were fired successfully including one from the two-seater with the C-in-C Fighter Command, Air Chief Marshal Sir D. Morris.
    Ten aircraft detached to Akrotiri using IFR in June 1964 followed by a three aircraft detachment to Bahrain, when one aircraft was taken by Jimmy Dell of BAC and demonstrated to the Saudis. This was the birth of the BAC Lightning sale to the Saudi Air Force. Needless to say, it was a very enjoyable five weeks in the Near East.

Four aircraft on a weekend visit to Rheims in France – What a headache!

The Squadron participated in Winston Churchill's funeral flypast along the Thames on the 30th January, 1965.

On the 12th April 1965, four aircraft were detached to Bodo in Norway, with a flypast over Narvik to commemorate the Battle of the 10th April.

The 2nd to the 13th May, missile firing at Valley. Four out of five Fireflash successful.

In July a four aircraft detachment to Akrotiri in Cyprus. I left the detachment to return home to hand the Squadron over to the first Wing Commander Boss – Brian Cox.

I can only say that the two years was a very happy period. We flew more hours than any other Fighter Command Squadron, had no major accident and nobody was hurt. We won the Aberporth Trophy both years for our results on the Missile Firing detachment at Valley and the Dacre Trophy for the best Squadron was on the shelf. Our success was due, I believe, to a professional approach to our flying and servicing".

In July Wing Commander B.R.A. Cox, A.F.C. assumed command of the Squadron.

In July a detachment of the Squadron flew to Akrotiri for the task of QRA.

On the 22nd September, the day before the move, the C-in-C Fighter Command, Air Marshal Sir Douglas Morris KCB, CBE, DSO, DFC flew to Leconfield to say farewell to the Squadron. Also present was the AOC 11 Sector, Air Commodore R.J. Pritchard CB, CBE, DFC, AFC. The C-in-C told us he was sorry to lose the best Squadron in his command.

On the 23rd the Squadron moved to Gutersloh, West Germany to become the first supersonic fighter Squadron of the RAF in the 2nd TAF. In brilliant sunshine at Gutersloh, the Station had turned out to welcome us. Present was the C-in-C RAF Germany, Air Marshal Sir Ronald Lees KCB, CBE, DFC, to whom all the pilots were introduced. After a quick turnround, the Battle of Britain four, gave an impressive display starting with a reheat stream take off and ending with a fast run over the airfield. The Squadron was briefed on the role they were to play in Germany – to provide a "Battle Flight" at a constant state of alert, in addition, as members of the Second Allied Tactical Airforce, we will be an intrigal part of the air defence of north west Europe. The Squadron has therefore, a realistic and vital task to perform. Flying began on the 29th to test the GCI control and recovery system.

On the 6th October, the Squadron was declared operational and on the 18th took over "Battle Flight".

1966

On the 25th February, Commander in Chief of the Group of Soviet Forces in Germany, General P.K. Koshevoi, visited Gutersloh with the Commander in Chief BAOR, General Sir William Stirling and the Commander in Chief RAF.Germany Air Marshal D.F. Spotswood. For the occasion four Lightnings from the Squadron were tasked to provide a formation display as part of a small air show. The team consisted of Flight Lieutenant Hopkins, Flight Lieutenant Ducket, Flight Lieutenant Leach, and was led by the Squadron Commander, Wing Commander Cox.

In April RAF Gutersloh had its Initial Tactical Evaluation – After the teams' assessment the Station Commander, Group Captain Evans announced that Gutersloh had achieved the best result ever recorded by any Squadron on their initial evaluation. To celebrate the occasion the Squadron flew over the station in a diamond nine formation led by Wing Commander Cox.

During May four aircraft from the Squadron flew at the Hanover Air Show

In September the Squadron had an unusual duty to perform when it was requested that the celebrated Belgian strip cartoonist, Monsieur Albert Weinberg be shown round the Squadron. It transpired that Monsieur Weinberg was collecting background material for a new series to be featured in the British Press involving his famous hero, Squadron Leader Dan Cooper of the Canadian Air Force, who used to be a member of No. 19 Squadron.

(Crown Copyright – Sqdn Album)

1967

On the 16th August, Wing Commander L.A. Jones assumed command of the Squadron

In October, the line of the month is claimed by the Station Commander who, upon returning from an instrument sortie in the T4, exclaimed that that was the first time he had inflated his anti-G suit on an ILS.

1968

On the 26th Feb, the first Lightning Mk 2A (XN781) re-entered service with the Squadron having been converted from the F2. Many pilots considered the F2a the best of the breed. Its safety record was now exemplary. The converted F2a featured a large ventral fuel tank, cambered leading edge wing, fin and arrester hook. It retained the four nose-mounted Aden cannons.

Wing Commander L.A. Jones (now Air Marshal Sir Laurence Jones, KCB, AFC, FBIM) recalls:-
"When I arrived in August 1967, the Squadron was equipped with Lightning F2s. They had moved out from the UK 'en masse' and therefore as I arrived and during the next six-nine months, the whole Squadron pilot population was replaced.

A large number of the new arrivals were first tourist and it was difficult to maintain a reasonable number of operational pilots. At the worst point we only had eight operational pilots (including CO and Flight Commanders) to run the training programme and to man the "Battle Flight" – two aircraft at five minutes, 24 hours per day alternated with 92 Squadron. It was a difficult few months.

The Squadron was short of spares and the groundcrew were working incredibly long hours when I arrived. I cut back the flying rate to enable them to recover and recover the servicing backlog. After 2 or 3 months the Squadron was back on course and began to approach and finally achieve the target. The appearance of the first one or two Mark 2a Lightnings with their increased endurance, after three months, also helped considerably. Within six months and with half the Squadron aircraft now Mark 2a's, the flying target was being achieved every month and usually with one or two days stand down which compensated for overtime worked.

With a very inexperienced bunch of pilots the first 18 months of my tour was spent teaching the 'basics'. It was only later that we were able to get on to more advanced work such as combat etc. Despite the lack of experience the Squadron participated in the annual AAFCE fighter competition providing one half of the 2 ATAF team which competed with the US and Germans of 4 ATAF and the other teams.

There were no major accidents during my tour although a number of minor incidents – including a spate of 'false' fires as per the rest of the Lightning force.

"Battle Flight" continued to provide an interesting sequence of scrambles as border incursions were relatively frequent albeit only just skimming across in most incidents as they made mistakes on their side. The other main source of trade was civil incursions into the ADIZ which we had to shepherd back. The most vivid memory was a trip by Flying Officer Ross Payne who had to try and intercept a light civil aircraft (presumably) in the middle of the night somewhere around Hamburg. He was asked to identify the aircraft which was flying at about 150 knots, not surprisingly he failed but had fun trying.

About midway through the tour, 92 Squadron from Geilenkirchen joined us at Gutersloh.

The competition became high spirited particularly in the mess. The Hunter Wing (2 & 4 Squadrons) were also stationed at Gutersloh as was 18 Squadron (commanded by the present CAS) for about a year or so".

1970

On the 22nd May Wing Commander R.L. Davis assumed command of the Squadron.

1971

On the 13th July, the Squadron launched 16 aircraft. This was the first time that a single Lightning Squadron has managed to get 16 aircraft airborne at the same time. Whilst airborne the aircraft flew in four boxes of four and a diamond 16 formation over the Squadron hangar. On the second sortie a formation depicting 19 aircraft was also flown.

1972

On March 27th Wing Commander P.C. Vangucci assumed command of the Squadron.

In May, Flying Officer Beadle, recently made Operational Pilot, was involved in an incident with XN786 a Lightning Mk F2A which suffered a double reheat fire warning. Flying Officer Beadle handled a very unpleasant situation with considerable skill and managed to recover the aircraft.

Wing Commander P.C. Vangucci (now Group Captain – retired) recalls:
"I arrived at Gutersloh in mid-March 1972 to take over command from Les Davies whom I had known for a number of years. In those days the Squadron operated from the hangar but had a dispersed area on the far side of the airfield. Quite recently the Squadron had built itself a dispersed HQ by semi-submerging an old mobile ops room. The result was not very elegant but was serviceable, much better than operating on the open ground and represented an immense amount of hard work by the Squadron and by Eng Wing who had installed the electrics.

Having arrived from the UK, I was unaware of the delights and mysteries of MINEVALS. I was soon to learn. The arrival programme consisted of meeting various worthies throughout the station, without whose help the day to day operations of the Squadron could not function smoothly, and an introduction to the Squadron itself. Much of the latter involved meeting people. Naturally, it started with the pilots and I soon came to the notion that I had met one too many. It took some time to work out that I had been introduced to Flight Lieutenant "Jack" Frost wearing a moustache which he promptly removed that night thus making himself unrecognisable the next day. The ground crew appeared to be a great bunch and I was able to confirm this time and time again over the next two plus years.

But back to Minevals. The evenings of my first week were punctuated by dinner parties and the like arranged so that I could get to meet, as quickly as possible, those who I should know. After a rather late affair I retired to bed only to be awoken by a dreadful, mournful, fog horn-like siren. I did not know its meaning but its intent was quite clear. I was being summoned somewhere for something. When in doubt, one should head for the Ops Room, the heart of every Squadron, so I did. The next twelve hours were spent enjoying the delights of NBC suits, gas masks and CS gas. I also discovered that a thin-skinned ops vehicle designed to operate above ground was not the warmest of places in North Germany in March. Although it was only a practice (called just for my benefit so you can imagine I was not the most popular of persons.) I could already see why the Squadron had achieved a rating of ONE at its latest taceval. There was undoubtedly a high standard to be maintained.

At the end of the week I signed for the classified material and monies, and Les Davies departed. On the Monday, my first flying day in command, Flight Lieutenant Martin "Stumpy" Stoner was returning to land while night flying when he heard and felt an explosion and found flames licking round the side of the aircraft from underneath. It was an unpleasant experience which he handled calmly and well. When we saw the aircraft on the ground we found that there had been an explosion in the ventral tank area and he had lost most of the tank. The fire had been caused by the small amounts of fuel that remained at the end of the sortie.

It was unusual to have any major problems with the Mark 2a Lightning. Those who flew it always reckoned it to be the best Lightning ever built and there is no doubt in my mind to that fact. It was fast, had the least restrictions, carried a good fuel load in the enlarged ventral and yet still had the twin Aden cannon in the nose. It also handled beautifully and, as we were allowed to practice combat in Germany, gave great satisfaction when flown well.

In September, the Squadron detached to Decimomannu in Sardinia for air-to-air firing. The detachment was not entirely successful as air-to-air firing and the guns themselves had been very neglected over the recent past. However, towards the end of the month-long visit the pilots started to get some reasonable scores and the groundwork was laid for the successes that followed in later years.

Two of the amusing parts of the detachment had nothing to do with flying. The pilots spent a weekend away at a hotel for wet dingy drill. After a very full and liquid lunch we gathered at the pool, jumped or fell off the top diving board, inflated our dinghies and climbed in. The other guests were mildly interested and amused but sat up to take notice when an unfortunate engineer who was with us tried the same drill. It quickly became clear that righting an upturned dingy and climbing in without finishing up like a ball of knitting from the goodies that were attached to the dingy or the Mae West, was not as easy as it seemed. We heroes preened ourselves in front of the admiring onlookers.

On the next weekend we were to be seen in a less fearless light. We borrowed the RAF detachment commander's Landrover and set off for the hills. I do not know what Sardinia is like now, but even in those days the hills were pretty wild and fairly mountainous for that matter. We arrived at a reservoir late in the afternoon and decided to camp for the night. Squadron Leader Pete Penfold, one of the Flight Commanders, and a couple of other pilots made off to a small village we could see perched on the side of a hill, to make some purchases – probably of wine. They returned some time later and regaled us with stories of the cut-throat inhabitants who were allegedly armed to the teeth. We decided they had drunk more wine than they had brought back and dismissed the episode from our minds. Next morning we were awakened by the sound of gunfire which we quickly realised was coming from the ridgeline of the circle of hills that surrounded us. It was a good job that the great British public could not see the performance of their heroic defenders of the west as we beat a hasty and ignominious departure.

By the time we returned from Deci the detachment had played havoc with our flying task. I seemed quite impossible for us to reach our end of year target in the time remaining. Some argued that this would not matter as it was "only a figure", but I was not so sure as the Squadron had reached its target for at least the previous two years, and our sister Squadron at Gutersloh, 92 Sqn, looked set to reach theirs. Not reaching the target could have an unwanted effect on morale and would give too many critics ammunition to aver that "Nineteen", always the quiet Squadron, really was second best. I announced that we would go for the target and erected a flying hours notice board in the hangar and waited for the complaints at the extra long hours worked and the weekend overtime. As the weeks passed into November it began to dawn on the Squadron, in particular the groundcrew, that we could make it. By December everyone was quietly confident and morale was high. We reached the target on December 21st and both Squadrons flew a celebratory flypast. It goes without saying that we enjoyed an excellent, and I like to think well-deserved, Christmas break.

Early in 1973 I experienced my first Taceval in command. To say that it was hard work would be an understatement. Everyone on the Squadron, including those attached to us from the station to undertake certain key ground tasks, worked flat out. At the end of the week we awaited news of our fate. When it came we found we had earned a resounding ONE. Celebrations were obviously in order and Group Captain John Howe, who had just taken over as Station Commander, was invited to join us. Imagine the embarrassment when we found that his new hat, acquired specially for his forthcoming interview with the Commander-in-Chief, had disappeared. Worse still, it was his only hat. Several telephone calls later I managed to borrow one from a friend at HQRAF Germany just for the interview and ordered a new replacement from London. For several months the Squadron was renowned for the hat episode and was also the butt of some good-natured humour.

Suddenly one day, out of the blue, the Squadron adjutant, WO Bill Wild, a legend unto himself, appeared in my office with a rather sheepish look on his face. If I were to find, on entering the office, that the Station Commander's "old" new hat had appeared, would I insist on knowing how and why and where it had been? It was quite clear that the wrong answer would result in the hat never seeing the light of day again, so I really had little choice. Besides, with careful stage-managing we could make the front page of the Zeitung 47, the excellent station magazine, innocently invite John Howe to a crewroom party and then unveil and return the offending headpiece. Despite some attempts by other people to sabotage our efforts and to steal the hat again, we pulled it off. The ensuing publicity was a fitting end to a story that had started with such an excellent Taceval.

Naturally, not all of the "characters" at Gutersloh were members of 19 Squadron, and one of the most respected and liked individuals was "The Sheriff". The Sheriff was the Warrant Officer policeman and received his nickname because his surname was Earp. He was respected and liked, but also feared. He seemed to be everywhere and had an uncanny knack of turning up just as trouble started off, or much more often, just in time to prevent trouble in the first place. You could always tell if The Sheriff was about as he rode a bicycle on the crossbar of which he had hung an RAF Police sign with a radio on the handlebars.

One weekend the WOs and SNCOs invited my wife, Gwenda and I to a barbeque they were holding in the dispersed area. It was a super evening, very informal and very relaxing. I like to think I always got on well with the SNCOs and it was quite clear that my presence was not inhibiting them at all. Suddenly the festivities stopped. What could have gone wrong? Several of the most senior and self confident of the Squadron's WOs and SNCOs had visibly paled. The door opened and in walked The Sheriff. I was surprised and amused that, despite my presence, the backbone of the Squadron were afraid they had been caught doing something wrong! Paradoxically, the Sheriff was a little embarrassed at interrupting a party attended by a Wing Commander. So he saluted smartly, bid us goodnight and rode off. I realised it was a glimpse of the bike that had caused the original blight to our festivities and the incident certainly showed me where the true power at Gutersloh lay.

I have mentioned how much I – and my wife for that matter – enjoyed the company of the

SNCOs. These good relationships spread right across the Squadron. One officers' Mess Guest Night coincided with the departure of a particularly popular Chief Technician, Abbott by name. He was being dined out of the Sergeant's Mess and had hoped to invite the Squadron officers to join him. He was most disappointed so I had a quiet word with the Station Commander and asked if the Squadron officers could be excused for a while if I promised to see them safely back within an hour. He readily complied and we withdrew. Without a word from me, all the officers formed up outside, dressed in threes and their "mess kit" uniforms. I gave the order and we marched down the road to the Sergeants' Mess arriving much to the delight of our departing colleague. After a very pleasant drink everyone formed threes outside again and to the good-humoured cheers and applause of the members of the Sergeants' Mess we marched back to rejoin our own guest night.

Towards the end of 1973 an amusing rumour was started that my tour was being extended in order to include the next Taceval which had been postponed for a few months. Shortly after Christmas the Squadron WOs and SNCOs dined out my wife and I from the squadron and their mess. It was a very special evening. Next day I was told that my tour had been extended to May so that I could go straight to the next Air Warfare Course at Cranwell. Later, when my time as CO came to an end my wife and I were invited to the Sergeants' Mess to be dined out for the second time and I was told of a conversation that had been overheard. Needless to say the story was anonymous. A new young sergeant was heard talking to one of the old hand SNCOs. "What's PVG done to deserve a second dining out night?" "Nothing" came the reply, "but his wife has"!

Battle Flight, with its two aircraft, pilots and groundcrew on duty 24 hours a day 365 days a year, was shared with 92 Squadron. I used to do my turn of duties, as much as anything to show the young pilots that the old man wasn't too old to hold a five minute state and get airborne in the time if required. Because of the pressure of work during the week I usually did my turn "in the shed" at the weekend. One peaceful Sunday morning I was quietly reading when, without any warning, the scramble bell rang. I am told that for an instant I did absolutely nothing, then turned quite pale from shock and then ran like hell. I checked in with the controller who ordered me to get airborne immediately. Once in the air I called on RT and was told to head straight for the border at maximum speed at 5000 feet. I was cleared through all the check zones and placed alongside the Iron Curtain which at 5000 feet is noticeable by its absence. What could it be? I soon caught sight of a small, old, West German, civilian twin-engined King Air and breathed a sigh of relief. After giving identification details I was instructed to return to base and make contact by landline, which I did.

The story ran as follows. The pilot of the King Air was a photographer and he had received permission to photograph from the air right up to the West German border. It was impressed upon him that this was a most unusual clearance so if he made a mess of the flight he would not have a second chance. He obviously thought long and hard as to how to ensure success and decided to rehearse his Sunday afternoon, once only, single flight by practising without a clearance in the morning! I have forgotten the actual time recorded but it took me something like 3.5 minutes from scramble to alongside the border. I rested for the remainder of my shift.

During 1973 the Squadron was host to Fred. Fred Archer was, as far as we knew, the oldest surviving member of 19 from when it was formed in 1915 at Castle Bromwich. He was in his seventies but from his letters seemed to be very alert, although having some trouble with his eyes. Little did we know how alert. We invited him to visit the Squadron at Gutersloh and he accepted. Fred stayed for the best part of a week and it would take me that long to recount the highlights of his visit. He gained a reputation for many things while he was with us, not least his ability to say what he meant pithily and with good humour. Two examples will give an idea of his wit.

On his arrival we had the local German press with us for a press call which was held out on the line alongside the Lightnings. The reporters were both interested and polite to an old warrior from the First World War. One asked Fred what he thought of Von Richthofen as a foe. "The Red Baron," exclaimed Fred, "he was only a figment of the press's imagination." Considering Fred had been shot down three times that was a bit steep, but the German reporters took it in good part.

On another occasion, Fred was in my office and I reminded him that he was due to visit 18 Squadron in five minutes. "I'm not going" said Fred and all my efforts could not get him to change his mind. Finally I asked him why he would not go although it was part of his published programme. "18 Squadron left Castle Bromwich in a mess in 1915. They were a shower then and they're a shower still. I'm not going." Faced with this determined view that had lasted nearly 60 years what could I do except telephone the CO of 18 Squadron and say that "Fred was not well".

At last, all too soon, the last few weeks of my tour came around. What had started as an amusing rumour now began to look more like fact. It appeared that I would catch the next Taceval, or rather it would catch me. What's more it became clearer still that for a number of reasons it would have to be in my last week. I was not amused. If it went well, the powers that would be would say it was the least to be expected after nearly two and a half years in command. If it went badly there would be literally no time to stage any sort of recovery as a saving grace.

I called all the Squadron together and appealed to their pride as British, RAF and members of 19 Squadron, because the Taceval would be by a NATO team with a large foreign contingent seeing just how good or bad we were. Finally, I explained my personal predicament and asked for their support. As events turned out I must have hit a sympathetic chord as the performance of the whole Squadron was magnificent.

On the Monday of the last week of my tour, my replacement, Bob Barcilon, arrived at 4pm – and the Taceval team at 5pm! The hand over of command took place in NBC suit and gas mask during the following five days.

The Flight Commanders, John Spencer and John May, started whipping in the pilots and the senior engineer, Charles Hopkins turned the groundcrew loose on the aircraft. I should perhaps explain that the Squadron had an establishment of twelve aircraft of which it had to prepare a percentage. By a strange quirk, the two spare aircraft that were normally in England on major refit had arrived back in Germany and the next two on the programme had been delayed as the Maintenance Unit was experiencing some difficulties. We had also, much to the annoyance of the RAF engineers, held back the last Lightning Mark 2 from the scrap yard with just four sorties left before everything became time-expired. Thus we actually had on the Squadron 15 aircraft. At the start of every session of the Taceval the groundcrew produced 15 aircraft from then on, fully serviceable and fully armed. The effort was enormous. The Taceval team were amazed and the Squadron too great delight in declaring on state 25% more aircraft than we were supposed to have on establishment.

The first day was long and hard as we had already done a full day's work before the team arrived. Next morning OC Eng wing told me that at half past two in the morning he had heard a great noise and had got up to quieten things down so that the pilots could get some well-deserved sleep. When he reached the source of the disturbance he found 19 Squadron pilots in high spirits celebrating their first day's Taceval. Clearly morale was high.

It was also quite clear as the evaluation progressed that everyone was pulling out all the stops to do well. It was for me one of the most intensely satisfying periods of my life. We were good, we knew it and we could deliver what was wanted time after time. When the results were announced by the visiting team, the Squadron had achieved the best results by any NATO air defence Squadron. A perfect end to my tour except for one last act.

On the 22nd May 1974, I climbed into XN 794 and flew the last Lightning Mark 2 sortie in the RAF.

On the final day of that last week I tried to hand in my NBC suit, gas mask and all the other accoutrements I had been using for the past 15 months. I wanted personally to thank Sergeant Wilson, the inventory holder, for all his help. He was not available. I would wait I said. That was difficult I was told, but I insisted I wanted to thank him myself. I knew something was afoot, but not what. Finally, I was told the full story.

At a critical stage in the Taceval we had needed a spare part from another area on the station. It was vital to have it immediately in order to keep our record intact. A young airman drove a Landrover to pick up the part and on the way back in the blackout, hit a tree and smashed one wing. Then it came to light that he did not have a valid RAF driving licence. Sergeant Wilson was the Squadron's "body" man and could make anything out of metal. He was building a new Landrover wing which was to be fitted to the damaged vehicle, resprayed by our painters and then returned in perfect condition to the Squadron MT. All this work was to save the young airman from being charged for the accident which occurred when he was working flat out for the Squadron.

On the 1st January 1975 I was awarded the Air Force Cross in the New Year's Honours List. I was both humble and proud. Humble that I should have been so honoured with the award that pilots respect the most, and proud to accept it on behalf of 19 Squadron, because it really belonged to them all."

1974

On the 24th May, Wing Commander R.L. Barcilon assumed command of the Squadron.

1976

On the 19th August, Flying Officer C.M. Rowley was awarded the Queen's Commendation for valuable service in the air. His aircraft had suffered a fire shortly after take off and severe structural damage to the fuselage, fin and to the No. 1 engine had resulted. The entry in the London Gazette read:- "For his outstanding courage, presence of mind and airmanship when, on the 4th August 1976 he brought his badly damaged Lightning aircraft safely back to base, had he abandoned it the aircraft could well have inflicted considerable damage causing injury on heavily populated areas. The Squadron was of course particularly pleased at the award of the Queen's commendation for valuable service in the air to Flying Officer Rowley who recovered his badly damaged aircraft safely to base after a major explosion in the fuselage.

The first air to air photograph of the green-camouflaged Lightning. Flying in the formation were: No.1 Wg Cdr Peter Vangucci; 2. Fg Off Ian Smith, 3. Flt Lt Jack Brown; 4. Sqn Ldr Peter Penfold; 5. Fg Off Colin Baldwin; 6. Flt Lt Terry "Muff" Hanlon; 7. Flt Lt John Bishop; 8. Flt Lt Martin Stoner; 9. Fg Off Ray Hodgson.

("Flight")

In November the Squadron started its last month of operational training.

Wing Commander R.L. Barcilon (Air Commodore AFC) recalls:-

"I commanded 19 Squadron from May 1974 until we phased out the Lightning at the end of 1976, handing over the Squadron Standard to the new Phantom Squadron at Wildenrath in the New Year, 1977, commanded by Wing Commander Bugs Bendell.

I served a previous tour as B Flight Commander from September 1967 to August 1970, under Laurie Jones. Pete Naz was the other Flight Commander. At that time we had the Mk2 Lightning, but converted to the 2A during the tour. The aircraft were kept in metal finish until about 1973-4, when they were camouflaged. On taking command I took over the same aircraft I had had as a Flight Commander, XN781 'B' Bravo. Some wag thought I looked like the Pink Panther and the ground crew painted the appropriate emblem over the fuselage roundel. The enclosed photo of yours truly, makes the point. I pass no comment on the Boss Kat – Often Licked but Never Beaten.

Wing Commander "Bob" Barcilon, AFC.

I think it is worth recording that during the whole of the Squadron's life as a Lightning outfit, none lost his life and to my knowledge none had to leave his aircraft in anger – not a bad record bearing in mind the early reputation of the Lightning.

Having flown Marks 1, 1A, 2, 2A, 3, 4, 5 and 6 I have no hesitation in saying that the 2A was by far the finest. Large ventral, extended leading edges, inbuilt Avons (30mm cannons),

Pilot Attack Sight, hook and refuelling probe made it the 'Complete Lightning', to my mind far superior to the Mark 6.

Finally, I was and remain very proud that during my tour first my B Flight Commander, then myself were both awarded AFCs – I suspect a double is quite rare. John Spencer spearheaded the squadron's air combat training programme and until the F15 came along, we were far and away the outstanding single seat air combat squadron in RAF Germany and surrounding area. We developed low level combat tactics which were of great value to our mud-moving brethren and the 'Dial a Lightning' line was the hottest around.

I was able, luckily, to command the UK Lightning force at Binbrook some years later."

The Welcoming Committee. Founder members of 19 (Phantom) Squadron.

THE PHANTOM YEARS
1976 to 1990

1976

Although the Phantom had been in RAF service for almost a decade, it's employment purely as an all weather, all altitude interceptor was relatively new when 19 Squadron began its conversion in the last quarter of 1976. The most dramatic change however, was the arrival on the Squadron, for the first time in its history of the Navigator. Whatever the single seat traditionalist may have felt about this, there was no gainsaying the overall effectiveness of the 2-crew Phantom, particularly in the difficult and demanding low level role, the increasingly hostile ECM environment and the crowded skies and adverse weather of the NATO Central Region.

The arrival of the first Phantom FGR2 flown by Wing Commander A.J. Bendell and Flying Officer S. Black.
(Jurgen Valley)

On the 1st October, the Squadron reformed at Wildenrath with ten Phantom FRG2 to replace No 19 Lightning Squadron on the 1st January, 1977. *The newly appointed Commanding Officer was Wing Commander A.J. Bendell, OBE, AFC,* who recalls;

"I arrived at RAF Wildenrath in September 1976 and was given three months to bring the Squadron up to combat ready status. There was to be no reduction in front line fighter strength, so each Phantom air defence squadron had to be combat ready before its equivalent Lightning squadron folded. As planned, we took over the hardened accommodation in the southeast dispersal at Wildenrath. I had an excellent team working for me: the aircrews were generally well experienced, although few were familiar with the air defence role in Germany and no-one had experience of operating out of hardened accommodation. In fact 19 Squadron was the first RAF Air Defence Squadron to do so. Our aircraft and most of the groundcrew, including the Senior Engineering Officer, were transferred with No 2 Squadron (a reconnaissance squadron) from RAF Laarbruch. So we had the advantage that the groundcrew were thoroughly familiar with the aircraft, but at the same time, the AI radars had not been peaked up to the high standards necessary for the air defence role.

As usual the works services were not complete on the dispersal, the taxiways and access aprons to the hardened aircraft shelters (HAS) were unfinished, but I was determined that we should start off as we planned to continue. On 27 September I collected the first aircraft, XV 488 from Laarbruch and delivered it to Wildenrath, Flying Officer Stuart Black flew as my navigator. We parked the aircraft in front of the only HAS ready for use and were greeted by Air Vice-Marshal Lloyd – Deputy Commander RAF Germany. For the next six weeks, 19 Squadron's dispersal was a strange – some would say unhealthy – mixture, of heavy earth moving equipment, and sophisticated front line fighter aircraft.

It would be difficult to summarise all the work that was done in the following months. Not only did we have to train crews up to combat ready (CR) status, but we also had to shake the bugs out of our accommodation and devise appropriate operating procedures. By the end of December eight of our 11 available crews were combat ready, two other pilots were qualified but unfit for duty due to injury. We were able to take over the Battle Flight commitment and the Squadron was declared operational. The Squadron Colour was handed over at RAF Wildenrath on 30 December 1976 and I arranged for an unofficial handover between OC 19 Squadron (Lightning) and OC 19 Squadron (Phantom) to take place in the air, at 2359 hours on 31 December 1976.

For the next three months we held the RAF Germany Phantom Battle Flight commitment at Wildenrath, in other words we maintained a pair of aircraft on state, one at five minutes readiness to take-off, 24 hours a day, while 92 Squadron completed their work-up. Fortunately we could just meet the alert state from a caravan parked alongside the HAS, which meant that we did not have to permanently man the cockpits, but it was tight. Our purpose built Battle Flight accommodation was completed some ten months later in October 1977 and by that time we had been joined by No 92 Squadron. The aircraft configuration for Battle Flight was: two external wing tanks; the Vulcan 20mm cannon on the centreline station; four Sparrow and four Sidewinder air-to-air missiles – one of the heaviest permissible Phantom configurations. We could be called to operate at any altitude within the flight envelope of the aircraft, but most of our training was done at low level.

In June 1977 the Squadron deployed to RAF St Mawgan for an armament practice camp where each pilot qualified up to NATO standards in air-to-air firing against the banner. Most NATO forces used the Dart target – all they had to do was score a hit – but the RAF persisted in using the low speed flag target and counted the holes. We achieved the desired results, of course, but it was a strictly academic exercise.

Meanwhile RAF Wildenrath's major commitment was to work up for its first annual no-notice NATO Tactical Evaluation (TACEVAL). Our proposed operating procedures had been accepted by the Command Staffs and had been returned to us as RAF Germany's Standard Operating Procedures. Each month the Station mounted a three day MINIVAL – which was the same as TACEVAL but assessed by Station personnel. We exercised continuous day/night operations sometimes under simulated nuclear, biological and chemical (NBC) warfare conditions. Wildenrath's TACEVAL was eventually called during the first week of November 1977 and the Squadron achieved the highest possible scores, across the board.

On 27 July 1977, two aircraft from 19 Squadron (myself leading with Flight Lieutenant N. Browne navigating) led the RAF Germany flypast, consisting of two Phantoms, two Buccaneers, two Harriers and five Jaguars, at Her Majesty's Silver Jubilee Royal Review at

RAF Finningley. We repeated the flypast again for RAF Finningley's Open Day on the 30 July.

Apart from our flying and other operational training, the Squadron also maintained a full social calendar. We concocted a near lethal cocktail called the Blue Dolphin, which guaranteed that any social function would get off to a lively start. And we actively liaised with the town of Erkelenz as part of Wildenrath's hearts and minds campaign to win over the local German population. Erkelenz's town colours were also blue and white – similar to 19 Squadron – so the twinning was particularly appropriate."

1977

In November No. 19 Squadron took part in the first tactical evaluation of RAF Wildenrath as an air defence station.

1978

In May Wing Commander T.J.L. Gauvain assumed command of the Squadron.

In November the Squadron had an exchange with 322 Squadron at the Royal Netherlands Air Force from Leeuwarden which was the first such event since the Squadron reformed in 1976. The exchange was extremely successful, however it was marred by the death of Lieutenant Heni Elbersen of 322 Squadron during a landing accident when two F104's collided.

1979

The Squadron spent its first detachment at RAF Akrotiri on the air-to-air gunnery practice against banners towed by Canberras of 100 Squadron.

1980

In January the Squadron became the first RAF Fighter unit to utilise the ACMI (air combat manoeuvring installation) at Decimomannu.

In July several sorties using aircraft from both 19 and 92 Squadrons were flown in support of a documentary television programme being produced by the BBC's Man Alive Team. The sequence involved a variety of manoeuvres which were filmed from a Phantom of 19 Squadron equipped with a cine camera mounted in the brake parachute compartment. It was unfortunate that on the 11th July during the filming a Phantom of 92 Squadron together with its crew was lost in a crash on the North German Plain.

In October, Wing Commander R.P. Hallam took command of the Squadron.

1981

At the beginning of September it was found that during recent operational flying, aircraft fatigue was being consumed at twice the allowable rate. Towards the end of the month all RAF Germany Squadrons were told to reduce their fuel consumption by 40% until March 1982. As a result the Squadron flew six aircraft in the clean configuration at reduced sortie rate.

Princess Anne visited RAF Wildenrath on 7th July.

Wing Commander R.P. Hallam recalls;
"The pilots during my tour were mad about motorbikes. This manifest itself when we went on the gunnery detachment to Cyprus. If we arrived there on Friday it took us only as late as Saturday noon for just about every man jack of them to have rented a Honda bundoo basher from down-town Limassol. These they rode around the island in a 19 Squadron Chapter wearing their blue and white checked scarves as headbands of course. Their activities included races over scrub lands around Akrotiri and the cliffs. The first briefing on Monday morning resembled the waiting room in the General Hospital – one or two broken limbs in plaster and a number of gravel rash cases, and not too many people available for flying.

The other problem was that they were pyromaniacs. A number of them had some very loud banger fireworks – a type you could buy in Germany and very loud indeed. Letting them off in Cyprus with its internal problems, was definitely not a good idea as it got the Police very excited. There had been a number of complaints and I had issued several warnings, but to no avail – the bangs continued. I then got exceedingly angry and said that I would be in my office at 1600 hours that afternoon and expected those who had these fireworks to be man enough to be there and bring their fireworks with them. I duly sat at my desk. There was a knock at the door and one of the most likely candidates walked in wearing a suitably straight face and a brown bag full of bangers. He was followed by another and another. Soon the whole Squadron was standing in my tiny office. Packed together fighting to keep straight faces as the pile of brown paper bags on my desk grew bigger and bigger. At last I could stand it no longer and burst out laughing (as did they) and I kicked them out of my office. I gave this enormous pile of fireworks to the Fiight Sergeant for destruction. He thought only the bomb disposal people could cope with this lot and duly shot off in that direction. I was pleased with myself at recovering all this loot and later in the bar said how pleased I was with the chaps, that they had been straight forward and had brought them in. "That's OK Boss" said one, "we wanted to get rid of that lot – we have got some better ones coming on Monday." Dammit if he wasn't right.

They were an excellent Squadron though and did extremely well while I was there, winning one or two trophies and thank God we had no accidents or hurt anyone."

Flight Lieutenant Robin Russell writes;
"I have just found these remarkable photographs taken in May 1982, whilst we were on APC in Cyprus. They show a Phantom wheel which locked on landing. The Boss, Wing Commander Reg Hallam who was flying it, will swear blind that his feet were off the brakes. Flight Lieutenant Andy Kirk was his navigator".

Wing Commander R. Hallam and Flight Lieutenant A. Kirk

(Robin Russell)

On 8th July Wing Commander M.P. Donaldson MBE assumed command of the Squadron.

In November Wing Commander M.P. Donaldson, was given the opportunity to fly the new Interceptor version of the Tornado, the F2. The flight lasted 55 minutes and was part of an engine performance test programme and included supersonic flight. Wing Commander Donaldson was invited by British Aerospace at Wharton, to fly the new Interceptor because of his previous appointment was at the Ministry of Defence in the Tornado F2 office of OR31 (RAF). His pilot for the flight was Mr P. Gordon-Johnson, the aeroplane's project pilot. After his flight, he was presented with a Tornado F2 badge by Mr J. Lee, British Aerospace Chief Test Pilot.

Wing Commander M. Donaldson (Air Commodore MBE) writes:-
   "The role of the squadron whilst I was in command was the policing of West German airspace in peacetime and the air defence of the 2ATAF area in war. The former of these tasks entailed having one aircraft and crew on a high state of readiness 365 days of the year round the clock to be scrambled within 5 minutes when directed by the controlling Sector Operations Centre for interception, identification, shadowing or shepherding tasks as required. Such events were not frequent, but most crews on the squadron would be involved in a 'live' scramble at some stage during their tour. The latter task of the squadron's role would

339

have involved mounting combat air patrols in the western part of West Germany to intercept and engage low flying enemy aircraft which had penetrated the missile belts. The majority of the squadron's flying was devoted to training for this task, so although an element of training involved flying at medium or high altitudes against both subsonic and supersonic aircraft, the primary effort of the squadron involved flying at low altitude in sections of two or flights of four aircraft and the interception and simulated engagement of low flying formations of fighter bomber aircraft. The squadron was thoroughly proficient in this role during the period, able to operate in mixed formations with other NATO aircraft and under total R/T silence, as tactics were totally standard and very well practised.

The main highlights of each year were the squadron deployments to Decimommanu for air combat training in the NATO instrumented range off the coast of Sardinia and to Akrotiri for air gunnery training in the range off the southern coast of Cyprus. The deployments to Sardinia were twice yearly and involved half the squadron each time. The air combat training was conducted against Royal Air Force Harriers or Hawks which accompanied the deployment and against other NATO aircraft also deployed to use the range such as USAF F–15 Eagles and F–5 Freedom Fighters of the Aggressor training unit. The deployments to Cyprus were once per year and involved the whole squadron. The objective on these deployments were to qualify each pilot to NATO standards at air to air gunnery firing against the banner target towed by Canberra aircraft which accompanied the deployment. The social aspects of these deployments were some of the highlights of the year and were truly memorable. The permanent supporting staff at Akrotiri had to put up with a lot of high spirited social behaviour from succeeding deployments of fighter squadrons, but I was always pleased to see that they accepted No. 19 Squadron's presence with good humour.

The operational training of each year culminated in a Tactical Evaluation carried out by NATO evaluators. The preparation for this evaluation was hard and arduous and concentrated more on ground operations at the main base than it perhaps should have done, but at the end of the day it was worth it as on both Tacevals the squadron was awarded excellent ratings.

Some light relief was gained from the main training routine, and the endless series of flying exercises, by NATO squadron exchanges, and in 1984 the squadron exchanged with a Danish F–16 squadron at RDAF Aalborg. All squadron pilots were treated to at least one sortie in a dual controlled F–16 and thus had a chance to experience a high tec aircraft and the discomfort of 9g whilst manoeuvring.

The highlight of 1984 for me was to lead a squadron display formation of four aircraft at a number of air shows during the summer months. The venues for these shows ranged from major airfield – such as Strasbourg airport – to little grass strips which were no more than a glider site. The demands of finding the venue, arriving on time, and performing the display on the right line and centred on the right point were great, and I was glad to be served always by an excellent navigator. Also, the pilots in the formation were very good, growing into thoroughly able and professional formation display pilots as the season progressed. I was fortunate that they were so capable, as it allowed me to devise and fly a spirited routine which showed off the Phantom, the formation and the squadron to great effect and which brought a deal of enjoyment to and commendations from many spectators who saw us."

Wing Commander M.P. Donaldson and Aircrew

1985

On 19th July Wing Commander F.S. Rance assumed command of the Squadron.

No 19 Squadron celebrated its 70th anniversary in November.

1986

On the 3rd July Flight Lieutenant Heames and Flying Officer Walters Morgan were briefed to carry out an inverted flight check on Victor 417 as part of a search procedure for a loose article in the cockpit. The aircraft subsequently suffered a double utility hydraulics failure. The crew elected to recover to Wildenrath and during final checks before landing an uncommanded pitch up which the pilot could not control. The crew ejected safely and the aircraft crashed and was destroyed. The crew returned to flying duties on 14th July 1986.

Wing Commander F.S. Rance (now Group Captain) recalls;

"I think like every Squadron Commander, it is their most satisfying tour. Not so much for the flying but commanding a team – aircrew and groundcrew – who are multi-talented in a way that no comparable body in civilian life seems to be; an expert on anything will step forward almost on request. I joined 19 Squadron in July 1985 and left in December 1987 with much in between. An exhausting round of commitments taking in many of the countries on the Continent and Cyprus.

A particular highlight for me was the first visit to Nevada of the Air Defence Squadrons for 'Red Flag' in October 1987. Flight refuelling across America being an adventure in itself, although my memories from the Mississippi valley westwards may seem idiosyncratic. I seemed to sit there thinking that the Western Pioneers must have been out of their minds as I watched the Great Plains unfold, across the Badlands of Northern Nebraska, and the age it seemed to take for the Rockies to show, and then the seemingly endless High Desert.

'Red Flag' itself is, of course, exciting with hundreds of aircraft pumping off two runways at Nellis AFB in constant use. The flights over the High Desert are a swirling and fleeting business conducted at high speed with opportunities come and gone in an instant – with always the need to be with friends or promptly shot! Ground features such as Irish Peat and Bear Pan became engraved on the soul, as favoured killing grounds or lifebelts for rapid re-orientation.

The officers and airmen on the Squadron were a super bunch. I had two different sets of people in my time at Wildenrath – latterly younger and more inexperienced, but equally talented. These were of course the time of the Blues Brothers (for the parties), the music was Dire Straits (forever associated with Jack Thompson, killed later rehearsing the Abingdon Air Show, and at ACMI in Sardinia tactical callsigns – still in use – from the vogue movie "Top Gun". For 19, of course, these were more of a homely sort with 'Big Ted' and 'Little Ted' replacing 'Iceman' and 'Maverick'.

Already it all seems a long time ago; like the air fights, suddenly come and gone, and dimming fast in the memory.

1987

Wing Commander R.L. Dixon ·ıssumed command of the Squadron on 14th December.

1988

On the 15th January a new Standard was presented to the Squadron by Air Marshal Sir Anthony Skingsley, KCB, MA, at Wildenrath.

In June the Squadron finally laid to rest its 32-year old standard in St Clement Danes Church.

1989

On the 6th July at 1400 hours, four Phantoms took off from Wildenrath. The number three of the formation was flown by Flight Lieutenant Al Thorogood, with Squadron Leader Geoff Yapp as his navigator. The aircraft, XV 430 (A), was on a low flying exercise when Flight Lieutenant Thorogood performed one of the frequent "belly-checks" which all fighter crews use to clear the outside of turns at low-level. He saw a Canberra at close range, and immediately bunted his aircraft to avoid a potential collision. Squadron Leader Yapp, who had been concentrating on the radar at this point, was subjected to a violent negative-g manœuvre at low-level. There was insufficient time for either the pilot or the navigator to discuss the situation, due to the proximity of both the Canberra and of the ground; consequently, the navigator decided to eject. The pilot was fortunately able to recover the aircraft from the manœuvre and subsequently landed safely back at Wildenrath. Squadron Leader Yapp was quickly picked up by a German Air Force rescue helicopter, initially he was admitted to a British Army hospital at Munster before being transferred to the RAF Hospital at Wegberg, and finally discharged the following day with nothing more than cuts and bruises. He flew again within a few days, and has subsequently flown in the same aircraft with considerably more success!

A degree of humour arose from the event: at the subsequent sortie debrief, the formation leader counted those present and asked who was missing: the reply was, "It's Geoff, he's in the middle of a field in Area 2." "Oh yes, I forgot about that!" Aircrew understatement at its best.

During October, RAF Germanys' Commander-in-Chief, Air Marshal Sir Roger Palin took the opportunity to fly with the Squadron when he visited the base. He was accompanied by Flight Lieutenant Steve Cheskin.

1990

Wing Commander Ray Dixon (the former Commanding Officer) writes;

"One of the most interesting events during my tour surrounded the ejection from a serviceable aircraft by one of our navigators, Squadron Leader Geoff Yapp. Geoff was right to leave the aircraft, as all the evidence pointed towards it being disastrously out of control at low level. The pilot, Flight Lieutenant Al Thorogood, had dived towards the ground to avoid a mid-air collision and Geoff, feeling the violence of the manœuvre, looked up from his radar set in the rear cockpit to find his field of view full of ground rushing towards him at an alarming rate. Now these are not the sort of things that pilots and navigators have extensive conversations about and so Geoff, unable to contribute towards preventing the apparently inevitable crash, ejected. The pilot, however, managed to recover from the dive and was able to return safely to base. Meanwhile, Geoff was left standing unhurt but unhorsed in a field with his parachute, watching his aircraft minus its rear canopy, ejection seat and him set course for home.

An ejection these days is quite a significant event and obviously the circumstances had to be reported to higher authority. Normally, however, there is some time available to collate all of the facts before making the report. Unfortunately, in this case there was not. The highest authority in the Royal Air Force, the Chief of the Air Staff, was at Wildenrath in the VIP lounge at Movements, having informal discussions with the Station Executives who, of course, were those who received the incoming incident messages hot off the press. The telephone in the lounge rang repeatedly and the amount of scurrying and whispering indicated without doubt that things were not 'routine'. OC Ops received the first message and passed it on to me. "There's been a mid-air collision and it's one of yours". Nothing I could do except wait for the next report. Seconds later, "It's alright, they both got out". The crews of both aircraft, I wonder, or both my pilot and navigator? If so, what about the other crew? All I can do is wait. Oh yes, tell the Station Commander, of course, and thus join in the scurrying and whispering. Next message, again, only seconds after the last, "Only your navigator has ejected and the pilot is flying home". Things are getting better – perhaps nothing has happened at all and so we continue our polite conversations whilst watching out of the window for the aircraft to land with only half a crew and at least get some kind of confirmation of the actual result of the incident. As time went on, the true story began to emerge and it was evident that a disaster had been narrowly averted. Squadron Leader Yapp had indeed ejected but there had not been a collision and both aircraft involved were recovering to RAF Wildenrath. Geoff was apparently unhurt but had been whisked off to hospital for checks.

At last, the right people knew exactly what was going on and although the circumstances surrounding the event required further investigation, now at least we knew what had happened, although not why and then the tension began to discipate. It had been a long afternoon, or so it seemed, until a glance at the watch revealed that just less than fifteen minutes ago, things had been as close to normal as a visit by the Chief of Air Staff permitted.

Squadron Leader Yapp returned to Wildenrath that evening in an Army Gazelle helicopter. I met him on the landing pad and he was wearing only an old dressing gown and little else, certainly nothing on his feet. For all the world he had just got out of the shower at home. Various pieces of his flying equipment had to be replaced after the ejection but he was very soon back on the flying programme and in the air again.

Now we have the dramatic change of circumstances that is destined to have a profound effect on millions of people throughout Europe. We were on detachment in the USA when, in Berlin, the first signs that the Wall was at last coming down, began to appear. The extent of TV coverage in the USA immediately confirmed the beginning of something of world-wide importance that both stunned and delighted those of us whose task it was to defend against the Warsaw Pact attack. Now, in the Spring of 1990, it seems that we indeed have sound grounds for optimism although surely the rate of change must now slow down. Nevertheless, the last six months are irreversible and sooner or later the impact of these changes will be felt by NATO forces and by 19 (Fighter) Squadron. It is too early to say what these changes might involve; the men, our location, or our equipment. One thing is certain, however, and that is that the spirit of the Squadron will remain. To sustain it, we have seventy-five years of history and the example of those who fought and died for those ideals that are at last sweeping across Europe. That history and these sacrifices are facts and they will serve as fine examples as to how we must strive during the uncertainties of the future so that in the end, we will all have contributed to lasting peace."

BACK ROW (L to R): Fg Off Loizou (J Eng O 'A'), Fg Off Fairbrass (Sqn Int O), Flt Lt Harris, Flt Lt Butterworth, Flt Lt Creber, Fg Off Squires, Fg Off Batey, Fg Off Wainwright, Flt Lt P-J, Taylor, Fg Off Carlton, Flt Lt Lewis, Flt Lt Hart, Fg Off Anderson, Fg Off Halden, Fg Off Cheesbrough, Fg Off Vallely, Fg Off Bone, Fg Off Stellmacher (J Eng O 'B') FRONT ROW (L to R): Flt Lt McGilvray, Sqn Ldr Dixon (S Eng O), Sqn Ldr Yapp (Nav Radar Ldr), Sqn Ldr Harrison (OC 'B' Flight), Wg Cdr R.L. Dixon (OC), Sqn Ldr Shaw (OC 'A' Flight), Sq Ldr Watson (Sqn Ldr Weapons), Flt Lt Giles, Flt Lt McMahon, Flt Lt Bartle. (18th April 1990)

"BATTLE FLIGHT"
"A fully armed 19 (Fighter) Squadron Phantom FGR2 (XV475 – H) on a defensive patrol during January, 1990".

(Derek Palmer)

347

The Squadron's 75th Anniversary celebrations due to take place on the 7th, 8th and 9th September, were postponed due to the Gulf crisis and the squadron was put on readiness.

On the 21st September, Wing Commander N.B. Spiller assumed command of the squadron.

The squadron with No. 92, moved to Akrotiri, Cyprus where they provided air defence of the Sovereign Base Area as part of Operation Granby.

ESCORT DUTY

Crewed by Squadron Leader Nick Watson and Flying Officer Jon Conway, the Phantom is escorting the Tristar through Cypriot airspace on its way from Hamburg to Dhahran, Saudi Arabia with men of the 7th Armoured Brigade. Taken by Flying Officer Ian Halden and Flight Lieutenant Richard McMahon in a second 19 Squadron Phantom.

1991

On the 8th January a 19 Squadron Phantom being flown by a 92 Squadron pilot, with Flying Officer Winwright (19 Sqdn Navigator), had to eject 20 miles south of Limassol, Cyprus. Pilot and navigator activated their homing beacons, climbed into their dinghies and were picked up within 30 minutes of the alarm being raised by a Wessex SAR helicopter of No. 84 Squadron. The aircraft (VX462 - G) went into the sea.

BASES

Castle Bromwich	1st September 1915
Netheravon	31st January 1916
Filton	4th April 1916
St Omer	30th July 1916
Fienvilliers	1st August 1916
Vert Galand	2nd April 1917
Liettres	31st May 1917
Poperinghe	14th August 1917
Bailleul	5th September 1917
St Marie Cappel	25th December 1917
Bailleul	13th February 1918
St Marie Cappel	23rd March 1918
Savy	31st March 1918
Cappelle	17th August 1918
Savy	23rd September 1918
Abscon	24th October 1918
Genech	9th February 1919
Ternhill	17th February 1919

Disbanded at Ternhill on 31st December 1919. Reformed at Duxford on 1st April, 1923 as a fighter flight attached to No. 2 FTS; brought up to full strength as a fighter squadron on 1st June, 1924.

Duxford	1st April 1923
Henlow	11th June 1935
Duxford	20th July 1935
Horsham St Faith	17th April 1940
Duxford	16th May 1940
Hornchurch	25th May 1940
Duxford	5th June 1940
Fowlmere	25th June 1940
Duxford	3rd July 1940
Fowlmere	24th July 1940
Detachment at Eastchurch	
Duxford	30th October 1940
Fowlmere	6th February 1941
West Malling	21st May 1941
Matlask	16th August 1941
Ludham	1st December 1941
Hutton Cranswick	4th April 1942
Perranporth	6th May 1942
Warmwell	1st June 1942
Perranporth	14th June 1942
Biggin Hill	1st July 1942
Perranporth	7th July 1942
Colerne	23rd July 1942

Perranporth	31st July 1942
Rochford (Southend)	16th August 1942
Perranporth	20th August 1942
Exeter & Fairwood Common	October 1942
Perranport	October 1942
Middle Wallop	1st March 1943
Membury	10th March 1943
Middle Wallop	13th March 1943
Fairlop	5th April 1943
Digby	18th May 1943
Matlask	4th June 1943
Gravesend	20th June 1943
Bognor	26th June 1943
Newchurch	2nd July 1943
Gravesend (Kingsnorth)	18th August 1943
Weston Zoyland	30th September 1943
Gatwick	15th October 1943
Gravesend	24th October 1943
Ford	15th April 1944
Rochford (Southend)	12th May 1944
Funtington	20th May 1944
Ford	15th June 1944
Martragny (B.7)	25th June 1944
Ellon (B.12)	15th July 1944
St Andre de l'Eure (B.24)	2nd September 1944
Nivillers (B.40)	3rd September 1944
Grimbergen (B.60)	9th September 1944
Matlask	28th September 1944
Andrews Field	14th October 1944
Peterhead	13th February 1945
Acklington	23rd May 1945
Bradwell Bay	13th August 1945
Molesworth	7th September 1945
Lübeck	2nd May 1946
Wittering	29th June 1946
Biggin Hill	10th September 1946
Wittering	16th September 1946
Church Fenton	23rd April 1947
Leconfield	29th June 1959
Gutersloh	23rd September 1965
Wildenrath	1st January 1977

COMMANDING OFFICERS

Major R.M. RODWELL	January 1916 – February 1917
Major H.D. HARVEY-KELLY, D.S.O.	February 1917 – April 1917
Major W.G.S. SANDAY D.S.O., M.C.	April 1917 – March 1918
Major E.R. PRETYMAN	March 1918 – November 1918
Major H.W.G. JONES, M.C.	November 1918 – December 1919
Squadron Leader P. BABINGTON, M.C., A.F.C.	July 1924 – July 1925
Squadron Leader H.W.G. JONES, M.C.	July 1925 – August 1928
Squadron Leader E.C. EMMETT, MC., D.F.C.	August 1928 – June 1929
Squadron Leader L.H. SLATTER, O.B.E.,, D.S.O., D.F.C.	June 1929 – October 1929
Squadron Leader C.R. KEARY	December 1929 – July 1931
Squadron Leader A.C. SANDERSON, D.F.C.	July 1931 – February 1934
Squadron Leader J.R. CASSIDY	February 1934 – January 1936
Squadron Leader J.W. TURTON JONES	January 1936 – December 1937
Squadron Leader H.I. COZENS	December 1937 – January 1940
Squadron Leader G.D. STEPHENSON	January 1940 – May 1940
Squadron Leader PINKHAM	May 1940 – September 1940
Squadron Leader B.J. LANE, D.F.C.	September 1940 – June 1941
Squadron Leader R.G. DUTTON, D.F.C. Bar	June 1941 – July 1941
Squadron Leader LAWSON, D.F.C.	July 1941 – March 1942
Squadron Leader P.R.G. DAVIES	March 1942 – September 1942
Squadron Leader M.C.B. BODDINGTON	September 1942 – December 1942
Squadron Leader V.H. EKINS	December 1942 – November 1943
Squadron Leader N.J. DURRANT	December 1943 – May 1944
Squadron Leader W. McM. GILMOUR, D.F.C., D.F.M.	May 1944 – August 1944
Squadron Leader W.W.J. LOUD, D.F.C.	August 1944 – October 1944
Squadron Leader M.J. WRIGHT	October 1944 – December 1944
Squadron Leader P.J. HEARNE	December 1944 – October 1945
Squadron Leader J.R. BROUGHTON, A.F.C.	October 1945 – April 1946
Squadron Leader C.I.R. ARTHUR, D.F.C. Bar	April 1946 – August 1948
Squadron Leader V.C. WOODWARD, D.F.C. Bar	August 1948 – September 1950
Squadron Leader B.L. DUCKENFIELD, A.F.C.	September 1950 – October 1952
Squadron Leader B. BEARD, A.F.C.	October 1952 – April 1955
Squadron Leader D.J. FOWLER, A.F.C.	April 1955 – August 1957
Major R. G. NEWELL (USAF)	August 1957 – July 1959
Squadron Leader L.W. PHIPPS, A.F.C.	July 1959 – July 1961
Squadron Leader R.M. RAW, A.F.C.	July 1961 – July 1963
Squadron Leader W.F. PAGE	July 1963 – July 1965
Wing Commander B.R.A. COX, A.F.C.	July 1965 – August 1967
Wing Commander L.A. JONES	August 1967 – May 1970
Wing Commander R.L. DAVIS	May 1970 – March 1972
Wing Commander P.C. VANGUCCI	March 1972 – May 1974
Wing Commander R.L. BARCILON	24 May 1974 – January 1977
Wing Commander A.J. BENDELL, A.F.C.	1 January 1977 – May 1978
Wing Commander T.J.L. GAUVAIN	16 May 1978 – October 1980
Wing Commander R.P. HALLAM	6 October 1980 – July 1983
Wing Commander M.P. DONALDSON, M.B.E.	8 July 1983 – July 1985
Wing Commander F.S. RANCE	19 July 1985 – December 1987
Wing Commander R.L. DIXON	11 December 1987 – September 1990
Wing Commander N.B. SPILLER	21 September 1990

THE
SQUADRON'S
AIRCRAFT

AIRCRAFT INSIGNIA

In the First World War the Squadron's Spads and Dolphins originally carried a white square aft of the roundels although for a while in 1917 the Squadron carried red, white and blue bands around the fuselage of the Spads. This was changed to a dumbell in the last year of the war. With its reconstitution after the war it assumed a blue and white check marking along the fuselage and across the upper wing. The Spitfires at first carried the squadron number "19" on the fin in red for "A" flight and white for "B" flight. This was changed to the code letters "WZ" in 1938 and from September, 1939, onwards "QV". During 1945 the Mustang spinners were yellow with black bands and in 1947 the blue and white check was unofficially restored on a Hornet and officially from 1951 onwards on the Meteors, Hunters, Lightnings and Phantoms.

(Sqdn Album)
MAURICE FARMAN
(September 1915 – December 1915)

Built in France as a Reconnaissance aircraft in 1913. It was powered by a Renault 8-cylinder air-cooled inline V. 70hp engine, giving it a maximum speed of 59mph (95km/h) at sea level, a ceiling of 13,123 feet (4,000m) and an endurance of 3 hours 30 minutes. It had no armament and a crew of two.

No known serial numbers.

(Sqdn Album)
CAUDRON G3
(September 1915 – December 1915)

Built in France as a Reconnaissance aircraft in 1914. It was powered by a Le Rhone 90hp engine, giving it a maximum speed of 67mph, a ceiling of 13,123 feet and an endurance of four hours. It had no armament and a crew of one.

No known serial numbers.

AVRO 504
(September 1915 – December 1915)

Built in Britain as a Reconnaissance/Light Bomber in 1914. It was powered by a Gnome 7-cylinder air-cooled rotary 80hp engine, giving it a maximum speed of 82mph (132km/h) at sea level, a ceiling of 12,000 feet (3,658m) and an endurance of 4 hours 30 minutes. It had one machine gun and a crew of two.

No known serial numbers.

(Sqdn Album)
R.E.7
(December 1915 – June 1916)

Built in Britain as a Bomber in 1915. It was powered by an RAF 4a 12-cylinder air-cooled inline V. 150hp engine, giving it a maximum speed of 85mph (137km/h), a ceiling of 6,500 feet (1,981m) and an endurance of six hours. It had one machine gun, 336lb of bombs and a crew of two.

No known serial numbers.

(J.M. Bruce/G.S. Leslie Collection)
RAF B.E.12
(June 1916 – February 1917)

Built in Britain as a Fighter/Bomber in 1916. It was powered by a RAF 4a 12-cylinder aircooled inline V. 150hp engine, giving it a maximum speed of 102mph (164km/h) at sea level, a ceiling of 12,500 feet (3,810m) and an endurance of three hours. It had one or two machine guns and a crew of one.

Serial Nos:

6145	6545	6572	6638
6513	6546	6579	6640
6530	6547	6588	6643
6531	6548	6591	6652
6532	6549	6594	
6536	6551	6619	
6537	6552	6622	
6538	6553	6624	
6540	6554	6626	
6542	6557	6627	
6543	6561	6632	
6544	6562	6635	

B.E.2c
(August 1916 – March 1917)

Built in Britain as a Reconnaissance/Light Bomber in 1914. It was powered by a RAF 1a 8-cylinder air-cooled inline V. 90hp engine, giving it a maximum speed of 72mph, a ceiling of 6,500 feet and an endurance of 3 hours 15 minutes. It had one machine gun and a crew of two.

Serial Nos:

2493	2635	2762	4545
2528	2756	4161	

(Sqdn Album)

B.E.2d

Serial Nos:
5869

B.E.2e

Serial Nos:
6758   7212

356

(Crown Copyright – MOD)
SPAD S.VII
(December 1916 – June 1917)

Built in France as a Fighter in 1916. It was powered by a Hispano-Suiza eight Ac 8-cylinder liquid cooled inline V. 175hp engine, giving it a maximum speed of 119mph (191.5km) at 6,500 feet (2,000m), a ceiling of 18,000 feet (5,485m) and an endurance of 2 hours 15 mins. It had one machine gun and a crew of one.

(June 1917 – January 1918)

It was powered by a Hispano-Suiza 8Ba 200hp engine, giving it a maximum speed of 138mph, a ceiling of 21,820 feet and an endurance of two hours. It had two machine guns and a crew of one.

Serial Nos:

A262	A263	A310	A312	A1263	A6607	A6619
A6627	A6632	A6633	A6634	A6706	A6712	A6714
A6746	A6749	A6749	A6753	A6795	A6802	A6871
A8863	B1564	B1565	B1573	B1578	B1581	B1585
B1586	B1588	B1593	B1620	B1622	B3471	B3492
B3507	B3508	B3520	B3528	B3531	B3533	B3534
B3535	B3552	B3553	B5337	B3559	B3562	B3568

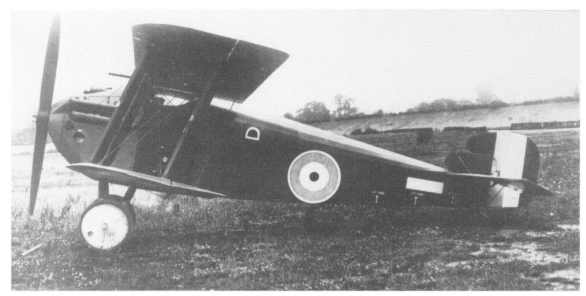

SOPWITH 5F1 DOLPHIN
(November 1917 – December 1919)

Built in Britain as a Fighter in 1917. It was powered by a Hispano-Suiza V.8 inline liquid cooled 200hp engine, giving it a maximum speed of 120mph, a ceiling of 19,000 feet and an endurance of 1 hour 45 minutes. It had two machine guns and a crew of one.

Serial Nos:

B7849	B7855	B7876	C3788	C3789	C3790	C3792
C3793	C3796	C3797	C3799	C3817	C3818	C3819
C3820	C3822	C3826	C3827	C3828	C3829	C3832
C3833	C3836	C3837	C3838	C3840	C3841	C3843
C3844	C3891	C3899	C3902	C3940	C3941	C4017
C4019	C4023	C4026	C4043	C4048	C4057	C4129
C4132	C4134	C8087	C8146	C8188	C8190	D3748
D3755	D3762	D3768	D3769	D3770	D5236	D5237
D5306	D5314	E4427	E4432	E4495	E4501	E4511
E4514	E4545	E4548	E4552	E4637	E4713	E4715
E4735	E4748	F7036	F7037	F7051		

(Crown Copyright – MOD – AHB)
SOPWITH 7F1 SNIPE
(June 1924 – December 1924)

Built in Britain as a Fighter in 1918. It was powered by a Bentley BR2 9-cylinder air-cooled rotary 230hp engine, giving it a maximum speed of 121mph (195km/h), a ceiling of 19,500 feet and an endurance of three hours. It had two machine guns and a crew of one.

Serial Nos:

E6943	E7605	E8245	F2444

(Crown Copyright – MOD – AHB)
GLOSTER GREBE
(December 1924 – April 1928)

Built in Britain as a Fighter in 1923. It was powered by an Armstrong Siddeley Jaguar IV 14-cylinder air-cooled radial 400hp engine, giving it a maximum speed of 152mph (245km/h), a ceiling of 22,900 feet (7,000m) and an endurance of 2 hours 45 minutes. It had two machine guns and a crew of one.

Serial Nos:

J7368	J7377	J7414	J7415	J7417	J7575	J7585

(Sqdn Album)
A.W. SISKIN IIIa
(March 1928 – September 1931)

Built in Britain as a Fighter in 1927. It was powered by a Armstrong Siddeley Jaguar IV 14-cylinder air-cooled radial 425hp engine, giving it a maximum speed of 156mph (251km/h), a ceiling of 27,000 feet (8,230m) and a range of 280 miles (450km). It had two machine guns and a crew of one.

Serial Nos:

J8394	J8846	J8888	J9347	J9901
J8825	J8886	J9193	J9892	

("Flight")
BRISTOL BULLDOG IIa
(September 1931 – January 1935)

Built in Britain as a Fighter in 1929. It was powered by a Bristol Jupiter VIIF 9-cylinder air-cooled radial 490hp engine, giving it a maximum speed of 174mph (280km/h), a ceiling of 27,000 feet (8,200m) and a range of 310 miles. It had two machine guns, 80lb (35kg) of bombs and a crew of one.

Serial Nos:

K2138	K2158	K2162	K2166
K2155	K2159	K2163	K2167
K2156	K2160	K2164	K2168
K2157	K2161	K2165	K2169

GLOSTER GAUNTLET I
(January 1935 – March 1939)

Built in Britain as a Fighter in 1934. It was powered by a Bristol Mercury VI S2 9-cylinder air-cooled radial 645hp engine, giving it a maximum speed of 230mph (370km/h), a ceiling of 33,500 feet (10,210m) and a range of 460 miles (749km). It had two machine guns and a crew of one.

Serial Nos:

K4081	K4084	K4087	K4089	K4094	K4097
K4082	K4086	K4088	K4092	K4095	

(Crown Copyright – MOD – AHB)

GLOSTER GAUNTLET II
(September 1936 – February 1939)

Differed in its construction to the Gauntlet I due to the merger of Gloster and Hawker Siddeley.

Serial Nos:

K5284	K5296	K5341	K7870

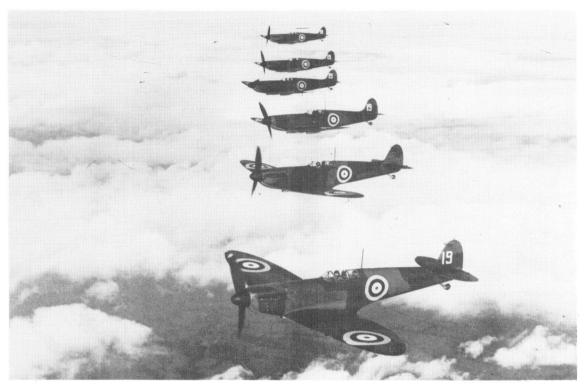

(Crown Copyright – MOD – IWM)
VICKERS-SUPERMARINE SPITFIRE I
(August 1938 – December 1940)

Built in Britain as a Fighter in 1938. It was powered by Rolls Royce Merlin II 12-cylinder V liquid-cooled 1,030hp engine, giving it a maximum speed of 355mph (571km/h), a ceiling of 34,000 feet (10,360m) and a range of 500 miles (805km). It had eight machine guns and a crew of one.

Serial Nos:

K9789	K9824	L1042	R6687
K9790	K9825	L1089	R6688
K9792	K9826	N3030	R6778
K9794	K9836	N3040	X4059
K9795	K9841	N3198	X4070
K9796	K9851	N3199	X4170
K9797	K9853	N3200	X4173
K9798	K9854	N3237	X4179
K9799	K9857	N3238	X4237
K9800	K9858	N3286	X4267
K9801	K9859	P9305	X4331
K9803	K9967	P9386	X4352
K9807	K9993	P9391	X4353

K9808	L1027	P9422	X4424
K9810	L1029	P9440	X4425
K9811	L1030	P9546	X4473
K9815	L1031	R6625	X4474
K9820	L1032	R6627	X4475
K9821			

VICKERS-SUPERMARINE SPITFIRE Ib
(June 1940 – September 1940)

Serial Nos:

R6761	R6889	R6917	R6991
R6762	R6890	R6919	X4159
R6776	R6897	R6923	X4231
R6809	R6904	R6924	X4279
R6833	R6911	R6958	X4342
R6888	R6912		

The armament was changed to two cannons and four machine guns.

VICKERS-SUPERMARINE SPITFIRE IIa
(September 1940 – November 1941)

A more powerful Merlin XII 1,175hp engine. It was armed with eight machine guns.

Serial Nos:

P7289	P7428	P7732	P8166
P7299	P7429	P7771	P8171
P7301	P7430	P7813	P8204
P7316	P7432	P7822	P8241
P7318	P7433	P7849	P8243
P7357	P7434	P7883	P8251
P7358	P7435	P7886	P8255
P7359	P7501	P7887	P8270
P7367	P7509	P7889	P8277
P7372	P7545	P7890	P8366
P7377	P7547	P7907	P8384
P7379	P7560	P7912	P8432
P7380	P7566	P7924	P8442
P7381	P7617	P7929	P8460
P7420	P7618	P7971	P8583
P7421	P7619	P7991	P8659
P7422	P7620	P8017	P8667
P7423	P7668	P8032	P8679
P7425	P7680	P8077	P8729
P7427	P7686	P8164	

VICKERS-SUPERMARINE SPITFIRE Vb
(October 1941 – August 1943)

It was powered by a Rolls Royce Merlin 45 12-cylinder V liquid-cooled 1,440hp engine was fitted, giving it a maximum speed of 374mph (602km/h) at 13,000 feet (4,000m), a ceiling of 37,000 feet (11,280m) and a range of 470 miles (750km). It had two 20mm cannon and four machine guns, and a crew of one.

Serial Nos:

P8561	AD191	BL755	EP183
P8715	AD231	BL810	EP298
W3370	AD237	BL830	EP354
W3432	AD307	BL851	EP393
W3439	AD323	BL852	EP394
W3638	AD332	BL854	EP398
W3644	AD385	BM117	EP445
W3771	AD416	BM147	EP447
W3898	AD458	BM203	EP465
W3966	AD461	BM233	EP504
AA764	AD476	BM238	EP506
AA868	AD478	BM333	EP516
AA915	AD500	BM381	EP523
AA931	AD514	BM425	EP548
AB272	AD556	BM509	EP552
AB274	AD571	BM516	EP601
AB467	AD572	BM522	EP603
AB524	AR364	BM526	EP604
AB848	AR422	BM531	EP605
AB939	AR451	BM535	EP637
AB971	AR463	BM542	EP639
AD132	BL380	BM565	EP715
AD184	Bl566	BM583	EP749
AD185	BL635	BM652	EP756
AD190	BL682	EN971	

(Crown Copyright – MOD)
VICKERS-SUPERMARINE SPITFIRE Vc
(September 1942 – March 1943)

This model was equipped with a universal wing which could accommodate all foreseeable kinds of weapons, and was the first to be used as a Fighter/Bomber.

Serial Nos:

AR505	AR516	AR605	EE613
AR507	AR517	AR608	EN767
AR509	AR552	BL263	EN768
AR513	AR604	Bl472	

VICKERS-SUPERMARINE SPITFIRE IX
(August 1943 – January 1944)

It was powered by the Rolls Royce Merlin 61 12-cylinder V liquid-cooled 1,515hp engine, giving it a maximum speed of 408mph (656km/h) at 25,000 feet (7,620m), a ceiling of 44,000 feet (13,400m) and a range of 434 miles (700km). The armament was two x 20mm cannon, and four machine guns.

Serial Nos:

BS409	MA818	MA842	MH354
BS461	MA819	MH316	MH355
BS512	MA833	MH319	MH375
MA750	MA837	MH330	MH871
MA806	MA841	MH352	MJ215
MA815			

NORTH AMERICAN MUSTANG III
(January 1944 – April 1945)

Built in the USA as a Fighter in 1943. It was powered by a Packard Merlin 12-cylinder engine, giving it a maximum speed of 440 mph, a ceiling of 42,000 and a range of 810 miles. It had four machine guns and a crew of one.

Serial Nos:

FB105	FB194	FX990	FZ164
FB110	FB198	FX999	FZ172
FB112	FB199	FZ112	FZ174
FB113	FB201	FZ133	FZ181
FB116	FB223	FZ139	FZ195
FB131	FX188	FZ140	HB827
FB148	FX887	FZ141	KH444
FB166	FX955	FZ144	SR433
FB168	FX974	FZ158	SR437

NORTH AMERICAN MUSTANG IV
(April 1945 – March 1946)

Built in the USA as a Fighter in 1944. It was powered by a Packard Merlin 12-cylinder engine, giving it a maximum speed of 437 mph, a ceiling of 41,900 feet and a range of 950 miles. It had six machine guns and a crew of one.

Serial Nos:

HB832	KH756	KH858	KM152
KH655	KH761	KH867	KM155
KH674	KH778	KM103	KM193
KH697	KH818	KM118	KM200
KH742	KH847	KM137	KM272

VICKERS-SUPERMARINE SPITFIRE LF.16e
(March 1946 – November 1946)

It was powered by the Rolls Royce Merlin 61 12-cylinder V liquid cooled 1,515hp engine, giving it a maximum speed of 408mph, a ceiling of 44,000 feet and a range of 434 miles. It had two 20mm cannons and four machine guns.

Serial Nos:

RW384	SL690	TE391	TE447
SL601	SL728	TE393	TE451
SL610	TE332	TE396	TE458
SL668	TE387	TE397	TE470
SL687	TE389	TE408	

D.H. HORNET F.1
(October 1946 – May 1948)

Data as the F.3. The F.3 had structural modifications and extra fuel capacity.

Serial Nos:

PX233	PX246	PX250	PX278

("Flight")
D.H. HORNET F.3
(May 1948 – April 1951)

Built in Britain as a Fighter in 1944. It was powered by two Rolls Royce Merlin 130s V-12 liquid cooled 2,030hp engines, giving it a maximum speed of 472mph, a ceiling of 37,500 feet (11,430m) and a range of 2,500 miles (4022km). It had four 20mm cannons and 2,000lb (907kg) of bombs and a crew of one.

Serial Nos:

PX293	PX332	PX389	PX390
PX306	PX343		

GLOSTER METEOR F.4
(January 1951 – June 1951)

Data similar to that of the F.8. The F.8 had modifications and a longer range. Built in Britain as a Fighter in 1946.

Serial Nos:
EE598

(Sqdn Album)

GLOSTER METEOR F.8
(April 1951 – January 1957)

Built in Britain as a Fighter in 1949. It was powered by two Rolls Royce Derwent eight Turbojets, 3,500lb (1,587kg) thrust each engine, giving it a maxium speed of 598mph (962km/h), a ceiling of 43,000 feet (13,106m) and a range of 980 miles (1,580km). It had four 20mm cannon and a crew of one.

Serial Nos:

VZ520	WA758	WA868	WA870	WA969	WA984	WB106
WB107	WB108	WE843	WE855	WE856	WE857	WE863
WE864	WE866	WE868	WE870	WE962	WE963	WE969
WF677	WH289	WH304	WH348	WH351	WH376	WK736
WK914	WK974	WK990	WL104	WL107	WL117	WL120
WL133	WL137	WL304	WL307			

(Sqdn Album)
HAWKER HUNTER F.6
(October 1956 – February 1963)

Built in Britain as a Fighter in 1954. It was powered by a Rolls Royce Avon 203 turbojet 10,000lb (4,536kg) thrust engine, giving it a maximum speed of 710mph (1,142km/h), a ceiling of 51,500 feet (15,700m) and a range of 1,900 miles (3,085km). It had four 30mm cannons, 2,000lb (907kg) of bombs and a crew of one.

Serial Nos:

XE557	XF449	XG159	XG187
XE561	XF525	XG167	XG188
XE583	XF527	XG169	XG191
XE590	XG133	XG172	XG195
XE603	XG135	XG185	XG196
XF439	XG152	XG186	XG199

HAWKER HUNTER T.7

Trainer version.

Serial Nos:

XL601	XL623

371

(Crown Copyright – MOD – AHB)
E.E. LIGHTNING F.2
(December 1962 – October 1969)

Built in Britain as a Fighter in 1961. It was powered by two Rolls Royce Avon 301 16,300lb thrust engines, giving it a maximum speed of 1,500mph. It had four 30mm cannons, two Firestreak AAM and a crew of one.

E.E. LIGHTNING F. 2a
(January 1968 – December 1976)

Forty four F.2s were built and 31 were converted to F.2a's, re-entering service in 1968. The conversion included the cambered leading edge to the wing, larger ventral tank, an extended leading edge to the fin and arrester hook.

Serial Nos:

XN 724	F. 2a
XN 726	F. 2
XN 727	F. 2
XN 730	F. 2
XN 731	F. 2a

XN 733	F. 2 later converted to F. 2a
XN 735	F. 2a
XN 771	F. 2 later converted to F. 2a
XN 774	F. 2
XN 775	F. 2
XN 776	F. 2 later converted to F. 2a
XN 777	F. 2a
XN 778	F. 2 later converted to F. 2a
XN 779	F. 2
XN 780	F. 2 later converted to F. 2a
XN 781	F. 2 later converted to F. 2a
XN 782	F. 2
XN 783	F. 2a
XN 784	F. 2 later converted to F. 2a
XN 786	F. 2a
XN 787	F. 2
XN 789	F. 2a
XN 790	F. 2a
XN 791	F. 2a
XN 794	F. 2

E.E. LIGHTNING T.4

Training version.

Serial Nos:
XM970   XM973   XM988   XM991

(P. Willis)
McDONNELL PHANTOM FGR.2
(September 1976 –   )

Built in the USA as a Fighter/Bomber in 1961. It is powered by Rolls Royce engines, giving it a maximum speed of 1,500mph, a ceiling of 62,000 feet (18,900m). It has a crew of two.

Serial Nos.

XT902	XV411	XV462	XV470
XV404	XV421	XV465	XV475
XV407	XV422	XV468	XV485
XV408	XV430		

Roll of Honour

ABBOTT, W.G. Flight Sergeant (1944)
ADAMS. J.S.L. Flight Lieutenant (1929)
ADAMS. N. Flight Lieutenant (1985/86)
ADAMS. W.S.C. Flying Officer (1930/31)
ADNAMS. A.G. Pilot Officer (1929/30)
AEBERHARDT. R.A.C. Pilot Officer (1940)
AGGETT. A.R. Sergeant (1936)
AINGER. H.C. Lieutenant (1917)
AITCHISON. Pilot Officer (1949)
ALCHIN. Squadron Leader (1971/73)
ALDRIDGE. J.A. Lieutenant (1917)
ALLABARTON. S.F. Second Lieutenant (1917)
ALLEN. G.W.D. Captain (1916)
ANDERSON. Pilot Officer (1941)
ANDERSON. D.M. Flying Officer (1989/90)
ANDERSON. G.F. Lieutenant (1918)
ANDREWS. Sergeant (1937)
ANDREWS. Pilot Officer (1941)
ANDREWS. W.A. Flying Officer (1928)
APPLIN. R. Second Lieutenant (1917)
ARMSTRONG. Lieutenant (1918)
ARTHUR. C.I.R. Squadron Leader, DFC and Bar (1946/48)
AUTY. Pilot Officer (1948)
AVERY. B.P. Pilot Officer (1944)

BABINGTON. P. Squadron Leader, MC, AFC, (1924/25)
BACON. P.A. Flying Oficer (1959/61)
BADER. D.R.S. Flying Officer (1940)
BAKER. G.B.A. Captain (1916/17)
BAKER. H.C. Pilot Officer (1939)
BAKER J.W. Second Lieutenant (1916)
BAKER. R.B. Lieutenant (1917)
BALDEN. D.W. Pilot Officer (1937)
BALDWIN. Major (1916)
BALDWIN. C. Flight Lieutenant (1973)
BALL. G.E. Pilot Officer (1938/40)
BANCROFT-WILSON. G. Flight Lieutenant
BANHAM. A.J. Pilot Officer (1939)
BANHAM E.G. Pilot Officer (1929/31)
BARAGWANATH J.D. Flight Sergeant (1943/44)
BARCILON. R.L. Wing Commander (1974/77)
BARKER. F.E. Lieutenant (1917)
BARLOW W.H. Lieutenant (1918)
BARMBY. A.S. Flying Officer (1957)
BARRETT. P.J. Squadron Leader (1990)
BARRETT. W.J. Sergeant (1928)
BARROW. S.H.A. Flying Officer (1931)
BARTLE. D.J. Flight Lieutenant (1989/90)
BARWELL. P.R. Flying Officer (1928)
BATES. Pilot Officer (1952)
BATEY. N.R. Flight Lieutenant (1990)

BAYES J.W. Flying Officer (1929)
BEADLE. T. Flight Lieutenant (1971/74)
BEAN. C.A.S. Lieutenant (1916/17)
BEARD. B. Squadron Leader, A.F.C. (1952/55)
BEAZLEY. R.H. Flight Lieutenant (1967/69)
BECKETT, Warrant Officer (1944)
BEDFORD. Flying Officer (1953/54)
BELCHEM. L.G. Pilot Officer (1931/33)
BELL. Warrant Officer
BELL S.H. Flight Lieutenant (1954/87)
BELL. G.N. Sergeant (1942)
BELL. M.H. Sergeant (1942)
BELL. P.H. Flight Lieutenant (1943)
BENDELL. A.J. Wing Commander, A.F.C. (1977/78)
BENNETT. Warrant Officer (1945)
BENNETT. A.L. Flight Lieutenant (1957)
BENNETT. L.V. Flying Officer (1930)
BENTLEY. R.R. Captain, M.C. (1919)
BERNARD. M. Sub Lieutenant (1942)
BEST. F.B. Lieutenant (1917)
BIGGS. D.A. Sergeant (1943)
BIGNAL. J.S.W. Sergeant (1935)
BILLING. J.E. Sergeant (1942)
BINCH. F.B. Second Lieutenant (1918)
BINNIE. Second Lieutenant (1916)
BIRCH. Sergeant (1940)
BIRD. Flight Lieutenant, D.F.C. (1944)
BIRMINGHAM. F. Sergeant (1930)
BISHOP. J. Flight Lieutenant (1973)
BJORKLUND. D.E. Captain USMC (1959/61)
BLACK. I. Flight Lieutenant (1981/82)
BLACK. S. Flying Officer (1976/77)
BLACKFORD. P.A. Flight Lieutenant (1976/79)
BLACKLEY. Flight Lieutenant (1965)
BLAIN. W.N. Pilot Officer (1928)
BLAKE. A.G. Sub Lieutenant (1940)
BLAKE. A.W. Lieutenant (1918)
BLISS. G. Flying Officer (1939)
BLYTHE. E. J. Lieutenant (1918)
BOBOLA. T. Flying Officer (1942)
BODDINGTON. M.C.B. Squadron Leader (1942)
BOEREE. A.R. Lieutenant (1917)
BOND. H.S.J. Flight Lieutenant (1942)
BOND. T.M. Flying Officer (1959/61)
BONE. D.J. Flying Officer (1989/90)
BONSEY. B.W.E. Pilot Officer (1930)
BOSWELL. Sergeant (1940)
BOTHAM. J.A. Squadron Leader (1985/87)
BOULTON. P.R. Pilot Officer (1953)
BOWEN. J.B. Captain (1916)
BOWRING. J.H. Pilot Officer (1939)
BOYD C.N. Lieutenant (1918)

BOYD. T. Sergeant (1939)
BOYLE. E.G. Second Lieutenant (1919)
BOZMAN. H.G. Second Lieutenant (1916)
BRACKENBURY. E.L. Pilot Officer (1930/31)
BRADLEY. C.F. Flight Lieutenant (1942)
BRADLEY. H.P. Second Lieutenant (1916)
BRADY. J. Flight Lieutenant (1975/76)
BRECKETT. Flight Sergeant (1953)
BRECKON. Sergeant (1951)
BRENTON. R.J. Sergeant (1942)
BRETT. M.J. Flight Lieutenant (1989/90)
BRIDGES. A.G. Pilot Officer (1956)
BRIGGS. S.P. Second Lieutenant (1916)
BRINSDEN. F.N. Flight Lieutenant (1938/40)
BROADHURST. H. Flight Lieutenant (1936)
BROADWAY. S. Flight Lieutenant (1985/86)
BROOKER. Pilot Officer (1942)
BROOKES. Flying Officer (1954)
BROUGHTON. J.R. Squadron Leader (1945/46)
BROWN. Sergeant
BROWN. J. Flight Lieutenant (1973)
BROWN. A.D.C. Lieutenant (1917)
BROWN. J.A.S. Flying Officer (1931)
BROWN. J.L. Sergeant (1942)
BROWN. V.S. Lieutenant (1916)
BROWNE. N. Flight Lieutenant (1977)
BROWNE. P.E. Squadron Leader (1962)
BROWNE. W.G. Second Lieutenant (1918)
BRUCE. A.E.A. Sergeant
BRYAN. R.B. Sergeant (1932)
BRYANT. S. Flight Lieutenant (1978/9)
BRYDEN. W.P. Lieutenant (1917)
BRYSON. O.C. Lieutenant (1917)
BUCHAN. A.C. Sergeant
BUCK. G.S. Lieutenant (1916)
BUCKNALL. G.A.F. Flight Lieutenant (1929)
BULLEMENT. T.J. Flight Lieutenant (1990)
BURDICK. G. Flying Officer
BURGOYNE. E. Pilot Officer (1940)
BURLEIGH. T.H. Flying Officer (1931)
BURNETT. Flying Officer (1954/55)
BURNS. B.R.A. Flying Officer (1956)
BURTON. D.P. Flight Lieutenant (1989)
BUSK. Captain (1919)
BUTLER. Flight Lieutenant (1945)
BUTTERWORTH. N.J. Flight Lieutenant (1987/90)
BYRNE. Flying Officer (1955)

CAIRNES. W.J. Captain (1917)
CALDWELL. Squadron Leader (1965)
CALLAGHAN. E. Second Lieutenant (1916)
CALVERT. Pilot Officer (1941)
CAMERON J.L. Flying Officer (1955/57)

CAMPBELL. Flight Lieutenant (1945)
CAMPEL. Flight Sergeant (1951)
CANDY. J.G. Lieutenant (1917)
CANNING. Second Lieutenant (1917)
CAPPER. E.W. Lieutenant (1916/17)
CARDEN. D. Flight Lieutenant (1975/76)
CARLINE. S.W. Second Lieutenant (1916)
CARLTON. P. Flying Officer (1989/90)
CARSON. Warrant Officer (1943/44)
CARTER. A.D. Major (1917/18)
CARTER. P. Sergeant (1942)
CARUANA. R. Flight Lieutenant (1946)
CASSIDY. J.R. Squadron Leader (1934/36)
CAYLEY. E.G. Pilot Officer (1929)
CEMPEL. M. Pilot Officer (1950)
CHADBURN. Flight Lieutenant (1942)
CHADWICK G. Captain (1918)
CHAPPELL. S. Second Lieutenant (1916)
CHARLTON. Flight Lieutenant (1985/87)
CHARNOCK. Sergeant (1940/41)
CHARTERS. S.C. Sergeant (1943)
CHEATLE. C.C. Second Lieutenant (1917)
CHEEK. L. Pilot Officer (1942)
CHEESBROUGH. P.D. Flying Officer (1989/90)
CHESKIN. S. Flight Lieutenant (1987/89)
CHILD. J.M. Lieutenant (1917)
CHILTON. S.N. Flying Officer (1943)
CHORLTON. S.N. Pilot Officer (1942)
CHRISTEN. J.R. Flight Lieutenant (1989)
CHRISTIE. Sergeant (1941)
CHRISTIE. C.M. Flight Lieutenant (1959/61)
CHUBB A. Flight Lieutenant (1984)
CIECHAMOWSIK. L.M.M. Pilot Officer (1942/43)
CLARK. G. Flight Lieutenant (1975/76)
CLAYTON. E. Flight Lieutenant (1944)
CLAYTON. J.E. Flying Officer (1928)
CLEE. P.A. Pilot Officer (1957)
CLEGG. J. Pilot Officer (1953)
CLELAND. R. Sergeant (1931)
CLIFFE. J. Squadron Leader (1985/87)
CLINCH. S.J. Sergeant (1917)
CLOUSTON. W.G. Flight Lieutenant (1937/40)
CLYDSDALE. A.B. Pilot Officer (1943)
COCKBURN. G.A. Lieutenant (1917)
COLE. Flying Officer (1945)
COLEMAN. Flying Officer (1954)
COLEMAN. J.H. Sergeant (1937/40)
COLLEY. M.P. Flight Lieutenant (1989)
COLLYER. T.H. Sergeant (1942)
COLLYNS. Flight Lieutenant (1944)
CONNOR. D.W. Flying Officer (1944)
CONNOR. J. Squadron Leader (1984/85)
CONWAY. J.B. Flying Officer (1989)

COOMBES. S. Flying Officer (1986.87)
COOPER. F.B. Flying Officer (1943/44)
COOPER. P. Flight Lieutenant (1975/76)
COOTE. M.H. Flight Lieutenant (1928)
CORBOLD. H.M. Lieutenant (1916)
COSGROVE. J.A. Squadron Leader (1977/78)
COTTON. R.D. Pilot Officer (1929/30)
COUTTS. Sergeant (1951/53)
COUZENS. D. Flight Lieutenant (1973)
COWARD. J. B. Flying Officer (1937/40)
COWLEY. Pilot Officer (1941)
COX. B.R.A. Wing Commander, A.F.C. (1965/67)
COX. D.G. Sergeant (1940)
COX. Flight Lieutenant (1943)
COZENS. H.I. Squadron Leader (1937/40)
CRANE. A. Flying Officer (1958)
CRANE. J.S. Flight Lieutenant (1957)
CRANE. J.W. Captain (1918)
CREBER. D.I. Flight Lieutenant (1989/90)
CRESWELL. Flight Lieutenant (1952/55)
CRICHTON. J. Flying Officer (1959/61)
CRISHAM. W.J. Pilot Officer (1929/30)
CRONYN. Lieutenant (1916)
CROOME. V. Flying Officer (1935)
CROSSLEY. D.M. Flying Officer (1957)
CROWCROFT. Pilot Officer (1942)
CROWDEN. C.T. Flying Officer (1926)
CUBITT. C.R. Flying Officer (1928)
CULLINGTON. G. Flight Lieutenant (1973)
CULLUM. Flying Officer (1955)
CUNNINGHAM. W. Flight Lieutenant(1940)
CURETON. C. Flying Officer (1959/61)
CUTTING. D. Flight Lieutenant (1964)
CZERWINSKI. B. Pilot Officer (1949)

DALY. Warrant Officer (1946)
DANNING. J. Flight Lieutenant (1975/76)
DAVIDSON. D.A.L. Captain (1917)
DAVIDSON. H. Flying Officer (1956)
DAVIDSON, J. Flight Lieutenant (1945)
DAVIES. Flying Officer (1945)
DAVIES. Sergeant (1941)
DAVIES. E.B.C. Pilot Officer (1933)
DAVIES. P.R.G. Squadron Leader (1942)
DAVIES. R.C. Second Lieutenant (1918)
DAVIS. R.L. Wing Commander (1970/72)
DAWSON. H.W. Second Lieutenant (1917)
DE LART. V.E.C. Flight Lieutenant (1931/32)
DE LASTANG. R.N. Flight Lieutenant (1942)
DE PENCIER. J. Lieutenant (1917/18)
DE S. BARROW. H.A.J. Flying Officer (1931/32)
DE SALIS. A.R.F. Flight Lieutenant (1938)
DE L'HAYE. R.A. Captain (1918)

DELAMERE. W.P. Second Lieutenant (1917)
DELANGE. P.G. Lieutenant (1942)
DENNISON. Flight Lieutenant (1985/86)
DENSTON. Sergeant (1941)
DENTON. D. Warrant Officer (1946)
DEVAR. Warrant Officer (1945)
DEVEREUX. Pilot Officer (1942)
DEVITALIS. Lieutenant (1918)
DEWING. Warrant Officer (1945)
DILKS. Flying Officer (1943)
DITCHFIELD. J. Lieutenant (1918/19)
DIXON. R.L. Wing Commander (1987/90)
DOBSON. J. Flight Lieutenant (1975/76)
DOLEY. A.S. Flight Lieutenant (1945/46)
DOLEZAL. Pilot Officer (1940)
DONALDSON. G.M. Flight Lieutenant (1947/48)
DONALDSON. M.P. Wing Commander (1983/85)
DOUGLAS. R.M. Lieutenant (1918)
DOWNING. F.G. Flying Officer (1928/30)
DOWNING. G.G.B. Lieutenant (1916)
DRAKE. R.E. Sergeant (1932)
DREWERY. A.B. Second Lieutenant (1916)
DRINKWATER. Flight Lieutenant (1943/44)
DRISCOLL. J. Flying Officer (1961)
DUCKENFIELD. B.L. Squadron Leader (1950/52)
DUCKETT. R. Flying Officer (1964)
DUFF. Lieutenant (1918)
DURRANT. N.J. Squadron Leader (1943/44)
DUTTON. R.G. Squadron Leader (1941)
DWERRYHOUSE. Second Lieutenant (1919)

EDMONDS. Pilot Officer (1941)
EDMONSON. D.J. Flying Officer (1957)
EDWARDS. Flight Lieutenant (1942)
EDWARDS. G. Second Lieutenant (1916)
EDWARDS. I.H. Flight Lieutenant (1942)
EDWARDS. R.H. Second Lieutenant (1916)
EDWARDS. S.A. Flying Officer (1959/61)
EILLS. Flight Lieutenant (1945)
EKINS. V.H. Squadron Leader (1942/43)
ELDER-HEARN. T. Second Lieutenant (1917)
ELLIOTT. R.S.V. Lieutenant
ELLISON. C.S. Flight Lieutenant (1933)
EMMETT. E.C. Squadron Leader (1928/29)
EVANS. D.V.S. Pilot Officer (1938/39)
EVANS. E.J. Second Lieutenant (1916)
EVANS. R. Flight Lieutenant (1986)

FABESCH. J.P. Pilot Officer (1950/51)
FAIRCLOUGH. A.B. Lieutenant (1917/18)
FARRAND. E.S. Lieutenant (1918)
FARRAR. B.C. Flight Lieutenant (1961)
FEATHER. A.E. Sergeant (1935)

FELLOWES. A.H.G. Second Lieutenant (1916)
FELLOWS. Sergeant (1943)
FERGUSON. J. M. Flying Officer (1959/61)
FIELD. C.P. Flying Officer (1958)
FIGGIS. C.L.D. Flying Officer (1944)
FILSON. Flight Lieutenant (1946)
FINDLAYSON. S.S. Sergeant (1943)
FINLAY. G. Flight Lieutenant (1985/86)
FITCHAT. Lieutenant (1918)
FLEMMINGS. M. Squadron Leader (1986/87)
FLETCHER. B. Flying Officer (1956)
FOES. Warrant Officer (1945)
FOLKARD. Sergeant (1941)
FOSTER. D.W. Sergeant (1942)
FOSTER. E. Pilot Officer (1931)
FOSTER. J. Flying Officer (1944)
FOSTER. M.M. Flight Lieutenant (1959/61)
FOWLER. D.J. Squadron Leader (1955/57)
FOWLER. M. Flight Lieutenant (1970)
FROST. I.E. Flight Lieutenant (1972/77)
FUCHS. B. Lieutenant (1942)
FULFORD. Sergeant (1940)
FULLER. M.J.D. Flying Officer (1959/61)
FURNEAUX. Flight Lieutenant (1945)

GALER. H.E. Second Lieutenant (1917)
GAPE. R.N.T. Flying Officer (1926)
GARDINER. C.H. Lieutenant (1916)
GARDNER. C.V. Lieutenant (1917/18)
GARTSIDE-TIPPINGE. F. Second Lieutenant (1917)
GAUVAIN. T.J.L. Wing Commander (1978/80)
GEEN. G. Second Lieutenant (1916)
GENDERS. D. Pilot Officer (1938)
GENT. A.J. Flight Lieutenant (1989)
GEORGE. Pilot Officer (1947)
GEORGE R. Flight Lieutenant (1984)
GERMAIN. Flying Officer (1944)
GIDNEY. J. Flight Lieutenant (1970)
GILES. J.A. Flight Lieutenant (1989/90)
GILMOUR. P.S. Flight Lieutenant (1980/83)
GLANVILLE. P.T. Flight Lieutenant (1944)
GLEADON. A.W. Flight Lieutenant (1957)
GLEAVE. M. Flight Lieutenant (1970/71)
GLOVER. A. Sergeant (1942/43)
GOADBY. A. Pilot Officer (1951/53)
GODDEN. S.F. Flying Officer (1933)
GOLDING. K.L. Second Lieutenant (1917)
GORDON. J.A.G. Pilot Officer (1939)
GORDON-KIDD. A.L. Captain (1917)
GOULBOURNE. Pilot Officer (1954)
GRAHAM. Major (1918)
GRAHAM. J.S. Sergeant (1935)

GRAHAM. R.L. Lieutenant (1917)
GRAINGER. B. Flight Lieutenant (1963)
GRANDIN. R.J. Second Lieutenant (1917)
GRANT. R. Flying Officer (1946)
GRAY. P. Squadron Leader (1986/87)
GREEN. A.D. Flight Lieutenant (1989)
GREEN. J. Flying Officer (1956)
GREENFIELD. Sergeant
GREENWOOD. E.W. Flight Lieutenant (1957)
GREGORY. L. Sergeant (1935)
GREGORY. M.P. Lieutenant (1918)
GREY. P.P. Flying Officer (1928)
GRIERSON. C.D. Second Lieutenant (1917)
GROSS. A. Flight Lieutenant (1970/71)
GROSSE. M. Flight Lieutenant (1970/71)
GUNNING. P.S. Sergeant (1938)

HAGON. A.C. Captain (1917)
HAINES. L.A. Flying Officer (1941)
HAINSBY. F.W. Lieutenant (1918)
HALDEN. I. Flying Officer (1989/90)
HALFORD. Pilot Officer
HALL. Lieutenant (1918)
HALL. Flying Officer (1944)
HALL. J. Flight Lieutenant (1962)
HALL. J. Flight Lieutenant (1975/76)
HALL. W.T. Captain (1917)
HALLAM. R.P. Wing Commander (1980/83)
HALLIDAY. Lieutenant (1918)
HAMELIN. L.L. Sergeant (1942)
HAMERSLEY. M.A. Captain (1919)
HAMILTON. J.S. Pilot Officer (1930/31)
HAMILTON. W.M. Lieutenant (1917)
HAMMELL. J. Flight Lieutenant
HANDFORD. Sergeant (1945/46)
HANLON. T. Flight Lieutenant (1973)
HANNAY. T.J. Flying Officer (1958)
HANSON. Flying Officer (1953/55)
HARDING. F.L. Second Lieutenant (1917)
HARDMAN. J.D.I. Lieutenant (1918)
HARNETT. B. Pilot Officer (1951/53)
HARPER. A. Flying Officer (1962)
HARRIS. K. Flight Lieutenant (1989/90)
HARRISON. Flying Officer (1951/54)
HARRISON. D.I. Squadron Leader (1989/90)
HART. D.F. Flying Officer (1944)
HART. R.W. Flight Lieutenant (1989/90)
HARTLEY. J. Second Lieutenant (1918)
HARVEY-KELLY. H.D. Major (1917)
HASLAM. S.J. Squadron Leader (1989)
HAWKE. J.R. Flying Officer (1959/61)
HAY. J.C.M. Captain (1917)
HAYR. K.W. Flight Lieutenant AFC (1963)

HAYWARD. Pilot Officer (1949)
HAYWOOD. Flight Lieutenant (1944)
HEADING. Second Lieutenant
HEAMES. Flight Lieutenant (1986)
HEANEY. S.R. Flight Lieutenant (1990)
HEARNE. P.J. Squadron Leader (1944/45)
HEATH. Flying Officer
HEATH. N.G.C. Pilot Officer (1937/38)
HEDDERWICK. G. Second Lieutenant (1916)
HEDGES. A. Flying Officer (1963)
HENDERSHOT. W.F. Lieutenant (1918/19)
HENDERSON. H.C. Sergeant (1942)
HENDERSON. I.H.D. Captain (1916)
HENDERSON. J. Pilot Officer (1942)
HERMAN. R.D. Second Lieutenant (1916)
HEWAT. R.A. Second Lieutenant (1917)
HEWITT. G. Flight Lieutenant (1985/86)
HEWSON. J.S. Lieutenant (1918)
HICKS. H.R. Second Lieutenant (1917)
HIGGS. G.W. Flying Officer (1928)
HIGSON. Flight Lieutenant (1947)
HILL. Pilot Officer (1933)
HILL. Squadron Leader (1945)
HILL. Flying Officer (1951)
HILL. D.G. Sergeant (1942)
HILL. T. Flight Lieutenant (1986/87)
HILL. T.E. Flying Officer (1958)
HINDLEY. Sergeant (1941)
HINTON. B.K. Flight Lieutenant (1987/89)
HOBBS. R.H. Flying Officer (1932)
HODGSON. G. Squadron Leader (1986/87)
HODGSON. P. Flight Lieutenant (1975/76)
HODGSON. R. Flight Lieutenant (1973)
HOLLOWAY. B.S. Lieutenant (1919)
HOLMES. H. Warrant Officer (1944)
HOLMES. J.D.V. Second Lieutenant (1917)
HOLT. R.G. Second Lieutenant (1917)
HOOK. L. Flying Officer (1954/57)
HOPE. A.T. Lieutenant (1916)
HOPKINS. Flying Officer (1953/55)
HOPKINS. Squadron Leader (1973)
HOPKINS. E.W. Flight Lieutenant (1964)
HORTH. H. Flight Lieutenant (1950)
HOUGH. D.G. Flying Officer (1957)
HOUGHTON. S. Flying Officer (1985/86)
HOWARD-WILLIAMS. P. Pilot Officer (1940/41)
HOWATT. Flight Lieutenant (1945)
HRADIL. Pilot Officer (1940)
HUBBARD. Flight Lieutenant (1945)
HUGHES. Flight Sergeant (1945)
HUGHES. E.S. Flight Lieutenant (1944)
HUNTER. W.A. Lieutenant (1918)
HURREL. I. Flight Lieutenant (1973)

HUSKINSON. P. Captain (1917)
HUSSEY. Flight Lieutenant (1944)
HUSTINGS. Lieutenant (1918)
HUTCHINSON. I. Sergeant (1943)

IKIN. Flying Officer (1953/55)
INGHAM. R.M. Flying Officer (1962)
INGLIS. Flight Sergeant (1945)
INGLIS. R.A. Second Lieutenant (1917)
IRVING. G.B. Captain (1917/18)
IRWIN. Sergeant (1940)
IVEY. Sergeant (1940)

JACOBS. Sergeant (1940/41)
JAMES. F.R. Flight Lieutenant (1953)
JARMAN. G.T. Pilot Officer (1931/32)
JARRETT. Sergeant (1952)
JELLETT. Flying Officer (1946)
JENKINS. S. Flight Sergeant (1943)
JENKINS. S.T. Pilot Officer (1952)
JENNINGS. Sergeant (1954)
JENNINGS. B.I.J. Sergeant (1939/40)
JENNINGS. D. Flight Lieutenant (1962)
JENNINGS. M.R.N. Lieutenant (1918)
JERRARD. A. Second Lieutenant (1917)
JOHNSON. B.C. Flying Officer (1959/61)
JOHNSON. E.G. Sergeant (1941)
JOHNSON. R.H. Second Lieutenant (1916)
JOHNSON. S.N. Pilot Officer (1942)
JOLLEFF. H.C. Flying Officer (1928)
JONES. Sergeant (1938)
JONES. R.L.Pilot Officer (1940)
JONES. C. Flight Lieutenant (1975/76)
JONES. D. Flight Lieutenant (1963)
JONES. H.W.G. Major/Sdn Ldr (1918/19 – 1925/28)
JONES. L.A. Wing Commander (1967/70)
JONES. P. Flight Lieutenant (1985/86)
JONES. W. Lieutenant (1917)
JONES. W.H. Sergeant (1942)

KAY. J.C. Sergeant
KEARY. C.R. Squadron Leader (1929/31)
KELLOGG. W.B. Lieutenant (1917)
KELLY. J. Flight Lieutenant (1970/72)
KELLY. P. Flight Lieutenant (1985/86)
KENNEDY. Sergeant (1942)
KENRICK. M.E. Flying Officer (1953/56)
KENRICK. P.C. Flying Officer (1955)
KENT. J.A. Pilot Officer (1936/37)
KIMBER. Sergeant (1954)
KING. Sergeant (1943)
KING. G. Pilot Officer (1942)
KING. L.V. Pilot Officer (1942)

KIRBY. F.W. Second Lieutenant (1917)
KIRK. A. Flight Lieutenant (1982)
KNIGHT . Flying Officer (1945)
KNIGHT. A. Flight Lieutenant (1986)
KNOX. J.C Sergeant (1955/57)
KONINA. Sergeant

LAING. J.D. Second Lieutenant (1917)
LAIRD. D.P. Lieutenant (1918)
LAMB. Flight Lieutenant (1943)
LANCE. W.G. Second Lieutenant (1918)
LANE B.J.E. Squadron Leader (1939/41)
LANE. W.A.N. Flight Lieutenant (1964)
LANGDON. P. Flight Sergeant (1945/46)
LANGHAM. Pilot Officer (1945)
LARDNER-BURKE. P. Pilot Officer (1940)
LARKIN. Second Lieutenant (1916)
LARSEN. S.J. Warrant Officer (1944/45)
LAWSON. W.J. Squadron Leader (1940/42)
LEACH. F.W. Lieutenant (1918)
LEACH. R. Flight Lieutenant (1965)
LEACROFT. J. Captain (1918)
LEE. H.H. Sergeant (1930)
LEE-COOPER. F. Sergeant (1943)
LENDON. D.F. Flight Lieutenant (1942)
LEWIS. D. Flight Lieutenant (1989/90)
LEWIS. E.C. Pilot Officer (1928)
LINDLEY. W.J.H. Flying Officer (1930)
LINTON. Flight Lieutenant (1942)
LITTELL. Lieutenant
LLEWELLIN. A.J.A. Pilot Officer (1938/39)
LLOYD. D.E. Sergeant (1940)
LOCK. J.H. Pilot Officer (1929)
LOGAN. Sergeant (1951/54)
LOGAN. D.C. Sergeant (1942/43)
LONG. G.R. Second Lieutenant (1917)
LONG. J.T.C. Flying Officer (1954/57)
LORD. C.W.R. Flight Lieutenant (1947)
LOTT. C.G. Sergeant (1929)
LOUD. W.W.J. Squadron Leader (1944)
LOVE. D.J. Sergeant (1942)
LOWE. Flying Officer (1949)
LOWE. M. Second Lieutenant (1917)
LYE. R.G. Lieutenant (1918)
LYNE. M.D. Pilot Officer (1939/40)
LYNN. F. Lieutenant (1918)
LYSICKY. Sergeant (1941/42)

MacDONALD. W.M.L. PIlot Officer(1930/33)
MacEWAN. K.A.K. Pilot Officer (1930/31)
MacFADYEN. I. Flying Officer (1964)
MacKENZIE. Pilot Officer (1933)
MacLACHLAN. J.R. Flying Officer (1937)

Mac NEIL. Flight Lieutenant (1944)
McARTHY-JONES. C.C. Flight Lieutenant (1942)
McCLURE. Second Lieutenant (1916)
McCONNELL. F.J. Lieutenant (1918)
McCORD. M. Pilot Officer (1957)
McCULLUM. Flying Officer (1955)
McDONALD. Flying Officer (1954/55)
McDONALD. J.M. Second Lieutenant
McEDMONSTON. D.J. Pilot Officer (1956)
McENTEGART. B. Lieutenant (1917)
McGILVRAY P.C. Flight Lieutenant (1989/90)
McGREGOR. A.N. Sergeant (1940/41)
McINTYRE. R.V. Pilot Officer (1929/31)
McKAY. Sergeant (1946)
McLEAN. D.D. Sergeant (1942)
McLEOD. Flight Lieutenant (1945)
McLEOD. Second Lieutenant (1917)
McLINTOCK. J.L. Lieutenant (1918)
McMAHON. R.M. Flight Lieutenant (1990)
McM GILMOUR. W. Squadron Leader, DFC,
    DFM, (1944)
McNAE. A.R.M. Flying Officer (1958)
McQUISTAN. F. Lieutenant (1918)
McRAE. W.G. Second Lieutenant (1917)
McSWEENEY, Flying Officer (1953/55)
McTAVISH. Pilot Oficer (1949)
MACEY. J. Captain (1918)
MACNAB. A.C. Pilot Officer (1942)
MAHONEY. M. Flight Lieutenant (1985/86)
MANLEY. J. Captain (1917)
MANN. D.J. Pilot Officer (1952/53)
MANNING. D.A. Pilot Officer (1957)
MANNING. R. Flight Lieutenant (1964)
MANSFIELD. Flight Lieutenant (1946)
MANWARING. D.H. Second Lieutenant (1916)
MAREK. Sergeant (1940)
MARLOW. Sergeant (1951/52)
MARPLES. R. Pilot Officer (1938/39)
MARSHALL. Pilot Officer (1952)
MARSHALL. D. Flight Lieutenant (1959/61)
MARSHALL. P. Flying Officer (1986/87)
MARTIN. A. Flight Lieutenant (1975/76)
MASKERY. Sergeant (1941)
MATHESON. A.W.S. Pilot Officer (1931/33)
MATHESON. G.C. Pilot Officer (1939)
MATSON. B.N. Pilot Officer (1930/33)
MAWHINNEY. J. Flight Lieutenant (1970)
MAY. J. Squadron Leader (1975/76)
MAY. J. Flying Officer (1945)
MAYNARD. J.M. Flying Officer (1944)
MEARNS. E.A. Second Lieutenant (1917)
MEDLAND. W. Flight Lieutenant (1986/87)
MEE. M.C.F. Pilot Officer (1937/38)

MERCER. Sergeant (1951/52)
MERCER. M. Flight Lieutenant (1984)
MERCER. T.H. Second Lieutenant
MILLER. Flight Lieutenant DFC (1949)
MILLER. M.E. Lieutenant (1918)
MILLS. Sergeant (1942)
MILLS. Flight Lieutenant (1951)
MILLS. G.D. Major (1917)
MILLS. W.H. Flight Lieutenant (1944) – (1948/50)
MILMAN. Pilot Officer (1941)
MILNES. P. Flight Lieutenant (1985)
MITCHELL. C.N.C. Flying Officer (1950/52)
MITCHELL. J.A. Lieutenant
MITCHELL. P.D. Flight Lieutenant (1952/53)
MOLLAN. P.F. Flight Lieutenant (1957)
MOORE. C. Captain (USAF) (1960)
MOORE. C.M. Lieutenant (1918/19)
MOORE. G.K. Flying Officer (1958)
MORFFEW. P.G. Sergeant (1936)
MORGAN. D. Flight Lieutenant (1985/86)
MORGAN. N. Flight Lieutenant (1985/86)
MORLEY. Flight Lieutenant (1952)
MORRIS. B.G. Pilot Officer (1937)
MORRIS. E.B. Second Lieutenant (1917)
MORRIS. J.C. Lieutenant (1918/19)
MORRIS. J.W. Flying Officer (1951)
MORRISON. Flight Sergeant (1945/46)
MOSELEY. P. Flight Lieutenant (1985/86)
MOSS. Flight Sergeant (1951)
MOSS. J. Pilot Officer (1948)
MOWATT. Flight Lieutenant (1945/46)
MOXON. Pilot Officer (1949)
MULLEN. C. Flight Lieutenant (1971)
MUMFORD. G.S.C. Flight Lieutenant (1957)
MUNDY. I.M. Flying Officer (1942/44)
MUNRO. A. Squadron Leader (1983)
MURRAY. H.C. Lieutenant (1918)
MUTTER. N. Flight Lieutenant (1946)

NASH. D.S. Sergeant (1928)
NATTA. B.M. Warrant Officer (1944)
NAZ. P. Squadron Leader (1969/70)
NEALE. A. Flight Lieutenant (1954/56)
NESBITT. W.J. Lieutenant (1918)
NETOPIL. Sergeant (1942)
NEVILLE. C.R.G. Flight Lieutenant (1953)
NEVILLE. T. Flight Lieutenant (1975/76)
NEWELL. R.G. Major (USAF) (1957/59)
NICHOLLS. D.M. Flying Officer (1959/61)
NICHOLS. H. Pilot Officer (1940)
NICHOLS. S.L. Second Lieutenant (1917)
NODDINGS. E.E. Flying Officer (1932)
NORRICE. Sergeant (1945)

NORTHRIDGE. G.W. Lieutenant (1918)
NOTMAN. S. Flying Officer (1985/86)

O'DONNELL. Sergeant (1940)
O'FLYNN. Flying Officer (1965)
O'LEARY. Flight Lieutenant (1942)
OLDHAM. T. Flying Officer (1957)
OLIVIER. E. Lieutenant (1917/18)
ONYETT. K. Second Lieutenant(1918/19)
OPENSHAW. E.R. Flight Lieutenant (1929/30)
OPIE. E.S. Pilot Officer (1943)
ORLEBAR. A.H. Lieutenant (1917)
OSBOURNE. G.H. Second Lieutenant (1918/19)
OUSTON. R.J. Flying Officer (1961)
OWEN. A. Flight Lieutenant (1984/85)
OWEN. P. Flight Lieutenant (1975/76)
OXLIN. Flying Officer (1941)

PABIOT. P. Sub Lieutenant (1942)
PACE. T.G. Pilot Officer (1937/40)
PADDLE. M. Flight Lieutenant (1943)
PADDON. F.W.J. Sergeant
PAGE. W.F. Squadron Leader (1963/65)
PAINE. M. Squadron Leader (1986/87)
PALMER. G.H. Second Lieutenant(1917)
PARK. A.J. Flying Officer (1959/61)
PARKIN. Sergeant (1941)
PARKINSON. Sergeant
PARR. J.J.E. Flight Lieutenant (1975/76)
PARR. R. Sergeant (1932)
PARROT. D. Flying Officer (1940)
PARRY-OKEDEN. H.G.P. Lieutenant(1917)
PARSONS. E.G. Sergeant (1928)
PARTRIDGE. F.A. Flight Lieutenant(1951/52)
PASCOE-WEBBE J.B. Pilot Officer (1936)
PATERSON. R.J. Second Lieutenant (1917)
PATON. Flying Officer (1944)
PAXTON. T.R. Flight Lieutenant (1975/76)
PAYNE. Flying Officer (1965)
PAYNE. A.A. Sergeant (1928)
PAYNE. J.M. Flying Officer (1954/56)
PAYNE. R. Flying Officer (1967/68)
PEACOCK. Pilot Officer (1933)
PEARCE. Sergeant (1943)
PEARSON. Pilot Officer (1952/55)
PEARSON. F.M. Squadron Leader (1977/78)
PEARSON. R.B. Pilot Officer (1938)
PEARSON-ROGERS. H.W. Flight Lieutenant (1930)
PEEL. J.R.A. Pilot Officer (1932)
PELLY. C.B.R. Flight Lieutenant (1953)
PENFOLD. P. Squadron Leader (1971/72)
PENMAN. W.M. Pilot Officer (1937)
PENTLAND. A.A.N. Lieutenant(1917)

PERDUE. G.S. Flight Lieutenant (1954/56)
PETERS. Flight Lieutenant (1949/50)
PETRE. G.W. Flight Lieutenant(1938/41)
PHIPPS. L.W. Squadron Leader, AFC (1951/53 –
    1959/61)
PICKERING. B. Flying Officer (1959/61)
PICKERSGILL. J.N.M. Flight Lieutenant (1959/61)
PIDDOCKE. B.G. Pilot Officer (1938/39)
PIERCE. P.J.E. Lieutenant (1918)
PINKHAM. P. Squadron Leader (1940)
PINOUS. J.D. Sergeant (1942)
PITTAWAY. S. Flight Lieutenant (1986/87)
PITTS. R. Flight Lieutenant (1986/87)
PLUMMER. H.A. Sergeant (1942)
PLUMRIDGE. Flying Officer
PLZAK. G. Sergeant (1940/41)
POTTER. J.H. Sergeant (1940)
POWERS. B.A. Second Lieutenant(1917)
PREBBLE. F.J.D. Sergeant (1943)
PRESCOTT. J. Flying Officer (1986/87)
PRETYMAN. E.R. Major (1918)
PUCKRIDGE. H.V. Second Lieutenant (1917/18)
PUGH. J. W. B. Flying Officer (1930/32)
PURVES. S.S.B. Lieutenant (1916/17)

RAFIQUI. S.A. Flight Lieutenant (1961)
RANCE. F. S. Wing Commander (1985/87)
RANDALL. Flying Officer (1953/54)
RANKIN. A.J. Flight Lieutenant (1929/30)
RANSLEY. R.A. Flight Lieutenant (1947/48)
RAW. R.M. Squadron Leader, AFC (1961/63)
RAY. L.H. Second Lieutenant (1918)
REDGATE. Sergeant (1943)
REED. W.E. Lieutenant (1917)
REES. D. Squadron Leader (1983/84)
REEVES. K. Flight Lieutenant (1984/86)
REID-WALKER. Lieutenant (1918)
REYNELL. A.W. Second Lieutenant (1916)
REYNOLDS. Pilot Officer (1949/50)
REYNOLDS. P. Flight Lieutenant (1969/70)
RICE. A.H. Second Lieutenant (1917)
RICHARDS. E. Flight Lieutenant (1956)
RICHARDSON. Sergeant (1942)
RICHARDSON. G. Flight Lieutenant (1985/86)
RICHIE. Sergeant (1943)
RICHMOND. Pilot Officer (1949)
RICHMOND. J.R. Sergeant (1951/52)
RIDINGS. Sergeant (1942)
RIGBY. Flying Officer (1965)
RIGGS. R.R. Second Lieutenant (1917)
RIPON. C.I. Sergeant (1942)
RIPON. T.J. Sergeant (1943)
ROBERTS. G.B. Second Lieutenant (1917)

ROBERTS. P. Flight Lieutenant (1985/86)
ROBERTSON. R.K.D. Lieutenant (1917)
ROBINSON. A.I. Pilot Officer (1937/40)
ROBINSON. L. Lieutenant (1915)
ROBINSON. P.G. Lieutenant (1916)
ROBINSON. S. Flight Lieutenant (1976/78)
ROBSON. Flight Lieutenant (1945)
RODEN. G.S. Lieutenant (1918/19)
RODEN. H.A.C. Sergeant (1940)
RODWELL. R.M. Major (1915/17)
ROGERS. Pilot Officer (1952)
ROGERS. G.H. Second Lieutenant (1918)
ROSIE. W. Flight Lieutenant. (1985)
ROSS. Lieutenant (1918)
ROUND. Pilot Officer
ROUSSELOT. M.A. Lieutenant (1942)
ROWELL. Captain
ROWLEY. C. Flying Officer (1975/76)
ROYER. R. Pilot Officer (1942/43)
RUSSELL. R. Flight Lieutenant (1982)
RUSSELL-RIGBY. J.S. Lieutenant (1919)
RUTLAND. C.P. Flight Lieutenant (1942)
RYAN. Flight Lieutenant (1953)
RYE. W.J. Sergeant (1932/35)

SANDAY. W.G.S. Major, DSO, MC (1917/18)
SANDERS. Pilot Officer (1941)
SANDERSON. A.C. Squadron Leader (1931/34)
SANDERSON. J.B. Pilot Officer (1939)
SANT. E.M. Second Lieutenant (1917)
SAVIJAR. N. Squadron Leader (1985/86)
SAVILLE. Flying Officer (1944)
SCHELL. F.S. Lieutenant (1916)
SCHOFIELD. Flying Officer (1944/45)
SCHOULAR. J.E. Pilot Officer (1937)
SCLATER. T.W. Second Lieutenant (1917)
SCORGIE. D. Pilot Officer (1932)
SCOTT. Sergeant (1940)
SCOTT. Sergeant (1951/52)
SCOTT. E. Flight Lieutenant (1963)
SCOTT. G.W. Pilot Officer
SCOTT. J.A. Flying Officer
SCOTT. L.A. Pilot Officer (1939)
SEARS. R. Flight Lieutenant (1973)
SELOUS. F.H.B. Captain (1916)
SEYMOUR. W.C. Lieutenant
SHACKLETON. Flight Lieutenant (1951)
SHARPE. M. Second Lieutenant (1916)
SHARPLES. Pilot Officer (1948)
SHAW. D. Squadron Leader (1989/90)
SHEPHERD. A. Flying Officer (1950/52)
SHEPPARD. R.W. Flying Officer (1942)
SHEPPARD. T.H. Flying Officer (1957)

SHEPPARD. W.P. Flight Lieutenant (1958)
SHIPWRIGHT. A.T. Second Lieutenant (1917)
SHIRREFF. A.C. Flight Lieutenant (1944/45)
SIMA. Pilot Officer (1944)
SIMPSON. H.A.L. Pilot Officer (1942)
SIMPSON. K. Flying Officer (1957)
SINCLAIR. G.L. Pilot Officer (1937/40)
SISON. Captain (1917)
SLATTER. L.H. Squadron Leader OBE, DSC, DFC
    (1929)
SLEE. R.A.B. Flying Officer (1944)
SLOAN. W.H. Sergeant (1942)
SMITH. Lieutenant
SMITH. Sergeant (1942)
SMITH. Warrant Officer (1945)
SMITH. Flight Lieutenant (1951)
SMITH. B. Flight Lieutenant (1970)
SMITH. B.H. Flight Lieutenant (1952)
SMITH. F.E. Flying Officer (1949)
SMITH. G. J.E. Flight Lieutenant (1985/86)
SMITH. G.M. Flight Lieutenant (1947/52)
SMITH. I. Flight Lieutenant (1973)
SMITH. T.W. Flying Officer (1957)
SMYTHE. E.J. Second Lieutenant (1916)
SNAREY. G.N. Flying Officer (1932)
SOKOL. Sergeant (1941)
SOWREY. F. Captain (1917)
SPARKES. T. Pilot Officer (1945)
SPARKS. M.N. Flying Officer (1949/50)
SPENCE. A. Flight Lieutenant (1985/86)
SPENCER. J. Squadron Leader (1975/76)
SPENCER. W.A.L. Second Lieutenant (1917)
SPILLER. N.B. Wing Commander (1990/91)
SPIRIT. H. Flight Lieutenant (1975/76)
SPIRO. S.G. Second Lieutenant (1917)
SPOOR. J. Squadron Leader (1975/76)
SQUIRES. D. Flying Officer (1989/90)
STAPLES. Flying Officer (1944)
STARKING. P.R. Pilot Officer (1948/50)
STEADMAN. Pilot Officer (1947)
STEER. J. Flying Officer (1956)
STEERE. Pilot Officer (1954)
STEERE. H. Flight Sergeant (1940)
STEPHEN. J.A. Flight Lieutenant (1952/53)
STEPHENSON. G.D. Squadron Leader (1940)
STEVENS. Pilot Officer (1940)
STEVENSON. J.G. Second Lieutenant (1917)
STEWART. A. Flight Lieutenant (1985)
STEWART. C.R.D Pilot Officer (1937)
STEWART. H.G. Second Lieutenant (1916)
STEWART. P.R. Second Lieutenant (1916)
STONE. H.J. Second Lieutenant (1917)
STONER. M. Flight Lieutenant (1973)

STOWELL. Pilot Officer (1953)
STRANG. R.M. Lieutenant (1917)
STRIHAVKA. Flight Sergeant (1941)
STUART. Pilot Officer (1941)
STUART-PAUL. R.I. Flight Lieutenant (1959/61)
SULLIVAN. Flying Officer (1954)
SUTHERLAND. Pilot Officer (1940)
SWAN. M. Flight Lieutenant (1985/86)
SWART. Squadron Leader (1965)
SYDNEY. Flight Sergeant (1940)

TALBOT. R.F.R. Second Lieutenant (1916)
TAP. Captain (RNAF) (1964)
TAYLOR. Sergeant (1951/52)
TAYLOR. A.H. Flight Lieutenant (1989)
TAYLOR. G. W. Captain (1918)
TAYLOR. J. H. Flight Lieutenant (1944)
TAYLOR. K. Pilot Officer (1949)
TAYLOR. P.J. Flight Lieutenant (1990)
TAYLOR. P.S Flying Officer (1945/46)
TAYLOR. P.B. Flight Lieutenant (1954/56)
TAYLOR. P.P.W. Flying Officer (1959/61)
TEAGER. J. Flight Lieutenant (1985/86)
TEALE. R.P. Pilot Officer (1930)
TELFORD. M.A.P. Flying Officer (1957)
TERRY. H.R.R. Pilot Officer (1937)
THIELE. Flying Officer (1945)
THOMAS. Flying Officer (1940)
THOMAS. E.H. Pilot Officer (1937/39)
THOMPSON. Flying Officer (1953/55)
THOMPSON. C.D. Lieutenant (1917)
THOMPSON. C.R.J. Lieutenant (1917)
THOMPSON. F. Second Lieutenant (1916)
THOMPSON. J. Second Lieutenant (1916)
THOMPSON. J. Flight Lieutenant (1985/86)
THORBURN. G. Flight Lieutenant (1985/86)
THOROGOOD. A.N. Flight Lieutenant (1989)
THREAPLETON. E. Squadron Leader (1981/82)
TIDSWELL. C.R. Captain (1916)
TINWORTH. M.R. Flying Officer (1990)
TOYLER. D.H. Sergeant (1942)
TOSTEVIN. O.C. Sergeant (1928)
TOWLER. P.E. Second Lieutenant (1918)
TOYLER. D.H. Sergeant (1942)
TRENCHARD. H.A. Pilot Officer (1939/40)
TRESIZE G.O. Pilot Officer (1948)
TREWEEK. A. Flight Lieutenant (1961)
TUCKER. Pilot Officer (1940)
TUNALEY. Flying Officer (1953/55)
TURBIN. R.W. Flying Officer (1959/61)
TURGOOSE. Pilot Officer (1952)
TURNER. Pilot Officer (1933)
TURNER. Sergeant (1942)

TURNER. G. Pilot Oficer (1947)
TURTON-JONES. J.W. Squadron Leader (1936/37)
TUTTLE. G.W. Flying Officer (1928)
TYLDESLEY. A. Pilot Officer (1957)

UNDERWOOD. Flying Officer (1985/86)
UNWIN. G.C. Warrant Officer (1940)
URQUHART. J.C. Second Lieutenant (1918/19)

VAIR-TURNBULL. A.P. Sergeant (1942/43)
VALLELY. I. Flying Officer (1989/90)
VAN DER BYL. R.I. Lieutenant (1917)
VANGUCCI. P.C. Wing Commander (1972/74)
VAN WYK. P.D. Flying Officer (1961)
VARLEY. P. Flying Officer (1949)
VASS. P. Sergeant (1943)
VASSILIADES. B. Flight Sergeant (1943/44)
VEALE. A.A. Second Lieutenant (1917)
VENABLES. Flight Lieutenant (1946)
VERNON. Flight Sergeant (1941)
VINCENT. A.W. Flying Officer (1932/33)
VINE. A. Warrant Officer (1945/46)
VIVEASH. J.F. Flying Officer (1942)
VOKES. A.F. Pilot Officer (1941)

WADHAM. N.W. Lieutenant (1916)
WAINMAN. Flight Lieutenant (1983)
WAITE. H.L. Lieutenant (1917)
WALKER. T.N.K. Pilot Officer (1936)
WALLACE. E.W. Pilot Officer (1942)
WALLACE. W. Sergeant (1932)
WALMSLEY. H. Second Lieutenant (1918)
WALSH. M. Flight Lieutentant (1983/85)
WALTERS-MORGAN. Flying Officer (1985/86)
WALTON. A. Flight Lieutenant (1984)
WALTON. B.K. Squadron Leader (1975/76)
WANT. N.D. Flight Lieutenant (1961)
WARREN. Flight Sergeant (1944)
WASS. R.E. Sergeant (1942/43)
WATSON. Sergeant (1941)
WATSON. Flight Sergeant (1951)
WATSON. C.W.D. Flight Lieutenant (1970)
WATSON. N.J. Squadron Leader (1989/90)
WATSON. P.V. Pilot Officer (1939/40)
WATTS. Flight Lieutenant (1986/87)
WATTS. I. Pilot Officer (1942)
WATTS. R. Second Lieutenant (1916)
WATTS. R.A. Flying Officer (1942)
WEARNE. A. Second Lieutenant (1917)
WEBLEY. D. Flight Lieutenant (1970/71)
WEBSTER. Flying Officer (1944)
WEDD. W.B.P.D. Flying Officer (1942)
WEIGHILL. R. Flight Lieutenant (1945)
WEIR. H.A. Second Lieutenant (1918)

WELD. D. S. Lieutenant (1917)
WELLS. Flight Sergeant (1944)
WELLS. F. Flying Officer (1929/30)
WENDT. Pilot Officer (1944)
WEST. T. Second Lieutenant (1916)
WEST. T.V. Flight Lieutenant (1924)
WESTLEY. Captain (1945)
WHEELER. A.B. Flying Officer (1944)
WHEELER. D. Flight Lieutanant (1946)
WHITE. G.A. Flight Lieutenant (1959/61)
WHITE. R.E. Lieutenant (1918)
WHITEHOUSE. S.L. Second Lieutenant (1917)
WHYTE. Pilot Officer (1946/47)
WIGLEY. P. Flight Lieutenant (1943)
WILD. I. Flight Lieutenant (1975/76)
WILDE. I.R. Flight Lieutenant (1974/77)
WILKINS. F.S. Lieutenant (1917)
WILKINSON. Captain
WILLENBRUCH. A. Squadron Leader (1986/87)
WILLIAMS. A.T. Lieutenant (1916)
WILLIAMS. C.P. Second Lieutenant (1917)
WILLIAMS. G.G.A. Captain (1916)
WILLIAMS. R. Flight Lieutenant (1946)
WILLIAMS W.G.B. Captain (1917)
WILLIAMSON. P.P. Flight Lieutenant (1969/70)
WILLIS. P.A. Flight Lieutenant (1983/85)
WILLS. Sergeant (1945)
WILSON. C.L. Lieutenant (1919)
WINTER. T.E. Sergeant (1942)
WINWRIGHT. G.A. Flying Officer (1989/90)
WITHALL. L.C. Pilot Officer (1937/39)
WOOD. M.H. Flight Lieutenant (1970/71)
WOODWARD. Warrant Officer
WOODWARD. V.C. Squadron Leader D.F.C. &
    Bar (1948/50)
WOOLLAM. R. Flight Lieutenant (1986)
WORMALD. A.W.G. Pilot Officer (1952)
WRAGG. Warrant Officer (1945)
WRATTEN. W (Bill). Flight Lieutenant (1964)
WRIGHT. M.J. Squadron Leader (1944)
WRIGHT. W. Pilot Officer (1945)
WRIGLEY. Flight Lieutenant

YAPP. G.D. Squadron Leader (1989/90)
YEARWOOD. F.C. Flight Lieutenant (1945)
YELDING. G.M.J. Pilot Officer (1953)
YEO. H.A. Second Lieutenant (1917)
YOUNG. J. Flight Lieutenant (1945)
YOUNG. N. Flight Lieutenant (1929/30)
YOUNG. W.E. Captain (1917)
WILSON JR FLT LT (1958) ATCHD